Faulkner's Media Romance

Faulkner's Media Romance

JULIAN MURPHET

OXFORD
UNIVERSITY PRESS

Oxford University Press is a department of the University of Oxford. It furthers
the University's objective of excellence in research, scholarship, and education
by publishing worldwide. Oxford is a registered trade mark of Oxford University
Press in the UK and certain other countries.

Published in the United States of America by Oxford University Press
198 Madison Avenue, New York, NY 10016, United States of America.

© Oxford University Press 2017

First issued as an Oxford University Press paperback, 2020

All rights reserved. No part of this publication may be reproduced, stored in
a retrieval system, or transmitted, in any form or by any means, without the
prior permission in writing of Oxford University Press, or as expressly permitted
by law, by license, or under terms agreed with the appropriate reproduction
rights organization. Inquiries concerning reproduction outside the scope of the
above should be sent to the Rights Department, Oxford University Press, at the
address above.

You must not circulate this work in any other form
and you must impose this same condition on any acquirer.

Library of Congress Cataloging-in-Publication Data
Names: Murphet, Julian, author.
Title: Faulkner's media romance / Julian Murphet.
Description: New York, NY : Oxford University Press, 2017.
Identifiers: LCCN 2016049616 | ISBN 9780190664244 (hardback : alk. paper) |
ISBN 9780190077808 (paperback : alk. paper)
Subjects: LCSH: Faulkner, William, 1897–1962—Criticism and interpretation. |
Mass media in literature.
Classification: LCC PS3511.A86 Z9188 2017 | DDC 813/.52—dc23
LC record available at https://lccn.loc.gov/2016049616

For Mary and Richard
Incipe, parve puer: qui non risere parenti,
Nec deus hunc mensa, dea nec dignata cubili est.

CONTENTS

Acknowledgments   ix

Introduction: Modernism and the Absent Event of Romance   1

1. A Folklore of Speed   48

2. Affect and spatial dynamics in *Flags in the Dust* and *The Sound and the Fury*   84

3. Currents of Consciousness; or, my mother is a graphophone   143

4. The Negative Plate; or, *Absalom, Absalom!* and the camera's voice   216

Index   283

ACKNOWLEDGMENTS

The research represented by this book was supported under the Australian Research Council's *Discovery Projects* funding scheme DP0985478 "William Faulkner Between Cinema and Literature," 2009–2013. I am grateful to the ARC for its trust in this project, and for the support it offered toward international travel, relief from teaching duties, and research assistance. During the life of the project, I was fortunate to enjoy the part-time services of the best research assistant in the world, Catriona Menzies-Pike, long may she prosper. As well, the grant funded a dedicated Ph.D. stipend for the redoubtable Stefan Solomon, whose doctoral thesis, "Faulkner, Form, and the Anxiety of Cinematic Influence" (University of New South Wales, 2014), should be seen as a companion piece to the present volume; as should our co-edited work, *William Faulkner in the Media Ecology* (Louisiana State University Press, 2015), which grew out of an international symposium similarly funded by the grant.

I acknowledge the role of the Centre for Modernism Studies in Australia, and the School of the Arts and Media, UNSW Australia, in aiding and abetting this work. Undoubtedly, without the collegiality of a remarkably healthy work environment, and the resources of an institution dedicated to good scholarship, several years would have been added to the already protracted period of gestation. James Donald, as Dean of the Faculty, and Andrew Schultz, as Head of School, have presided over a notable resurgence in Humanities research during my tenure at UNSW. I have particularly appreciated the interlocution of my colleagues and students: Sean Pryor, Grace Hellyer, Baylee Brits, Ronan McDonald, Mark Steven, George Kouvaros, Helen Groth, Chris Danta, and the late Peter Alexander.

Faulknerians are a uniquely convivial and genial folk, and I have been fortunate to enjoy the conversation and critical intelligence of a number of them. Don Kartiganger took us on a personal tour of the key sites in Oxford, Mississippi. Jay Watson led the inevitable nocturnal delegation to the gravesite, for ritual libations. Sarah Gleeson-White, perhaps the only other Faulknerian in Australia (though she swears she isn't one), has been a constant friend. Peter Lurie has been very kind and liberal in his engagement with this project, and I am grateful to him. Richard Godden has rewarded and perplexed in the most enabling of manners. Mike Zeitlin and Robert Jackson provided extremely helpful feedback. And few things can compare to the civility and generosity of the late, great Noel Polk, whose untimely death is still a spiritual sore; all serious students of Faulkner owe him an incalculable debt.

Sascha Morrell, whose work has sailed very close to mine over a number of years, remains a remarkably lively and knowledgeable friend in Faulkner, for whose critical eyes I am enduringly grateful. Above all I wish to thank Jack Matthews for his extraordinary generosity with my work in progress, his tireless enthusiasm for the project, and the peerless quality of his work in the field. It is a privilege to call him a friend.

Two anonymous Press readers offered truly constructive feedback on an earlier draft and contributed substantially to its improvement. The copyeditor also made invaluable improvements. The constant support of Brendan O'Neill, former commissioning editor at OUP New York, was a lifeline; as have been the kind efforts of his successor, Sarah Pirovitz.

To Ruth Jennison I owe the inexhaustible thanks of a comrade in arms. My son Gabriel has been the coeval companion of the full life of this work: his remarkable accomplishments, height, and maturity are its more flattering mirror in the Real. My dog Ezra Pound has helped keep me sane. But this book is for my parents who between them, and separately, set me on my way. I love them both.

Introduction

Modernism and the Absent Event of Romance

This book develops a usable definition of modernism as a family resemblance of formal procedures that crystallized during a systemic media revolution and a series of crises specific to world industrial capitalism, roughly between 1880 and 1940. It focuses on the extended prose narrative form of the printed book, in particular the novel—specifically, the work of William Faulkner. Why Faulkner? Primarily due to his status as the canonical modernist writer most thoroughly immersed in the narrative DNA of romance. The argument of the book turns on Faulkner's formal strategies for managing this passionate attachment to what he could no more simply abandon or transcend, in the manner of a Beckett, than he could identify with it outright.[1] What is so endlessly intriguing about Faulkner's work is how this lifelong fixation on romance is worked through, in a staggering variety of ways, without ever being renounced. It is pointless to try to conscript him as a modernist in any way committed to aesthetics of subtraction or purification. Rather, Faulkner's oeuvre stands out because it never pronounced itself as superior to those romance elements that it sought to preserve against the grain of the very formal devices used to displace and conceal them. Faulkner's is, at least for that "matchless period" of its most intense efflorescence, a romantic imagination put through the mangler of a modernist sense of form. The question is how, and in what shape, it might have survived that grueling passage.

This book addresses that question by proposing an underlying form taken by his various solutions to this problem. Simply put, that form is *mediatic*. In some key places where Faulkner's material is most palpably steeped in the ideological substance of romance (a lurid murder, an incident of incest, a revenge plot),

---

[1] For a sterling account of Beckett's remorseless campaign against the contents and formal apparatus of romance, see Pascale Casanova, *Beckett: Anatomy of a Literary Revolution* (London & New York: Verso, 2007).

there emerges a recurrent practice of masking it in the trappings of technological media that are incompatible with, and anachronistic to, romance's social basis in a feudal order. Time and again (though assuredly not always), what threatens to tilt over into sheer melodrama or sensationalism is treated with a technological fix, which sidesteps those aesthetically exhausted traps and becomes enmeshed in ideological currents belonging to another world entirely. And the value of this strategy is that it retroactively alters the very coordinates through which we understand the romance elements seeking admittance to the text in the first place. For now they appear, not as drawn intact from an extinct antebellum cultural milieu or fossilized chivalric codex, but from the strictly contemporary afterlife of romance in the commodified materials of mass culture, where they circulate by way of entirely new technologies, new media, new cultural economies. That is to say, Faulkner's devious masking strategies allow him to eat his romance cake while having it too, because they rightly indicate that romance is alive and well—on the big screen, as popular song on the radio and phonograph, and in the mass market for dime novels and magazines. It is a dialectical situation that behooves this novelist not simply to renounce or abstract from the romance origins of all Western storytelling (either as folktale or aristocratic quest), but to reflect formally on the uncanniness of mass-cultural romance as modernism's conjoined twin.

This is not meant, however, as yet another critical relativization of modernism's technical audacity and difficulty by way of the more enjoyable corpus of mass culture. I am the last person to want to underestimate the extraordinary aesthetic achievement of William Faulkner, or belittle it by recalling the debts it owes to cinema, popular song, and bestselling books. Rather, what I think needs to be better determined is how his modernism *works*: how, by introjecting the material it most reviles, and exposing it to the labor of the negative, it develops unprecedented technical means for circumventing the most harmful ideological effects of what he called "moron's pap,"[2] mass culture's *toujours déjà-lu*—which is to say laziness, inattention, mindless submission to prefabricated norms and values, and hatred of the unknown. This book attempts to demonstrate how ingenious and resourceful Faulkner was at putting certain elements to work that, left to themselves, were perhaps most likely to have had such pernicious effects, but which, exposed to his formal *Verfremdungseffekte*, developed among his readers styles of aesthetic attentiveness, engagement, and openness to novelty that were second to none in the American literary tradition. I make the argument that, in order to appreciate this resounding success, we need to comprehend more precisely the variable forms that Faulkner's labor of the negative took. His modernism requires a deeper acknowledgment

---

[2] William Faulkner, *If I Forget Thee, Jerusalem*, in *Novels 1936–1940* (New York: Library of America, 1990), 577.

of the very things it wants us to be better than, by not being altogether better than them itself.

And yet, the persistence of romance in Faulkner cannot simply be decoded as a contextual negotiation of present-day mass cultural forms; it also stubbornly references a historical and regional matrix of ideologemes which, despite the seventy or so years that separated his best work from the end of the Civil War and thus the military defeat of this ideology's *raison d'être*, lingered in an undead fashion underwriting the renaissance of Southern romance and gothic forms in the late nineteenth and early twentieth centuries. There is no study of Faulkner that does not somehow engage this edifice of zombie concepts and values, of romance as a well-nigh imperishable discursive web adhering to the work of every Southern writer. But the virtue of Faulkner's "technological fix," his habitual reaching for media metaphors to cloak his romance *topoi*, is that it permits another and more materialist way of understanding the South's relationship to that genre. Because nothing was less immediate than the collapse of Southern romance's ideological legitimacy after the removal by force of its economic infrastructure in chattel slavery; indeed, indicating a theoretically fascinating "cultural lag" with few precedents in history, romance survived the passage into systematic "agri-peonage" and then again into the more fully rationalized and wage-based classical capitalism of the modern period, not exactly intact, but presumably with tenacious roots in the very dominance of the agricultural sector itself. The additional complication, much explored by Richard Godden,[3] that the South of Faulkner's own moment was undergoing another radical economic reconstruction only sharpens our appreciation of how an image of the past can continue to "flash up" at moments of emergency, and is retroactively reconfigured in turn by the contours of the present it is developed in.[4] The incessant, though periodically reformatted, crisis affecting the South's mode of production is, ironically, what allowed romance to persist, as the dominant class again and again reached back to the future, both to idealize the imaginary lost plenitude and to underscore an ongoing real difference in economic modes between industrial and agrarian sectors of the national economy. In successive stages the South's dominant forces of production shifted from slaves and manual tools, to peons and manual tools, to sharecroppers and manual tools, to wage hands and machines; these formal and technological breaks, each responding to and triggering a new mode of crisis, are the vertebrae in the material backbone supporting the persistence of romance, less an "organic" ideological expression of the mode of production, than an executive PR campaign to dissemble continuity.

---

[3] Richard Godden, *Fictions of Labor: William Faulkner and the South's Long Revolution* (Cambridge: Cambridge University Press, 1997).

[4] Walter Benjamin, "Theses on The Philosophy of History," *Illuminations: Essays and Reflections*, ed. Hannah Arendt, trans. Harry Zohn (New York: Schocken, 1968), 255.

And it is this subterranean history of crisis, breaks, and technological fixes that Faulkner allows us to glimpse in allegorical flashes, via his recourse to the mediatic tropes that mask his romance proclivities. Anachronistic techno-mediatic tropes help to expose the material truths that subtended the perdurable anachronism of romance itself.

Here, at any rate, we have in barest outline the coiled argumentative spring of what follows. Combined and uneven development is configured, in Faulkner, as a palimpsestic textuality in which three disjunctive modes of production are, not juxtaposed, but fused into unstable ideological friezes. Their key is an insistent troping of romance materials in the language of modern mediatic technologies. Or, as I will demonstrate, Faulkner obliges us to come to terms with the logic of *mediation* itself, such that apparently simple or disposable rhetorical figures—for example, voices like phonograph records, bodies like Kodak prints, or dreams like magazine stories—insist on straddling two or three historical layers, and on their strange capacity to effect transpositions between and among them. Ultimately, I argue that Faulkner simply could not have achieved what he did at the level of novelistic form without the techno-mediatic tropes that peppered his characteristically multidimensional historical landscapes. And that by learning to appreciate that fact, we can teach ourselves valuable lessons about history's inscription through mediatory means. In order to say what they say, these texts have to say something else; and the truth of what they say consists in that strange tropological displacement.

The persistence of romance

At the risk of appearing to sell coals to Newcastle, I need to rehearse a theme that ran stubbornly throughout Faulkner's contemporary reception, namely his profound debt to the genre of romance. Of course, there is a long-standing tradition of approaching Faulkner from just this angle. Irving Howe's *The Southern Myth and William Faulkner* (1951), the work of Cleanth Brooks in *William Faulkner: The Yoknapatawpha Country* (1963) and *Toward Yoknapatawpha and Beyond* (1978), Olga Vickery's *The Novels of William Faulkner* (1964), W. L. Miner's *The World of William Faulkner* (1963), E. M. Kerr's *William Faulkner's Gothic Domain* (1979), and of course the concerted curatorial and promotional efforts of Malcolm Cowley—all these and many more besides made considerable efforts to situate Faulkner's achievement in relation to the subgenres of romance, especially, but not exceptionally, its regional forms in the South. But this initiative, which was non-systematic and far from exhaustive, seems to have been confined on the whole to the first long stage of the critical consolidation of Faulkner's reputation after he received the Nobel Prize for literature in 1949. As I have pointed out elsewhere, however, something radical happened in the late 1970s to the ways in which Faulkner was constructed as an "author function," and this involved the sudden obsolescence of that kind of attention to genre, in preference to the jostling problematics of historical materialism, psychoanalysis, feminism, race studies, popular culture, regional and area studies, queer studies, and so on.[5] Periodic forays into Faulkner's romance proclivities have continued to appear, as in Jeff Karem's *The Romance of Authenticity*,[6] Taylor Hagood's *Faulkner's Imperialism*,[7] or indeed Judith Sensibar's spin on it in her *Faulkner and Love*[8]—but that these remain minority and scattered pursuits is nowhere better proven than by the fact that the indexes of such notable additions to scholarship as Philip M. Weinstein's *Faulkner's Subject: A Cosmos No One Owns* (1992), Richard Godden's *Fictions of Labor: William Faulkner and the South's Long Revolution* (1997), David Minter's *Faulkner's Question Narratives: Fiction of His Major Phase, 1929–42* (2004), Peter Lurie's *Vision's Immanence: Faulkner, Film, and the Popular Imagination* (2004), Charles Hannon's *Faulkner and the Discourses of Culture* (2005), Ted Atkinson's *Faulkner and the Great Depression: Aesthetics, Ideology, and Cultural Politics* (2006), or even John T. Matthews's comprehensive *William Faulkner: Seeing Through the South* (2009), do not contain a single entry on "romance." This absence is amplified in the capacious coverage of the new scholarship's terrain in the Richard C. Moreland–edited *Companion to William Faulkner*, which, though it dedicates a section to "Genres and Forms," signally omits romance as a subject worth thinking through in its own terms. That this is a reversal of fortunes is clear, as is, to be sure, the general rationale for a tendency to downplay formalistic and relatively abstract generic concerns in the age of Theory and after. But the late return to formal preoccupations in literary scholarship, slowly consolidating alongside the growth of the "New Formalism" in American poetry circles, cannot long delay its inevitable rediscovery of Faulkner, whose pride of place in the New Critics' canon of prose writers will already have drawn significant attention to an oeuvre long since saturated by an apolitical, de-historicized formalist critical history. The point, I take it, is to outflank this inevitable return, by way of a historical formalism that takes seriously the material dynamics of form in the framing of history itself.

This is why we need to review the omnipresence of romance in Faulkner, not as some timeless formal essence instantiated like a Platonic Idea in the textual particulars of this body of work, but as an allegorical key to these works'

---

[5] See my "Introduction" to Stefan Solomon and Julian Murphet, eds., *William Faulkner in the Media Ecology* (Baton Rouge: Louisiana University Press, 2015), esp. 7–9.

[6] See Jeff Karem, *The Romance of Authenticity: Cultural Politics of Regional and Ethnic Literatures* (Charlottesville, VA & London: University of Virginia Press, 2004), 17–60.

[7] Taylor Hagood, *Faulkner's Imperialism: Space, Place, and the Materiality of Myth* (Baton Rouge: Louisiana State University Press, 2008).

[8] Judith L. Sensibar, *Faulkner and Love: The Women Who Shaped His Art* (New Haven, CT: Yale University Press, 2009).

resonance in social history. If, as I suggest, Faulkner's use of romance is characterized by a mediatic tropology that, Janus-faced, looks simultaneously to the regional uses of the genre over time and to the afterlives of romance in the new mechanical and electronic media themselves, then we are justified in rediscovering its deep, pervasive place in his fictions. For here lies an as-yet-unformulated modality of the political unconscious itself: the way in which modern literature used its own ecological endangerment and looming precarity as a medium to unearth those aspects of its prehistory (in romance above all) that had survived despite the many virulent efforts to extirpate them, and so cast a critical light on the cultural logic of a mode of production that routinely deployed anachronism as a means of dissimulating what Walter Benjamin called its permanent "state of emergency."[9] It must be stressed that such complex political aesthetics proceed by way of what look to be purely formal procedures, as texts assimilate often quite contradictory kinds of material into unstable formal syntheses in order to discharge the "truths" peculiar to their role in history. Such truths cannot be reduced to mere content, to the topics or themes being rehearsed on the narrative or representational level; rather, they inhere in the gaps and fissures, the irreconcilable dissonances, between the ideological presumptions encoded in the genres and forms themselves. At any rate, for the argument that follows to make any consistent sense, we now require a quick detour through the history of reception of Faulkner's work, to specify how inextricable it had always been from the coils of a romance plot that no end of formal modernization campaigns could loosen. Recovering this vital strand of Faulkner's authorial identity—a strand we thought we knew so well that we had forgotten it—is critical to a materialist account of how his fictions actually worked.

For his contemporary readers, Faulkner was perceived only intermittently as a modernist, and predominantly as a writer pulled back and forth between the aesthetic ideology of romance and the formal protocols of realism. Indeed, so persistent was this classificatory schism that it more or less defined Faulkner's Anglophone critical reception over his entire writing life. Since in what follows I am interested in how the cultural technology of the novel was understood within the discourse network of its modernist moment, it seems worthwhile to establish this point more fully, the better to analyze what is at stake in Faulkner's work in the form. John Bassett is perhaps typical of our presumptive amnesia with regard to changing aesthetic ideologies when he suggests, condescendingly, that although Faulkner's "reviewers seem to have been ill at ease dealing with fiction that could not be fitted into the two traditional categories of Romance or Realism, some were at least receptive to Faulkner's originality."[10] But the

---

[9] Walter Benjamin, "Theses on the Philosophy of History," trans. Harry Zohn, *Illuminations*, ed. Hannah Arendt (New York: Schocken Books, 1968), 257.

[10] John Bassett, ed., *William Faulkner: The Critical Heritage* (London: Routledge, 1997), 7.

problem is rather our own, since if such a critical "fitting" dogged this writer from the publication of his first novel to his dying day, then surely it not only spoke to something perdurable in the fiction itself, but more important, it was a dialectic in which Faulkner must have felt himself, and his precious "originality," implicated. Romance was part and parcel of the aesthetic discourse network in which the novel as a form was construed and contested across the modern period, and nobody knew that better than Faulkner.

As a Southerner, of course, Faulkner was early on conscripted into a group of younger regional novelists generally proposed as "romantic rather than realistic."[11] A frequent reviewer like Clifton Fadiman would return repeatedly to the fact that Faulkner "has a set of romantic obsessions which he treats in a highly intellectual manner" (apropos of *As I Lay Dying*), that his work is "curiously akin to the eighteenth-century Gothic tale of horror. It makes use of similar mechanisms—dark hints, desolate backgrounds, unrelievedly black villains" (of *Sanctuary*), and that *Absalom, Absalom!* itself is "a penny dreadful tricked up in fancy language and given a specious depth by the expert manipulation of a series of eccentric technical tricks."[12] Matthew "Monk" Lewis was perhaps the early critics' favorite point of comparison, along with Poe and the Jacobean tragedians; but this Gothic tradition having devolved by the late nineteenth century into lurid sensation and melodrama, it was in those terms above all that critics tended to perceive and scold Faulkner's inclinations to romance. James T. Farrell spoke to a certain division of labor in the reading mind upon taking up a Faulkner novel. "It is his sheer ability to write powerfully that carries many readers through the consistently melodramatic and sensational parts that occur regularly in his writings."[13] His elaboration is worth repeating:

> For instance, when one strives to reconstruct or to tell a Faulkner plot in retrospect one sees this melodrama clearly, but when one is reading, one is swept along by the man's driving pen. Technically, he is the master of almost all American writers who fit under such a loose and general category as "realists." (165)

So, the technical "realism" offsets and masks the dime-store melodrama that runs like thick treacle through the plotlines. If that operation was generally successful for Farrell, it was less so for Geoffrey Stone, who put the matter far

---

[11] Donald Davidson, "Two Mississippi Novels" (1929), in M. Thomas Inge, ed., *William Faulkner: The Contemporary Reviews* (Cambridge: Cambridge University Press, 1995), 27.

[12] Clifton Fadiman, reviews in Nicholas Fargnoli, ed., *William Faulkner: A Literary Companion* (New York: Pegasus, 2008), 72, 112, 221.

[13] James T. Farrell, "The Faulkner Mixture," in Fargnoli, ed., *William Faulkner: A Literary Companion*, 165.

more severely. "Realism," he reiterated, "is romanticism going on all fours, and at times the debased posture has been a rather effective disguise."[14]

> Faulkner, we presume, lays claim to the title of realist (if he does not, then his rapine, insanity, mutilation, et cetera stamp him as a special sort of pornographer), yet his latest novel [*Light in August*], in common with his earlier ones, is reminiscent of nothing so much as the work of the Gothic writers in England, the men of the forties in France, and the fiery-eyed poets of the *Sturm und Drang*. Mr. Faulkner is a thorough romantic; it is evident in his love of violence for its own sake and the pretentiousness with which he loads almost every paragraph. (184)

As a result, the balance all wrong, the work "does not give a true or 'realistic' picture of the world. The picture that it does give is an entirely romantic one, replete with *frissons* for both the senses and the emotions, and all overshadowed with vague indications of some deep meaning" (186).

This "pure romantic emotion" (186) was felt at a maximum in *Absalom*, where, as Bernard DeVoto wrote in his long and fascinating review, one finds the usual "fiction of families destroyed by a mysterious curse [. . .], of ruined castles in romantic landscapes, of Giaours and dark 'unwill,'" one long "parade of Grand Guignol tricks and sensations," the whole "just a series of horror stories that are essentially false—false because they happen to grotesques who have no psychology."[15] But Farrell's point—of a schism in the text itself—kept suggesting itself, so that Lewis Gannett could write in the idiom of antinomy and paradox, "You may accept it as an astonishing exercise in literary technique. You may see it as the wild ramblings of a Gothic mind."[16] Paula Snelling put it in the same baffled idiom: "No one can read William Faulkner's books without arriving at the conclusion that the man has truly remarkable powers. No one can read these books without recognising that the stigmata of the third-rate recur in them with a frequency which cannot be dismissed."[17] Or, most concisely, Cameron Shipp: "The story is the starkest melodrama. [. . .] His method of telling the story is unique."[18] And few were going to resist the opportunity

---

[14] Geoffrey Stone, "Keeping Up with the Novelists," in Fargnoli, ed., *William Faulkner: A Literary Companion*, 184.

[15] Bernard DeVoto, "Witchcraft in Mississippi," in Fargnoli, ed., *William Faulkner: A Literary Companion*, 215, 217.

[16] Lewis Gannett, "Sunlight and Shadows Alternate in Faulkner's World," in Fargnoli, ed., *William Faulkner: A Literary Companion*, 222.

[17] Paula Snelling, "Mr. Faulkner Adds a Cubit," in Fargnoli, ed., *William Faulkner: A Literary Companion*, 236.

[18] Cameron Shipp, "Confederacy's Hamlet: Faulkner's New Novel," in Fargnoli, ed., *William Faulkner: A Literary Companion*, 226–27.

to point up the obvious coincidence of the novel's publication within a year of Margaret Mitchell's bestseller, as Gannett could not: "I doubt very much if the guilt-obsessed South of his fiction ever had any more concrete reality than the romantic world created out of Southern tradition and history for 'Gone With the Wind'" (224).

It then fell to Malcolm Cowley, eight years before the two would correspond and forge their more durable relationship, to draw the inevitable conclusion from the evidence of *Absalom*'s perverse aesthetic matrix. Faulkner belongs

> with the "satanic" poets from Byron to Baudelaire, and with the "black" or "terrifying" novelists from Monk Lewis and the Hoffman of the "Tales" to Edgar Allan Poe. The daemon that haunts him is the ghost of the haunted castle—though it is also Poe's raven and Manfred's evil spirit. And the daemon is especially prominent in his new novel. Not only is *Absalom, Absalom!* in many ways the strongest, the most unified and characteristic of his twelve books, but it is also the most romantic, in the strict historical sense of the word.[19]

Here some literary historical detail was in order. As Cowley put it, "romantic novels are likely to be written on two planes, with one subject below, in the foreground, and above it another subject that is half-revealed by conscious of unconscious symbolism" (230). Faulkner's textual world was an intrinsically dualistic one, whose upper and lower levels were bound by symbolic ligatures. Lionel Trilling was particularly keen to proclaim Faulkner's achievement in terms of that "world" or cosmos of which he had, in *Absalom*'s frontispiece, proclaimed himself "sole owner and proprietor," since precisely its separateness and unity was what distinguished the class purview of his romanticism and indeed all romance topographies.

> Like every aristocracy, this one is hostile to the generalization of experience, to ideas; hence the unilluminating unarticulateness of so many of Mr. Faulkner's people; hence, too, their quaintness, their mere melodrama and lack of significance [...]. A will to secede, to cherish its apartness and live out of the present is characteristic of Mr. Faulkner's particular aristocracy and to this one may trace the specialness and apartness of his artistic worlds.[20]

---

[19] Malcolm Cowley, "Poe in Mississippi," in Fargnoli, ed., *William Faulkner: A Literary Companion*, 229.

[20] Lionel Trilling, "Mr. Faulkner's World," in M. Thomas Inge, ed., *William Faulkner: The Contemporary Reviews* (Cambridge: Cambridge University Press, 1995), 70.

This condensation of decades of critical reaction must stand for sufficient evidence that during Faulkner's life his work was insistently understood as romantic, or at best as a field of dynamic aesthetic interplay between romance and realism, tricked out with modernistic style elements. What requires further theoretical determination is why the egregious "predilection for Gothic horror, melodramatic violence, macabre humor and an almost complete absence of sweetness and light" that were seen to have characterized Faulkner's literary sensibilities could have co-existed with an impulse toward realism such that the net result was a "unique quality among writers which has earned Faulkner a preeminent place among modern novelists" by the 1940s.

Most important here is the sense of "trouble" that most critics and commentators felt obliged to address in Faulkner's literary aesthetic. Incompatible with the finer discriminations of a regnant and Jamesian novelistic orthodoxy, Faulkner's susceptibility to romance was felt as an embarrassing (but secretly pleasurable) hangover from a paradigm whose extirpation was the *raison d'être* of the art novel and professional literary criticism to begin with, and explained away most often by way of stereotypical references to the South's incurable cultural proclivities and aristocratic heritage. How might we better understand this trouble in its material, historical dimension? One answer is to propose Faulkner as an exemplary instance of the *becoming-modern* in modern letters: not the modern's heroic achievement, but the unfinishable torment of its coming into being. In order to pursue that hypothesis, we need to be clearer about the dialectical interplay between modernism, realism, and romance.

The aesthetic ideology of modernism has turned, classically, on its negation of realism, with which it is often declared to be incompatible in a strong formal sense.[21] But what is not adequately addressed in this account is how bifurcated and internally contradictory that "realism" always was, its epistemological vocation and insistence on the undesirable aspects of social life matched by an equally apparent "pleasure principle" in the orchestration of providential rewards and the libidinal currents of narrativity as such. Modernism, on the whole inimical to these latter properties of its realist inheritance, cannot so easily be separated from the more austere philosophic inclinations toward formal omnipotence and thematic unhappiness that had distinguished the realist work of fiction from its prehistory in romance. But it is this latter residue that one can already feel being

---

[21] From György Lukács's fulminations against the modernist rejections of realism in *Studies in Contemporary Realism, Writer and Critic*, and *The Historical Novel*, and Brecht's rebuttals (collected in *Aesthetics and Politics*), through Barthes's distinction between the "readerly" and the "writerly" and Kristeva's anti-realist reading of Joyce in *James Joyce and the Revolution of the Word*, through Jameson's remarkable theorizations of this distinction as an historical mutation of the culture of capitalism, and down into the latter-day accounts of Moretti, McKeon, and others, no item of faith has seemed so unshakable as that modernism stages its various revolutions against the prevailing orthodoxies of realism.

adapted and given an entirely new lease of life in the realist novel's narrative economy, its momentous climactic episodes and sentimental tableaux, where archetypal romance forms and figures are allowed an anachronistic life-after-death, suitably scaled down to a more manageable size. If modernism represents a refusal of realist aesthetic norms, that rejection must be understood as a complex engagement with a paradigm already internally divided against itself, inheriting certain features intact and doubling down on a denunciation of elements only inconsistently contained within realism's economy of means.

To arrive at a better understanding of modernism's intensely critical relationship to this residual baggage of romance, then, we need briefly to revisit the standard accounts of the realist novel's engagement with that same ideological and aesthetic freight. Taking only the most recent and compelling instances of a long-standing critical convention that understands the novel's realism as a displacement and ironic negation of the narrative edifice of romance, we find Fredric Jameson proposing this displacement in terms of a momentous stabilization of the categories of "everyday life": "The nineteenth century, indeed, may be characterized as the era of the triumph of everyday life, and of the hegemony of its categories everywhere, over the rarer and more exceptional moments of heroic deeds and 'extreme situations.'"[22] The existential excess of the banal and ordinary, the calculating bourgeois lifeworld, over any remaining opportunities for adventure (outside of war and the colonial situation) then seals the fate of romance as a mode of discourse in need of internal overcoming. Jameson remarks that "realism is opposed to romance only because it carries it within itself and must somehow dissolve it in order to become its antithesis: the *Quijote* is a laborious work on the romance it still contains, and the later Spanish tradition might cause us to wonder whether the dissolution of romance leaves us with something radically different or merely with an *Aufhebung* of the impulse onto a higher and perhaps unrecognizable level" (139). On this account, realism is what we call the negation of romance from within, such that (speculatively at any rate) the latter is transformed from a sociopolitical worldview into a libidinal and wish-fulfilling impulse that realism cannot entirely do without.

In similar terms, Franco Moretti advises that we see the opposition between banality and adventure in the nineteenth century in the strongest possible terms, as a contradiction generative of immense narrative energies. "The everyday functions in other words as *the opposite of narrative*; a weight that cannot always be avoided (every now and then, horses must be brushed, even in novels), but has to be quickly overcome for the 'real' story to be told."[23] The mounting weight of inertia and boredom within the frame of the novel is the index of a successfully

---

[22] Fredric Jameson, *Antinomies of Realism* (London & New York: Verso, 2013), 109.

[23] Franco Moretti, "Serious Century," in Moretti, ed., *The Novel, Vol. 1: History, Geography, and Culture* (Princeton, NJ: Princeton University Press, 2006), 370.

achieved bourgeois hegemony, which cannot perceive itself as revolutionary and "eventful," but must immediately seal over its historical emergence by way of the ideological gravity of the status quo. "This collapse of 'adventure' into everyday banality," best observed in Flaubert, can be correlated technically with the rise of one particular formal device, "the only narrative invention of the entire nineteenth century," the *filler*, which succeeds so well because these descriptive pauses "offer *the kind of narrative pleasure compatible with the new regularity of bourgeois life* . . . turning [the novelistic universe] into a world of few surprises, fewer adventures, and no miracles at all" (378, 380). Summing up these internal paradoxes, Moretti writes:

> One is reminded of the antithesis evoked in the Protestant Ethic between "adventure capitalism"—impulsive, violent, confiding in fortune, and present in almost every epoch, like those narratives that in English are called "romances"—and the sober, predictable, repressed ethos of bureaucratic-rational capitalism, which is instead, like the "novel," a recent European invention. (384)

On this reading, then, once capitalism has developed out of its feudal conditions of possibility, and overcome or at least regulated the "primitive accumulation" of its adventure-capitalist modes, its privileged cultural vessel—the novel—is charged with the responsibility of normalizing its hegemony through the technical conquest of something never yet attempted in prose or rhyme: monotonous regularity, tedium, and everyday repetition. That this form, the novel, is still tied genetically to its origins in feudalism opens it to multiple levels of irony, which will turn out to have been the very purpose of the form—the constant act of cultural revolution whereby such feudal genetics are exposed to the withering grey light of actuarial tables, stock reports, and the working day.

In nuce, our argument is that the successive cultural dominants under capitalist relations of production—realism, modernism, postmodernism—designate an increasingly successful, though never fully victorious, war of position against the feudal DNA of romance. Modernism is a continuation by other means of the already established and immensely generative formal tensions that drive the great century of realisms: between narrative pleasure and sensory data, satisfying plots and miserable fortunes, totalizing depictions and the empty contingencies of everyday life. For modernism, those "other means" are, exactly, the various realisms themselves, which it can now round upon and expose as governed by an aesthetic ideology in their own right, available for deconstruction. For unlike realism, which maintains a dutiful fidelity to narrative pleasure, modernism (so we are told) learned to revile the underlying genesis of all narrative in what Sir Walter Scott had called the "common origin" of "Romance and real history,"[24] and what Andrew Lang in 1887 was bold enough to have associated with the most "primitive" and atavistic layers of civilized literary culture.[25] Romance, in Nicolas Daly's paraphrase, was thereby exposed as "the original core of the novel," and preserved within realism's formal apparatus the contaminating "traces of a primitive consciousness in the modern self."[26] With its intimidating arsenal of technically sophisticated means, aesthetic modernism is all too readily grasped as the final elimination and humiliation of this genetic hangover from an age of patriarchal barbarism and feudal superstition. And yet what could be more modernist than the very libidinal appeal of the "primitive" itself, lodged like the glistering kernel of a lost world in the gray gridworks of enlightenment: the thrilling "techno-primitivism" of its semisynthetic material substances,[27] the polymorphous appeals of a Freudian unconscious, and the combined and uneven developments specific to imperialism, generating surplus value out of violent material expropriations of the "savage" peripheries? If the primitive persists as romance within the realism of the nineteenth century, the modern's affective relationship to that survival was powerfully ambivalent, for strong historical reasons. For such reasons, as Joyce made clear in the "Nausicaa" chapter of *Ulysses*, the "negation" of romance within the modern novel might well be achieved, not by acting as if it did not exist, but by a satirical passage through its perdurable discourses. And that meant keeping these latter at least temporarily alive within the laboratories of literary modernism—even as the Freudian analysand was encouraged, by way of hazardous symbolic reconnaissance missions through its archaic ruins, to map the repressed infantile materials secretly manifesting its symptoms in the present.

In order to come to grips with what romance must still have meant in the modern period, such that its management and repression would become definitive of a new aesthetic regime, we need to adopt a flexible and adaptive historical account of the fortunes of a genre or mode that, at the outer limit, seems indistinguishable from narrative in general—or, as Jameson paraphrases Frye at his most grandiose, romance is at some level "the ultimate source and paradigm of all storytelling. On this view, the oral tales of tribal society, the fairy tales that are the irrepressible voice and expression of the underclasses of the great systems of domination, adventure stories and melodrama, and the popular or mass culture of our own time are all syllables and broken fragments of some single immense

---

[24] Walter Scott, "An Essay on Romance," in *The Complete Works of Sir Walter Scott*, Vol. 1 (New York: Conner & Cooke, 1833), 27.

[25] Andrew Lang, "Realism and Romance," *Contemporary Review* 52 (1887), 690 [683–93].

[26] Nicolas Daly, *Modernism, Romance, and the* fin de siècle: *Popular Fiction and British Culture, 1880–1914* (Cambridge: Cambridge University Press, 1999), 21.

[27] See David Trotter, *Literature in the First Media Age: Britain between the Wars* (Cambridge, MA: Harvard University Press, 2013), 86–119.

story."[28] It will be advisable to keep this view in mind throughout what follows, for its implication is that the purifying aesthetic aspirations of the modernist art-novel are fated to seek an exit strategy from narrative itself, at the cost of its own sustaining element in storytelling (which is ultimately traceable down to the smallest syntactical units of prose as such). Moreover, that the fundamental genetic structure of romance concerns the utopian dimension—reversals of ill fortune, ultimate ascensions and rebirths, entrances into the heavenly city—surely suggests a baby in this bathwater that will be flushed away only at great cost to the imaginative and political yield of narrative art. In any event, on this outer circumference, romance as wish-fulfillment is better conceived of as a barrier that literary aesthetic experimentalism breaches at its own peril—perhaps Stein's *Making of Americans* can here emblematize the risks, as the further that text recedes from the narrative promises with which it opens, the less readable and more physically unbearable it becomes.

If we can regard both literary realism and its modernist negation as attempts to work alongside in order to overcome the romance-germ of the narrative impulse itself, then it becomes possible to recognize both as moments in an ongoing imaginary management, in the domain of prose fiction, of the "persistence of the old regime." How is a middle-class culture predicated on rational exchange and formal liberty supposed to reserve any place for the aristocracy's romance—for dynastic plots, courtly intrigues, demonized Others, surprise encounters, happy endings, noble military sacrifice, and so forth—in a mode of production whose logic is pitted against such rank anachronisms? I propose that there have been three dominant answers to that question. First and foremost, in realism and popular culture, by clinging to narrative as the dimension in which this superannuated worldview attains its universal, utopian vocation, negating via atavistic wish-fulfillments the spiritual deformities and inequalities of capitalism itself. Second, in modern satire, as an ambivalent formal operation that reads modern reality in the light of romance valuations, and romance tropes in the light of modern conditions. And third, in modernism, by occluding and masking romance, as a mark of a still deeper fidelity to its utopian vocation—as we shall see.

If capitalism is always a mode of production in some ways unevenly combined with others (both within national markets and in the sense of international lags and differentials), then it is never simply a question of the modernity of the aesthetic regime immediately displacing or substituting itself for the now defunct system of "magical narratives."[29] Rather, capitalism's halting emergence from within the womb of the old order means that there is *never* any sudden rejection

---

[28] Jameson, *The Political Unconscious: Narrative as a Socially Symbolic Act* (Ithaca, NY: Cornell University Press, 1981), 105.

[29] Jameson, *Political Unconscious*, 103–50.

of the *ancien régime*'s *Weltanschauung*, but instead its tactical reinvention within the nascent structure-in-dominance, and its repurposing as a semi-autonomous instance or ideological level of the new order.[30] So, just as the agricultural sector of the old feudal economy is subsumed into the new capitalist mode of production without entirely ridding it of its older class integuments (in Europe[31]), so too the ideological matrix of feudalism (romance) is retroactively reinserted into the wider web of capitalist cultural discourses and value systems—indeed, dialectically, and with two principal valences. On the one hand, romance is newly available for the expression of nostalgic anti-capitalist sentiments generated by capitalism itself, in that new species of discourse called Romanticism. On the other, it is reconfigured as an explicit ideological instrument of the new system, in the new market for mass-produced cultural materials among the lower-middle and working classes. Romance is doubly preserved against its logical extinction, thanks to combined and uneven development; but in the event it is completely reinvented, so the residual gene structure is more active than ever, only in forms that make it useful to an inhabitation of the modern. What we call modernism is the protracted critical aesthetic realization that both of these dynamics are current in the cultural and imaginative life of the present: romance is offering a nostalgic corrective to, and a potent ideological justification for, the conditions of existence that progressively make it impossible in the first place. Modernism is the attempt to conceptualize this double spectrality of romance, in its radical uncanniness. It wants to conjure away what it is detained by as a node of pure fascination. But how it will do so must be very different in societies where the old feudal class never existed in the first place.

Functions of romance

On American soil, the tensions between realism and romance were played out in the nineteenth century with a peculiar emphasis on the latter's capacity to engender a properly artistic effect, as against the paltry aesthetic yields of what Frank Norris ridiculed as "the drama of a broken teacup, the tragedy of a walk down the block, the excitement of an afternoon call, the adventure of an

---

[30] "The capitalist economic order emerged from the entrails of the feudal economic order. The dissolution of the latter set free the constitutive elements of the former." Marx, translated by Ben Brewster from Joseph Roy's 1872 French edition of *Capital, Vol. 1*, as overseen by Marx, in Louis Althusser and Étienne Balibar, *Reading Capital*, trans. Ben Brewster (London: Verso, 1970), 279. Marx used the figure of the womb to metaphorize capitalism's emergence from feudalism in *A Contribution to the Critique of Political Economy* (1859), and the *Critique of the Gotha Program* (1875), as well as *Das Kapital*.

[31] Here see the definitive discussion in Louis Althusser and Étienne Balibar, *Reading Capital*, esp. Part III by Balibar, "The Basic Concepts of Historical Materialism," 199–307.

invitation to dinner."[32] Norris's defense of romance's capacity to map "the wide world [...], the unplumbed depths of the human heart, and the mysteries of sex, and the problems of life, and the black, unsearched penetralia of the soul of a man"—as against its ghettoization in the ranks of bestsellerdom where it is confined to "the castles of the Middle Ages and the Renaissance chateaux"—chimes with a long-standing tradition in the most esteemed American literature. Brockden Brown stands at the head of this tradition, but its more reputable disciples form the very backbone of the national library. From Hawthorne's stirring bid for liberty from the novel's "very minute fidelity, not merely to the possible, but to the probable and ordinary course of man's experience," in order romantically to attempt "to connect a by-gone time with the very present that is flitting away from us," suitably draped in "a legendary mist,"[33] and the moonlit synesthesia of his account of "a neutral territory, somewhere between the real world and fairy-land, where the Actual and the Imaginary may meet,"[34] through Fenimore Cooper's historical adventure tales, Poe's explicit invocations of the fantastic, Melville's ambivalent navigations of the distinction at issue, down to the curiously self-conflicted figure of Henry James himself (who declared that the "celebrated distinction between the novel and the romance" was a "clumsy" separation doubtless invented "by critics and readers for their own convenience"[35]), this canonical lineage is precisely what the critical consensus hails as "American literature," and Richard Chase is only the first of a long line of intellectuals to make the case that this national literature is romantic before it is realistic.[36] But if that is the case, and if American realism emerges into a literary

[32] Frank Norris, "A Plea for Romantic Fiction," *Boston Evening Transcript* (December 18, 1901), reprinted in *The Literary Criticism of Frank Norris*, ed. Donald Pizer (Austin: University of Texas Press, 1964), 76.

[33] Nathaniel Hawthorne, "Preface," in Robert S. Levine, ed., *House of the Seven Gables* (New York: W. W. Norton, 2006).

[34] Hawthorne, "The Custom House," *The Scarlet Letter*, reprinted in *The Norton Anthology of American Literature*, 4th ed., Vol. 1: Beginnings to 1865, eds. Nina Baym et al. (New York: Norton & Co., 1994), 1268.

[35] Henry James, "The Art of Fiction," in *Literary Criticism, Vol. 1* (New York: Library of America, 1984), 55.

[36] Richard Chase, *The American Novel and Its Traditions* [c. 1957] (Baltimore: Johns Hopkins University Press, 1980); but see also Joel Porte, *The Romance in America* (Middletown, CT: Wesleyan University Press, 1969), Michael Davitt Bell, *The Development of American Romance* (Chicago: University of Chicago Press, 1980), Evan Carlton, *The Rhetoric of American Romance* (Baltimore: Johns Hopkins University Press, 1985), George Dekker, *The American Historical Romance* (Cambridge: Cambridge University Press, 1987), Robert S. Levine, *Conspiracy and Romance: Studies in Brockden Brown, Cooper, Hawthorne, and Melville* (Cambridge: Cambridge University Press, 1989), William Ellis, *The Theory of the American Romance: An Ideology in American Intellectual History* (Ann Arbor: University of Michigan Press, 1989), Emily Budick *Nineteenth-Century American Romance: Genre and the Construction of Democratic Culture* (New York: Twayne, 1996), Stephen Frye, *Historiography and Narrative Design in the American Romance* (Lewiston, NY: Edwin Mellen Press, 2001), among many others.

space much more heavily mortgaged to the mists and legends, "the enormous, the formidable, the terrible,"[37] of romance than a national literary scene presided over by the twin figures of Jane Austen and Anthony Trollope, then the challenge for a materialist criticism is to account for this surprising tenacity of feudal specters and mythemes in a social and economic landscape from which the aristocracy is missing.

That task cannot possibly be undertaken here, but a more manageable subtask can at least be assayed, and that concerns the specific clustering of romance fictions in the antebellum and Reconstruction South, which was to have exerted the most direct pressures upon the literary productivity of William Faulkner. Faulkner understood the arguments of Hawthorne and Norris enough to have written, in 1922 at the age of twenty-four, "We have, in America, an inexhaustible fund of dramatic material. Two sources occur to any one: the old Mississippi river days, and the romantic growth of railroads."[38] This unselfconscious conflation of the new and the old, the realistic and the romantic, speaks to a national literary preoccupation, but it stems particularly from the extraordinary concentration of popular literary romance forms in the South, where Faulkner's own grandfather had penned one of the most popular romantic fictions of the 1880s, *The White Rose of Memphis* (1881). Writing in 1883, two years after that novel was published, Mark Twain satirically attributed all of the blame for the social simulacrum of Southern romance to the influence of Walter Scott: "It was Sir Walter that made every gentleman in the South a Major or a Colonel, or a General or a Judge, before the war; and it was he, also, that made these gentlemen value these bogus decorations. For it was he that created rank and caste down there, and also reverence for rank and caste, and pride and pleasure in them."[39] He was to develop that observation in a core section of his masterpiece, *The Adventures of Huckleberry Finn*, and it is substantiated in any number of novels published between 1830 and 1860, which Richard Chase argues constitute an entire secondary stream to the lauded American romance tradition of Hawthorne, Poe, and Melville:[40] a bastard form of the novel, got on the body of European romance by Scott's "historical novel," and reared into a uniquely reactionary political space by men who were openly pro-slavery, opposed to industrialization, and fiercely culturally conservative.

---

[37] Frank Norris, "Zola as a Romantic Writer," in Donald Pizer, ed., *Novels and Essays* (New York: Library of America, 1986), 558.

[38] William Faulkner, "American Drama: Inhibitions," in *The Mississippian* (March 17 & 24, 1922), reprinted in *Essays, Speeches & Public Letters*, ed. James B. Meriwether (New York: Modern Library, 2004), 318.

[39] Mark Twain, *Life on the Mississippi*, Ch. 46, in *Mississippi Writings* (New York: Library of America, 1982), 501.

[40] Chase, *American Novel and Its Traditions*.

According to Chase and Twain, the cultural backwater of the Old South supposedly made it possible for a completely distinct literary formation to establish itself with little if any connections to the emergent lineage of romance in the North—based on an ideological matrix of the cavalier ethos, agrarian gentility, courtly gender roles, and categorical racism, the prose romances of the antebellum South manufactured an ersatz aristocracy out of the brutal slave-owners of the plantation economy and endowed them with a class glamor put to the test in various narrative trials. The political effort represented by such fictions was to foster a vivid sense of cultural cohesion and visceral difference from the increasingly abolitionist Yankee North, a habitable enclave of romance ideologemes that were, in fact, irreconcilable with the presiding economic situation and the demands of history, and which, in that sense, tended to rehearse over and again the very quixotic nature of the task on which they were bent. That is to say, the romance of antebellum Southern novels is espoused and affirmed in accents of mounting secessionist pride, but often enough in a manner that forces a formal crisis, which Scott's borrowed narrative machinery was guaranteed to effect: a nostalgia for the present, seen as historically doomed in advance. Just as Scott's highlands were, for all their glorious and rebellious patriotism, destined to be absorbed into the imperial United Kingdom, so these Southern revisions of Scott tended unselfconsciously to mobilize their romance modes in the key of glorious failure. Indeed, the most important early such fiction, George Tucker's *The Valley of Shenandoah* (1824), has been described as a "suicidal 'romance' of cultural difference; [its] insistence on the material reality of a 'romantic' southern past results in the abortion of 'romance' as a means for coming to terms with the present."[41] Subsequent Southern romances only deepen the paradoxes. John P. Kennedy's *Swallow Barn* (1832), for instance, which more than any other text is responsible for formulating the "plantation legend" as "a nostalgic re-creation of a way of living being lost in an expanding America,"[42] has long been seen as a text woven of incommensurable ideological and narrative elements: picturesque picaresque, pastoral, social satire, pro-slavery tract. But this hybrid nature is evidence of the instability of romance as a viable form: "The ideological and aesthetic heterogeneity of the narrative is not merely the (unintentional) expression of ideological crisis. Rather it is the very strategy by which the text seeks to overcome crisis."[43] Meanwhile, William Gilmore Simms, probably the most successful and outspoken of all the antebellum romancers, publicly defended the vocation of the romance artist to confabulate a "perfect ideal" out

---

[41] Zeno Ackermann, *Working at "Romance": Poetics and Ideology in Novels of the Antebellum American South, 1824–1854* (Doctoral Dissertation, Regensburg University, 2004), 49.

[42] J. V. Ridgely, *John Pendleton Kennedy* (New York: Twayne, 1966), 53; William S. Osborne, "Introduction," *Swallow Barn* (New York: Hafner, 1962), xix.

[43] Ackermann, *Working at "Romance,"* 50.

of the meaningless chronology of events;[44] and yet his novel *The Partisan* (1835) "marks a transition from the 'romance' of national history to the 'romance' of secession"—that is, its "perfected" history is increasingly pitched in the optative mood, and has one eye firmly set on the future of an independent Confederacy. As Ackermann puts it, the "national history constructed by Simms was really an unusable past, and especially through the attractive character of Porgy, the novel even betrays a vague consciousness of the fact."[45] Or again, while Nathaniel Tucker's "inversion of the time scheme of the historical novel, his writing about a past that is really a future" in *The Partisan Leader* (1836), seemingly results in a "profound epistemological shift" away from the Scottian prototype, such that its romance is promoted as an achievable historical fact, a call to arms in the present, nevertheless it cannot escape the irony that its political "realism" obeys a template steeped in the feudal codes and militarism of an aristocracy that does not exist outside of its own pages.[46]

Here, then, we see a rather distinctive pattern being nurtured by the immanent tensions between romance and "reality" in the nineteenth-century novel. If there is only ever, as John Frow writes, a "continuing, genre-defining structural tension between the romance and the novelistic modes," then this tension took on a very peculiar form in the South.[47] The critical operation here was less the invocation of a heroic past, and of a class capable of sustaining such heroism in a world unburdened by the weighty implications of a bourgeois daily life, than it was the invention from whole cloth of such a class, capable *in the imaginary* of filling in the empty slot of a counter-revolutionary force against the rationalized "floor plan" of modernity.[48] The latter would never tolerate the continuation of slavery in an economy defined by contract law and the extraction of surplus value from marketable labor-power. Romance came to the service of a reactionary slaveholding class by symbolically endowing it with a ready-made glamor and history that it lacked in reality, where its more evident characteristics consisted in a vulgar brutality of manner, a determinate distance from the increasingly hegemonic industrial class, a dependency on chattel slavery rather than peonage, and a consequent lack of any "organic" consistency in its relations of production (which is to say, a dependency on force rather than consent to maintain the division of labor). If Scott was in any way right to suggest that the ruling

---

[44] William Gilmore Simms, "The Epochs and Events of American History, as Suited to the Purposes of Art in Fiction," *Views and Reviews in American Literature, History and Fiction* (n.p.: Wiley & Putnam, 1845), 41.

[45] Ackermann, *Working at "Romance,"* 106.

[46] Ackermann, *Working at "Romance,"* 119.

[47] John Frow, *Character and Person* (Oxford: Oxford University Press, 2014), 197.

[48] See Fredric Jameson, "The Realist Floor-Plan," in Marshall Blonsky, ed., *On Signs* (Baltimore: Johns Hopkins University Press, 1985), 373–83.

class of the Middle Ages modeled itself on the romances of its greatest writers, then Twain was surely not wholly in error to suppose that the descendants of those uncultivated second and third sons of the minor British gentry who settled in the South to make their fortunes came to model their own class aspirations in the terms laid down by Scott himself, either unaware of or unwilling to look too deeply into the ironies implicit in that self-fashioning. With secession and civil war looming as inevitable historical tests of this class's destiny, the romance form mutated as it was called upon to articulate the political fantasies of a faction whose future was logically incompatible with the growth of capitalism itself, and which was therefore obliged to project its fortunes "back to the future" by way of a trebly simulated cavalier ethos: Simms adapting Scott adapting the *chanson de geste*.

It is possible to grasp the active legacies of romance in nineteenth-century America as dialectically intertwined. On the one hand, in the North, a self-conscious adaptation of the literature of the marvelous and the elevated to contest the insidious normality of a spreading industrial culture, in much the same way that, in Europe, a folk past and the aristocratic regime that was its historical counterpart were revived in order to check the ideological ascendancy of abstract rationalism and utilitarian philistinism: Romanticism as romantic anti-capitalism. What Robert Sayre and Michael Löwy call "the deeply antagonistic relationship of Romanticism to industrial society" as evinced by writers who "*because* they turn their gaze toward the past ... are able to criticise the present with such acumen and realism,"[49] or what Raymond Williams celebrates such nostalgic artists for embodying—"certain human values, capacities, energies, which the development of society towards an industrial civilization was felt to be threatening or even destroying"[50]—was as pertinent a structure of feeling in the United States as in England, Germany, or France; if not more so, since America lacked even the built environment of a world antedating the rule of capital on which to dream. In the South, on the other hand, there was a deliberate exercise in class self-fashioning on the basis of Scott's extremely successful novelistic implementations of nostalgic romance. This wishful identitarian fantasy of the slave-owning plantocracy flourished in the absence of any more viable realism for the class in question, since "the real" (the bourgeois everyday, with its practical roots in the generality of exchange) was exactly what imperiled its existence in the first place. However pervasive and persistent this extraordinarily successful romantic projection—not only is early Faulkner criticism peppered with references to a landowning "aristocracy," for example, but no less

---

[49] Robert Sayre and Michael Löwy, Figures of Romantic Anti-Capitalism," *New German Critique* 32 (Spring–Summer, 1984), 46, 49 [42–92].

[50] Raymond Williams, *Culture and Society, 1780–1950* (London: Penguin, 1976), 53.

an acerbic critic than Richard Wright classified the Southern economy in 1941 as "feudal" in essence[51]—there can be no denying its social function as a self-serving literary wish-fulfillment on the part of a class unable to find satisfactory rhetorical resources in the anti-royalist and pro-bourgeois Constitution, even as they sought to re-enact one of the founding principles of the Declaration. The novels written under the impress of this doomed wish-fulfillment are evidence of a failed collective effort to preserve a mode of production whose pseudo-organicism could then be offered as a potent, material force of resistance to the spreading fragmentations of modernity itself. "There was," writes Richie Watson, "a perfect sympathy between the time-transcending paradigm of the plantation romance and the implicit need of southerners to believe that their culture could escape the imperatives of modernity";[52] or in other words, "the attempt to stay the historical dynamics of disintegration and alienation by means of an aesthetic intervention that was to be based on the conserving power of (literary) style," as Ackermann puts it.[53] Eugene Genovese once controversially wrote, "At their best, Southern ideals constituted a rejection of the crass, vulgar, inhumane elements of capitalist society," insofar as these ideals were the manufactured discourses of "precapitalist, quasi-aristocratic landowners who had to adjust their economy and ways of thinking to a capitalist world market."[54] But in that case, the "utopian" dimension of Southern romance, and the utopian moment of Hawthornian romance, are two sides of a divided whole whose name is capitalist modernity itself, and whose most persistent critical specter is the lingering literary corpus of a class doomed by it to extinction. If Northern romance conjured its aristocracies out of the venerable families of old Mayflower money, or projected them in high fantasy from Europe itself (recall the mysterious husband to Pearl, who writes with "armorial seals ... though of bearing unknown to English heraldry"[55]), then Southern romance tried the wholly illegitimate, but prodigiously successful tack of manufacturing one from whole cloth on the back of an actual dominant class. Both forms were deeply uneasy with the cultural consequences of an economic system predicated on free, anonymous labor-powers, but while one speculated in more or less empty aesthetic abstraction from historical forces, the other explicitly aligned its cavalier ethos with the military credentials of a regional elite whose ultimate weakness and poverty, in comparative terms, served only to burnish the romance of

---

[51] See Richard Wright with Edwin Roskam, *12 Million Black Voices: A Folk History of the Negro in the United States* (New York: Basic Books, 2008).

[52] Richie D. Watson, *Yeoman versus Cavalier: The Old Southwest's Fictional Road to Rebellion* (Baton Rouge: Louisiana State University Press, 1993), 83.

[53] Ackermann, *Working at "Romance,"* 6–7.

[54] Eugene Genovese, *The Political Economy of Slavery: Studies in the Economy and Society of the Slave South* (New York: Pantheon, 1965), 30, 19.

[55] Hawthorne, *Scarlet Letter*, 1385.

an anti-capitalist crusade lost in advance. Its indefensible basis in slavery (which not even the oldest of chivalric romance forms would endorse) could thus durably be screened by the very pathos of the lost cause.

Romance itself should not be understood as any kind of trans-historical, fixed ideological matrix, but seen instead from the very beginning as a field of narrative and political vectors pressed into service to manage social contradiction and crisis. Michael McKeon insists on twelfth-century romance as "a method of investigating the substance of status categories at a time of pressing status inconsistency. It is a technique designed to anatomize 'aristocratic honor' into its constituent parts without acknowledging that such a labor is needed—indeed, without acknowledging that its parts are truly separable."[56] In this way, newly available ambitions for upward class mobility could be "spiritualized" into personal quests and proofs of internal merit that were separable from birth: romance translated nobility from a birthright into a function. Contrarily, Fredric Jameson argues that

> Romance in its original strong form may then be understood as an imaginary "solution" to this real contradiction [between distinct warring clans who now, for the first time in the twelfth century begin to recognise themselves as a single class], a symbolic answer to the perplexing question of how my enemy can be thought of as being evil (that is, as other than myself and marked by some absolute difference), when what is responsible for his being so characterized is quite simply the identity of his own conduct with mine, the which—points of honor, challenges, tests of strength—he reflects as in a mirror image.[57]

Whether or not we accept Jameson's or McKeon's sense of the historical dilemma to be definitive of twelfth-century socioeconomic reality, the point is that romance evolved as a creative response to real exigencies that limited the capacities of prevailing ideological norms to perceive them in the first place. Romance is not a timeless essence, but an improvised system of narrativization in which invariable categories such as self and other, friend and foe, high and low, honor and infamy, are tested in relation to valorized character traits and trials of spiritual worth against a perdurable backdrop of charismatic rule and the obeisance of agricultural labor.

And throughout modernity, this flexible, adaptive semiological apparatus continued to respond creatively to the irresistible rising tide of secularization

---

[56] Michael McKeon, *The Origins of the English Novel, 1600–1740* (Baltimore: Johns Hopkins University Press, 1987), 142–43.

[57] Jameson, *Political Unconscious*, 118.

and disenchantment, as a means of attending to, or papering over, its own contradictions. Maturing like realism's disreputable twin, romance enjoyed a new lease of life in the commercial modes of melodrama and sensation fiction, catering to readerships and audiences already fully adapted to the stipulations of modernity and seeking there the thrills and rushes of what Baudelaire ironically dubbed the "heroism of modern life,"[58] or what Frank Norris sneered at as the vulgarization of romance in the "cut-and-thrust stories" of the middle class's obsession with "cloaks and daggers, or moonlight and golden hair."[59] This is no residual afflatus of an aristocracy which, as Baudelaire put it in 1859, "is only just beginning to totter and fall,"[60] but a mode of sensation fully internalized to the ubiquity of market relations themselves. For just as the industrial commodity brought with it a "fetishism" whose apparent archaism masked a completely modern form of enchantment, so too bourgeois commercial culture nurtured a pulse of outrageous overstimulation within forms marked from without by the deadening repetitions of industrial production. Where realist forms battened onto a dying feudal semiotic system in order to generate from within its webs the genuine critical energies of negation, these other forms stimulated trade through the cultivation of ersatz excitations. What we call modernism marks the irreversible moment in cultural history at which realism and its superannuated twin stand revealed as conjoined in the final instance, most particularly in the mode of "Naturalism," where it is henceforth impossible to tell what is art from what is trash, what is critical from what is merely monstrous and exploitative. Even the very greatest achievements of the realist tradition stand charged in retrospect by their inevitable affiliations with narrative modes, character types, and scenic situations that cannot fully be distinguished from commercial melodramatic corruptions: something perhaps not felt at the time of the publication of works by Dickens, Balzac, and Stendhal, but which, by the end of the nineteenth century, cannot be unseen. The arrival of the "bestseller" is the crowning moment of systemic reabsorption of hitherto critical narrative strategies, since in it, what was once residually feudal has been fully translated into the "mere sentimentalism" of romance's "misuse" at the hands of the publishing industry.[61] Modernism's rejection of realism is thus a visceral reaction against its "real subsumption" into romantic bestsellerdom.

---

[58] Charles Baudelaire, "Salon of 1846," in Jonathan Mayne, trans. and ed., *Art in Paris 1845–1862: Salons and Other Exhibitions Reviewed by Charles Baudelaire* (Ithaca, NY: Cornell University Press, 1965), 116.

[59] Norris, "A Plea for Romantic Fiction," 558.

[60] Baudelaire, *The Painter of Life and Other Essays*, trans. and ed. Jonathan Mayne (London: Phaidon, 1995), 28.

[61] Norris, "A Plea for Romantic Fiction," 559.

Faulkner and the place of modernism

If we think of the nineteenth-century novel as an institution in which the rising tide of bourgeois quotidianness or the "sober, predictable, repressed ethos of bureaucratic-rational capitalism"[62] was set in productive formal tension against a tenacious romance infrastructure of adventure motifs, narratological pleasures, and a pervasive moralism, then we can begin to perceive the strange symmetry between this "uneven and combined development" of the form and the objective situation from which Faulkner might be said to have entered modernism itself. The pervasive cultural hostility much noted in the South's adversarial attitude toward the North's capitalist norms—what Jennifer Greeson calls the distinctive *"ideological juxtaposition"* that sutures the South disjunctively to the North within an unstable national formation[63]—is mapped, as a geographical tension, onto the historical antagonism that defines the relationship between realism and romance. This regional configuration, in which the South as "internal other" refracts the larger national ideological norms, provides a particularly opportune framework for the continued flourishing of romance, but also suggests a uniquely Hegelian optic through which to observe Faulkner's modernism. Greeson writes that the "South gives writers a backward glance, a conduit to the American colonial past against which they may gauge the rise of the independent, developing republic. As writers posit the South as premodern and undeveloped [...] it comes to serve a forward-looking function as well."[64] On this argument, it is almost as if the passage of the diachronic realism-romance agon through the regional prism of the "backward" internal other is precisely what supercharges it with the internationalist, universalist potentialities of modernism itself: a means of looking at modernity from the far side, a beyond reached only through this ideological particle accelerator built under the South's cotton- and tobacco-yielding topsoil. As everything that was not (yet) industrial, the South (as much a fantasy as a region) proved hospitable to modes of textual production that saw modernization as a Fall into alienation, ennui, and anomie; offered succor to the residual affective and epistemological embrace of the "knowable community"; nurtured cultural resistances based on accentual, ethnic, and religious specificities; and, in some potent and suggestive ways, gestured beyond capitalism itself as an inevitable structure of social relations.

The New Southern Studies has been particularly generative of dialectical figures for considering these national tensions and contradictions. Jay Watson describes the South as "a region that has functioned in the national imagination

---

[62] Moretti, "Serious Century," 384.

[63] See Jennifer Rae Greeson, *Our South: Geographic Fantasy and the Rise of National Literature* (Cambridge, MA: Harvard University Press, 2010), eBook edition, loc. 33 of 4114.

[64] Greeson, *Our South*, loc. 68 of 4114.

for over two centuries as the basis for idiosyncratic modes of American identity (psychic forms), as a problematic topography within the geographic space of the nation, and as a specific social formation bearing an uneasy inside-outside relation to US society more broadly considered."[65] His analyses of the many ways the figure of the human body has been repurposed by Southern writers in order to literalize and develop these larger, structuring antinomies are suitably dialectic in method. Leigh Anne Duck's explorations of the productive tension along the "temporal divide between the South and the larger nation," between a larger search for national continuities and a regional agenda of modernizing change, take on "the central frameworks through which southern exceptionalism was routinely asserted—devolution, folkloric authenticity, romanticism, and gothicism," and show how writers "tested and challenged a model of binding and determinate group identification that was simultaneously courted and disavowed in US nationalism."[66] Meanwhile, Scott Romine demonstrates the tenacity of what he calls the "mechanical reproduction" of a South "full of fakes—Civil War reenactments and plantation tourism, to name two"—flourishing alongside the inevitable social "progress" that such disenchantment betokened over parochial forms of authority and tradition. His is a "double narrative of continuity and rupture, a doubling [he wishes] less to adjudicate than to preserve, since it is precisely in this liminal space that [...] contemporary southern narrative has found something like a home ground."[67] Liminal space, temporal divide, inside-outside: in this ambivalent critical tropology the South is less an abiding substance than an unstable, dynamic moment within the consolidation of larger "antipodal images" that make the "national" and the "regional" distinct in the first place, within a broadly disseminated discourse network.[68] So the South's "tortured and complex relation to contemporary economic pressures and to flows of culture that are increasingly global and dispersed in nature; its acute absorption and production of declension and progress as culture-stories; and its fraught and anxious relation—in which most of the above are embedded— with authenticity" become modalities of a necessary fiction against which the contours of the nation as such can be made brilliantly salient.[69] Cleanth Brooks' long-standing case that Faulkner's dominant theme was one of agrarian resistance to the unstoppable spread of Northern industrialization, and Lawrence H. Schwartz's cynical account of Faulkner's rise to prominence in national

---

[65] Jay Watson, *Reading for the Body: The Recalcitrant Materiality of Southern Fiction, 1893–1985* (Athens, GA & London: University of Georgia Press, 2012), eBook edition, loc. 254 of 9716.

[66] Leigh Anne Duck, *The Nation's Region: Southern Modernism, Segregation, and US Nationalism* (Athens, GA: University of Georgia Press, 2006), 3–4.

[67] Scott Romine, *The Real South: Southern Narrative in the Age of Cultural Reproduction* (Baton Rouge: Louisiana State University Press, 2008), eBook edition, loc. 91 of 7111.

[68] Duck, *The Nation's Region*, 2.

[69] Romine, *The Real South*, loc. 115 of 7111.

letters as coincident "with United States political and economic hegemony" after the Second World War, can today be thought of together, as a dialectical argument in which regional separatism and outward-facing continental nationalism are the obverse and reverse of a coin stamped "exceptionalism" and "anti-communism."[70] The South served, as Taylor Hagood makes clear, a very useful ideological function in the Cold War years, for the way in which it preserved an anti-industrial, pro-agrarian matrix of mythemes in its accepted regional identity, and yet proved resistant to any overlay of socialist political semes.[71] Which is not to say, of course, that projections of its polyvalent charms did not, despite this overt anti-political use-value, emanate strong utopian and proto-political signals in a situation characterized by the glaciation of political currents outside of the "developing world" (where, as we know, Faulkner assumed a very different aspect indeed from the Cold Warrior of the national scene[72]). What is most modern and "modernist" about Faulkner's fiction in particular is its tendency to gene-splice the realist and romantic rudiments of its narrative DNA, generating in the result a series of baffling mutations, distorted hybrids that defy existing classificatory schemas, but which recapitulate many of the underlying tensions and antinomies that make the "South" America's region par excellence.

If, ideologically, the USA required "the South" to play a certain, immanently negative part within the *Realpolitik* struggles it was engaged in against the Soviet Union, then that provides a strong materialist explanation of the perseverance of romance within a national culture tending officially more and more toward rational and modernist formal structures (including the CIA's sponsorship of abstract expressionism and the State Department's secret friendship with any number of modern poets). Faulkner's eventual place at the very apex of the nation's sense of its own postwar literary bearing—his emergence as what Jameson calls (not without irony) "the greatest American novelist"—thus turned on his capacity to weave mythic forms out of a conjunctural sense of "the US South as a liminal space situated between and participating simultaneously in the cultures of the global North and the global South."[73] And yet it also turned, as this book will argue in substantive detail, on his remarkable sensitivity toward the infrastructural developments underpinning the ascent of the U.S.

---

[70] Cleanth Brooks, *William Faulkner: The Yoknapatawpha Country* (Baton Rouge: Louisiana State University Press, 1990), 1–10; and Lawrence H. Schwartz, *Creating Faulkner's Reputation: The Politics of Modern Literary Criticism* (Knoxville, TN: University of Tennessee Press, 1988), 4.

[71] See Taylor Hagood, *Faulkner's Imperialism: Space, Place, and the Materiality of Myth* (Baton Rouge: Louisiana State University Press, 2008), 7–9.

[72] See *Jameson on Jameson: Conversations on Cultural Marxism*, ed. Ian Buchanan (Durham, NC & London: Duke University Press, 2007), 87.

[73] Hagood, *Faulkner's Imperialism*, 8.

State as world hegemon: specifically, the physical mediation of nationhood made possible by photomechanical print technology, celluloid, gramophone recordings, electromagnetic propagation by wire, radio signals, electric streetcars, the combustion engine, paved roads, and aviation, to name a few. For not since the military defeat of the South's secessionist bid in the 1860s had the very questions of nationalism and regional difference been as accentuated and politicized as they were during the extraordinary spread of interconnectedness made possible by these technologies in the 1910s, '20s, and '30s. As we shall see in chapter after chapter below, these new media (very much including motorcars and airplanes)—thanks to their unprecedented ability to compress time and space, and articulate a congeries of diverse regional topographies around the commonality of a syndicated broadcast schedule, a bus timetable, or a bestseller list—made the abstract "nation" more of a material reality for more millions of people than at any moment in human history. Conceived as a vast palimpsestic web of arterial roadways, flight paths, radio waves, telephone wires, and vertically integrated distribution networks, "America" was coming rapidly into being, less as a verbalized "discourse" of values and sentiments, and more as an integrated simultaneity of industrially fabricated point-to-point stimuli taking mechanical, electrical, and petrochemical forms.

Yet this extraordinary development of the machinery of nationalism (a machinery whose accent on ideological consistency was less than its emphasis on technique, monopoly, and signal strength) met inevitable regional impedances, resistances predicated both on "cultural" factors such as those rehearsed above and on the material limits presented to such modernization by geographical hazards and scale, the relative extent of human settlements, the state of economic development, investment structures, taxation schemes, and many other factors besides. The promise of a simultaneous, real-time dissemination of national sensibilities across a distributed network of relay stations and franchise operations remained, in many regions, just that, for years to come, giving rise to a situation that can only be characterized as one of "combined and uneven development" in the means of media production. The inevitable development of underdevelopment that was a consequence of corporate decisions about concentration and reach, production and distribution, meant that certain regions remained more regional than others, while isolated outposts of the core locales across the periphery (like Memphis, for instance) provided graphic and sonic reminders of just how regional they were. Take Jason Compson's rage at the sluggishness of the wire service that articulates his speculations on cotton futures with the actual movements of the market in New York. So frustrating is the 15-minute periodicity of the market news-feed in Jefferson that, at one key point (which I will explore in Chapter 3), he finds himself complaining that he was "within sixty-seven miles of [Memphis] once this afternoon," where "they have it on a blackboard every ten seconds."⁷⁴ The significant material differentials in the rate of information flow between towns not 40 miles apart (the refresh time is 90 times faster in Memphis) mean that, in certain terms, Memphis is now closer to New York than it is to Jefferson, while Jefferson feels its relative distance ramified in the atrocious state of the roads (exacerbating Jason's headaches), the absence of a local radio station, the cluttering of the town square with mules and wagons, the absence of an electric streetcar system, and so on. Yoknapatawpha is thus a "region within a region," a further dialectical twist of the knife whereby the "national" feeds off the negative moment of its antinomy in the underdeveloped South, here distinctly felt as a lag in the rate of development of media and transport infrastructures.

Historically, this period between the two World Wars has tended to be characterized in terms of large cultural abstractions such as the "jazz age," in the demographic terms of immigration and internal migration, or in the standard "boom and bust" narrative of the Great Depression and the war against international Communism. But there is another story here with as much, if not more, to tell us about the interanimation of nation and region, North and South, as these more familiar tales. And that is the history of media, with which, I argue, William Faulkner was intimately and almost obsessively acquainted. It is this history—of the growing stabilization of the abstract concept of the nation within an integrated system of new technologies allowing for a real-time simultaneity of consumption—that presents a particularly vivid and dynamic picture of the uneven development that made the South the period's privileged vantage point from which to measure the achievements and limitations of modernization itself; since there, for most of the inhabitants and for longer than most of the rest of the nation, this transformation of daily life encountered obstacles that threw its logic into sharp relief. This was a protracted period in which, for all intents and purposes, the *media were the message*, and that message was one of participating in a genuine common mass culture as consumers, rather than producers, of prefabricated national values, habits, and sentiments. In a dialectic that would find its distorted geopolitical echo some sixty years later in Eastern Europe, around the end of the 1920s Southerners were confronted with an irresistible invitation that was simultaneously a prohibition: the movies, the radio networks, the recording industry, the automobile industry, and the nascent airways, all projected a humming immanence of belonging (to modernity, to America) from which they, by virtue of a determinate underdevelopment, were in part excluded. And yet the message (of the media) was nonetheless inescapable and ubiquitous; even filtered

---

[74] William Faulkner, *The Sound and the Fury*, in *Novels 1926–1929* (New York: Library of America, 2006), 1065.

through the various impedances of the "nation's region," it got through: "The sunny air was filled with competitive radios and phonographs in the doors of drug- and music-stores. Before these doors a throng stood all day, listening."[75] Or recall the deputy's wife in "Pantaloon in Black" who, after listening to the shattering story of Rider's fate, simply states "'I'm going to clear this table and then I'm going to the picture show."[76] Or that uncanny vision of "a bungalow, a tight flimsy mass of stoops and porte-cochères and flat gables and bays not five years old and built in that colored mud-and-chickenwire tradition which California moving picture films have scattered across North America as if the celluloid carried germs."[77] In so many subtle ways, as we shall see, for Faulkner the "regional" is always already undone by the "national" that propagates itself, not as a consistent ideological weave of discourses, but as a mediatic insertion of the prefabricated and "identical" within the recalcitrant, local, and different. Anticipating the baseline situation of postmodernity by half a century, in the 1920s the South bore uncomfortable witness to the penetration of media "corporations into the very heart of local and regional culture," making it "difficult to decide whether it is authentic any longer (and indeed whether that term still means anything)."[78] The uneven development of this process makes for gaps and schisms in which a critique can take root, but not for an outright declaration of independence: there can no longer be a secessionist cry. And here again we can see the anachronistic serviceability of romance as a regionally resonant system of representative norms from which to conduct doomed reconnaissance missions over the inevitable subsumption of the very difference at stake. But how much more delicious the irony, or salted the wound, when it is realized that these "competitive radios and phonographs," these picture shows and cinematically mediated suburbias, are thronging with undead romance motifs all along, thanks to the unbreakable grip of the melodramatic imagination over the industries of mass-produced entertainments at this time. It is from within such bizarre torsions of the prevailing conditions of cultural production that "the South" can, at one and the same time, offer the succor of some last vestige of chivalric honor in a disenchanted age, and cast a withering, disenchanted light on imported, mass-produced romance thanks to its "underdeveloped" status as the nation's most impoverished and therefore "realist" locale. The history

---

[75] William Faulkner, *Sanctuary*, in *Novels 1930–1935*, eds. Joseph Blotner and Noel Polk (New York: Library of America, 1985), 257.

[76] William Faulkner, *Go Down, Moses*, in *Novels 1942–1954*, eds. Joseph Blotner and Noel Polk (New York: Library of America, 1994), 120.

[77] Faulkner, *Pylon*, in *Novels 1930–1935*, eds. Joseph Blotner and Noel Polk (New York: Library of America, 1985), 984.

[78] Fredric Jameson, *The Seeds of Time* (New York: Columbia University Press, 1993), 203, 204–05. Romine discusses this same passage in his *The Real South*, loc. 134 of 7111.

of media offers an extremely productive lens through which to attend to these perverse and interminable turns of the screw of modernization, and some particularly suggestive arguments about the flourishing of modernism here at the heady confluence of two disjunctive streams of romance: one inherited and literary, the other imported and mass-mediatic.

It is crucial to conceive of Faulkner's position as an artist of a certain class and complexion coming of age in the Great War, in touch by way of a certain New Orleans intelligentsia with the major currents in modernist thought and practice, but colored in his most intimate imaginative wellsprings by the lingering phantoms of romance, local and international. It is not only the military romance that dictated the public performance of his fictional experiences as an RAF pilot, or the gradual construction of that redoubtable romance protagonist he made of himself as a "gentleman farmer" far removed from the vulgar world of literary fame and profit; it is the innermost impulse of his earliest art, which can then be charted in a lifelong course, now subterranean, now snaking up to the surface, through all his works, whose retroactively proclaimed "modernism" has to be understood as a formal management of just this virulent strain. "L'Après-Midi d'un Faune" (1919) establishes a tenacious early commitment to the protocols of late romanticism and aestheticism. *The Marionettes* (1920) arranges its weak effects in an undergraduate pastiche of Mallarmé by way of a romanticized idea of the *commedia dell'arte* and a layering of pseudo-Beardsleyan graphics. *The Marble Faun* (1924), that seasonally orchestrated verse pastoral consisting of nineteen leaden eclogues, is as flagrant an episode of superannuated late romanticism as anything in American letters, a lame Keatsian derivation that develops Faulkner's persistent anachronism in lurid style. *Mayday* (1926) then explicitly carries through his first and only full exercise in the medieval romance mode, featuring that standard Faulkner protagonist, a wounded veteran of war (Sir Galwyn of Arthgyl), and arranging a fatalistic scenario around his courtly ambitions and desires. This is a seven-year-long history of efforts within a style that, as "Hugh Selwyn Mauberley" (1919) has it, "strove to resuscitate the dead art/Of poetry; to maintain 'the sublime'/In the old sense. Wrong from the start—."[79] But if it is "wrong," it is not so on the ground that most touched Faulkner to the quick, since it could be said to have been "genetic": that is to say, in the sense represented by his great-grandfather William Clark Falkner, author of *The White Rose of Memphis* (1881). For none of this early "wrong" romance material is in any recognizable sense Southern; it participates in the international vogue of symbolist aestheticism whose ultimate source is Parnassian Paris, and in the vulgar streak of cod medievalism descending in a degenerating line from Scott himself, but it nowhere touches on the powerful regional currents that old

---

[79] Ezra Pound, *Early Writings: Poems and Prose*, ed. Ira B. Nadel (London: Penguin, 2005), 127.

Colonel Falkner had adapted from Simms, Kennedy, and Tucker. And it is here that we find, of course, the quintessence of Faulkner's more germane heritage, summed up in a description of the contents of Chick Mallinson's grandmother's library, those "sombre tomes,"

> through which moved with the formal gestures of shades the men and women who were to christian-name a whole generation: the Clarissas and Judiths and Marguerites, the St Elmos and Rolands and Lothairs: the women who were always ladies and men who were always brave, moving in a sort of immortal moonlight without anguish and with no pain from birth without foulment to death without carrion, so that you too could weep with them without having to suffer or grieve, exult with them without having to conquer or triumph.[80]

"So the legend was his too," the narrator continues in a self-referential sigh. But rather than subject *The White Rose of Memphis* to any sustained critique, it will be more useful to extract from it a single passage that can represent for us, as a talismanic prodigy, Faulkner's vexed and overdetermined relationship to Southern romance, since it is everything that the younger novelist would learn to mask in his mature work. Here is a passage from near the end of the novel, in which the crescendos of romance narrativity are heard in all their climactic thunder.

> As Bowles uttered the last sentence, he snatched a large navy revolver from under his coat, and cocking it as he brought it round, levelled it at Wallingford's breast; but the lady in the black domino, who was standing near, seized his arm and instantly jerked it round; a short scuffle ensued—the loud report of the pistol rang out through the saloon—a cloud of blue smoke gushed up—a column of red flame blazed out—a loud scream escaped the mysterious woman's lips, and she fell bleeding into Navarre's arms. As the body of the lady dropped forward against Navarre's breast, he saw a crimson stream gush out from her left side and trickle over his vest. As her head fell back across his arm her mask fell off, and her dark brown hair dropped unconfined about his shoulders.
>
> "Merciful God!" exclaimed Wallingford, "it is Viola, and the cruel villain has killed her!"[81]

---

[80] William Faulkner, *Knight's Gambit* (London: Chatto and Windus, 1960), 124.

[81] William Clark Falkner, *The White Rose of Memphis*, 35th ed. (Chicago & New York: M. A. Donohue & Co., 1912), accessed online at http://www.gutenberg.org/files/41134/41134-h/41134-h.htm.

Faulkner would likely have known this passage from the Donohue edition of 1912, with the copyright renewed by his own father in 1909, printed from entirely new plates, and which bore the publishers' astonished preface: "For thirty-one years, this book has met popular favour, and a sale of *one hundred and sixty thousand copies*. Its sale now is steadily increasing, notwithstanding the worn condition of the plates."[82] With its breathless accumulation of action-based clauses, its paratactic transitions from one to the next, and its shameless deployment of verbal cliché upon cliché, the old Colonel's prose had maintained an undiminished popularity on a literary market whose appetite for realism had sunk beneath a prodigious romance revival. What it represents here, in flagrant fashion, is the very archetype of a narrative mode predicated on the *delivery of the goods*: episodes of high drama, violent explosions, noble sacrifices made in blood, aghast utterances over dead bodies, a cornucopia of overripe romance shaken from the laden branches of melodrama and sensation fiction.

It is this florid style of high incident, associated in retrospect with an extinct class of slave-owners, but also animating the narratives of early cinema and the bestseller lists, that the young William Faulkner felt as his gravest threat and dearest temptation; even the early late-romantic efforts may be seen as a relatively sophisticated warding-off of the familial and regional curse that this prose betokened on his own bookshelves. For as an aspiring writer poised to enter a literary field dominated commercially by the progeny of this very style, though increasingly governed intellectually by a cadre of elite aesthetic warriors for whom it was anathema, Faulkner had not only to navigate the treacherously complex woof and weft of romance ideologemes threaded through the living body of the modern word in Paris, London, and New York, and flickering across cinema screens the world over, but also to wrestle with the lamentable focusing device for all those narrative hangovers that was his own family's one historic claim to literary greatness. What we take to be his modernism, then, is, of all the various and inconsistently related modernisms, subject to far and away the most pressure from its antithesis: there is simply no other modernist writer whose creative energies were more closely filiated to the very thing modernism had evolved to expunge once and for all from its new aesthetic "equations for the human emotions."[83] Elsewhere I have argued that Ezra Pound's modernism turned, in some crucial respects, on a rejection of Tennyson, the embodiment of a romanticism no longer equal to what "the age demanded"; and that the rejection left its formal scar tissues, which in turn proved instrumental to the

---

[82] Ibid., emphasis in original.

[83] Ezra Pound, *The Spirit of Romance* (New York: New Directions, 2005), 14. See also Eric Homburger, "Modernists and Edwardians," in Philip Grover, ed., *Ezra Pound: The London Years: 1908–1920* (New York: AMS Press, 1978), 14.

modernism he was championing.[84] That is, the repudiation of romance is not just a symptom of the modern, but determinant of certain formal effects not otherwise imaginable and immensely generative. Faulkner's case is different again, for reasons here developed, but of comparable status. Both writers were at an early age immensely impressed with and adept at the idiom bequeathed them by a generation now dying or dead. They were both apt pupils in the late romanticism that would scarcely survive their late teens as an aesthetic paradigm. But, thanks to the legacy of Southern romance that impinges uniquely upon him, Faulkner's learned taboo against romance is simply not the same as it was for any other modernist; the residual pull is felt the more profoundly for its regional and so structurally adversarial relation toward the modern as such. While it cannot be openly endorsed (in the serious longer fiction), it can certainly be maintained in ironic and masked guises throughout, and here and there (in the short stories, the screenplays, and the early work) openly espoused.

Moreover, given the manner in which this undead aesthetic paradigm confronted him in the masks of the modern media system, Faulkner grasped the situation as a propitious one for the re-establishment of the aesthetic credentials of literature itself. The circumambient pressure of new media forms, their aggressive competition for attention and consumption, was not something merely to be represented or adapted as inert "content" for literary labor; rather, the labor would consist in a systematic formal recalibration of literary techniques and devices, in an effort to outflank the untold new speeds and scales of mass culture. Unless these problems of inheritance and mediatic interference were raised to the level of formal conundrums, and solutions for them sought in a purely immanent, holistic fashion, there would be no "modernism" to speak of.

My sense is that Faulkner's vocation for modernism privileged two critical strategies to discipline and punish the romance residuals that could not finally be abandoned:

1. Omission, ellipsis, the "absent event" or repressed incident, which registers only in its wake or aftershocks, but very much happens within the diegetic frame.
2. Tropological containment or masking, which, I will argue, often assumes the guise of modern mediatic carriers of romance.

It is the last of these management strategies that is the real subject of this book, but, since it will frequently reappear as a major formal characteristic from chapter to chapter, it will be worth our while to explore, briefly and cursorily, that more obvious technique adapted by Faulkner from a long-standing tradition for managing romance tropes and temporalities—ellipsis, or the absent event.

[84] See Julian Murphet, *Multimedia Modernism: Literature and the Anglo-American Avant-Garde* (Cambridge: Cambridge University Press), 80–122.

The absence of the event

That Faulkner was anything but immune to the lures of the adventure incident, or the heightened narrative event or Act as such, is abundantly clear from his fiction. Consider the following list of melodramatic episodes internal to the narrative worlds of his major work: a romantic suicide, a gelding, and grand larceny in *The Sound and the Fury*; a corncob rape and a lynching in *Sanctuary*; the near-beheading of Joanna Burden in a "crime of passion" and the castration of its perpetrator in *Light in August*; and more delirious romance tropology than we could economically recount here in *Absalom, Absalom!* Yet the critical point about most of these narrative moments is that they are not presented in their own right, but only wrestled with before and after. In Faulkner, the romantic incident is present chiefly as an absence, and this amounts to a major formal achievement, with a notable prehistory.

> Then it was over, gone like a furious gust of black wind, leaving a peaceful vacuum in which they moved quietly about.[85]

Whatever it is, *it has already happened*. In Faulkner, as Sartre once put it, "everything has already happened."[86] The event, though actual, is lost to narrative time, and the prose occupies that "peaceful vacuum" of its wake. But in that occupation, it opens up another space. We will later take up Jameson's compelling account of the fate of the narrative *récit* in realist fiction, and of the forcing of gaps and seizures of affective "presentness" into its foreclosed and irrevocable temporality—and here in Faulkner, one can already sense the dual commitment both to the "time of the preterite, of events completed, over and done with, events that have entered history once and for all,"[87] and to something exterior to that, something that cannot or must not be recorded, since to do so would violate the truth of it. There was a before, and now there is an after. But in between there falls that something, which registers as a nothing.

> [H]e was travelling at a fair gait when he saw suddenly, leaning against a tree beside the road, the man whose face he had seen in the window of the house. One moment the road had been empty, the next moment the man stood there beside it, at the edge of a small copse—the same cloth cap, the same rhythmically chewing jaw materialised apparently

---

[85] Faulkner, *Sanctuary*, in *Novels 1930–1935* (New York: Library of America, 1985), 228.

[86] Jean-Paul Sartre, *Literary and Philosophical Essays*, trans. Annette Michelson (London: Methuen, 1955), 73.

[87] Fredric Jameson, *Antinomies of Realism*, 18.

out of nothing and almost abreast of the horse, with an air of the complete and purely accidental.[88]

Then it happened. I know what did happen, but even now I don't know how, in what order. [...] All I know is, one second he was standing there in his muddy Confederate coat, smiling at us [...]; and the next second there were two bright orange splashes, one after the other, against the middle of the gray coat and the coat itself swelling slow down on me.[89]

One moment, it was so; and the next moment, it was other. In between, unnoticed, comes the event—the something that happens. It is whatever makes the difference between state A and state B that fails to be recorded, and this is something every inveterate Faulkner reader knows to expect. It is the absence of the event, the vanished mediator between two states of affairs, such that, whether it is described as "pure accident" or registers as a temporal confusion in the grammar, what has happened strikes with the traumatic shock of the utterly unexpected, that has therefore somehow not quite happened—even though it has.

At the most abstract narrative level, what makes the difference between narrative states of affairs is the technical principle of *transition*. As Gérard Genette reminds us, for the most part, "up to the end of the nineteenth century" the most usual transition from one scene to another remained the "summary" of events, "the 'background' against which scenes stand out, and thus the connective tissue par excellence of novelistic narrative, whose fundamental rhythm is defined by the alternation of summary and scene."[90] Faulkner is, by and large, obedient to these well-established dictates, and alternates between scenes and summaries with classical decorum.[91] But what is so often missing from his work is internal to scenes themselves, and usually the most critical or charged moments at that. Here, Faulkner subjects his scenic elaborations to a principle of elision, cutting away at the moment of maximum tension and pictorial intensity to leave a glaring gap in the narrative fabric of the scene. That is to say, he has shifted the technical locus of transitionality from a macrological structuring principle (moving between scenes) to a micrological one (in which each scene is now perceived as a concatenation of aspects) and surgically removed the most potent moments. This tactic strikes at the very heart of traditional narrative discourse, since it demonstrates that scenes are themselves constituted of major

---

[88] Faulkner, *The Hamlet*, in *Novels 1936–1940* (New York: Library of America, 1990), 749.

[89] Faulkner, "Vendée," in Joseph Blotner, ed., *Uncollected Stories* (New York: Vintage, 1997), 114.

[90] Gérard Genette, *Narrative Discourse: An Essay in Method*, trans. Jane E. Lewin (Ithaca: Cornell University Press, 1980), 97.

[91] Although Benjy's monologue in *The Sound and the Fury* and the entire performance of *As I Lay Dying* test this decorum extensively.

and minor nodes of intensity and consequence, and that it is possible to expel the most consequential nodes without damaging the narrative texture—indeed, with the paradoxical effect of raising the stakes.

This is of the highest importance to any theory of modernism. How, after all, is a modernist supposed to narrate? Ever since Wordsworth first recoiled from the gross sensationalism, the "craving for extraordinary incident" exploited in "frantic novels, sickly and stupid German Tragedies, and deluges of idle and extravagant stories in verse,"[92] the drift of literature into the domain of high art had come at the expense of what Henry James, too, dismissed as mere "incident." Indeed, the *Lyrical Ballads* can be said to stand at the threshold of a modern era of narrative form actively attempting to distance itself from the category of incident, as witness "Hart-Leap Well," which begins as a medieval romance and then dispenses with its narrative machinery in order to dwell on its "meaning":

> The moving accident is not my trade;
> To freeze the blood I have no ready arts:
> 'Tis my delight, alone in summer shade,
> To pipe a simple song for thinking hearts.[93]

James's revulsion, in "The Art of Fiction," at any too voluptuous appetite for stories "full of incident and movement, so that we shall wish to jump ahead, to see who was the mysterious stranger," and at the mere "multiplication of 'incident'" as such, though it is not offered in any overt partisan support for the "novel of character," is taken in useful directions in the "Preface" to *The Portrait of a Lady*. Discussing Isabel Archer's memorable fireside vigil in that novel, James writes that

> it throws the action further forward than twenty "incidents" might have done. It was designed to have all the vivacity of incident and all the economy of picture. [...] It is a representation simply of her motionlessly *seeing*, and an attempt withal to make the mere still lucidity of her act as "interesting" as the surprise of a caravan or the identification of a pirate.[94]

---

[92] Wordsworth, "Preface" [1800], in Samuel Taylor Coleridge and William Wordsworth, *Lyrical Ballads 1798 and 1800*, eds. Michael Gamer and Dahlia Porter (Toronto: Broadview, 2008), 177.

[93] Wordsworth, "Hart-Leap Well," *Lyrical Ballads*, 296.

[94] Henry James, "Preface to *The Portrait of a Lady*," in Leon Edel, ed., *Literary Criticism: French Writers, Other European Writers, The Prefaces to the New York Edition* (New York: Library of America, 1984), 1084.

Thus, "incident" proper, for modern literature, has to be relocated away from external events and exciting scenic episodes, and into a less immediately narratable territory (of mood, perception, affect, and other unrepresentable regions). As a result the novelist can abandon all those trappings, of pirates and caravans, of the earlier romance tradition, now tarnished by commerce; indeed, he can increasingly abandon outward action per se in favor of what must take place in order for it to happen. As it is with Isabel, so it is with Browning's Artemis, whose final lines are: "While I/Await, in fitting silence, the event."[95] As Browning's syntax studiously defers the word "event" to very the end of his poem, so the very narrative organization of modern letters learns to adopt a "fitting silence" toward events.

Meanwhile, in a development still closer to the young Faulkner's heart, Mallarmé's immensely consequential clearing of a poetic space beyond mere incident, where *"rien n'aura eu lieu que le lieu,"* can be considered as homologous to James's strictures, but distinct in the radical skepticism it has begun to cast upon the category of the present itself. Led by his ecstatic vision of Loïe Fuller to imagine a stage cleared of "the traditional permanent or stable stage-set" and delivered over to "a central nothingness," Mallarmé declares such a stage "freed for any fiction, cleared and instated by the play of a veil with attitudes and gestures; the site, all movement, becomes the very pure result."[96] Meanwhile, the mime Paul Margueritte evokes simply "the idea, not any actual action, in a Hymen (out of which flows Dream), tainted with vice yet sacred, between desire and fulfillment, perpetuation and remembrance; here anticipating, there recalling, in the future, in the past, *under the false appearance of a present*."[97] These apprehensions of a pure Scene herald a "space of the event that never happens, or once did happen, or is to come."[98] Here in Mallarmé's visions of the *fin-de-siècle* Parisian stage, which were so formative on his poetics, we arrive at a "new idea of fiction: this substitutes the plot with the construction of a play of aspects, elementary forms that offer an analogy to the play of the world," and not to the logic of romance plots and classical verisimilitude.[99] In place of the play of representations, we have a play of forms. "These forms can be called abstract because they tell no stories."[100] What is "imitated" in this new mimesis is the complex of forces and pulsions that subtend the world itself, not its surface appearances. And, paradoxically enough, even the "violence of naturalism

---

[95] Robert Browning, "Artemis Prologizes," in *The Poems of Robert Browning* (Hertfordshire: Wordsworth Editions, 1994), 422.

[96] Stéphane Mallarmé, *Divagations*, trans. Barbara Johnson (Cambridge, MA: The Belknap Press of Harvard University Press, 2007), 136, 137.

[97] Mallarmé, *Divagations*, 140.

[98] Fredric Jameson, *The Modernist Papers* (London & New York: Verso, 2007), 310.

[99] Jacques Rancière, *Aisthesis* (London & New York: Verso, 2013), 100.

[100] Ibid.

is acceptable as the sign of the unrepresentability of this new impersonal life of drives and instincts; and thereby rejoins the general absence of the Event on stage."[101] There is a modality of romance (the violent act) which, suitably exaggerated, violates the constraints of narrative propriety and leaps the very traces of the representational order (a formula not without strong echoes in Faulkner's art). In any event, in Mallarmé's aesthetics "we cannot tell whether a thing is being affirmed or denied and take up a place at the very vanishing point of meaning as such, which the poet dramatizes as the empty stage, or else the scene which breathlessly awaits its Event to come."[102]

What we then find happening in Conrad is another uncomfortable melding of the two impulses, a vitally unstable interpenetration of romance and Art. In *Lord Jim* especially this uneasy synthesis of modernist foreclosure and romantic excess is felt as a definitive structural tension. And what makes the first part so exquisitely "modernist" in these terms is precisely its suppression or elision of the central narrative incident, the absent kernel or missing Act, the pulse of decision and transition ripped out of scenic time. Who can forget it?

> "'The ship began a slow plunge; the rain swept over her like a broken sea; my cap flew off my head; my breath was driven back into my throat. I heard as if I had been on the top of a tower another wild screech, "Geo-o-o-orge! Oh, jump!" She was going down, down, head first under me....'
>
> "He raised his hand deliberately to his face, and made picking motions with his fingers as though he had been bothered with cobwebs, and afterwards he looked into the open palm for quite half a second before he blurted out—
>
> "'I had jumped...' He checked himself, averted his gaze.... 'It seems,' he added."[103]

Just where the principles of romance would dictate an avowal of decision and act, this account suppresses it. The elision that erases the pivotal choice similarly deranges the temporal coordinates of the *récit*, since by suggesting that the first-person voice does not know the most elementary thing about what happened (its root cause in his own psyche), it is as if the present as a mediation between present and past has been subtracted, leaving only a chronicle-like sequence of facts, without motivation or meaning. The narrative voice here fails to coincide with itself as an ethical agent, cannot yield the most critical information about its own presence. "There is no present tense of the act, we are forever always

---

[101] Jameson, *Modernist Papers*, 318.
[102] Ibid., 330.
[103] Joseph Conrad, *Lord Jim* (Oxford: Oxford World Classics, 2008), 80–81.

before or after it, in past or future tenses, at the stage of the project or those of the consequences."[104] And this unravels the narrative economy of romance itself, which requires a suturing of the chain of events to a responsible agent enduring in time.

Eagleton is right to say that in Conrad's fiction more generally, "many of the key narrative events—Lord Jim's crucial jump, the unspeakable rites surrounding Kurtz in *Heart of Darkness*, Winnie Verloc's murder of her husband in *The Secret Agent*, the blowing up of Stevie in the same novel, Decoud's gradual disintegration in *Nostromo*—take place, so to speak, behind the back of the reader, squinted at sideways rather than viewed head-on."[105] But the formal consequences of this excision of the central event are exhilarating, since in that absence something else is allowed to wax and mutate, namely style itself. As Jameson puts it, around this central non-narrated incident proliferates a writing which, "approaching its narrative presence, its anecdotal centre, at once denies the possibility of such presence and spills over into yet further sentence production and the further frustration of presence affirmed and denied."[106] Modernist *écriture* senses its opportunity in the repression of what had been fundamental to the development of the novel out of romance: the incident.

It is an event in the history of the form to which Faulkner remains strikingly faithful. Sartre's analysis was precise: "Faulkner disappoints us [. . .]; he rarely describes acts, because he encounters and by-passes an old problem of fictional technique. Acts are of the essence of the novel. They are carefully prepared, and then, by the time they happen, they are utterly simple, as smooth and polished as bronze. They slip between our fingers. There is nothing more to say about them; the mere mention of them suffices. Faulkner does not speak of acts, never mentions them, and thus suggests that there is no naming them, that they are beyond language. He shows only their results."[107] This structural disappointment is exacerbated by the fact that his novels are strewn with romance materials and the palpable outlines of "incidents," without ever properly delivering them. What goes unremarked by Sartre is that this triggers a crisis in the art of narrative transition. Romance had always functioned according to a more or less physical and expressive temporal causality; crudely put, the domino theory of action. Which is why what Roland Barthes called the "proairetic code" of narrative could function in a fundamentally automatic and thus invisible manner: all the little actions that make up any narrative act are articulated according to an

---

[104] Jameson, *Political Unconscious*, 264.
[105] Terry Eagleton, *The Trouble with Strangers: A Study of Ethics* (Oxford: Blackwell-Wiley, 2009), 261.
[106] Jameson, *Political Unconscious*, 222.
[107] Sartre, *Literary and Philosophical Essays*, trans. Annette Michelson (New York: Collier Books, 1962), 80.

"already-read" sequential logic. In Barthes's words, "Actions (terms of the proairetic code) can fall into various sequences which should be indicated merely by listing them, since the proairetic sequence is never more than the result of an artifice of reading; [...] the sequence exists when and because it can be given a name [...]. TO BE DEEP IN: 1: to be absorbed. 2: to come back again. HIDING PLACE: 1: to be hidden. 2: to come out of hiding." [108]

What we frequently find in Faulkner is a disturbance of this basic narrative code. "One moment the road had been empty, the next moment the man stood there beside it." Proairetic articulation comes undone once the category of the event has been subtracted from narration: acts are dismembered into sudden jerks and jolts; transition becomes awkward. Think of *As I Lay Dying*'s Darl Bundren imagining his brother Jewel on horseback:

> They stand in rigid terrific hiatus, the horse trembling and groaning. Then Jewel is on the horse's back. He flows upward in a stooping swirl like the lash of a whip, his body in mid-air shaped to the horse. For another moment the horse stands spraddled, with lowered head, before it bursts into motion. They descend the hill in a series of spine-jolting jumps, Jewel high, leech-like in the withers, to the fence where the horse bunches to a scuttering halt again.[109]

The romance proairesis of RIDING A HORSE is here convulsively disarticulated; what results is something like an image of Chaplin's tramp going comically about the business of mounting, cantering, stopping, and starting.[110] And it will take no great leap of the critical imagination to see this microscopic derangement of the mechanics of transition as being intimately related to the larger experimentations in form that we see on display in *The Sound and the Fury*, *As I Lay Dying*, and *Absalom, Absalom!* The severing of the automatic links that articulate the proairetic code has broader amplifications at the level of episodic autonomization and fragmentation, where autonomous aesthetic laws and codes determine (à la *Ulysses*) the various chapters. It is in the gaps between *these* units that the larger narrative events (Quentin's suicide, Joanna's murder, Sutpen's murder)

---

[108] Roland Barthes, *S/Z*, trans. Richard Miller (Oxford: Blackwell, 1990), 19, 255.

[109] Faulkner, *As I Lay Dying*, in *Novels 1930–1935*, 9.

[110] "The innovation of Chaplin's gestures is that he dissects the expressive movements of human beings into a series of minute innervations. Each single movement he makes is composed of a succession of staccato bits of movement. Whether it is his walk, the way he handles his cane, or the way he raises his hat—always the same jerky sequence of tiny movements applies the law of the cinematic image sequence to human motorial functions." Walter Benjamin, "The Formula in Which the Dialectical Structure of Film Finds Expression" (1935), *Selected Writings, Volume 3: 1935–1938*. Trans. Edmund Jephcott, Howard Eiland, and Others. Edited by Howard Eiland and Michael W. Jennings (Cambridge, MA & London: Belknap Press of Harvard University Press, 2002), 94.

fall silently. By the moment of Faulkner, then, it would seem that actions and events—what used to be so simple, because so basic to the novel—have so far receded from the proper domain of literary narration that they have vanished "beyond language" in the mists of a rhetorical pleonasm.

This cannot, however, be altogether right: after all, Faulkner is full of incident, as we have said: duels and murders and thefts and rapes and battles, any number of sensational plot materials, in some kind of daemonic counterpoint to the mesmeric voice. As in Conrad, we have here an unstable and uneven development at the level of form, only further intensified. Popular adventure and romance elements are there, but also *not* there, suspended just beyond the discursive surface in opaque aspic, stylistically interstitial and absent but palpable regardless. Moreover, there is an obvious genetic link between the romance narrative form and Faulkner's de-transitionalized prose, since in this latter we frequently come across those very adverbial markings of "adventure-time" in Bakhtin's sense that proclaim at least a ghostly inheritance.[111] "Suddenly" is an adverb that Henry James rarely uses outside of psychological descriptions of shifting states of mind; but in Faulkner it all too often modifies narrated actions, encounters, and states of affairs. And well it may, since, with the intervening transitional moments subtracted, and the resultant activity rendered akin to Chaplin's spasmodic *Gestus*, how else to greet the news that B has replaced A in the sequence of things? At the pitch of his most egregious capitulations to romance, this tendency is rife: "Then it was afternoon. [...] All of a sudden we began to hear them [...] It went fast like that, every time [...] Because all of a sudden it was sunset [...] and all of a sudden there was an officer [...] I don't know what happened to him; he just vanished,"[112] is a sequence of locutions packed into a page and a half of one of the *Unvanquished* stories (which he called a "pulp series" of "trash"[113]). But what Faulkner calls in both "Death Drag" and "Mule in the Yard" "that apparition-like suddenness" with which, say, "two men in helmets and lifted goggles emerged suddenly around the corner of the barn," is a frequent rhetorical device, covering Quentin's racial anxieties about the way people of color emerge into white lives "in sudden sharp black trickles" ("and suddenly I saw Roskus watching me from behind all [Deacon's] whitefolks claptrap"[114]), Jason's apprehensions of spatial action ("I had just turned onto the street when I saw a ford coming helling toward me. All of a sudden it stopped," 1060), the narrator's sense of Jason's headaches ("and suddenly

---

[111] Mikhail Bakhtin, *The Dialogical Imagination: Four Essays*, ed. Michael Holquist, trans. Caryl Emerson and Michael Holquist (Austin: University of Texas Press, 1981), 86–110.

[112] Faulkner, "Raid," in *Uncollected Stories*, 48.

[113] Quoted in Joseph Blotner, *Faulkner: A Biography* (Jackson, MS: University Press of Mississippi, 2005), 335.

[114] Faulkner, *The Sound and the Fury*, in *Novels 1926–1929* (New York: Library of America, 2006), 1008, 953.

with an old premonition he clapped the brakes on and stopped and sat perfectly still," 1113), Horace Benbow's acknowledgment of the sublime ("he knew suddenly that it was the friction of the earth on its axis, approaching that moment when it must decide to turn on or to remain forever still"[115]), the Reporter's constantly amazed sensorium ("suddenly he realized that now [...] it was himself who was the nebulous and quiet ragtag and bobend of touching and breath and experience"[116]), a nameless cab-driver's realization of where he has driven ("during that moment he seemed to have become caught in that sort of instantaneous immobility like when a sudden light surprises a man or an animal out of darkness. Then it was gone"[117]), up to and including as apotheosis Thomas Sutpen, who "out of quiet thunderclap abrupts" even into age itself ("The flesh came upon him suddenly"[118]). This is a narrative universe in which everything is sudden because nothing is properly continuous; all motion is crippled from within by a subtraction from it of all the articulating links and hinges, the way a waiter removes the bones from a fish. Note the constant proximity of "sudden" and "still" in these extracts. The entire phenomenon is allegorized in *Pylon* by one remarkable passage:

> There was a second hand on the clock too—a thin spidery splash; he watched it now as it moved too fast to follow save between the intervals of motion when it became instantaneously immobile as though drawn across the clock's face by a pen and a ruler—9. 8. 7. 6. 5. 4. 3. 2. and done; it was now the twenty-first hour, and that was all. No sound, as though it had not been a steam train which quitted the station two seconds ago but rather the shadow of one on a magic lantern screen until the child's vagrant and restless hand came and removed the slide. (969)

"Between the motion/And the act," Eliot wrote, "Falls the Shadow."[119] Elsewhere I have argued for this heavy-handed insistence on the shadow or void that "falls" between moments in Faulkner's prose to be related to the technical realities of film projection—for what is the Maltese Cross but a "vagrant and restless hand" behind the back of the viewer that snatches away one frame in a moment's blackness before allowing the projector's light to project another, subsequent one?[120] Here, however, it is enough to draw attention to this disarticulation of

---

[115] Faulkner, *Sanctuary*, in *Novels 1930–1935*, 333.
[116] Faulkner, *Pylon*, in *Novels 1930–1935*, 968.
[117] Ibid., 984.
[118] Faulkner, *Absalom, Absalom!*, in *Novels 1936–1940*, 66.
[119] T. S. Eliot, "The Hollow Men," in *Collected Poems 1909–1962* (London: Faber, 1974), 92.
[120] Julian Murphet, "Faulkner in the Histories of Film: 'Where Memory is the Slave,'" in Peter Lurie and Ann J. Abadie, eds., *Faulkner and Film: Faulkner & Yoknapatawpha 2010* (Jackson, MS: University Press of Mississippi, 2014), 197–219.

proairesis to see it as a technical extension of the basic wish to avoid falling into the traps of romance narrativity as such. With *all* motion constantly falling into a stricken "instantaneous immobility" like the second hand on *Pylon*'s clock face, and "abrupting" back into motility again with "sudden" alarm, there can be no question of the larger narrative from succumbing to the temptations of "incident"—rather, the Event (murder, theft, abduction, suicide) is rendered absent but still more potent by virtue of the Shadow that falls across its form.

If, then, in Faulkner "the 'spontaneity' of literary language has already been dissociated into the establishment of a visual, nonverbal content, on the one hand, and a well-nigh interminable rhetorical evocation, on the other,"[121] our further specification is that the "visual, nonverbal content" (invariably a sensational and romantic frieze) has to be approached asymptotically through the formal taboo placed upon incident itself. Insofar as his narrative voice returns compulsively to "this gesture out of time, desperately accumulating its adjectives and qualifiers in an attempt to conjure, from the outside, what is virtually a seamless gestalt in its own right that can no longer be constructed by the movement of the sentences,"[122] it is an ingenious formal development of the strictures against romantic incident that had extended from Wordsworth, through James and Conrad, to become one of the central tenets of modernist aesthetics. Faulkner's modernism consists above all, I would argue, in the unprecedented lengths he took in order to shelter a romance imaginary that his aesthetic intelligence would not permit him formally to indulge, other than *sous rature*. His language can only conjure up this element *bodily*, in affective seizures traceable in the repetitions and excesses of the style, since to present them "objectively" would be to watch them come apart in one's hands—the big scenes, the extraordinary incidents, the extravagant actions, of an extinct and impermissible representational regime. The other option is to mask it, in technological figures.

Technological troping

That there were other means available to Faulkner for managing his incalculable debts to romance is the larger argument of this book. That argument will be elaborated extensively in the chapters that follow, but we have already indicated its basic claim. Namely, where Faulkner is able neither to resist nor to put *sous rature* his inclinations towards romance, he will typically issue his impulse under the masking device of one or other of the various media technologies of his day: photography, mass-circulation newsprint or magazines, popular song,

---

[121] Fredric Jameson, *Postmodernism, or, the Cultural Logic of Late Capitalism* (London & New York Verso, 1991), 133.
[122] Ibid., 134.

radio, phonograph, cinema, aviation, electrified public transport, and the private motorcar. The economy of this measure is remarkable and doubly rewarding: not only does it allow the author to get away with indulging a moment's sensationalism or melodramatic plot device, it simultaneously allows him to cast a withering glance sideways at the contemporary culture industry that thrives on the recirculation of such exhausted materials. The novel is able to eat its romance cake and have it, too, since this ironic critique of the contemporary source of romance is an unimpeachable screen behind which the inadmissible materials are nevertheless exploited.

In the first chapter, we consider Faulkner's insistent fascination with aviation, and approach it in relation to his equally perdurable (though distinctly unacceptable) investment in the romance figure of the cavalier. Again and again, we find that his texts manage to cloak and displace the figure of the *chevalier* by way of the various institutional forms in which human flight had become available to representational activity at the time: the military ace, the test pilot, and the "flying gipsy" or barnstormer. Faulkner's debts to romance are thus discharged via a complex mediation of its residual functions through objective social and institutional, not to say technological, forms that helped him to recast romance in the key of irony and (at the upper level) as part of a social critique of dehumanization. Of particular interest here is the remarkable transition affecting the ideological discourse of mechanized flight in the immediate postwar period, away from a chivalric language of individual valor and gallantry and toward an anonymous and bureaucratic discourse of corporate efficiency and reliability, a shift explained by the sudden diminution of flight's military function and its irresistible rise as a commercial medium of goods, bodies, and information. The establishment of a nascent national network of airports, flight paths, and timetables in the 1920s, in which the South was inserted unevenly, made aviation a critical instrument for thinking about the technological realization of a stable coast-to-coast media and transport system, even as it continued to resonate with the anachronistic mythic grandeur of the Lindbergh-type aviator and the reckless barnstormer. It thus served as a perfect "mask" for Faulkner's incurable proclivity toward romance semiotics and allowed him to project a unique form of nostalgia in the accents of futurology. He did so, however, on the basis of what thus inevitably emerged as a problem of literary language itself, since this protracted engagement at the seam of two largely contradictory discourses had disclosed a crisis in the discourse of humanism. What aviation had done with the chivalric code was to present an opportunity for transcending those limits altogether, outside the imperturbable continuity of narrative language in the long shadow of Homer: a post-humanist technophilic eschatology.

Chapter 2 accounts for the striking evolution of Faulkner's technique in 1928 by observing the radical decline in regional descriptive prose in his work between the writing of *Sartoris* (*Flags in the Dust*) and *The Sound and the Fury*. Making sense of that diminishment comes to turn on an analysis of the ways in which Faulkner was learning to incorporate the fact of rapid automotive transport into fictional forms at the time, and how this decisive reconfiguration of the rhythms of daily life had altered, at a stroke, the conventional chronotopes of romance. While in the prior book, the textual antinomy between romance chronotopes and the spreading space-time of modernity is condensed into a figural antagonism between horse- and mule-drawn surreys and wagons and new private automobiles as "viewing platforms" for Southern scenery, in the breakthrough novel about the Compson family, things get altogether more complicated. Associating each brother with a different mode of transport—gig, electric streetcar, and motorcar—Faulkner orchestrates an extraordinary chronotopic virtuosity in the way he elaborates his "new South" without the luxury of descriptive prose. By placing a formal taboo on what had been the most dependable rhetorical vestment of regional romance—its lyrical evocations of the dreamy, timeless landscape itself—Faulkner nevertheless manages to persevere with its subtending ideological apparatus. And what makes this remarkable transaction possible is the inexorable rise of private automotive transport as the dominant "media" paradigm of its moment in the late 1920s: a literal "masking" of the somnolent dirt-road infrastructure of the older space-time under clouds of tire-churned dust and a new paving campaign designed to stimulate Northern motor tourism. Once again, these profound modifications of the speeds and technologies of quotidian human movement are seized as opportunities, not only to screen an underlying commitment to romance, but to jettison the standard narrative techniques concerned with motion, progress, and change. *The Sound and the Fury* emerges as an experimental laboratory in which to improvise entirely new literary mechanics of scenic transition and articulation, all stimulated and underwritten by the momentous revolutions in human intercourse and urban design made possible by street railways and motorcars.

Chapter 3 takes a more recognizably media-historical turn toward the convoluted and often adversarial commercial struggles between two types of audio technology: the gramophone and the radio, the former dependent mechanically upon groove-inscriptions and analogue data-storage, the latter on the uncanny propagation of wireless electromagnetic radiation at near light-speed through the air. Attending to a brace of novels dominated by questions of audition, reception, playback, and tuning—by the extraordinary apparition of "voices from the air"—we see how deeply invested Faulkner had become in matters of mediation and technique throughout the wider media ecology. His representational strategies in *Sanctuary* and *As I Lay Dying* are shown to be shot through with figures and devices (such as the weird propagation of bodiless voices, and a radical development of the first-person present-tense narrative voice) that are borrowed laterally from the audio niche of that ecology. If what is thereby "masked" in *Sanctuary* amounts to the obscene, non-representable kernel of a debased romantic imaginary (the corncob rape), along with an array of melodramatic subjective repercussions of that signal absent event, then *As I Lay Dying* sets the stage for a fully elaborated allegory of the narrative voice in the age of mechanical and electromagnetic mediation, "masking" a formidable Oedipal romance ideologeme to do so. In this astounding *tour de force*, Faulkner exposes literary artistry to the technical demands made by a relocation of the very source of the nation's authoritative voice, from print technology to the radio phenomenon. Rather than throwing in the towel to the hegemony of new media, this novel allows the radio voice to infiltrate the inner sanctum of literature's own residually sacred authority, and follows the implications through to their most radical conclusions. The first novel that is also a "radio play for voices," *As I Lay Dying* emerges as one of the era's most inventive solutions to the sudden mediatic obsolescence of literature's claim for social eminence.

Finally, Chapter 4 turns its attention (after a transitional passage through *Pylon*'s thinking about photography and newsprint) to the case of *Absalom, Absalom!*, which I argue is the single greatest work of art to have been subsidized by the market for scripts and treatments in the Hollywood studio system. This material underpinning is refracted in the novel's abiding structural tension between a lurid gothic "story" and a plot that tends to hide and distort all its most egregious romance tableaux behind media screens—a tension played out, more often than not, in the shared narrative duties of a garrulous superannuated romance poet and a young man of the coming age whose spontaneous tendency is to "see" the flood of melodramatic verbiage as so many expertly developed photographs. More than any other novel of its moment, *Absalom, Absalom!* exploits the full range of metaphorical and symbolic potentialities opened for literature by the suturing of sound to image in the nascent sound cinema and the vogue for photographic essays during the Depression years. And in so doing, it discovers many new tactics for screening and dissembling melodramatic passions behind techno-mediatic figures, whose formal function is to forestall the looming charge of aesthetic illegitimacy as regards an excess of narrative cliché through an affective transfiguration of that temporal dimension into friezes of visual immediacy. Faulkner's masterpiece takes the technical hybridity of the period's various "imagetexts" (in cinema and mass publishing) and repurposes it for the novel form by allowing that artificial synthesis between sound and picture both to stand as a means of reflecting on literature's shifting place in the media ecology and to generate new technical figures for thinking about Southern romance's most pernicious ideological symptom: the racism that made slavery and Jim Crow possible.

Thus this book traces the intricate and multi-layered impression left on one major body of work by a reconfiguration of the media and transport systems in the America of the 1920s and 30s. But it does so by attending to a specifically literary concern, namely, a rapidly evolving management campaign undertaken by

Faulkner to discipline and punish the tendencies toward romance that ineluctably manifest themselves every time he puts pen to paper. In brief, the argument is that in order aesthetically to manage this irresistible return of the repressed, Faulkner looked outward to the transformation of his life-world, and borrowed from its transforming media ecology the figures and devices—the disembodied radio voices, the scratchy grooves of a graphophone, the photomechanical reproduction of a moment in time etched onto silver halide crystals, the paving of a town street, or the buzz overhead of a Flying Jenny—that might allow him to dissemble his atavisms behind the screen of a mechanical and electronic modernity. In the event, his evolving habit of patching the post-literary means of mediatic production, as so many potent literary tropes, onto an anachronistic pre-realist narrative system, give him the wherewithal to produce one of the greatest and most distinctive of all literary modernisms. Out of the combined and uneven development of the contemporary media system, which was doubly ramified in the objective anachrony of the "nation's region" itself, Faulkner produced a string of masterpieces of such arresting stature that they would have to be read and evaluated in France, by the most luminous intellects on the face of the earth, before "America," let alone the "South," would know what to do with them.

1

A Folklore of Speed

Chivalric vestiges

In the Introduction, it was argued that Faulkner's formal complexion as a literary artist turned more than anything else upon his simultaneous commitment to, and negation of, a romance topos whose stubborn persistence in his mature narratives was vouchsafed by deft tropological substitutions—the older figures and types being henceforth masked by some technological aspect of the new media ecology of the 1920s, '30s, and '40s. The problematic centrality of the cavalier figure to Southern romance forms is no exception to this general rule; indeed, so conspicuous is it as an illustrative case in point that the present chapter will use it to crystallize our method and begin to map the complex formal dialectics at issue. The challenge here is not merely to show the various ways in which Faulkner remained beholden to perhaps the Southern romance's most irrecusable narrative element—its mounted military hero-agent—but how this commitment was managed formally through symptomatic displacements, distortions, and abrogations of ideological use-value, all of which came freighted with historical and political significance peculiar to the time of writing. The task is to show how such formal management achieved *more*, aesthetically, than the simple suppression or erasure of this romance element might have done, for it is precisely through the reprocessing and retrofitting of figures from one exhausted regime of sense to another that "modernism" can be said to have worked in the first place, its various taboos and "don'ts" managing to "make it new" on the basis of these ingenious transferences at the levels of figure and ground.[1]

Of the cavalier figure in general, as far as American literary history is concerned, it has been proposed that its origins lie in a mythic conception of

---

[1] Elsewhere I have shown, for instance, how Ezra Pound's uneven management of one of Romantic verse's more stubborn ideological figures—the lovesick abandoned woman at the shore—served as an occasion for the demonstration of his more exorbitant "modernist" effects. See my *Multimedia Modernism: Literature and the Anglo-American Avant-Garde* (Cambridge: Cambridge University Press, 2009), 80–122.

immigrant-settlers arriving in Virginia between 1645 and 1675 as the entitled and defeated supporters of the decapitated Charles I, craving land after Cromwell's victory.

> By the 1830s writers eager to explain why the inhabitants of the northern states and those of the southern states appeared to be so different in values and temperament had begun to seize on the idea that the people of the two regions were simply heirs to the dramatically different class, religious, cultural, and political traditions delineated by the English Civil War. The northern states were populated, so many believed, by the descendants of the middle-class Puritan "Roundheads" who had routed the defenders of the monarchy, the aristocratic Cavaliers, supposedly of Norman descent, who had then settled in the southern states.[2]

The fomenting of this loosely historical Southern origin myth in the 1830s (just as Abolitionism began to make serious political headway) thus allowed for the development of romance forms that privileged this cavalier figure as their central agent. William R. Taylor has speculated, with dialectical lucidity, that this figure evolved throughout the central decades of the nineteenth century in lockstep with that other national stereotype, the Yankee, whose puritanical common sense and narrow practicality were ideal ideological foils for the insouciant worldliness and hauteur of the Southern cavalier.[3] So if the "concept of the Southern gentleman is inextricably mingled with that of the southern cavalier,"[4] so too was it implicated in the coeval myth of its political and cultural antipode; that is, while "southerners could take refuge in their image of the South as an aristocratic society organized in quasi-feudal fashion and blessed with remarkable stability and cohesion,"[5] they did so on the imaginary basis of this figural inversion of the industrial Yankee—the gentleman planter mounted in armed resistance to an inexorable Northern leveling. It was the escalating political and economic tensions over the institution of slavery, and the felt inevitability of civil war in the decade leading up to that crisis, that sharpened this opposition and gave crisp ideological salience to a figure wrought of anachronism, literary fancy, and an anti-modernizing utopia. So it is that the cavalier, "the

---

[2] James C. Cobb, *Away Down South: A History of Southern Identity* (Oxford & New York: Oxford University Press, 2007), 22.

[3] William R. Taylor, *Cavalier and Yankee: The Old South and American National Character* (New York: George Braziller, 1961).

[4] Ritchie D. Watson, "Gentleman," in Joseph M. Flora and Lucinda H. Mackethan, eds., *The Companion to Southern Literature: Themes, Genres, Places, People* (Baton Rouge: Louisiana State University Press, 2001), 292.

[5] Daniel J. Singal, *William Faulkner: The Making of a Modernist* (Chapel Hill: University of North Carolina Press, 1997), 6.

living embodiment of a political and economic struggle to preserve the South's many changing institutions,"[6] and wrought to a pitch in the fictions of John P. Kennedy and William Gilmore Simms, among others, was galvanized by an historical crisis that ironically brought it off the pages of romance and into the theatre of military engagement. The doomed secessionist ambitions of the Confederacy gave ample opportunity to the planter class to test their mettle in the vestments of fantasy and imitate the artistic figure their collective fantasy had nurtured on the field of battle, with catastrophic results in a context of industrialized warfare.

That Faulkner knew how to draw this figure—was in fact compelled to do so by the force of some inner daemon—is a critical commonplace, usually harnessed to biographical speculations about the Old Colonel and the anxiety of influence in the Southern literary economy.[7] His masterpiece, *Absalom, Absalom!*, can scarcely resist tracing its recurrence across its pages, not only in the striking inaugural image of Sutpen's "abruption" out of "quiet thunderclap" into a mythic "ogre-shape" bearing only the most abstract generic accoutrements—"a man who rode into town out of nowhere with a horse and two pistols and a herd of wild beasts," a portentous cavalier-cum-desperado[8]—but in those hyperstitional Civil War scenes where the breathless confabulation of Charles Bon's and Henry Sutpen's dilemma revolves around the absent figure of their father, heroic at last, mounted and magnificent and bearing a citation of valor from General Lee himself. But the novel is particularly sharp about the always and already anachronistic nature of the chevalier figure on the fields of the world's first industrialized war, the Confederacy's generals having "the divine right to say 'Go there' conferred upon them by an absolute caste system," but "never liv[ing] long enough to learn how to fight massed cautious accretionary battles, since they were already as obsolete as Richard or Roland or du Gueslin" (284–85). It is a version of that same obsolescence, perhaps, that fixates *Light in August*'s Reverend Gail Hightower's fevered imagination upon "his grandfather, a cavalryman, who was killed" in the Civil War, so that his sermons turn to a chaotic jumble of "his religion and his grandfather being shot from the galloping horse all mixed up, as though the seed which his grandfather had transmitted to him had been on the horse too that night and had been killed too and time had stopped there and then for the seed and nothing had happened in time since, not even him."[9] Here the sense of anachronism forces something like a

---

[6] Emmeline Gros, "The Southern Gentleman and the Idea of Masculinity: Figures and Aspects of the Southern Beau in the Literary Tradition of the American South," doctoral dissertation, Georgia State University & Université Versailles St Quentin-en-Yvelines, 2010, 9.

[7] See, for example, Lori Watkins Fulton, "Knight's Gambit: Gavin Stevens and Faulkner's Critique of the Cavalier Tradition," doctoral dissertation, University of Southern Mississippi, 2007.

[8] Faulkner, *Novels 1936–1940*, 6, 10, 12.

[9] Faulkner, *Novels 1930–1935*, 443, 445.

narrative arrest, a seizure of the storytelling faculty, such that the figure is cast out of time altogether and into an hysterical present tense, not unlike the photographs the good reverend offers to develop on the sign outside his property. If all of this mature revaluation of the cavalier figure then seems undone by *The Unvanquished*'s open appeals to the heroism of Colonel John Sartoris, still, we must remark the undisguised relish with which passages such as the following must have been written:

> He was on Jupiter now; he wore the frogged gray field-officer's tunic; and while we watched he drew the sabre. Giving us a last embracing and comprehensive glance he drew it, already pivoting Jupiter on the right snaffle; his hair tossed beneath the cocked hat, the sabre flashed and glinted; he cried, not loud yet stentorian: "Trot! Canter! *Charge!*" Then, without even having to move, we could both watch and follow him—the little man (who in conjunction with the big horse looked exactly the right size because that was as big as he needed to look and—to twelve years old—bigger than most folks could hope to look) standing in the stirrups above the smoke-colored diminishing thunderbolt, beneath the arcy and myriad glitter of the sabre.[10]

There is little enough in the way of irony here—though Noel Polk has made much of the horseman's diminutive stature[11]—and the only sure formal dissonance is that implicit in the qualifier "to twelve years old," since by attributing this romanticism to a wide-eyed son, the narrator at least maintains some minimal distance from the dashing figure he is evoking. In *The Unvanquished* Faulkner allows his text—compiled from "a pulp series" of "trash," in his own estimation[12]—to approach dangerously close to the very fetish on whose formal dissimulation I have said his artistry depended. The "obsolescence" noted previously is encoded tentatively in the indeterminate gap between the narrator's present tense and this lost past, but never truly impedes the palpable ideological charge of the figure itself.

Which is why it is notable that this same character, Bayard Sartoris (1849–1919) had already been granted the privilege of telling his cavalier father's story, ten years previous in *Flags in the Dust*, but preferred not to, cajoled only into minor glosses by the indefatigable exhortations of old Simon Strother. This Bayard, septuagenarian and brittle, prefers to delegate narrative authority to the

---

[10] Faulkner, *Novels 1936–1940*, 327.

[11] Noel Polk, "Faulkner and the Commies," in *Faulkner and Welty and the Southern Literary Tradition* (Jackson, MS: University Press of Mississippi, 2008), 9–10.

[12] Quoted in Joseph Blotner, *Faulkner: A Biography*, one-volume edition (Jackson, MS: University Press of Mississippi, 2005), 335.

old Sartoris coachman, who relishes the romance of the colonel's daring escape from Yankee troops on "the stallion" held for him "in the willers" by that same twelve-year old Bayard.[13] His aunt, Virginia Du Pre, née Sartoris, the widow Miss Jenny, aids and abets the chivalric demiurge of old Simon's tales about those titanic Sartoris brothers.

> [A]s she grew older the tale itself grew richer and richer, taking on a mellow splendour like wine; until what had been a hare-brained prank of two heedless and reckless boys wild with their own youth, was become a gallant and finely tragical focal-point to which the history of the race had been raised from out the old miasmic swamps of spiritual sloth by two angels valiantly fallen and strayed, altering the course of human events and purging the souls of men. (549)

And nowhere is her version of the vision splendid so developed and focused as it is in the figure she draws of the true-to-life cavalier and General Lee's matchless cavalry reconnaissance expert J. E. B. Stuart. The story itself, related with heightened free indirection, though it ends up replaying old Bayard's uncle Bayard's end, is a comic one concerning a raid for coffee and anchovies, all foolish gallantry and reckless bravery; however, its aesthetic apex consists in a sudden figural flourish:

> The captain freed his stirrup and hauled the prisoner up behind him. "Forward!" the General said and whirled roweling his bay, and with the thunderous coordination of a single centaur they swept down the knoll.... Stuart now carried his plumed hat in his hand and his long tawny locks, tossing to the rhythm of his speed, appeared as gallant flames smoking with the wild and self-consuming splendour of his daring. (552)

But, as if the textual matrix can no longer truly support such figural plenitude, a note of dissonance is allowed to sound in the form of his captive's running commentary. "'No gentleman has any business in this war,'" the federal major quips. "'There is no place for him here. He is an anachronism, like anchovies.'" (554) And again, "'Forward, Sir, I beg,' the captive major added. 'What is one man, to a paladin out of romance?'" (555).

So it is with the cynical voice of the inevitably victorious North, and his perfect antitype the Yankee, ringing in his ears that the gallant chevalier is obliged to feel his own figural obsolescence, at least as Miss Jenny tells it. At all events,

---

[13] Faulkner, *Novels 1926–1929*, 559.

it cannot have escaped notice that old Bayard himself has recused himself from the narrative proceedings altogether and refrained from making any comment on the sentimental depositions of his old aunt and coachman. The latent affinity between the text's sense of complicit inauthenticity with regard to these romance materials (left to a black servant and a woman) and Bayard's own steely silence clarifies an implicit aesthetic compact that, at this early stage (1928), permitted Faulkner to eat his cake and have it too, but whose cynical suspension ten years later for *The Unvanquished* awkwardly obliges Bayard himself to utter the unutterable, write out the clichés he would never have endorsed in the first Yoknapatawpha (or Yocona County) novel, and so exposes the frailty of the stratagem in the first place.

Transposition

But what has any of this to do with mediation and technology? How could this tendency in Faulkner be said to participate in what I have described as a strategy of techno-mediatic displacement and distortion, when it appears that the mature fictions adopted a variety of far less outrageous management techniques, none of which required the sorts of elaborate aesthetic red-shifting I have outlined? The clue to solving this riddle is announced in the early novel at issue, where, in a symptomatic Faulknerian *mise en abîme* around the Proper Name, John and Bayard Sartoris are reduplicated twice in the space of four generations, a twinned intergenerational brace of brothers—"two heedless and reckless boys wild with their own youth"—rushing headlong into a war that will claim one of them and leave the other to hang on in a state of dissociated melancholia some few years after the armistice; and not just any war either, but one in which (with distinct inflections) the perdurable chivalric codes of honor and glory are put through an industrial shredder. For with this nominal fold in space-time, and the formal repetition it aggressively signals between the Civil War and World War I, a link is forged in which we can clearly discern the figural replacement in question, namely, the substitution of the *airplane* for the *steed*, the flying corps or air force for the cavalry as such. It is, then, the suicidal romanticism of the first Bayard, whirling his horse around to recover the forgotten anchovies, that finds its belated and now fully technological echo in the last John's death in the skies over France—which young Bayard is forced to recapitulate mentally in what Freud called the death drive of traumatic repetition,[14] just as Miss Jenny is obliged to repeat the first Bayard's death as a fable: "[A]nd he recalled that

---

[14] See Sigmund Freud, *Beyond the Pleasure Principle, Group Psychology and other works*, trans. James Strachey with Anna Freud, Vol. XVIII of the Standard Edition (London: Hogarth Press, 1955), 18–23.

morning, relived it again with strained attention from the time he had seen the first tracer smoke, until from his steep sideslip he watched the flame burst like the gay flapping of an orange pennon from the nose of John's Camel and saw his brother's familiar gesture and the sudden awkward sprawl of his plunging body as it lost equilibrium in midair" (824). Of course it is this same unmanageable image that finally drives Bayard to his own lethal rendezvous above a government airfield at Dayton, Ohio, "in the wildest skid he had seen since his hun days" (863), where the wings shear away and dislodge the tail, and from one thousand feet he at last descends to his fate as the "MISSISSIPPI AVIATOR" (866) who reaches Miss Jenny and his wife Narcissa on a sensational headline in the local newspaper.

Joel Williamson once speculated that this link can be thought of equally in the other direction; if, biographically, around 1946, "horses had replaced flying as his passion," and if "[j]umping horses, like flying airplanes, was an exhilarating and very dangerous proceeding,"[15] then the fiction testifies to the various ways in which one pursuit transposes into the other, in a dialectic of mutual transformation. It is not as if young Bayard does not attempt to cut the figure of the traditional cavalier (his very namesake, the Chevalier de Bayard) upon his return home (though he prefers his motorcar, as we shall see); he does, but the organic fit between man and beast has been fatefully compromised, such that the rhetoric of figuration is now constantly urging the animal toward the aeronautical domain where the newer breed of chevalier belongs: "[T]he animal soared like a bronze explosion . . . swirled in a myriad flicking like fire . . . whipping his body like a rag upon its flashing arc. . . . The beast burst like bronze unfolding wings: a fluid desperation" (648). This futurist morphing of the "centaur" figure of the chevalier, its transformation into an explosive metallic line of flight, is made perfectly explicit as an historical torsion later on, when Miss Jenny compares "my Bayard" to the one just returned from the front in 1918: "'Look what he did with just a horse. . . . He didn't need any flying machine'" (737). To which Bayard sharply retorts: "'Little two-bit war. . . . And on a horse. Anybody can go to war on a horse. No chance for him to do anything much'." "'At least he got himself decently killed', Miss Jenny snapped. 'He did more with a horse than you could do with that aeroplane'" (738). Within a few months of this exchange, of course, he will have done just enough with it to lie alongside all the other Sartorises in the family plot.

That Faulkner was being explicit about this substitution, this shift within the figural economy of the cavalier from an equine to an aeronautical register, can scarcely be denied, but what this has to do with technical mediation is, for the moment, unclear. Here it bears remembering that "Jeb" Stuart, the most

---

[15] Williamson, *William Faulkner and Southern History*, 285, 345.

celebrated chevalier of the Confederate Army, was himself none other than "General Lee's eyes" (554)—which is to say a prosthetic *medium*, if not yet a technological one. By the 1860s, the role of the cavalry in modern warfare had become as much an informational as a strictly military one, the relative speed of the mounts permitting swift circumnavigations of enemy camps, mapping of terrain and embedded forces, counting of large guns, routine interception of orders, audacious pursuits, sabotage and tapping of telegraph lines, and basic reconnaissance, and so in general could be said to have acquired mediatic capacities in excess of any other component of the armed forces. In fact, its information-gathering function would diminish only once the airplane itself, suitably rigged with semi-automatic photographic equipment, had assumed its primary function within the army—which was informational before it was military, as Paul Virilio points out:

> [C]ontrary to what is generally thought, the air arm grew out of the reconnaissance services, its military value having initially been questioned by the general staffs. Indeed the reconnaissance aircraft itself, whose function was to supply ground troops with information, to direct artillery barrages or to take photographs, gained acceptance merely as a "flying observation post," almost as static as the old balloon with its cartographers, pencils and paper. Mobile information remained the province of the deep-penetrating cavalry until Joffre, at the Battle of the Marne, turned to the aviators for the first time in deciding on the offensive dispositions necessary for victory. The lot of the airborne crews was not an enviable one, since they had to maintain a constant altitude and thus expose themselves to enemy fire in order that the photographic scale should remain the same.[16]

So the airplane enters warfare not as an armed machine, but as a medium of photographic images and tactical information for the artillery, which was transmitted back to the ground by wireless telegraphy.[17] "Early in 1915, British generals at Neuve-Chapelle derived immense benefit from systematic photo reconnaissance that yielded a detailed look at German positions ranging from 700 to 1,500 yards in depth along the entire line of opposing trenches."[18] Military strategy was transformed by these omnipresent eyes in the sky (8,000

---

[16] Paul Virilio, *War and Cinema: The Logistics of Perception*, trans. Patrick Camiller (London & New York: Verso, 1989), 17.

[17] It is worth recalling that the autobiographically based story in Jean Renoir's *La Grande Illusion* (1937) concerns the capture of two French air officers by a German flying ace; the French craft was engaged in a reconnaissance mission.

[18] Roger Bilstein, *Flight in America: From the Wrights to the Astronauts*, 3rd ed. (Baltimore: Johns Hopkins University Press, 2001), 34.

buzzing the Western Front alone by the summer of 1918); the logistical concepts of war altered under the weight of mediatized information brought down from the heights. To be sure, by the time the United States joined the effort in late 1917, flight in Europe had been properly militarized (with bomb loads and mounted machine guns), industrialized, and transformed in public perception from a quaint pastime into a fully romantic uniformed vocation—perhaps the only one available above the prolonged attrition and meaningless mass slaughter of the trenches. As Blotner puts it, the war in the air was "so different" from the horrors of the trenches that it proffered "a form of conflict in which one could still hear echoes of knightly combats of men descended from that ideal...: the legendary Chevalier de Bayard, the sixteenth century '*chevalier sans peur et sans reproche.*'"[19] But flight's informational and mediatic prehistory, which it shares with the cavalry it quickly replaced, haunts the chivalric "rebranding" of aeronautics throughout and beyond its ideological and military functions in the Great War. And indeed, Faulkner himself, who would return from Canada in the autumn of 1918 high on his own afflatus of self-confabulated aeronautical derring-do, first endeavored to join the U.S. Army's Signal Corps, Aviation Section, in 1917; which is to say, to become the airborne eyes of the armed forces.[20] Of course he would end up enlisted as a pilot cadet in the Royal Air Force, no longer "the romantic, glamorous Royal Flying Corps of the early years of the war," but a vast administrative unit consisting of 4,000 combat aircraft and over 110,000 personnel distributed over 150 squadrons, many of whose roles remained informational and mediatic. Faulkner's main curriculum was in "wireless telegraphy, topography, and air-force law," his notebooks full of "signalling, artillery observation, reconnaissance, and photography" (62–63).

In what follows I will make the case that, while war cemented the romantic prestige of flying for a new mechanical age, transferring the residual glamor of the cavalry to the vertical third dimension by way of petroleum-fueled propellers and ailerons, and moreover forced the evolution of the machines themselves from amateur leisure craft to high-tech and high-speed precision weaponry, nevertheless it was flight's functional return in peacetime to a critical *mediator* of modernity that truly characterized the inter-war period. And just this curious paradox, between a public perception steeped in romance and heroism and a pragmatic intensification of airborne transport and communications on the home front, shaped Faulkner's passionate investment in figures of flight from his first published story to the screenplays and treatments for the Hollywood studios in the 1940s—since it was in the gap opened up by this objective contradiction in national ideological space that his own compulsive transpositions

---

[19] Blotner, *Faulkner*, 62.

[20] See Blotner, *Faulkner*, 60; and Joel Williamson, *William Faulkner and Southern History* (New York & Oxford: Oxford University Press, 1993), 176.

between feudal and futuristic structures of feeling could take ambiguous shape under the rubric of the chivalric aeronaut.

But more needs to be said first about the remarkable success of aviation's repertoire of potent romantic tropes and scenarios in the postwar period—about the contemporary representation of aeronautics, retrofitting an exhausted system of ideologemes and figures to a thoroughly secularized and commodified modernity, converting one of its dominant industrial drivers into a symbol for a vanishing and endangered archetype: the solitary hero. If Yeats's elegiac 1919 lyric for the Irish airman encapsulates a late romantic seizure of possibility in the conditions of airborne warfare—juxtaposing the self-sacrificial "lonely impulse of delight"[21] against the mounting obscenities of sublunary *Realpolitik*—then everywhere in the modern, the air pilot took on a glow of splendor radiating from the romance of dangerous individual endeavor. Delaunay's *Hommage à Blériot* (1914) (Fig. 1.1), imagines a heroic line of flight rotated on its axis into rainbow-hued quadrants and semicircles, the pilot reimagined as a spectrum of gay tones traversing polycentric arcs to a rhythm coordinated by the radio-signal beacon of the *Tour Eiffel*.

A generation later, with the cult of Lindbergh at its peak, no less a dramatist than Bertolt Brecht would premiere his production of *Der Lindberghflug* (1929) to celebrate the heroism of the nonstop transatlantic flight of May 1927. Hart Crane's great paean to manned flight, in the "Cape Hatteras" fourth section of *The Bridge* (1930), indulges in a feverish, ecstatic aeronautic romanticism that only the context of a dialogue with Walt Whitman could sustain:

> O Corsair of the typhoon,—pilot, hear!
> Thine eyes bicarbonate white by speed, O Skygak, see
> How from thy path above the levin's lance
> Thou sowest doom thou hast nor time nor chance
> To reckon—as thy stilly eyes partake
> What alcohol of space .. ! Remember, Falcon-Ace,
> Thou hast there in thy wrist a Sanscrit charge
> To conjugate infinity's dim marge—
> Anew .. ![22]

Finally, note should be taken of Auden's remarkable "Journal of an Airman," included as Book II of *The Orators* (1932), which explores with unflinching intimacy the psychological complexion of a pilot who portrays himself as the

---

[21] W. B. Yeats, "An Irish Airman Foresees His Death," in Daniel Albright, ed., *The Poems* (London: Dent, 1994), 184.

[22] Hart Crane, *The Bridge*, in *Complete Poems and Selected Letters*, ed. Langdon Hammer (New York: Library of America, 2006), 56–57.

Figure 1.1 Robert Delaunay, *Hommage à Blériot* (1914). Source: Kunstmuseum Basel.

antitype of "the Enemy" and his craft as a moral necessity "owing to the progress of enemy propaganda" (and who takes "Aerial photography of earthworks")[23]— provoking a review in the *Times Literary Supplement* claiming that the poem "describes measures of hostility against safe and organized society so reckless, so violent and capricious that they are surely beyond the imagination of any political revolutionary."[24] So the poetic image of the romantic pilot achieved its apotheosis in a figure so bent out of society's warp that its thoughts had become fully, and dangerously, irreconcilable with it.

At the same time that this romantic streak was being developed, the mechanical nature of aviation tended to predispose another species of aeronautical rhetoric away from the human and toward the machine itself. Beginning with Marinetti's *The Propeller* (1915), this tendency steadily finds its voice: "In the airplane, sitting on the gas tank, my stomach warmed by the pilot's head, I sensed the ridiculous inanity of the old syntax inherited from Homer. A burning need to

---

[23] W. H. Auden, *The Orators: An English Study* (London: Faber & Faber, 2015), 31, 52, 53.

[24] A. C. Brock, review of *The Orators*, TLS, 9 June 1932, 424. Reprinted in John Haffenden, ed., *W. H. Auden: The Critical Heritage* (London: Routledge, 1983), 99.

liberate words, to pull them out from the prison of the Latin period."[25] Kasimir Malevich's *Suprematist Composition: Airplane Flying* (1915) makes a similar point in the visual language of geometry and form: the recognizable figure pixelating into abstract rectangles and oblongs of black and yellow, intersected by a severe red horizon. Marsden Hartley's *The Aero* (1914) deploys an exuberant color scheme derived from overlapping flag patterns, stripes, and checkerboards, composing one striking field of textural and tonal juxtapositions, "the centre of which depicts the fireburst of a flying machine's engine."[26] This is probably the end result of a work in progress about which he wrote to Steiglitz in 1913, "I have one canvas 'Extase d'Aéroplane' if it must have a title—it is my notion of the possible extasy [sic] or soul state of an aeroplane if it could have one," indicating the state of confusion between pilot and craft even before the outbreak of war.[27] By 1931, Marinetti was openly advocating a new genre for poets, "aeropoetry," demanding in his *Manifesto for Aeropoetry* that poets emulate the aeropainters (Balla, Depero, Crali, Dottori) who two years before had heeded their master's call to give themselves over to "the immense visual and sensory drama of flight"[28]—and according to Marinetti, the best medium for aeropoetry was not the printed page but the radio transmission, proving that the airplane was more than anything else a medium of media.[29]

Nowhere would this be more evident than in the felt connection between aeronautics and cinema itself. As Peter Wollen points out, this spontaneous cultural affinity was both pervasive and perfectly logical:

> In 1933 the great modernist painter Fernand Léger observed that "Cine and aviation go arm in arm through life." "The cinema," he announced, "is the machine age." For Léger, aviation and the cinema were the two great contemporaneous mechanical inventions which had revolutionized the realm of human perception—allowing us to move through space with unprecedented velocity, to look at the world with a completely new perspective, and to change point-of-view in an instant while remaining seated in the same row of plush chairs. In [Jean Renoir's 1939 film] *Rules of the Game*, the aviator is the crucial representative of modernity,

---

[25] Filippo Tommaso Marinetti, quoted in Dominick Pisano, ed., *The Airplane in American Culture* (Ann Arbor, MI: University of Michigan Press, 2003), 254.

[26] Elizabeth Mankin Kornhauser and Ulrich Birkmaier, *Marsden Hartley* (New Haven & London: Yale University Press, 2002), 51.

[27] Letter week of May 18, 1913, in James Timothy Voorhies, ed., *My Dear Stieglitz: Letters of Marsden Hartley and Alfred Stieglitz, 1912–1915* (Columbia, SC: University of South Carolina Press, 2002), 77.

[28] Marinetti, quoted in Willard Bohn, *Reading Visual Poetry* (Teaneck, NJ: Fairleigh Dickinson University Press, 2010), 103.

[29] See Willard Bohn, "The Poetics of Flight: Futurist 'Aeropoesia,'" *MLN* 121 (2006), 210 [207–24].

the prospect of rapid and uncertain change. He is also a celebrity, a star, in the same sense that a film star is a celebrity, because of his command of the mass media. Unlike a film star, however, he is an authentic hero, one who has achieved fame, not as a vehicle for the fantasies of others, but for his extraordinary exploits, the realization of his own fantasies, his palpable authenticity. Jurieu is the modern hero—as the aviator was the modern hero for Brecht in his radio plays or for Auden or for Faulkner. *Rules of the Game* is cognate with . . . Faulkner's 1935 *Pylon*, with its ironic contrast between tragic barnstorming aviators and the carnival world of Mardi Gras.[30]

But the preconditions for this affinity were wrought in the crucible of the most advanced technological event in history to that point: the First World War, as Virilio insists.

> Distance, depth, three-dimensionality—in just a few years of war, space became a training-ground for the dynamic offensive and for all the energies it harnessed. And since "the harsh accents of its forward motion impel us towards a new clarity, the metallic roar of its matter plunges us into a new light," cinema became the metaphor for this object-shaping geometry, this fusion/confusion of genres which prefigured the terrifying species mutation of later years, and for the exorbitant priority accorded to speed of penetration by war and the war industry which, after 1919, converted to producing means of communication and transport and commercializing air space.[31]

Cinema as "metaphor" for the War's ushering of modernity into the age of flight, reshaping the standard geometries of logistical vision, and preparing the "tiny, fragile human body"[32] for monstrous mutations to come: it is in the maelstrom of cultural energies conjured by these momentous events that the repurposed cavalier figure served an invaluable role, surcharging the "terrifying" transition with an air of romance, allowing for a certain "modern heroism" (qua Baudelaire) in the act of overcoming the limitations of the human itself. And as Wollen attests, few were more aware of the extraordinary flexibility and polyvalence of that heroic figure than William Faulkner, who in his first published novel—which features a veteran airman blinded and doomed by his exploits—includes, hard on the heels of a verbal montage of all the clichés about the Front

---

[30] Peter Wollen, *Paris, Hollywood* (London & New York: Verso, 2002), 156.
[31] Virilio, *War and Cinema*, 27.
[32] Walter Benjamin, "The Storyteller," in Hannah Arendt, ed., *Illuminations: Essays and Reflections* (New York: Schocken Books, 1968), 84.

to be found in the films of 1919, this notable exchange on the cultural significance of "being a pilot" in the First World War:

> "What," said a beautiful painted girl, not listening, to James Dough who had been for two years a corporal-pilot in a French chasse escadrille, "is the difference between an American Ace and a French or British aviator?"
> "About six reels," answered James Dough glumly ... who had shot down thirteen enemy craft and had himself been crashed twice....
> "How nice. Is that so, really? You had movies in France, too, then?"
> "Yes. Gave us something to do in our spare time."[33]

That war, aviation, and cinema formed one dynamic ideological and technical unity was a fact not lost on Faulkner, who nevertheless persevered with a tragic cavalier figure, in Donald Mahon, in order to stabilize the explosive communicational energies condensed into the "metaphor" of cinema. Mahon's immobility, his blindness, and his death work to offset the mounting technological pressures of "massification" on everyday life by carving out a quiet space of romance *inside* the emblematic figure of those very pressures.

All the dead pilots

If the Great War had fostered a widespread neo-romantic rebranding of the pilot as cavalier, the representational question—as it had been for the Southern cavalrymen fifty years before—was what became of the demobbed veterans of the air upon their return home to an increasingly de-romanticized America. Such was undoubtedly Faulkner's question, which he asked with a characteristic repetitiveness in text after text following his own return from the RAF training base in Toronto in 1918. And, as we have already begun to note, in doing so, he was unable to refrain from a certain mediatic figuration. The opening of the story that most openly stages the question at hand, and repurposes John Sartoris to do so, "All the Dead Pilots" (1931), makes this figuration palpable:

> In the pictures, the snapshots hurriedly made, a little faded, a little dog-eared with the thirteen years, they swagger a little. Lean, hard, in their brass-and-leather martial harness, posed standing beside or leaning upon the esoteric shapes of wire and wood and canvas in which they flew without parachutes, they too have an esoteric look; a look not

[33] Faulkner, *Novels 1926–1929*, 150.

exactly human, like that of some dim and threatful apotheosis of the race seen for an instant in the glare of a thunderclap and then forever gone.[34]

Photographic reification, with its subsequent aging process, serves as a convenient trope for the sudden ejection of a noble figure from the amniotic sac in which it had found ideological nourishment, and into a two-dimensional caricature of itself. The keyword "esoteric" at once reinforces the unbridgeable sense of distance that a mere thirteen years has turned into an historical abyss, affirms a fundamental caste distinction, and denotes a regime change at the level of representation: to the modern, to 1930, the romance of 1916 is precisely esoteric.[35] Flash photography amplifies the passage's closing figure, of glare and thunderclap—which will also speak to the infamous "abruption" of Thomas Sutpen on horseback, and the Rev. Hightower's ancestor frozen in whirling equine motion—and asks that we read the romantic "threatful apotheosis of the race" carved out by these figures as a work as much of modern mediation as of gothic chiaroscuro. It also opens a portal to the beyond, these images amounting to so many ghostly vestiges, as the next sentence insists: "Because they are dead, all the old pilots, dead on the eleventh of November, 1918" (511). Photography embalms the pilot-cavaliers in a technical process of mummification that demobilization and the return to civilian existence has already exposed them to existentially.[36] Faulkner's account of the civilian undeath of these once-larger-than-life aeronauts is secured by way of a photographic trope that recurs at the story's end: "The courage, the recklessness, call it what you will, is the flash, the instant of sublimation; then flick! the old darkness again. . . . [B]eing momentary, it can be preserved and prolonged only on paper" (531).

Nor should we overlook in this context the remarkable textual fact that our narrator, adapting to a mechanical leg and so disqualified from further flying, both likes to chat with the gunnery sergeant of a Camel squadron "about the synchronization of the machine guns" mounted on the planes (513) and spends his spare time "experiment[ing] with a synchronized camera on which I was

---

[34] Faulkner, "All the Dead Pilots," in *Collected Stories* (London: Vintage, 1995), 511.

[35] Nietzsche writes that the "distinction between the exoteric and the esoteric . . . was found everywhere that people believed in an order of rank and *not* in equality or equal rights. . . .[T]he exoteric sees things up from below—while the esoteric sees them *down from above!*" Friedrich Nietzsche, *Beyond Good and Evil: Prelude to a Philosophy of the Future*, §30, trans. Judith Norman (Cambridge: Cambridge University Press, 2001), 31.

[36] The obvious reference here is to Bazin: "Those grey or sepia shadows, phantomlike and almost undecipherable, are no longer traditional family portraits but rather the disturbing presence of lives halted at a set moment in their duration, freed from their destiny; not, however, by the prestige of art but by the power of an impassive mechanical process: for photography does not create eternity, as art does, it embalms time, rescuing it from its proper corruption." André Bazin, "The Ontology of the Photographic Image," trans. Hugh Gray, *Film Quarterly* 13.4 (Summer 1960), 8 [4–9].

working" (512). This timely conceptual fusion of flight, automatic weaponry, and photography around the technical achievement of synchronization elevates the narrative out of its incorrigible predisposition to romance and establishes an awareness of flight's rapid development during the First World War, from which vantage point the airborne cavaliers themselves look always-already absurd. The tactic is critical, if relatively undeveloped in the given tale, since by associating the narrative voice with the war-driven technical breakthroughs in synchronization at the Front (and with mechanical prosthetics), it establishes a foothold in disenchanted modernity that—not unlike the photographic trope of embalming already discussed—tends to consign the narrative contents to a zone of nostalgia from which it is itself exempt. What is more, the narrator's official function at Wing Headquarters is "the censorship of mail from all squadrons in the Wing" (512), which is to say that he is an ideological media filter applied by the armed forces to its communications. Faulkner adopts a clear strategy of "masking" the deeply inauthentic materials on display in this short story—the sexual duel between Spoomer and Sartoris, the ribald contest over the publican's daughter with its bedroom-farcical climax, the dive-bombing of the dog—behind an exemplary cover of routine reconnaissance patrols, technical jargon, the daily practicalities of the aerodrome, and so on, all of which permits the narrative to indulge a tendency to lurid romance by vouchsafing its non-romantic provenance via a paraphernalia of modernity conceived as mediatory. And the final orchestration of its bizarre and wildly uneven affective economy under the sign of death—the death of the airborne Southern cavalier in battle, which happens "offscreen"—is managed by way of a Poundian Malatesta "post-bag," an editorial sampling of the correspondence between Sartoris, Aunt Jenny, and the Wing Commander, justified by the narrator's function as censor; thus, the narration of the tragic denouement is filtered through a modern media ecology of letters, parcels, flight, and the photographic figure in which the tale culminates.

Within a year of this story's publication, Faulkner was again recycling its Sartoris aeronaut-cavalier figure in his treatment for Howard Hawks at MGM of Major Elliot White Spring's cognate property "War Birds" (itself a redacted version of the real-life RFC pilot John McGavock Grider's diaries). It wasn't his first attempt to upload this material onto something ready for the screen: the treatment of "Absolution" had been delivered to the bosses at Culver City in June of 1932, and it too featured a violent, hot-headed young "John" and his sexual rivalry over a small-town Southern belle with a blue-blood son of Dixie—a rivalry that can be settled "only in flight combat."[37] But the work he did on "War Birds" in November and December of that year explicitly grafts material from *Flags in the Dust*, "All the Dead Pilots," and another story, "Ad Astra," onto

---

[37] William Faulkner, "Absolution: original story (treatment)," (Culver City: MGM June 1, 1932), University of Virginia acquisition number 10,211, folder 5, 3422, p. 7.

the pre-existing Springs treatment that Hawks wanted revised, making it a vivid demonstration of how Faulkner's debt to romance was repaid along a complexly recycled mediatic chain; and of how, in a strange inversion of the general law, writing for the screen tended to make him drop the technical mask he otherwise held up to obscure his deeper complicity with the material—since the cinema already *was* that mask.

One of the more remarkable, though properly unfilmable, features of this first "War Birds" treatment is its unusually insistent figuration of the act of writing itself: long stretches of flashback recapitulation told literally through close-up images of John Sartoris's writing hand making entries in his journal, mostly without any double-exposures or any other special effect to mitigate this extraordinary violation of the central aesthetic canon of the modern: *show, don't tell*. Later, a tight shot of a nervous Adjutant typing in agitation gives us "THE SHEET OF PAPER IN TYPEWRITER: A jumble of letters that make no sense at all as the Adjutant taps them out," as if to underscore the affinity of handwriting with "spirit" and of typewriting with post-human babble.[38] But things really get interesting when we come to the shots numbered (by Hawks, most likely) 190–91; for here, as the outline of the tragedy comes fully into focus, we find Bayard Sartoris mounting a camera on his airplane prior to undertaking a reconnaissance mission. He cannot make it work, however, and is obliged to fix the apparatus instead onto Spoomer's plane, which is what the disgraced John Sartoris is desperately looking to shoot out of the sky in his Camel. This diegetic reference to aerial reconnaissance in a war story was to have occasioned the use of many thrilling (and prohibitively expensive) aerial shots in the film itself, speculatively motivating the device that not Hawks but Howard Hughes had perfected in *Hell's Angels* (1930). It also initiates an important distinction within the film's conception of the brothers themselves, since Bayard will here survive his ancestral fate precisely by committing his flight time to the work of mediation, whereas John's doom is sealed by his commitment to the feudal code of honor. By far the most audacious of the treatment's many contrived effects, however, is the repeated airborne apparition of "JOHN'S GHOST SHIP" after his demise, as Bayard desperately hunts the skies for his brother's German killer before the Armistice arrives to exculpate him. This flying ghost ship, Faulkner's imprimatur on the treatment, is a remarkable attempt to think through again the complex relationships between flight, romance, photography, haunting, and cinema that subtend his entire fascination with the material. Its recurrence, no fewer than five times, underscores not only the debt contemporary romance owes to the modern media but the very "mummification" of change itself that cinema institutionalizes, and which can find no more

---

[38] Faulkner, "War Birds," first dialogue script (Culver City: MGM, January 12, 1933), shot 136, University of Virginia acquisition number 10,211, folder 1, p. 54.

fitting figure than an undead airplane in motion, superimposed upon an empty sky. Bazin's great formula—"Now, for the first time, the image of things is likewise the image of their duration, change mummified, as it were"[39]—finds in this treatment its *cine qua non*: an image of a plane without a pilot, haunting the sky where not only the archetypal "heedless and reckless boy" fell out of it, but the very martial romance of flight met its historical quietus above the mechanical slaughter of the trenches, just as the War itself came to an end and flight was transformed from a military into a civilian and commercial operation again. And in a final flourish of his own unfilmable pen, Faulkner ends his scenario on yet another telltale juxtaposition, a truly impossible framing of Bayard taking a jump in the saddle of the Sartoris horse (descended, no doubt, from Jupiter himself) and this: "IN DISSOLVE there passes behind Bayard the ghost of John's ship, John looking down at them, his face bright, peaceful. The ship goes on in dissolve; sound of an engine dies away."[40] All the dead pilot-cavaliers will return, this image avers, in a peacetime sky buzzing with a redeemed vocation for flight: not as a threat of decimation, but bearing messages of "bright" benignity. As a medium of media.

Flying the mail

In late 1931, Faulkner had published a story entitled *Idyll in the Desert* as a standalone Random House signed special edition. Much of its narration is given over to old Lucas Crump, a mail rider, "a fellow hauling government mail, government property."[41] Lucas insists up front upon the privilege of that vocation in terms of a certain prophylactic against "getting cracked in the head," namely the fact that, vested with the responsibilities of horseback mediation, "he ain't riding alone. He's got Uncle Sam right there to talk to whenever he feels like talking: Washington and the big cities full of folks, and all that that means to a man," as he puts it (399). The tale concerns a tragic romance unfurling in Blizzard, Arizona: a consumptive man sends a telegram via Lucas Crump to his lover in New York, who abandons her family to come care for him; he recovers, but she ails, and he leaves her to a lonely death in this town well off all the grids of "Washington and the big cities full of folks." In fact, Lucas is (with his horse) the only "medium" connecting Blizzard to that network of urban centers, now articulated by entirely new mediatic techniques: newsprint, automobiles, movies, telephone, radio, and commercial flight, alongside the older railways and

---

[39] Bazin, "Ontology of the Photographic Image," 8.
[40] Faulkner, "War Birds," shot 323, p. 143.
[41] Faulkner, "Idyll in the Desert," in Joseph Blotner, ed., *Uncollected Stories* (New York: Vintage, 1997), 399.

telegrams (all of which are assimilated into Lucas's narrative). Putting aside its melodramatic content, the story is an allegory of mediation itself, as the following passage makes particularly plain:

> News passes Blizzard about four times before it ever lights. News happens in Pittsburgh, say. All right. It gets radioed, passing right over us to Los Angeles or Frisco. All right. They put the Los Angeles and Frisco papers into the airplane and they pass right over us, going east now to Phoenix. Then they put the papers onto the fast train and the news passes us again, going west at sixty miles an hour at two A. M. And then the papers come back east on the local, and we get a chance to read them.[42]

It is one of the exemplary moments in Faulkner where what I would tendentiously call his *mediatic unconscious* is dredged up from the depths to assume unwonted prominence at the textual forefront. And its point is to sketch something like the fate of localism or regionalism itself—of any parochial district somehow sequestered or seeking to secede from the spreading, abstract national space—in the new media ecology whose vectors and velocities are here summarily mapped.

In the present context, the principal interest must lie in how aviation is inserted into the diminishing scale of speeds, from radio's light speed down to the ambling local train, at which "news" travels in 1930. As second only to electromagnetic propagation, air speed's superiority to rail transport has henceforth displaced all other "carriers" in the mediation of information in the new petrochemical economy. And what it carries is, of course, another *medium*: the newspapers printed with information conveyed virtually immediately by a nascent radio network from one metropolitan hub to another, then decelerated from wavelengths into paper and ink, so that it can eventually trickle out via physical transportation into the backwaters and standing pools of the media ecology as the morning edition—a day late in the "real time" of modern transmission, but right on time according to the uneven development of a modernizing media system. And this representation of postwar aviation as being above all a matter of *remediation*, or the housing of one medium inside another, is shaped not only by a need internal to the story itself (in which one character leaves a major city to grind to absolute stasis in a tiny hamlet, and another manages the reverse, thanks to a complex relay of media signals) but by the circumambient media system itself, in which flight is being recast as a medium of media, the emblematic instance of which is the story of the U.S. air mail.

---

[42] Faulkner, *Idyll in the Desert* (New York: Random House, 1931), 15.

After the Armistice, while much of the technological development of manned flight in America remained with the Air Force (and in particular, the astonishing advance of floating runways or aircraft carriers), in fact the cultural and economic logic of flight's role in the accumulation of capital during the 1920s depended on distinct civilian, utilitarian applications: in industry, trade, distribution, advertising, and above all, communications. Army surplus airplanes flooded the market to fuel the mounting appetite for faster and more targeted mail delivery services. The U.S. Post Office Department began offering regular airmail service between New York, Philadelphia, and Washington, D.C. in May 1918, just three months before the cessation of hostilities in Europe. "By the summer of 1920, the Post Office Department had improved reliability, took over all air-mail operations, and hired its own pilots. War-surplus DH-4 biplanes, extensively modified for air-mail service, replaced the slow, frail JN-4 trainers. By the autumn of 1920, the POD had forged a coast-to-coast air-mail route between New York and San Francisco."[43] But this continent-spanning service depended during the night hours on trains to carry the mail on long legs till the rising of the sun; until reliable and well-lit airfields could safely accommodate the landing and departure of these planes, the mechanical mediation of the U.S. mail was a hybrid affair. "By 1924, a system of flashing beacons had gone into service on the Chicago-Cheyenne segment, expanding to a transcontinental network in two years. A series of floodlighted main terminals, plus a string of intermediary emergency fields, added to air-mail's reliability" (50). With this 24-hour conquest of the nation's skies, the POD had achieved a truly remarkable feat: a network of brilliant nodes and pathways that articulated the vast landmass of the United States into a single integrated circuit of physical communications. And what could have been more valuable to a booming economy, not least in finance capital:

> As the sophistication of air mail improved during the twenties, the volume of banking and other financial mail began to mount. Clients included the Federal Reserve Bank and its branches as well as major banks across the country. In addition to sending drafts, securities, bonds, and stocks via air mail, a variety of companies used the service to speed delivery of manifests, bills of lading, advertising, and miscellaneous commercial correspondence. (51)

This mounting pressure from the private sector rapidly obliged the state's monopoly over aerial communications to cede to privatization; the Kelly Bill of

---

[43] Roger Bilstein, *Flight in America: From the Wrights to the Astronauts* (Baltimore: Johns Hopkins University Press, 2001), 50.

1925 allowed the government's working transportation system to be operated by a proliferation of new, private companies competing via contract to carry the nation's mail. Growth, the great capitalist fetish, was the result:

> [T]he recently formed airlines took over the routes pioneered by the POD and grew into mature transportation systems. By the spring of 1929, new aviation facilities in the United States included 61 passenger lines, 47 mail lines, and 32 express lines serving trade areas that contained 90 million people; the volume of air mail ballooned from 810,555 pounds in 1926 to 7,772,014 pounds in 1929. (52)

But so too was unionization, which led reactively to a trend of larger businesses, such as Ford Motors, incorporating their own private airlines, especially after new design modifications opened up aviation to freight transportation. Indicatively, the first commercial freight run from Chicago to New York City in 1927 was loaded with a "motley consignment of newsreels, machinery parts, advertising copy, trade journals, candy, and Paris garters" (58)—which is to say, *media* and other trade goods. Indeed, beginning auspiciously with the air mail service, American commercial aviation succeeded in large measure after the War by mediating the physical media, the information that couldn't be converted into electromagnetic pulses, but which, in an age of analog technologies, assumed mass and weight and volume: paper, celluloid, film canisters, shellac, and so forth.

Alongside this consolidation of private airline services specializing in the transportation of information, passengers, and consumer goods, so-called general aviation also fostered an informational prerogative among flyers returned from the Front and looking for a trade. Apart from crop-dusting in rural areas and the inevitable "flying gypsies" or barnstormers (to whom we shall return), the main branches of such "aerial service" work were in surveying and photography, not to mention skywriting and the routine transportation of journalists from one breaking news event to another. Aerial surveying assisted in the federal government's mission to assess property tax liabilities: accurate reassessments in a period of wildfire urbanization and an unprecedented construction boom were made much simpler after the introduction of aircraft to the task in 1927. Nor should the more exotic expeditions of flying survey teams into remote Alaska be dissociated from the media ecology's web, since the naval photographers who returned in 1929 with detailed aerial photographs of 23,000 square miles of territory discovered therein "important watersheds for power sites, coupled with accurate timber estimates, [and] prompted negotiations for new pulp mills in Ketchikan. With an estimated capacity for pulp production equaling one-third of the daily requirements in the United States, this promised to be an important source of indispensible newsprint." (68) Flight, photography, paper pulp, newsprint: the ecology of media veritably *subsumed* the natural ecology into its insatiable hunger for profits.

All of the foregoing illustrates the prodigious spread of civilian aviation in the decade and a half after the War in a manner that tended radically to diminish the aura of romance with which flight had been endowed at the Front, replacing it with a depersonalized logic of bureaucratic mediation. Flight entered mainstream American life, not as a perilous vocation for doomed knights, but as a "becoming-medium" in an unblinking material hook-up with those other forces—radio, telegraphy, photography—that were converting the patchwork of states into a national network. Moreover, as so many of Faulkner's stories and screen scenarios attest, airplanes were now not only media in themselves, carrying information and materials from point to point across the national grid, but they were also (and simultaneously) media of media, conveying mail, parcels, newspapers, advertising copy, films, newsreels, money, bonds, and so on, along the same paths. They were as well the occasion for a great deal of "media" attention, and here and there formed a symbiotic relationship with certain species of journalism and cinema ever on the lookout for new sensations and motor-sensory affects. The vestigial figure of the pilot-chevalier would apparently have nowhere to go in this new national space, other than in retrospective evocations of the now distant war; the new dispensation absorbed individual heroism into corporate stability and flattened the prehistory of commercial aviation into the ahistorical mask of this or that airline "brand"—American, TWA, United, Delta, and the rest. That Faulkner knew all of this perfectly well, and yet strove to find anachronistic opportunities within the rationalizing web of mechanical mediation for the flourishing of a now-extinct romance stereotype, is attested to first of all by his collaborative work on another scenario for MGM, in 1932, "Flying the Mail."

This property, developing a treatment by Ralph Graves and Bernard Fineman and based on a series of magazine articles by airmail pilot Bogart Rogers, was to have been a vehicle for MGM stars Wallace Beery and Marie Dressler (and so related to the wrestling picture commission lampooned by the Coen Brothers in *Barton Fink* [1991]). Faulkner's job was to provide heightened dramatic tension, especially in the rivalry between the "Wally" figure, an early airman of the 1910 vintage, and his adoptive son, Bob, who becomes another pilot under his tutelage. This intergenerational dynamic is played out over two decades in the history of American flight, with the Great War clearly separating two periods of civil aviation, and driving a wedge between Bob, who goes to fly in France, and Wally, who does not. Here the question is precisely what to do with the pilots who came home from the front, and with those of an earlier generation of pioneers and aging legends. With Bob, "a natural combat pilot,"[44] demobbed after

---

[44] Faulkner, "Flying the Mail," 6.

18 months at war, the Oedipal tension is raised when both he and his ersatz father enter planes at the same air show, unknown to each other. "[Wally] enters his ship as a meet where it is laughed at. The other entries are the new types developed in the war. [. . .] He is like a plow-horse strayed onto a race track in the middle of a race" (8). In Europe, Bob has come to realize that "the plane in which he practically grew up is an obsolete man-trap" (6), but it is this very same flying deathtrap that inevitably collides with his more streamlined craft during the show, and "father" and "son" are reunited. The rendezvous is supercharged by the fact that not one of the letters that Bob sent home from France has reached its destination, and this chronic failure of mediation prompts him to enter the Post Office's nascent airmail service. The motto of the U.S. mail—"Nor rain, nor storm, nor any dark of night shall stay these couriers from the swift completion of their appointed rounds" (7)—underwrites the remainder of the drama. Wally's determined skepticism ("It can't be done. Mail goes from one set place to another set place like a train. But who in hell wants to fly like a train? Who can? You can't fly by a lot of gadgets with needles, you fly by the seat of your pants" [8–9]) is countered by Bob's professional zeal; Bob's impersonal dedication finds him landing a plane on a cow and meeting his love interest on a train;[45] while behind this, a wealth of documentary background is adduced: "We see the crudities of the air mail at this time, with obsolete war ships and strips of burning gasoline for field markers and beacons" (9).

The historical drive is paramount, and particularly at stake is the integration of flight into a modern media ecology that leaves the likes of Wally alienated:

> The Government has sold the air mail privilege to private companies. Bob and Wally now have a franchise for their division. The girl is a clerk operating the new radio, of which Wally is contemptuous. He says that if a man cannot fly and land a plane by himself, how can another man on the ground tell him how to do it on the telephone. (13)

Privatization and commercialization dovetail with mediation and the absorption of aviation into media conglomerates and techniques. The older emphasis on chivalric mastery is rapidly displaced by a depersonalized and bureaucratic sensibility and the efficiency of a technological system. As monopolization proceeds apace—"TIME PASSES, THE BIG COMPANIES ARE BUYING IN THE little ones" (13)—efficiencies of scale engulf the horizon in which heroism seemed possible: "The airport is now a terminal of a modern line. It has electric field markers and beacons and radio in tough [sic] with the ships at all times" (14).

---

[45] This detail is a reference to the famous telegram dispatched by pilot Dean Smith to his superiors at the Post Office: "On trip 4 west-bound. Flying low. Engine quit. Only place to land on cow. Killed cow. Wrecked plane. Scared me. Smith." See Bilstein, *Flight in America*, 53.

Wally, now reduced to managing an airport restaurant, regales the younger pilots with tales of former times: "At every opportunity, he tells them of the old days when a man flew by sheer guts and optimism" (14). Meanwhile, Bob "rises in the service of a syndicate" (13). Only a melodramatic twist in the plot can allow for an anachronistic reflux of chivalric glamour: Bob flies his love interest through a blizzard and crashes, providing Wally the chance to take his venerable crate out of mothballs and ride to the rescue one final time. But the denouement is unforgiving: "SOME TIME HAS PASSED, we see a huge modern airport with the planes coming and going like trains. Bob is the manager of it" (16).

That this treatment was never produced, and was cleared off Faulkner's desk in a manner of days, should not detract from the remarkable testimony it provides of his thoroughgoing awareness of the history of civil aviation after the War, and its steady insertion into the modern media system of which it became a critical strut. The "Wally" figure, a stock studio stereotype of comical retrograde middle age, is aligned with a conception of flight that Faulkner himself, in his short fictions and early novels, had already been busy relegating to the superannuated stockpile of exhausted ideologemes, while the figure of the ambitious and younger Bob delineates a position that none of his published works would endorse: the socially dominant role of aviation in the postwar period, namely, its bureaucratic subsumption within monopolizing corporations as a source of surplus value. "Wally" is a hardy pioneer who becomes a garrulous restaurateur, while "Bob" advances from "born combat pilot" to zealous airmail flier to the manager of a vast urban airport—the march of capital leaves only tall stories in its wake, where romance floats to the surface like the wreckage of a plane the "vintage of 1910, a pusher. Flimsy as a box-kite, where the pilot sits out in front of it on a slat like a fence rail and flies with a wheel a little larger than a dollar watch" (3). Technical and engineering specifications allegorize the historical realities of media change; characters function as instantiations of the mechanical uneven developments implicit in that history.

A folklore of speed

Faulkner's sustained engagement with aviation as a contested ideological terrain, where romantic and bureaucratizing forces coalesced in dangerous cyclonic formations, is thus informed by a deep understanding of the drift of material history in the 1920s, towards a systematizing logic of media integration and the accumulation of monopoly capital. It is the accelerated and condensed history of this booming sector of the postwar economy—from Army surplus to an indispensable element within the new media ecology—that, I believe, appealed to his fictional imagination. This history offered an exemplary lesson in the obsolescence of certain paradigms within the space of a generation, an existentially palpable sense of cultural transformation—a felt torque—rooted in the irresistible spread of capitalist modernity. It was the figure of the aeronaut-cavalier, itself a manifest derivative of the perdurable Southern ideologeme that was his inheritance, that particularly attracted Faulkner, in what can be described as a symptomatic repetition straddling the three major genres of his voluminous work in the decade 1928–1938: novels, short stories, and screenplays and treatments. For this torque in the national ideological space permitted him to discharge the accumulating pressure of his irrepressible Southern romanticism in forms that were no longer merely regional, but could speak to wider and more systemic phenomena. Faulkner found, in the vestigial, doomed pilots of the postwar period, a ready-made palimpsestic figure on which to project chivalric and mediatory connotations simultaneously, their "tragic" comportment counterpointed by an insistence on their absorption into information systems in which tragedy was unthinkable.

Nowhere did he more avidly pursue these opportunities than in the sequence of stories concerned with the infamous barnstormers of the period, culminating in his least typical novel, *Pylon* (1935)—about which we can say only a few things here. In the 1920s, there were above all two species of aviator in whom there lingered the aura extinguished from the profession in ways that "Flying the Mail" had made palpable: the charismatic exhibition or endurance flier of the Lindbergh type (Lindbergh himself being a graduate of the airmail service), in whom Faulkner expressed not a shred of interest (much to his credit, as witness the subsequent embarrassment of Brecht and others); and the "flying gypsy" or daredevil pilot engaged in high-altitude risk-taking of the most alarming sort, perhaps the most conspicuous and suicidal of the "career" paths available to the demobbed pilots of 1919. Their craft of choice was the Flying Jenny, which had cost the government $5,000 per item, but was released as surplus for only a few hundred dollars. On these planes, the pilots and their stuntperson attendants routinely (and for minimal reimbursement) performed feats unprecedented in human history, before which the inherited arsenal of literary tropes, genres, forms, and figures wilted helplessly. As Marinetti put it, "I sensed the ridiculous inanity of the old syntax inherited from Homer. A burning need to liberate words, to pull them out from the prison of the Latin period,"[46] was the consequence of such aeronautical acts as dives, spins, loop-the-loops, barrel rolls, and the accompanying stuntwork of wing walks, mid-flight plane jumps, parachuting, aerial tennis, target shooting, and wing dancing. The riskier these stunts became under pressure of competition, the higher the fatality rate, so that by the beginning of the 1930s federal regulation and a mounting public intolerance for spectacles of death and destruction led swiftly to the decline

---

[46] Filippo Tommaso Marinetti, quoted in Dominick Pisano, ed., *The Airplane in American Culture* (Ann Arbor, MI: University of Michigan Press, 2003), 254.

of the type. "The gypsy/barnstormers were popular as picturesque figures, but the sensational stunts and attendant fatalities created a misunderstanding and fear of aviation that took years to erase. By mid-decade, the penchant for sensational aerial showboating had begun to wane."[47] That is, these vestigial figures of romance did not fit well with the progressive rationalization and transformation of aviation into a commercial industry of transportation and mediation. Their savage displays of incomparable skill and pointless grace contradicted an ideology of safety and normalcy that were critical to the success of flight as a source of corporate profits and as an indispensable modality of the infrastructure of monopoly capitalism.

Faulkner's barnstormer stories elaborate erotic triangulations of the core personnel, in a lingering echo of the romance forms they distantly convoke, but the interest lies in his extraordinary efforts to supersede the "old syntax inherited from Homer" and bestow upon the machinery itself the figural dynamism it deserves. In "Death Drag" (1932), we read: "The airplane appeared over town with almost the abruptness of an apparition. It was travelling fast; almost before we knew it was there it was already at the top of a loop ... with that apparition-like suddenness."[48] In a typical Faulknerian temporal conceit, there is an insistent lag between the phenomenology of perception and the speed of the machine (the adverbs "almost," twice, and "already" working overtime to induce this lag in the grammar) in a manner that bears comparison with the "abruption" of Thomas Sutpen himself, that other cavalier-misfit who appears without warning or precedent. But this is the tactic with which Faulkner prefers to engage the romance "event" itself, as we saw in the previous chapter: it is rather the event's *absence*, its reconstruction after the event, that we are dealing with here in the "apparition-like" distillation of the airplane out of the empty skies. Dissociated from all human intention and the "proairetic" logic of appearance that governs narrative norms,[49] this mechanical apparition is outside time itself. And when "we" (gaping children drawn to this apparition like flies to manure) finally catch up with it, we find this lag or rift to be incarnate in the object itself, now at rest: "There was no one in sight at all. Resting there, empty and dead ... it gave again that illusion of ghostliness, as though it might have flown there and made that loop by itself" (185). Now it is no longer the exceptional GHOST SHIP of John Sartoris's downed plane hovering over his brother's civilian life, but a ghostliness immanent to the aircraft itself, not only seemingly invested by an uncanny autopilot function but ghostly as well in its exception from the rules of continuity and contiguity that stitch the narrative "syntax inherited from Homer" into recognizable sequences. Moreover, the machine is always

---

[47] Bilstein, *Flight in America*, 61.
[48] Faulkner, *Collected Stories*, 185.
[49] Roland Barthes's term; see *S/Z*, trans. Richard Miller (Oxford: Blackwell, 1990), 19, 255.

already its own ghost, independent of human will and law, a synthesis under duress of Gilbert Ryle's figural congelation of Cartesian dualism, "the ghost in the machine"—the ghost *is* the machine. And this feature of mechanical self-hauntedness is contagious, passed down the new chain of being into its human appendages, who now live and move according to fully mechanical aesthetic dicta: "From around the corner of the barn there now appeared a third man, again with that abrupt immobility, as though he had materialized there out of thin air; though when they saw him he was already moving toward the group" (188). Ineluctably ensnared in a logic of motion and appearance with no human coordinates, this "third man" is veritably presented as a series of photograms on a roll of film, each moment of "abrupt immobility" succeeded by another whose projection onto the phenomenological frame is felt as a kind of "already moving," secretly decomposed from within. Here the logics of aerodynamics and cinematics coincide with a fateful intertwining in that double helix of cine-aviation that Léger was the first to herald.

Indeed, the story's most expressive agent is the vessel itself, all potential energy coiled into a taut kinesis of form:

> It reared on its muddy wheels, the propeller motionless, rigid, with a quality immobile and poised and dynamic. The nose was big with engine, the wings taut, the fuselage streaked with oil behind the rusting exhaust pipes. (188–89)

Bearing some comparison with the already-quoted description of the wild stallion under Bayard Sartoris in *Flags in the Dust*—"like a bronze explosion . . . burst like bronze unfolding wings: a fluid desperation"—this presentation of the stilled airplane participates in a figural economy where the "explosion," the "burst," is entirely implicit, latent in the immobility of the form. That is to say, it insists upon the latency of the "dynamic" within the "motionless," of the event within the state of rest, and so answers to one of Faulkner's most pressing problems of form. For the dissatisfying quality of organic forms is their never being sufficiently still, frozen, to make any sudden "apparition" of movement satisfactorily miraculous. Faulkner's syntax has to work overtime and with varying degrees of success in order to adduce for the human the "abrupt immobility" that inheres in this machine as a fact of mechanical design. For a frustrated romantic working under the proscriptive regime of a new law of form, the value of such an apparatus is immediately clear: it is an object whose obstreperous narrative "eventality" simmers as a sprung "standing reserve" (as Heidegger might put it) in the rearing "poise" of its engineered shape. It does not need to move in order to vibrate with the potentiality of something already drastically happening. Romance in a state of arrest, and dressed to look like its technological obverse: this kind of self-masking object serves a felt representational need with admirable precision. But it does so only if the "human" fuel it requires is stripped of the cavalier audacity and adventurousness that romance battens on as its actantial base. Instead, the real value of this "evental" airplane figure consists in the degree to which it has absorbed these chivalric virtues into its own "ghostly" form and contaminated its human counterpart with the machinic and inhuman qualities that should be its own.

Of course, what I am adumbrating here is an argument for the chiasmic transference of properties between people and things, in the spirit of Marx's inaugural chiasmus in *Capital*: people become things, and things people, under the dominion of the commodity. Flann O'Brien's infamous part-man-part-bicycle in *The Third Policeman* comically underlines the tendency in modernist culture to confuse and invert the properties of human and machine:

> The gross and net result of it is that people who spend most of their natural lives riding iron bicycles over the rocky roadsteads of this parish get their personalities mixed up with the personalities of their bicycle as a result of the interchanging of the atoms of each of them and you would be surprised at the number of people in these parts who nearly are half people and half bicycles. [. . .] And you would be flabbergasted at the number of bicycles that are half-human almost half-man, half-partaking of humanity.[50]

Such atomic displacements and substitutions, allowing for the dehumanization of the human and the humanization of the machine, are underwritten in Marx's chiasmic account of factory labor by the sublime scale of the machines themselves:

> In handicrafts and manufacture, the worker makes use of a tool; in the factory, the machine makes use of him. There the movements of the instrument of labour proceed from him, here it is the movements of the machine that he must follow. In manufacture the workers are the parts of a living mechanism. In the factory we have a lifeless mechanism which is independent of the workers, who are incorporated into it as its living appendages.[51]

The modern industrial machine converts all the "special skills" of former craftspeople into insignificant and "infinitesimal" quantities "in the face of the science, the gigantic natural forces, and the mass of social labour embodied in the system of machinery" (549). Once such topsy-turvy redistributions of properties

---

[50] Flann O'Brien, *The Third Policeman* (London: Flamingo/Harper Collins, 2001), 93.
[51] Karl Marx, *Capital, Vol. 1*, trans Ben Fowkes (London: Penguin, 1990), 548.

are established as inviolable laws in the forces of production, their logic begins to apply everywhere, filtering down into such everyday acts as riding a bicycle, or such economically marginal acts as piloting an Army surplus Jenny in death drags to entertain the rural poor. And here among the barnstormers, perhaps uniquely, the quantity of "special skills" is so high as to force the issue of to what extent becoming a Jenny's "living appendage" entails an alienation of human properties to the industrial machine, and to what extent it signifies an epochal "becoming-machine" that challenges the humanist orthodoxies of modernity.

In a book review published in November, 1935, of James "Jimmy" Collins's *Test Pilot* (1935)—an autobiography of the Communist airman-journalist written in terse telegraphese with lurid headlines[52]—Faulkner complained that the book was "tinged with a kind of sentimental journalese [...] you have seen it before a hundred times and it has been phrased just that way in ten thousand newspaper columns and magazines."[53] What particularly pained the author of *Pylon* (published in March of the same year) was the degree to which journalistic limpidness had quashed Marinetti's imperative to "liberate words" from "the old syntax inherited from Homer." The only phrase in the whole volume that excited Faulkner's ear was this one, from the self-written obituary: "The cold but vibrant fuselage was the last thing to feel my warm and living flesh" (190) Like something from a Ballard novel, the sentence rings with the chiasmic force of perverse qualitative transferences at the interface between man and machine. And it prompts Faulkner to express a wish: "I had hoped to find a kind of embryo, a still formless forerunner or symptom of a folklore of speed, the high speed of today which I believe stands [near] to the end of the limits which human beings and material [are] capable of" (191). In extremis, it is not the machines that will be tested, but their human appendages: "the limit at which blood vessels will burst and entrails rupture in making any sort of turn that will keep you in the same county, not to speak of co-ordination and perception of distance and depth" (191). He goes on to envisage an eugenic perfection of the pilots of the future, genetic engineers contriving "to create a kind of species or race" who, in time, "would produce a folklore" indecipherable to us mere mortals. But it is not this folklore that finally interests Faulkner so much as its correlative, "which might exist even now and of which I had hoped that this book might be the symptom, the first fumbling precursor":

> It would be a folklore not of the age of speed nor of the men who perform it, but of the speed itself, peopled not by anything human or

---

[52] The text is available at Project Gutenberg, at http://www.gutenberg.org/files/34589/34589-h/34589-h.htm.

[53] Faulkner, review of *Test Pilot*, in *Essays, Speeches and Public Letters*, ed. James B. Meriwether (New York: Modern Library, 2004), 189.

even mortal but by the clever willful machines themselves carrying nothing that was born and will have to die or which can even suffer pain, moving without comprehensible purpose toward no discernible destination, producing a literature innocent of either love or hate and of course of pity or terror, and which would be the story of the final disappearance of life from the earth. I would watch them, the little puny mortals, vanishing against a vast and timeless void filled with the sound of incredible engines, within which furious meteors moving in no medium hurtled nowhere, neither pausing nor flagging, forever destroying themselves and one another[,without love or even copulation forever renewing].[54]

Here we face a crisis in the humanistic imagination to which, in almost all other public contexts, Falkner subscribed unequivocally and dutifully. For with this philippic exacerbating the chiasmus of modernity (human machines, inhuman people), Faulkner delineates a truly posthuman horizon, where "human" qualities (clever, willful) persist in a "vast and timeless void" peopled only by self-piloting airplanes, and where the "little puny mortals" are snuffed out by "incredible engines" driven by that Kantian "purposiveness without a purpose" which had once stood for aesthetic experience. The "folklore of speed" stored in the coiled energy of a stalled biplane now emerges into view as the song of a science-fictional utopia where "machinery" attains to an autotelic aesthesis only on the basis of a final elimination of its "appendages"—"a literature innocent of either love or hate and of course of pity or terror," and so of "the old syntax inherited from Homer."

Aviation is finally a matter of mediation precisely because of what it betokens for the means of literary production. Within two decades of the end of the First World War, Faulkner had pursued the "line of flight" of this conspicuous symbol of modernity, from its appropriation in a remediation of chivalric heroism, to an apocalyptic and dystopian harbinger of the "disappearance of life from the earth." There is a dim echo here of Dean Swift's equine utopia in Houyhnhnm-land, where the former mounts of an unworthy noble class accrue to themselves the rationality and civility cultivated by the latter, and accede to species dominance while the "humans" devolve into chittering Yahoos. But Faulkner's aerotopia pushes the thought experiment the necessary extra step in a context of unfettered industrial capitalism: what becomes of language once machines are able to do our living for us, and we subside into "dead labour"?

The answer to that question is his novel *Pylon*, in which experimental solutions at the syntactic and lexical levels are hazarded to paper over the

---

[54] Faulkner, *Essays*, 192. The final phrase is taken from the unexpurgated text, 333.

ideological cracks of a world where noble qualities can now circulate independent of any human bearer, at the strange interface between these classless "gypsies" and their new "species" of mount. The novel opens with a prototypical tableau of framed mediation, a shop window in which "posed countrylife photographs in the magazine advertisements" sit adjacent to the street-front bunting of Mardi Gras and its ubiquitous placards: "the same lettering, the same photographs of the trim vicious fragile aeroplanes and the pilots leaning upon them in gargantuan irrelation as if the aeroplanes were a species of esoteric and fatal animals not trained or tamed but just for the instant inert."[55] As befits the torrid narrative that follows, here already it is impossible to distinguish the anthropomorphic, or at least zoological, qualities of the airplanes from the fact of photographic reification and the garish splash of publicity; the unwonted "inertness" that permits them to be seen in their snarling menace, magnified to "gargantuan" stature, is a staple of the photographic mode of production. The "motionless" rigidity of the propeller in "Death Drag," its "quality immobile and poised and dynamic," here assumes its proper mediatory form—that of the photograph-cum-photogram, which will jerk into vicious motion once the projector-propeller subjects it to the mechanical rhythms of modern speed. The term "esoteric" reappears to characterize the lofty machine "species" whose native habitat is this mediatory complexion of photograph, cinema, magazine, air show, and commodity fetishism—framed by a shop window behind which Jiggs the mechanic has his gaze riveted onto a pair of riding boots that will comically suture the regime of aeronautics to the (vanished) equestrian regime of chivalry for the duration of the book.

The narrative voice finds it impossible to allow for this plebeian body anything more than a thoroughgoing capitulation to the mass-mediating forces that compel Jiggs's gaze and regulate his movements. The act of reaching into his pocket to pay for the boots is rendered continuous with cinematic apperception: "When Jiggs put his hand into his pocket they could follow it, fingernail and knuckle, the entire length of the pocket like watching the ostrich in the movie cartoon swallow the alarm clock" (781). And even his walking away from the storefront is always-already mechanical: "walking in his fast stiff hard gait like a mechanical toy that has but one speed" (782). For the repetitive, reflexive point of *Pylon* is to account for its own perverse "folklore of speed" by way of a figural chiasmus that apportions mechanical qualities to its "barnstorming" agents, and zoological characteristics to its aircraft. Our first view of the main hangar likens it to "a mammoth terminal for some species of machine of a yet unvisioned tomorrow, to which air earth and water will be as one" (786). Meanwhile, our first vision of

---

[55] Faulkner, *Pylon*, in *Novels 1930–1935* (New York: Library of America, 1985), 779.

a plane that is not a photographic representation cannot resist further zoological figuration:

> Unbonneted, its spare entrails revealed as serrated top-and-bottomlines of delicate rocker-arms and rods inferential in their very myriad delicacy of a weightless and terrific speed any momentary faltering of which would be the irreparable difference between motion and mere matter, it appeared more profoundly derelict than the halfeaten carcass of a deer come suddenly upon in a forest. (787)

The torture to which the syntax is here exposed—the "pile-on" of adjectives and adverbs; the extreme delay of the main clause, buried under mounds of proliferating, appositive predicate clauses; a baroque detour through the subjunctive—is a measure of the degree of stylistic "life" that this kind of cross-sectioned mechanical *nature morte* can generate in its host text. A degenerate kind of commodity fetishism, peering greedily into the splayed anatomy of the product, finds in the "myriad delicacy" of the airplane's innards the *inference* of its animation—its "weightless and terrific speed"—but only because the syntax has already congealed to an absolute stasis around it. Style takes root in these cessations of narrative propulsion that obliterate literary aesthetics. What doesn't move, the prose, is then the negative promise of a movement beyond the "old syntax inherited from Homer." It takes as its phenomenological point of departure the unblinking techno-fetishist regard of a flying machine's exposed "rocker-arms and rods," and ends in a comparison with venison carrion—neither of which can really do justice to the quality of speed being invoked.

And that is because, finally, not vision but audition turns out to be the privileged mode of sensory access to this curious new race of creature. The airplane in flight is after all not an object fit for sight (which at best merely catches the "crates" at rest), but sensible above all as an aural apocalypse winging the pseudo-Wagnerian air in a veritable *twilight of the human*:

> Within the domed steel vacuum the single report [of the starting bomb] became myriad, high and everywhere about the concave ceiling like invisible unearthly winged creatures of that yet unvisioned tomorrow. Mechanical instead of blood bone and meat, speaking to one another in vicious highpitched ejaculations as though concerting an attack on something below. There was an amplyfier [sic] in the rotundra too and through it the sound of the aeroplanes turning the field pylon on each lap filled the rotundra. (791)

Now the folklore of speed comes into proper definition. "[P]eopled not by anything human or even mortal but by the clever willful machines themselves," this folklore is martial and terrible, "concerting an attack" on the "little puny mortals" who still populate the earth below. Its awful medium is sound, borne aloft beyond all embodiment, indefinitely multiplied, and remediated by the mechanical echo of the amplification system that binds Feinman Airport into a single horizon of Armageddon:

> the announcer's voice harsh masculine and disembodied; then at the end of each lap would come the mounting and then fading snarl and snore of engines as the aeroplanes came up and zoomed and banked away, leaving once more the scuffle and murmur of feet on tile and the voice of the announcer reverberant and sonorous within the domed shell of glass and steel in a running commentary to which apparently none listened, as if the voice were merely some unavoidable and inexplicable phenomenon of nature like the sound of wind or of erosion. (791–92)

As the modern medium lapses into a "second nature" of the droning wasteland ("as if the voice actually were that natural phenomenon against which all man-made sounds and noises blew and vanished like leaves," 792), the animalistic "snarl and snore" of the planes orchestrate an assault on the "tiny, fragile human body"[56] that nothing can resist.

But in fact the amplified voice is itself the privileged medium of flight's new "folklore of speed," since the "running commentary" that it vocalizes, and to which nobody listens, volatilizes the planes' malevolent hostility toward life with a futuristic syntax in which we can hear without hearing the collapse of our existential horizons.

> [T]he amplified voice still spoke, profound and effortless, as though it were the voice of the steel-and-chromium mausoleum itself talking of creatures imbued with motion though not with life and incomprehensible to the puny crawling painwebbed globe, incapable of suffering, wombed and born complete and instantaneous, cunning intricate and deadly, from out some blind iron batcave of the earth's prime foundation (793).

Without this incessant mediation, the roar of airplane engines would never amount to a "folklore," since it would merely be a victory yell; but, transposed into the mechanical, sourceless, disembodied, broadcast voice, the assault from the skies can assume, one last time, the imagery of the folk: batcreatures sprung from lethal cunning and primordial hunger. It is the voice itself

---

[56] Benjamin, "The Storyteller," 84.

that promotes such images, and renders them, oddly, visual: "he was now staring at the amplifyer above the door as though he were actually seeing in it what he merely heard" (886). Because the modern media system is a ceaseless synesthesia of sense data, transforming sound waves into electronic pulses and back again, celluloid into photograms and sound tracks, print into halftone photography, record grooves into radio signals, and so on, such translations are critical to the imaginary of the citizenry in an age of mass media, and to any novel that would treat of it.

While Michael Zeitlin is surely right to associate this grim emphasis on the electronic mediation of voice in *Pylon* with the "explicitly post-1933 fascist media ecology and the so-called 'ether war' that is gaining in intensity in this period,"[57] we cannot neglect the determinate path of development taken in Faulkner's own work toward this apotheosis of "heroism" in a post-human mediascape. The Reporter's dispatches to his editor circle madly around this central knot:

> "Because [the pilots] ain't human like us; they couldn't turn those pylons like they do if they had human blood and senses and they wouldn't want to or dare to if they just had human brains. Burn them like this one tonight and they dont even holler in the fire; crash one and it ain't even blood when you haul him out: it's cylinder oil the same as in the crankcase." (804)
>
> "... they aint human. It aint adultery; you cant anymore imagine two of them making love than you can two of them aeroplanes back in the corner of the hangar, coupling." (933)
>
> "Yair; cut him and it's cylinder oil; dissect him and it aint bones: it's little rockerarms and connecting rods—" (933–34)

To the extent that animal attributes have bled out into the machines, and mechanical qualities are stubbornly retrofitted onto the ground of the human, we can now take the full measure of this radical development of Faulkner's enduring preoccupation with the cavalier figure. For it is as if, having initially seized hold of that figure's fateful anachronism as a way of thinking ironically about the South's dislocation from the nation's main lines of force, Faulkner's perseverance with it, under the technological mask of aeronautics, has allowed him to attain a rare and properly futurist perception of those very lines of force. His initial interest in the aviator as hero, gathering up into itself as a figure the vestigial ideological trappings of the Southern cavalier, participated in a widespread aesthetic current in modernism—the enthusiasms of Yeats, Brecht,

---

[57] Michael Zeitlin, "Faulkner, Adorno, and 'the Radio Phenomenon,'" in Julian Murphet and Stefan Solomon, eds., *William Faulkner in the Media Ecology* (Baton Rouge, LA: Louisiana State University Press, 2015), 125.

Crane, Delaunay, Auden and others already rehearsed—but was then propelled away from the wellsprings of romance by an historical trend in aviation toward more mediatory and transportational functions. Yet the figure could be temporarily retained thanks to the sudden appearance in the field of "general aviation" of that evanescent class of barnstorming pilots who fascinated Faulkner with their unique blend of pointless heroics, technological aesthetics, and military superannuation; their strange subsidence into a class of Depression performance artists making a spectacle of their precarious bodies for negligible economic returns. In them, any echoes of a hereditary aristocracy were cancelled out and "heroism" lost its martial as well as its civil significance. Rather, their "heroism" was to have consisted principally in the very ruthless bravery with which, for "entertainment," they undertook their own extinction behind the controls of machines that, thanks to the pressures of competition and the lawlessness of the conjuncture, broke them over the wheel of capitalist futurity. In this development of Faulkner's long-standing engagement with the cavalier figure, "heroism" and "gallantry" are turned inside out under the figural gravity of a presiding chiasmus, evacuated from human agents and assimilated to that mechanical futurism that Marinetti had long since augured from the very form of the aircraft themselves. So it is that the central "hero"-pilot of *Pylon*, Roger Shumann, not only meets his fully expected demise in a terrible air-show accident, but has already suffered the routine verbal humiliations to which his character is subject by the narrative voice:

> singlepurposed, fatally and grimly without any trace of introversion or any ability to objectivate or ratiocinate as though like the engine, the machine for which he apparently existed, he functioned, moved, only in the vapor of gasoline and the filmslick of oil. (892)

Moreover, there is not a moment of his fate that is not articulated through a fourfold distantiation from its "Homeric" actuality: relayed "live" through the incessant "commentation" of the PA system's ubiquitous "radio voice"; printed and mimeographed as pamphleted bills of fare by the Feinman group; dispatched as daily news items by the Reporter to his editor via telephone; and snapped, at the moment of catastrophe, by a photographer onto a negative plate. For to be a pilot is to be a mere moment in a distributed, interconnected media system working at post-human speeds to instaurate a horizon of immanence in which literature itself has become a cumbersome irrelevancy. The airplanes themselves finally devolve into figures of this larger system, where every human sentiment and thought is converted into ephemeral fodder for its inexorable expansion:

> the rotundra was full of people and with a cavernous murmuring sound which seemed to linger not about the mouths which uttered it but to

float somewhere about the high serene shadowy dome overhead; as they entered a newsboy screamed at them, flapping the paper, the headline: PILOT KILLED. Shumann Crashes Into Lake. SECOND FATALITY OF AIRMEET, as it too flicked away. (939–40)

And in such wise does Faulkner's extended labor with the romance figure of the cavalier evolve, from a confrontation with aviation as a new modality of martial chivalry, into a realization of the inexorability of a media ecology where romance has been sublated and the human itself annihilated by a malevolent futuristic species. Having first "masked" the stealthy novelistic investment in romance, the mediatory figure of the airplane eventually vouchsafes its extirpation. It is an exemplary lesson in the revenge of the mediatic unconscious against its conservative novelistic management; and it took, in Faulkner's extraordinary surge of productivity, a mere six years to work its way out.

2

Affect and spatial dynamics in *Flags in the Dust* and *The Sound and the Fury*

Bad roads mean bad morals.[1]

There are few aesthetic breakthroughs in literary history as momentous as that achieved by Faulkner between the initial rejection of his manuscript of "Flags in the Dust," and his subsequent writing and delivery of the text of *The Sound and the Fury*, all in the space of a year or so. From a novel that, for all its maturity of ambition and scope, is mired in the worst kinds of ideological reaction and technical embarrassments, to a work so free from the bonds of conventional novel-writing as to represent a *sui generis* miracle, the passage is dramatic enough to demand some explanation. Faulkner's own—that commercial rejection finally liberated him to "shut a door between me and all publishers' addresses and book lists" and say to himself, "Now I can write"[2]—only raises the question of why a novel that he had already claimed to be "the book which will make my name for me as a writer" (namely *Flags*),[3] had not itself been written with the same conviction and autonomy from commercial constraints. This chapter will test the hypothesis that the "shock," "blind protest," "consternation and despair" that characterized Faulkner's reaction to Liveright's rejection of the *Flags* manuscript,[4] and the subsequent redactions of it, first on Faulkner's own time—"Every day or so I burn some of it [*Flags*] up and rewrite it, and at present it is almost incoherent" (206)—and then via Ben Wasson's slashing away a quarter of the fourth, 600-page draft for Harcourt, Brace, in New York, fed directly into

---

[1] Henry Adams, *The Education of Henry Adams*, Ch. 3 at; http://xroads.virginia.edu/~hyper/HADAMS/eha03.html, 47.

[2] Joseph Blotner, *Faulkner: A Biography*, one-volume edition (Jackson, MS: University Press of Mississippi, 2005), 212.

[3] Blotner, *Faulkner*, 206.

[4] On the grounds that it was and "diffuse and non-integral with neither very much plot development nor character development," see Blotner, *Faulkner*, 205.

Faulkner's contemporary aesthetic labors on *The Sound and the Fury*.[5] It is not the capitulation to commercial considerations per se that was decisive here, but the fact of cutting itself: the mutilated emergence of *Sartoris* from the bloated carcass of *Flags in the Dust* was proof that novels could indeed be carved out of novels, that a more chiseled and leaner artifact could be retrieved from an extant mass of prose, many of whose indulgences then stood exposed as inessential or redundant in the light of a new aesthetic dominant. The question of whether the published novel was "better" than its massy prototype is at this level irrelevant, as is the exact roster of cuts applied; what matters is the excruciating, loudly resisted passage through the discipline of excision and reduction, since it is this that accords with an emergent "modernist" discomfort with rhetoric, verbiage, redundancy and superfluity, and sets the stage for *The Sound and the Fury*'s astonishingly lapidary construction. What Hugh Kenner called Faulkner's innate discursive "copiousness, a garrulousness, a quality of psychic overflowing," which he purportedly "prized above any satisfactions to be obtained from erasure, paring, spareness,"[6] received its most extreme checks in that charged apartment on Christopher Street near Sixth Avenue, where, side by side, Ben Wasson attacked the manuscript of "Flags" and Faulkner completed his novel about the Compson family.

My contention is that a particular type of prose suffers an absolute decline, indeed something approaching an extinction, in Faulkner's novelistic work across this remarkable period, namely, *Southern topographical description*. On the face of it, this is not the first thing to strike anyone who reads these two novels in sequence; the more likely first reaction is to remark what binds them together. Both texts take as their ostensible "subject" the decline and fall of a landed Jefferson family; but technically and formally so much has changed that the theme itself seems oddly destabilized in its very consistency, as if the identical topic might simply have provided a convenient scaffolding on which to ring the changes. Motivation of the device, the formalists might have termed it; except that here the similarity of the theme serves to motivate entirely distinct sets of devices, which subsequently come to appear all the more autonomous and arbitrary in relation to the underlying substance on which they have battened. To be sure—and yet, what if, in a cunning ruse of reason, the apparent common theme were itself a feint, and that beneath its comfortable, archetypal familiarity an altogether unsuspected theme, also shared, could be discerned: one whose

---

[5] As Faulkner summed up his arguments with Wasson, "A cabbage has grown, matured. You look at the cabbage; it is not symmetrical; you say, I will trim this cabbage off and make it art; I will make it resemble a peacock or a pagoda or 3 doughnuts. Very good, I say; you do that, then the cabbage will be dead." See Blotner, *Faulkner*, 222.

[6] Hugh Kenner, "Faulkner and the Avant-Garde," in Evans Harrington and Ann J. Abadie, eds., *Faulkner, Modernism, and Film: Faulkner and Yoknapatawpha, 1978* (Jackson, MS: University Press of Mississippi, 1979), 185.

subjection to the trials of historical change was far more determinate and sensitive to the roughly nine years difference between the two novels' settings? What follows will explore this hypothesis in relation to what I have taken to be the "secret history" of these two novels. Specifically, I will consider transport technology and infrastructure, perhaps the most striking communicational "fact" of the South's transformation over the years 1915–1925, since both novels have an extraordinary amount to tell us about this aggressively material aspect of modernization as it swept through the region at this time.

That transport technologies and infrastructures should be thought of as media is not as outlandish a claim as it might first appear. What Jameson called "an expanded concept of the media as such, encompassing both transportation and communication," has been in order these many years.[7] As David Trotter observes, the "idea of transport as telecommunications medium" is in fact a venerable one:

> For centuries, the term "communication" referred equally to the movement of people and goods and to the movement of information. The second meaning displaced the first. The development this change of emphasis records is the supersession of travel by transit as a key modern experience.[8]

Trotter's point is that modernity's constitutive experience of time-space compression "converted transport systems into communications media: most notably, in the period between the world wars, the automobile and the airplane. Speed allied to directness and versatility meant that these two modes became during the period a primary mechanism for the principle of connectivity" (219). In the previous chapter, we considered in telescoped form some of the implications of flight as a communications medium in Faulkner's work; this chapter turns to the automobile as perhaps the more decisive media institution of the interwar years, at least insofar as the redrawing of a literary "cognitive map" might have been concerned.

The Introduction argued that the novel, in its ongoing critical engagement with romance as a narrative form, had as its most urgent duty the formal contestation of romance narrative conventions. The most irreducible of these are what Bakhtin calls the "chronotopes" of romance, which is to say the ways in which the "inseparability of space and time" is conveyed in stable generic indicators of

---

[7] Fredric Jameson, *The Cultural Turn: Selected Writings on the Postmodern 1983–1998* (London & New York: Verso, 1998), 125.

[8] David Trotter, *Literature in the First Media Age: Britain Between the Wars* (Cambridge, MA: Harvard University Press, 2014), 218.

the "livedness" of a world.⁹ Such chronotopes had sunk particularly stubborn roots into the Southern literary imagination, where an anachronistic limitation to "the locomotive power of human or animal legs," as Trotter puts it, had permitted a romance imaginary to flourish well into the twentieth century.¹⁰ Specifically, those chronotopes predicated on the free-roaming cavalier figure, on travel between locations by horseback, on the industrial use of mulepower, on the leisurely pace of equipage and wagon, and so forth, are not simply incidental to the world of romance; rather, they actively construct its spatio-temporal horizon and enable its most typical effects—the logic of "adventure time," the glorification of the hero, the chance encounter, the lyrical reverie in a landscape, the sudden appearance of rogues and fools, and so forth. Without the horse and ass as the primary means of topographical navigation in the romance, its ethos and mythos would be unimaginable, as that greatest of early novels, *Don Quixote*, makes particularly vivid by way of parody.

But neither, for that matter, would its most typical passages of spatial description be able to flourish. The counterpoint to romance action is romance scenography, best seen in rolling vistas from a horse-mounted summit, or glimpsed from the driver's seat of a carriage, which allows the narrative activity to halt and an ambrosial, changeless "natural" environment (i.e., one produced by serfs or slaves) to exude its ideological aura. Yet it is precisely these passages that disappear from Faulkner's prose in 1928, never to return. As Sean Latham has written,

> Faulkner's cartographic impulse is everywhere evident in his fiction's fascination with space, which rarely functions conventionally as mere backdrop or landscape. Land—its acquisition, maintenance, and loss—pervades the major novels, but it is striking how rarely this land is actually described, how little of it is surveyed by a narrative consciousness.¹¹

The observation that, in Faulkner, space is no "mere backdrop," will prove to be of the greatest importance in coming to understand the aesthetic transition from *Flags in the Dust* to *The Sound and the Fury*; but only because this concerns the relative absence of description from the latter text, when read against its predecessor, at least as regards the South. What this suggests is that, rather than some kind of built-in authorial disposition, the aversion from regional

---

⁹ See M. M. Bakhtin, *The Dialogical Imagination: Four Essays*, ed. Michael Holquist, trans. Caryl Emerson and Michael Holquist (Austin, TX: University of Texas Press, 1981), 84–85.

¹⁰ Trotter, *Literature in the First Media Age*, 219.

¹¹ Sean Latham, "An Impossible Resignation: William Faulkner's Post-Colonial Imagination," in Richard C. Moreland, ed., *A Companion to William Faulkner* (Oxford: Blackwell, 2006), 254.

description is in Faulkner a *learned* intolerance, and the moment at which he learns it is in the interval between these two texts of 1927–28—or better yet, in the charged imaginative space of their compositional overlap. And that this has everything to do with the motorcar as a medium, "a primary mechanism for the principle of connectivity" (in Trotter's words), is the burden of this chapter's larger argument, which will then have to take up the correlative matter of mass public transport as the "road not taken" in rural Mississippi.

In the dust of old chronotopes

In his review of the belated 1974 publication of the unexpurgated draft of *Flags in the Dust*, Richard Adams remarks Faulkner's evident sympathy for the "glamour of nostalgia for the virtues and the values of classical and medieval aristocracy" as embodied by the Sartoris clan, but suggests that, in the end, the novel asks us to let the flags of "feudal pride" lie trampled in the dust of war and "the destruction of slavery and the plantation system."[12] Perhaps; but there is another kind of dust swirling in these pages, churned up by the passage over unsealed dirt roads of a new sort of private vehicle, which in its own way is as inimical to the values of a quasi-feudal aristocracy as the disappearance of the mode of production that sustained it. The motorcar doesn't do away with that class (although Faulkner will contrive to have old Bayard Sartoris die of heart failure in the passenger seat of one); rather, it invalidates the world in which that class had had time and space to move. The automobile emerges upon the residual infrastructure of an agrarian plantocracy with not merely the symbolic but the literal and physical force of a new economic order of things—dependent upon the steady supply of petroleum, the sealing of roadways, highway networks, rubber, and a ubiquity of garages, service stations, and mechanics—whose most insidious portent in relation to the established regime of accumulation was the tractor itself.

The historical relationship between automotive transport and Southern romance is a properly contradictory one. Touring south in a Pierce-Arrow from his Connecticut home in 1910, Seymour Cunningham got as far as South Carolina before his troubles started: "south of Charlotte, the macadam paving ended, and from there on Cunningham described the driving as 'simply fearful, [with] nothing but mud [which was] so soft and soapy" that he was reduced to crawling forward in first gear.[13] Yet it was the unblemished Southern environment of cotton plantations, white mansions, and steamboats that had drawn him there in the

---

[12] In Nicholas Fargnoli, ed., *William Faulkner: A Literary Companion* (New York: Pegasus, 2008), 25.

[13] Howard Lawrence Preston, *Dirt Roads to Dixie: Accessibility and Modernization in the South, 1885–1935* (Knoxville, TN: University of Tennessee Press, 1991), 105.

first place. Representative of a new wave of Northern tourism that the faltering Southern economy could scarce afford to repel in the new century, Cunningham remarked: "If you will improve the bad places in your roads, automobilists in the hundreds will come from the North every spring," to see what remained of that "impressionistic view" of the territory "cultivated for more that a half-century by nineteenth-century writers, artists, and illustrators whose aim was to depict the South from a romantic perspective."[14] This projected invasion was intuited as epochal as regards the vested interests of the plantocracy, as for instance in the words of Josephine Anderson Pearson, who railed against the isolation of women in the South:

> I seem to hear "the whirr" of the automobile as it climbs the mountains and dashes along, recklessly determined of its mission to set us free, free from isolation and mud! We women are worse than slaves, considering everything, than the negroes [sic] were before the Civil War—(17)

Alabama senator John Hollis Bankhead spoke of how better public roads would

> open up new and improved channels to marts of trade and commerce, stimulate industrial enterprise, inspire every citizen of the rural districts with a brighter hope and a higher ambition, and add a new tie to bind him with increased loyalty and patriotism to his country. (35)

Improved roadways were portrayed as conduits for federal nationalism, the franchise, consumerism, and Northern capital, a paradigm explicitly counterposed to the entrenched regional interests of a still dominant agrarian class whose dependency on "rural idiocy," violent racial subjugation, and relatively enslaved women was manifest in the underdeveloped arterial infrastructure of their dirt roads.

The improved road system that began to be constructed around 1910 was motivated much less by the convenience for local farmers (the economic promise of hauling crops to market in bad weather, prolonging the lifespan of livestock, and avoiding extortionate railroad rates) than by the profitability of enhanced tourism from the North and the flow-on effects on real estate and capital accumulation. This prospect alone was finally sufficient to overturn decades of federal and state negligence with regard to the South's road infrastructure, openly admitted to be "the worst in the entire country,"[15] and convince Congress and state legislatures to levy the taxes required to invest in what would be a vast

---

[14] Preston, *Dirt Roads to Dixie*, 108, 110.
[15] Preston, *Dirt Roads to Dixie*, 36.

enterprise of improvement and new construction. "Prospect" was a loaded word; as William S. Gilbreath wrote in the Atlanta *Constitution* in 1914:

> You people in the South have wonderful scenery that is most unusual and attractive to owners of automobiles in the middle western states, and we are only waiting for an opportunity to drive through your country.... It is [the] lack of a thoroughly connected highway leading through the South which discourages tourists.[16]

It was the "wonderful scenery" of which the roads in question were to have been the primary delivery systems that made them economically valuable. The scenery, so the rhetoric went, would remain the same as it was in the antebellum South—supposedly unmodified by the mode of transportation exploited to experience it. Of course it would be much truer to say that the transformation in the transportation network encouraged by New South boosterism necessarily destroyed or evacuated the very painterly "scenery" being used to peddle it.

Preston remarks upon the fate of pictorial romanticism in this mix:

> At the turn of the century, the picture-postcard South, popularized in advertisements, landscape paintings, magazine articles, travel accounts, guidebooks, investment schemes, and woodcut illustrations, was the most visible impression Americans had of the region. By the time motorists began driving into the South, romanticism remained the standard upon which travel writers relied when describing places of interest.... As highway associations succeeded in promoting routes leading into the South, thereby raising Americans' expectations about the possibility of making a trip there in a motorcar, thousands upon thousands of tourists flooded the region, bringing the outside world with them. By 1930 the combination of interstate highways and automobility had greatly accelerated the pace of cultural conformity, so much so that some perceived this to be the end of the South.[17]

Such "acceleration" had everything to do with the national imaginary itself, specifically the spur of the 1924 Federal Road Act, which poured funds into state legislatures in order to stimulate commerce, tourism, and communication; such that, by the end of the decade, "highway construction programs employed more men and spent more money than any single private industry."[18] Indeed,

---

[16] Gilbreath, quoted in Preston, *Dirt Roads to Dixie*, 54.
[17] Preston, *Dirt Roads to Dixie*, 110–11.
[18] Kenneth Bruce, *Yowsah! Yowsah! Yowsah!: The Roaring Twenties* (Belmont, CA: Star Publishing Co., 1981), 79.

in 1928, Faulkner bore witness through the eyes of his own brother in Oxford, Mississippi, to the changes attendant upon this acceleration of "cultural conformity" via road improvement. As his official biographer puts it, "Johncy Falkner and his crews had transformed the muddy streets with gravel and tar. Sidewalks went in as new streets were laid down. More than two dozen houses had been built within the last half-year."[19] Moreover, "Uncle John moved the old house and sold the corner lot to the Standard Oil Company, which soon put in a modern service station" (207). The automobile had infiltrated every pore of the American economy, and every region of the federation, drawing it all together into one integrated web of petroleum capital: rubber distributors, tyre manufacturers, car dealers, "parts suppliers, oil companies, service-station owners, road builders, and land developers."[20]

It is this pace of petro-driven modernization that Faulkner was above all concerned to address in the novel written just previous (and set ten years prior) to these momentous changes in Oxford, but still hanging over him in a cloud of publishers' uncertainty as they took place all around him. For *Flags in the Dust* had concluded, in part, on a withering satiric depiction of the town of Kinston—a portrait of imported suburban dystopia to which, indeed, the whole work had covertly been tending in its none-too-subtle symbolic registration of the effects of modern transportation in Yocona (not yet Yoknapatawpha) County. That final vision of "crude and blatant newness" springing as if overnight from a once swamp-surrounded hamlet in craven "imitation of something else," and "financed by eastern capital,"[21] had been implicit as a spatial tendency throughout the text's engagement with the way of the automobile: a collapse of "the picture-postcard South," as represented by the Sartoris estate, into the impoverished civic imagination of real estate capital—"People in the neighboring counties ... moved there and chopped all the trees down and built themselves mile after mile of identical frame houses with garage to match: the very air smelled of affluence and burning gasoline" (849). The roads bring the people; the people take away the view. Identikit urban topographies usurp the parochial "romanticism" of Southern scenography, garages replace stables, improved roads seal over dirt tracks, and the rule of "eastern capital" is everywhere inscribed into social space. As the author wrote of Jefferson itself in 1945, "the old square mile [of what had been Compson land for over a century] was even intact again in row after row of small crowded jerrybuilt individuallyowned demiurban bungalows."[22]

---

[19] Blotner, *Faulkner*, 206.

[20] Kenneth T. Jackson, *Crabgrass Frontier: The Suburbanization of the United States* (Oxford: Oxford University Press, 1985), 164.

[21] Faulkner, *Flags in the Dust*, in *Novels 1926–1929*, 847, 849.

[22] Faulkner, "COMPSON 1699–1945," in David Minter, ed., *The Sound and the Fury* (New York: W. W. Norton & Co., 1994), 207.

The challenges facing the novelist in the midst of such a prodigious transformation of the social production of space are many, but become acute around the issue of finding the appropriate chronotopes to use when putting it into narrative shape. *Flags in the Dust* is an aesthetic failure for many reasons, but not for want of serious labor in this regard (much more serious than the previous two novels, which skirt the issue entirely): in it, we find Faulkner hard at work wrestling with the inherited romance chronotopes associated with families such as the Sartoris clan, struggling to find the means to make their obsolescence feel tragically (or ironically) inevitable, while also ushering in a new narrative machinery whose predication on the combustion engine is not simply satiric. In this novel, the ideological economy that underlies all of Faulkner's work is particularly close to the surface—the nostalgia for and inalienable affinities with patrician romance are acutely felt; at the same time, the urge to deface and denounce these spurious hangovers in the name of some new "aesthetic regime" is also conveyed with affective intensity. It is only that Faulkner has not yet perfected a formula in which these two tendencies can be managed in their contradiction. So, here they merely alternate along an axis whose privileged allegorical vessel is the body of young Bayard Sartoris himself—an embodiment, on the one hand, of the destructive energetics of a ferocious "headlong violence" (873), and, on the other, of the residual "sober rhythms of the earth" (715) into which he becomes temporarily (and ancestrally) absorbed during a domestic idyll after his first accident. The alternation of these two tendencies, rather than their paradoxical fusion, characterizes the narrative economy of the novel.

That alternation governs the various literal confrontations between horse- and mule-drawn modes of transportation (implicated in an agrarian mode of production) and the automobiles that have invaded the streets of Jefferson; and so between the distinct kinds of chronotope that each makes possible in the first place—both of which Bayard is given to occupy from the privileged vantage point of the hero himself—and the styles of spatial description specific to each. As the roadways of Jefferson (not yet named as such) are described, their population by automobiles is essentially the only thing that can be said of them, and what matters to the narrative economy of romance is to put them at as great a distance as possible:

> [A]t a dashing, restrained pace [Simon] drove among the tethered wagons about the square and swung into a broad street where what Bayard called paupers sped back and forth in automobiles, . . . until the town was behind them and they trotted on across burgeoning countryside cluttered still with gasoline-propelled paupers but at greater intervals, and his employer had settled back for the changing and peaceful monotony of the four-mile drive. (545)

The motorcars put pressure upon the visible order of things, interfering with the romantic "distribution of the sensible," as Jacques Rancière might put it. Insofar as they throng the roads where the now anachronistic Sartoris carriage would pass, they thwart the romance chronotope's "changing and peaceful monotony," obliging us to pay attention to the affront they present to the presumed patriarchal rights of mobility. Old Bayard's insistence on class distinction is telling here, since what the sudden availability of cheap automotive transport means to him is that "paupers" will pass him on the roads, and that the gentry's right of passage between town and estate is thereby obstructed by the town-to-town mobility of the white middle class.

Once out of town, however, the Sartoris equipage reverts to type and becomes representative of that most Faulknerian of oxymoronic chronotopes, "motion without progress":

> Dust spun from beneath the horses' feet and moiled in a sluggish cloud behind them. Against the thickening hedgerows their shadow rushed in failing surges, with twinkling spokes and high-stepping legs in a futility of motion without progress. (546)

Here the dust is merely atmospheric, "sluggish" and monotonous, while the shadow of the conveyance "rushes" along the hedgerows only to indicate the "futility" of what now looks, to the automobilic eye sharpened in town, like going nowhere at all. But going nowhere is the very point of such movement, since it is calculated not to give rise to incident or action, but to enable the narrative prose to relax into the gear of description, which is not long in coming. In town, where perception is monopolized by the competition between old and new types of transportation *on* the road, it is to that extent not free to wander away to the *side* of the road and make a landscape out of its field of sense data. It is only when the frequency of automobiles thins out to "greater intervals" away from town that descriptions of the landscape become possible.

> The road went on between hedgerows paralleling them with the senseless terrific antics of their shadow. Beyond the bordering gums and locusts and massed vines, fields new-broken or being broken spread on toward patches of woodland newly green and splashed with dogwood and judas trees. Behind laborious plows viscid shards of new-turned earth glinted damply in the sun.
>
> This was upland country, lying in tilted slopes against the unbroken blue of the hills, but soon the road descended sheerly into a valley of good broad fields richly somnolent in the levelling afternoon, and presently they drove upon Bayard's own land, and from time to time a plowman lifted his hand to the passing carriage.[23]

---

[23] William Faulkner, *Flags in the Dust*, in *Novels 1926–1929* (New York: Library of America, 2006), 546, 547.

The first passage is archetypal in its structured articulation of a three-dimensional rural topos: from the "hedgerow" and the "bordering gums," through the "massed vines" on through to the fields themselves, and beyond them some outer limit of "woodland newly green." The second passage then encompasses even that horizon with its upward tilt to the "unbroken blue of the hills," before returning to earth and descending into the valley, and thence into the Sartoris plantation itself, near which labor is obliged to hail the passing gentry. Labor has been remarked in both passages, once in a venerable hypallage (Blake's "laborious plows"[24]), and then again in this ritual of obeisance to what Simon will call the "Gent'mun equipage" (633). A rounded topography, this view engineered by the romance chronotope of the road is reinforced at periodic moments: again in the carriage ("Old Bayard brought his attention back from where it wandered about the familiar planted fields and blue shining hills beyond," 753), from the front door of the big house (the drive "descended in a cool green tunnel to the gates and the sultry ribbon of the highroad. Beyond the road fields spread away shimmering, broken here and there by motionless clumps of wood, onto the hills dissolving bluely in the July haze," 750), on horseback ("Behind him the earth rolled away ridge on ridge blue as woodsmoke, on into a sky like thin congealed blood. He turned in his saddle and stared unwinking into the sun that spread like a crimson egg broken upon the ultimate hills," 812), and given its definitive statement in the novel's final pages, this time seen from the vantage point of the dead Colonel John Sartoris's effigy in the cemetery: "his back to the world and his carven eyes gazing out across the valley where his railroad ran and the blue changeless hills beyond, and beyond that, the ramparts of infinity itself" (870).

Jameson's claim that "romance is precisely that form in which the *worldness* of *world* reveals or manifests itself, in which, in other words, *world* in the technical sense of the transcendental horizon of our experience becomes visible in an inner-worldly sense,"[25] is here vindicated by a recurrent topographic description whose central orientation-point is the plantation, but which recedes ever further, layer upon layer, into the "ramparts of infinity" itself. The "world" of plantation romance stands disclosed as a nested sequence of vegetable and geologic planes, best visible from the drowsy "motion without progress" that a negro-driven carriage makes over the roads leading toward one's "own land," from which, indeed, the bent class of black laborers will rise to acknowledge the master in a brief cessation of toil. This "world" is a narcissistic mirror in which

---

[24] See William Blake, "The French Revolution," l.226, *Complete Writings*, ed. Geoffrey Keynes (Oxford: Oxford University Press, 1972), 144.

[25] Fredric Jameson, *The Political Unconscious: Narrative as a Socially Symbolic Act* (Ithaca, NY: Cornell University Press, 1981), 112.

the plantation owner sees reflected back his own essence as so much new-turned earth and good broad fields peopled by beings who, if they are not slaves, are yet "field niggers" emplotted within a Master's "somnolent" self-image. The scene is not pastoral, precisely, but an eclogue or, better, a georgic—which means that this "world" is not exactly a landscape either. As Raymond Williams once categorically put it, "A working country is hardly ever a landscape."[26] Properly fantastic pastoral scenes, always evoking "a rural landscape emptied of rural labour and of labourers; a sylvan and watery prospect . . . from which the facts of production [have] been banished" (125), are not to be confused with the labor-filled "world" of romance. The Faulknerian touch is to allow his narrator's description of the landscape to morph imperceptibly into a narration (of the laborers' lifted hands), which for that reason converts the landscape into georgic, something industrious and defined by class.

Indeed, *Flags in the Dust* is not shy to demonstrate the degree to which this vision of the "world" of Southern romance is implicated in an entire mode of production. For example, witness the scene in which young Bayard and his new wife attend an annual folk event:

> The gin had been running steadily for a month, now, what with the Sartoris cotton and that of other planters further up the valley, and of smaller croppers with their tilted fields among the hills. The Sartoris place was farmed on shares. Most of the tenants had picked their cotton, and gathered the late corn; and of late afternoons, with Indian summer upon the land and an ancient sadness sharp as woodsmoke on the windless air, Bayard and Narcissa would drive out to where, beside a spring on the edge of the woods, the negroes brought their cane and made their communal winter sorghum molasses. (779)

Here the sharecropping mode of production is glimpsed from the moment of its annual hiatus, the cotton picked and the winter rituals commencing, so that labor can at last be witnessed as such, and the "world" it sustains exonerated of all charges, transposed into a sickly-sweet communal syrup of folk affect.

But Bayard's pacification at this stage of the novel, his physical enfeeblement after two serious injuries (one on horseback, the other in a motorcar) and conscription into the family plot of marriage and dynasty, is nevertheless felt as a temporary suspension and interlude in what everybody feels confident in proclaiming to be his fate and his doom, which is to die in some exceptionally violent mechanical accident. For this last scion of the great clan of chevaliers, back from the mechanized Western Front where his twin sibling has been shot down

---

[26] Raymond Williams, *The Country and the City* (London: Hogarth Press, 1993), 120.

over France, is existentially resistant to the chronotope in question, as we see during his excruciating ride home on a wagon after his most serious accident (a virtual parody of old Bayard's earlier trip in the carriage):

> At times it seemed to him that they were traveling backward, that they would crawl terrifically past the same tree or telephone post time after time; and it seemed to him that the three of them and the rattling wagon and the two beasts were caught in a ceaseless and senseless treadmill, a motion without progress, forever and to no escape. (721)

Here again is that "motion without progress" that had first disclosed the "world" to which young Bayard is nominally heir; only now it yields nothing but the most galling frustration, mired in an infernal repetition of Sisyphean torment. The "somnolent" chronotope has been disabled as a landscape-delivery device and transformed into an incorrigibly "backward" narrative element conducive not to the "*worldness of world*," but to an uncoordinated wordlessness.

This is because Baryard Sartoris the younger is identified above all with the automobile that he travels to Memphis to purchase on what is effectively his first act back from military duty. Faulkner's technical fetishism is all to the fore in the introduction of this potent symbolic presence in the text:

> Young Bayard came back from Memphis in his car. Memphis was seventy-five miles away and the trip had taken an hour and forty minutes because some of the road was clay country road. The car was long and low and gray; the four cylinder engine had sixteen valves and eight spark-plugs, and the people had guaranteed that it would run eighty miles an hour, although there was a strip of paper pasted to the windshield, to which he paid no attention whatever, asking him in red letters not to do so for the first five hundred miles. (604)

Frustrated by his average of only 45 mph on the road home, Bayard will later clock 54 mph (608), then 60 mph and more (660); consider 45 mph as "merely cruising speed" (715); heap scorn on Narcissa's car for not being able to exceed 20 mph (761); and finally end his grandfather's life in a nameless excess of velocity in collision with a "ford car's" relative speed the other way (810)—before sublating this terrestrial rush into an aerial apotheosis, as his great-aunt had predicted: "When he finds that car wont go fast enough … He'll buy an aeroplane" (612). Faulkner's description of the vehicle dwells on technical specifications that were truly avant-garde in 1918—4 cylinders with 16 valves and 8 sparkplugs did not become available in a mass-produced engine until 1973.

The question is, what chronotope will this new mode of transport make possible? What will it have engendered for the descriptive impulse that threads its way through this text like a pervasive scent of magnolia or honeysuckle? How will the "world" of romance accommodate its combustible mechanical energy? Old Bayard's first impression of the vehicle's movement does not bode well: "old Bayard watched them move soundlessly down the drive and watched the car pass from sight down the alley. Presently above the trees a cloud of dust rose into the azure afternoon and hung rosily fading in the sun, and a sound as of remote thunder died muttering behind it" (604). Unlike the "sluggish" dust of the carriage, this dust rises to obscure a landscape to which its motorized cause seems perfectly indifferent, thundering away in a cloud of unknowing with ominous portent. As the narrator puts it on the automobile's return to the drive, "After that the significance grew slowly" (604). Indeed, shortly after, as Simon is once again "sedately" transporting the old man homeward in the carriage, with "warning thunder" the car "burst upon him on a curve, slewed into the ditch and on to the road again and rushed on: and in the flashing instant he and Simon saw the whites of Isom's eyes and the ivory cropping of his teeth behind the steering wheel" (611). What more deleterious portent for romance topography than this Cheshire cat grin of mechanical democratization, Simon's own grandson steering the prodigious engine at speeds sufficient to obliterate the consistency of his own face, let alone the "drowsy" plantation chronotope of the road? The verbs are telling: "burst," "slewed," and "rushed." They pepper the text from this moment on, as the motorcar "abrupts" (the word is Bayard's before it is Sutpen's) upon a scenography than can scarcely register it other than as a blur or smudge.

Old Bayard's ambivalent decision to retire the horse and surrey for the time being and allow young Bayard to convey him to and from the bank, both to restrain his grand-nephew's propensity toward excessive speeds and to satisfy what Miss Jenny calls his liking "to ride in that car, only you wont admit it" (609), has a dusty consequence for "the carriage motionless in its shed" (632), for the horses getting "shabbier and less prideful with idleness" (632), and for Faulkner's most deplorable figure of a "house nigger," Simon, who grumbles: "Ridin' in dat thing, wid a gent-mun's proper equipage goin' ter rack en ruin in de barn" (633). There are simply no descriptions of what the two Bayards see on their regular way to and from town; it is as if space disappears in the mechanical fold created by the daily commute (and we will see this pattern repeated in Jason Compson's chapter a year later). But when young Bayard finally lures Simon into "the gleaming long thing, dynamic as a motionless locomotive and little awesome" (634–35) for a ride, we are at last treated to the novel's first genuine motorized chronotope of the road, focalized through the very coachman whose function it has supplanted:

> they shot forward on a roar of sound like blurred thunder. Earth, the unbelievable ribbon of the road, crashed beneath them and away behind

into dust convolvulae: a dun moiling nausea of speed, and the roadside greenery was a tunnel rigid and streaming and unbroken. (635–36)

This fierce reduction of the "world" opened up by the carriage's "motion without progress" to an indistinct green "tunnel" of speed is properly epochal and loaded with all kinds of historical and political freight. The automobile, reprising its leitmotif of thunder, orients its spatial horizon in comic-book two-dimensionality. Gone now is that complex and multi-planar scenography of hedgerow, "sluggish" dust, trees, fields, laborers, hills, unto the "ramparts of infinity." In its place, we have this "unbelievable" chronotope of a road being "crashed" into "dust convolvulae"—literally chewed up, atomized, and expelled by a velocity that relates to no "world" whatsoever, just an affect: that "dun moiling nausea of speed." It is precisely this transfiguration, of romance "world" into modernist affect, that the motorcar makes possible, and that *Flags* stages as the irreversible crisis of the Southern plantocracy. For once you have cashed in a world for an affect, it is spent at once, in the very intensity of its consumption as a bodily sensation.

The affect is contagious and communicable. In one of the many moments of allegorical encounter between the machine that generates it and the mode of transport it is displacing, we see this clearly. This one takes place during Simon's first ride:

> The wagon was moving drowsily and peacefully along the road. It was drawn by two mules and was filled with negro women asleep in chairs. Some of them wore drawers. The mules themselves didn't wake at all, but ambled sedately on with the empty wagon and the overturned chairs, even when the car crashed into the shallow ditch and surged back onto the road again and thundered on without slowing. The thunder ceased, but the car rushed on under its own momentum, and it began to sway from side to side (636).

After Simon finally extricates himself from this monster of thunder and speed, he is left to contemplate the consequences for the wagon:

> After a while the wagon emerged from the dust, the mules now at a high flop-eared trot, and jingled past him, leaving behind it upon the dusty insect-rasped air a woman's voice in a quavering wordless hysteria, passive and quavering and sustained. (637)

The spatially evacuated chronotope of automotive transport is transposed onto the medium of a voice; this "quavering wordless hysteria" is what the motorcar communicates to the body as so much unassimilable affect. It erases the "world" and substitutes for it a "sustained" vibration in the fibers of the body, ranging "chromatically up and down the bodily scale from melancholy to euphoria, from the bad trip to the high" in the eternal present of a singular sensation.[27]

In that case, the very possibility of descriptive prose—of any landscape emerging from this hysterical dust—seems quashed in advance by the motorcar's affective subsumption of space itself; a curious result, given what we have seen as the principal draw of the romantic "picture-postcard South" for the tourist motorists of the North. In this novel, it would appear, there are to be no views from the car at all, apart from an abstract "tunnelling" of the roadside into an unbroken green blur—to which one may well compare the automobilic experience of scenery in *Howards End* (1910): "Did not a gentleman once motor so quickly through Westmorland that he missed it? . . . She looked at the scenery. It heaved and merged like porridge. Presently it congealed. . . .[A]gain she lost all sense of space."[28] And yet, as David Trotter points out, in the way it was promoted as a consumer item at the time, "the motorcar . . . could be understood as a representational medium—as a platform for the production and potential storage of individually selected 'views.'"[29] Certainly that argument applies to the case made for road improvement in the South as a lure for Northern tourism; here too, as in England, "[a]esthetic appreciation, or departure from the main highways in search of the picturesque, became an important element in the definition of landscape" (233). But the only aesthetic appreciation to be had from the motorcar in *Flags* is the exclusively modernist one of affective chromaticism; the picturesque is liquidated. Faulkner's emphasis on "blur" and "thunder," nausea and dust, may be taken as a political contestation of the very origins of the "heritage industry" that converts uneven development into opportune windows upon lost time, provided the roads and amenities are good enough. For if you cannot see what you have come to gaze at in the first place, if your coming is what spoils it, it may be best to stay home. Bayard's car could be anywhere when it "rushes" and "flashes" past, and converts the landscape into abstract smears of color and line; so it may as well remain where it was sold.

To be sure, there are exceptions to this rule, as when Bayard, beaten temporarily back into his hereditary chronotope, takes Narcissa out driving in her car (which cannot exceed 20 mph)—"the road mounted presently in long curves among dark pines in the slanting afternoon. The road wound on, with changing sunshot vistas of the valley and the opposite hills at every turn," (762)—but only until he can mount a summit, pull out the clutch, and roll with the force of gravity down the next steep gradient: "they flashed with a sharp reverberation

---

[27] Fredric Jameson, *The Antinomies of Realism* (London & New York: Verso, 2013), 42.
[28] E. M. Forster, *Howards End* (London: Penguin, 2000), 168, 169, 170.
[29] Trotter, *Literature in the First Media Age*, 233.

like hail on a tin roof, between willows and a crashing glint of water and shot on up the next hill" (762). Scenery is contingent upon a velocity to which Bayard finds it existentially impossible to restrict himself behind the wheel. Or again, on a long night-time drive through the county with a band of black minstrels, as Bayard goes drunkenly serenading, we are given rare glimpses of a moon-dappled motorcar picturesque:

> The sandy road hissed beneath the broad tires of [the car] and rose shaling into the woods again where the dappled moonlight was intermittent, treacherous with dissolving vistas. Invisible and sourceless among the shifting patterns of light and shade whip-poor-wills were like flutes tongued liquidly. The road passed out of the woods and descended, with sand in shifting and silent lurches, and they turned on to the valley road and away from town. (658)

Which again ends abruptly in an irresistible quest for affect:

> The road fell from beneath them like a tilting floor and away across a valley, straight now as a string. The negroes clutched their instruments and held to one another. The speedometer showed 55 and 60 and turned gradually on. Sparse houses flashed slumbering away, and fields and patches of woodland like tunnels. (660)

At which, like the "hysterical wailing" earlier, we read that "the negroes' concerted wail whipped forlornly away" (661).

Hybrid formations

This recurrent registration of black affect in relation to the motorcar may be said to spring directly from the deepest layers of the text's political unconscious, especially since it is framed by the supposedly comical Simon Strother's anachronistic nostalgia for "de ole times comin' back" (864). Simon's considered judgment is that "De ottomobile ... is all right fer pleasure en excitement, but fer de genu-wine gen'lemun tone, dey aint but one thing: dat's horses" (738). His contempt for "field niggers" is best projected from his place at the reins of the Sartoris equipage: "Simon turned on the seat and clucked to the horses and drove on, his cigar tilted toward his hatbrim, his elbows out and the whip caught smartly back in his hand, glancing now and then at the field niggers laboring among the cotton rows with tolerant and easy scorn" (738–40). And this, too, is part of the romance chronotope that *Flags* is concerned both to memorialize and to contest. Simon's repudiation of the motorcar is first and foremost a clinging to his ancestral privilege as a coachman and domestic servant, as a lineal descendant of Sartoris house slaves, and to his light workload; but second, it is a confirmation of his utter stereotypicality as a clownish "nigger" in Faulkner's hands, a figure incapable of the affect in question, incapable of modernity, and so "comically" dispensable in a last-minute murder over sexual access rights—the last Sartoris being the clan's most ludicrous member.

His skepticism and resistance to motorized transport is not shared by his son, Caspey, who returns from the front as a demobbed soldier full of the anti-aristocratic and anti-racist sentiments of militarized modernity, sharpened by his experiences in France "ridin' about de country on dat private truck" with a French schoolboy who collects him AWOL at the side of the road (590). For Caspey, the automobile is a symbol of what it means to "take nothin' offen no white man no mo,'" especially the violent Jim Crow strictures against interracial sexuality: "I got my white in France, and I'm gwine get it here, too" (592). The "white" he turns his eye to is Narcissa, or rather her car: "He slowed in passing Narcissa's small car and examined it with a disparagement too lazy to sneer even, then he slouched on" (592). But the threat, the affect, is contagious, passing from vehicle to body and back again, so that when Narcissa drives home and is obliged to pass this discriminating son of the South, we read:

> The negro had moved down the road, slowly, and had stopped again, and he was watching her covertly as she approached. As she passed he looked full at her and she knew he was about to hail her. She opened the throttle and passed him with increasing speed and drove swiftly on to town, where she lived in a brick house among cedars on a hill. (595)

The act of hitchhiking is automatically translated into the idiom of rape, and interracial rape at that, the new mobility of the unaccompanied white middle-class woman resistlessly conjuring up the pernicious Southern romance mytheme of the marauding "black beast," only to put it behind her again by the power of a well-maintained engine.

The articulation of black desire with the automobile is felt within the persistent Southern romance plot as profoundly "unnatural" and threatening, at least until old Bayard and Simon both finally die, and Miss Jenny can allow Isom to become the driver of what is now effectively the family automobile (since young Bayard has disappeared to Mexico)—"And you drive this thing careful, boy," she told him, "or I'll get over there and do it myself" (868)—the very thing he has been itching to do since first seeing the vehicle: "Isom appeared around the corner and circled the car quietly with an utter and yearning admiration. . . . Isom stood like a leashed hound beside it" (604). But Isom-as-chauffeur is a moment of semi-tragic conclusion, and it contravenes the prevailing ethos according to which black men and automobiles shall not mix. There is something so wrong with the relationship that it cannot even be mentioned, until the infamous rhapsody on the mule, where we are finally given to understand the taboo against black car worship. Not only have black characters and mules been established as figuratively linked by the wagons that Bayard repeatedly disturbs in his passage, and by the turning of the molasses mill (637, 648, 715, 779), but in the "saga of the mule," the narrator outdoes himself in an argument for the homology between the two beings: "Misunderstood even by that creature (the nigger who drives him) whose impulses and mental processes most closely resemble his, he performs alien actions among alien surroundings" (780).[30] Ontologically proximate as he is to a mule, a black man's desire for automotive transport is a symptom of civilizational catastrophe.

Earlier, by explicit contrast, we have been regaled with an episode taken direct from the annals of Southern romance, stimulated by the appearance of Old Man Falls but told by Miss Jenny herself, concerning the "hare-brained" raid on the federal army coffee supply, the kidnapping of a Yankee major, and Bayard's tragicomic return for the anchovies—a tale "become a gallant and finely tragical focal-point" through frequent retelling, and the genetic origin of all young Bayard's woes (549). Only the central figure of the tale is not Bayard, a mere "reckless boy," but the dandy cavalier General Jeb Stuart, "a paladin out of romance," as the federal Major puts it (555). For it is Stuart who embodies not only the principles and charisma of the gallant knight, but facilitates the inscription of genuine romance chronotopes as such. "They now galloped along a faint trace that was once a road.... Stuart whirled his party and plunged back into the forest. Pistol-balls were thinly about their heads and the flat tossing reports were trivial as snapping twigs above the converging thunder of hooves. Stuart swerved from the road and they crashed headlong through undergrowth" (553). Or again, "above the strong and rapid breathing of the horses and the sound of their own hearts in their ears, was a nameless something—a tenseness seeping from tree to tree like an invisible mist, filling the dewy morning woods with portent though birds flashed swooping from tree to tree, unaware or disregardful of it" (533).

Nowhere but in moments like this will the landscape in Faulkner come to such extraordinary sensory life. It is by virtue of the fusion of human sense perception and equine motility that such phenomenological intensities are possible in the first place, since it is "the rhythm of his speed" (552) that brings the forest stillness to such vivid animation. Trees emerge as such—"vicious with minnies like wasps," their "dappled branches" no longer a mere backdrop to action,

---

[30] Charles Hannon makes the point that the whole passage "represents the efforts of the dominant classes to elide this fact [of black property ownership] and to represent the black Other as an object of ritual scorn." See Hannon, *Faulkner and the Discourses of Culture* (Baton Rouge: Louisiana State University Press, 2005), 6.

but complicate with it (552)—from a matrix of utopian possibility: "The glade dreamed quiet and empty of threat beneath the mounting golden day; laked within lay a deep and abiding peace like golden wine; yet beneath this solitude and permeating it was that nameless and waiting portent, patient and brooding and sinister" (554). All the potent elements of Southern landscape are here preserved against their technological dissipation in the rehearsed memory of old Bayard Sartoris and his aunt Virginia Du Pre. And they come to a focus in the figure that overarches this entire episode: "'Forward!' the General said and whirled roweling his bay, and with the thunderous coordination of a single centaur they swept down the knoll" (552).

Just as the mule and the "nigger" are fused into a single racist palimpsest, so too the cavalier and his stallion are made one in the classical figure of the centaur. The problem with the automobile is its substitution for both beasts and consequent erasure of the "essential" class and racial differences between them. And yet, a certain tropological "trouble" has here crept into the frame, such that precisely what distinguishes the classes and races (their imaginary hybridization with different equine beasts) is also what differentiates them from themselves: the centaur is a figure of monstrous coupling and the grotesque as much as it is of the romantic nobility, which is why it was also available to Faulkner for satirical purposes, as in his description of the techno-human hybrid figure of *Pylon*'s Jiggs being "like a cartoon comedy centaur." And throughout the text of *Flags in the Dust*, figures of the monstrous and the hybrid appear to disturb the essentialist matrix of romance with intimations of abortive, grotesque fatality—just as the mule itself is incurably an infertile bastard son of horse and donkey, "Father and mother he does not resemble, sons and daughters he will never have" (780). Think of the dead possum, "such a paradox, its vulpine, skull-like grin and those tiny, human-looking hands, and the long, rat-like tail of it" (785), gesturing at a limit of the grotesque that is then breached by the bizarre pups sired on Ethel the fox by the hound General: "a hound's wind and bottom, and a fox's smartness and speed" (827), "Neither fox nor hound; partaking of both, yet neither; and despite their soft infancy, there was about them something monstrous and contradictory and obscene" (828). Such impossible cross-breeds speak clandestinely to a persistent mytheme about "miscegenation" that is raised by the figure of the centaur, confirmed by the association between mule and "nigger," and set loose by the salacious eye that Caspey seems to cast upon Narcissa's vehicle and, by default, on her. But the extraordinary thing about motorcars, in this context, is that they fail to adhere to any caste-based dreams of organic integrity, and participate in the most promiscuous logic of exchangeability and transposition.

So it is, for instance, that Harry Mitchell can find himself playing alone with a car "out in the garage" (564) while his wife substitutes him with Horace Benbow, or "doing something to the engine of it while the house-yard-stable boy held a patent trouble-lamp above the beetling crag of his head and his daughter and Rachel, holding tools or detached sections of the car's vitals, leaned their intent dissimilar faces across his bent back" (704). This new domestic circle, fiddling with the "vitals" of a machine that is fast becoming the middle-class family's most critical asset, exposes the innermost fungibility of all relations, internal and external, in a nascent monopoly-capitalist space of "mile after mile of identical frame houses with garage to match" (849). Every part of an automobile is replaceable, as are the elements of the family group and the entire edifice of social relations.[31] But that very fungibility is also the secret utopian potential of mechanical reproducibility itself, as when V. K. Surrat appears in his magical vehicle to transport the wounded Bayard away to a kingdom of moonshine and inebriation—a perfect hybrid of motorcar and wagon:

> It was a ford body with, in place of a tonneau, a miniature one room cabin of sheet iron and larger than a dog kennel, in each painted window of which a painted house-wife simpered across a painted sewing machine, and in it an actual sewing machine neatly fitted, borne thus about the countryside by the agent. (649–50)

They end up in a barnyard "where stood a wagon with drunken wheels and a home-made bed, and the rusting skeleton of a ford car. Low down upon its domed and bald radiator the two lamps gave it an expression of beetling patient astonishment, like a skull" (651); and this evident refiguration of Harry Mitchell (bald, beetling) as a car's skeletal remains suggests that the cuckolded cotton speculator, who doubtless also drinks Surratt's sour mash, is to be understood as a human projection of the automobilic economy his fetishes sponsor.

So the motorcar gathers into its figural vicinity the logic of grotesque hybridization that anxiously patrols the eroding boundaries between the races and classes throughout the text, and seems to typify it; the utopia it projects is one where anything can be built out of the generic parts made in a northeastern or a midwestern factory—a *worldless world* indifferent to the peculiarities of its region, where a Snopes can send anonymous love letters to a Benbow and take off in a Ford by night, a Mitchell can divorce a Mitchell and marry a Benbow who will beg a Mitchell for a car, a Sartoris can kill a Sartoris through the medium of speed, a Strother can look a Benbow in the eye to hitch a "ride," and a Du Pre can take a car to town to telegram her already dead great nephew about his newborn

---

[31] Here we may recall E. L. Doctorow's exemplary summation of Henry Ford's historical achievement: "From these principles Ford established the final proposition of the theory of industrial manufacture—not only that the parts of the finished product be interchangeable, but that the men who build the products be themselves interchangeable parts." Doctorow, *Ragtime* (London: Picador, 1985), 104.

son. But it can only do so, of course, given a determinate investment in infrastructure like that overseen by Johncy Falkner and "his crews" in 1928. "By 1910, every southern state legislature had authorized local governments, both county and municipal, to make use of convicts incarcerated within their jurisdictions in the building and maintenance of public thoroughfares."[32] Convict or otherwise, there is no doubt about the racial complexion of the team that Johncy's brother William drafted in to improve the roads of Kinston, Mississippi, to remind his reader about what happens to black labor once a typical scene on the plantation can run as follows: "he tinkered with farming machinery and with the tractor he had persuaded old Bayard to buy" (712). Displaced—like the "mule" they supposedly resemble—by the combustion engine from one mode of production to another, black workers can thus be conscripted to seal the roads:

> The street from curb to curb was uptorn. It was in the throes of being paved. Along it lines of negroes labored with pick and shovel, swinging their tools in a languid rhythm. Steadily and with a lazy unhaste that seemed to spend itself in snatches of plaintive minor chanting punctuated by short grunting ejaculations which died upon the sunny air and ebbed away from the languid rhythms of picks that struck not; shovels that did not dig. Further up the street a huge misshapen machine like an antediluvian nightmare clattered and groaned. It dominated the scene with its noisy and measured fury, but against this as against a heroic frieze, the negroes labored on, their chanting and their motions more soporific than a measured tolling of far away bells. (851–52)

Another residual plantation chronotope, that of the field slaves' paradoxical "unhaste" and "soporific" labor under the whip, is here projected onto the most modern of scenes—back-breaking road work under the sun, where although pick and shovel are duly swinging, nevertheless these are "picks that struck not; shovels that did not dig." *Plus ça change*. And all this toil-that-is-not-toil is in the service of an altogether novel chronotope of the road, whose purpose it is not to afford a greater mobility between farm and town, but to get the fragile luxury goods from the train station to the private home as quickly as possible. Horace muses in the kind of syntactically fractured Joycean interior monologue that motorcars presumably foment in the modern subject:

> He lived on this street, and it was still open: motors could run on it, and he went on, dripping his trailing moisture along the sidewalk. With a motor car now, he could have Soon; perhaps next year; then things But

---

[32] Preston, *Dirt Roads to Dixie*, 22.

naturally Belle would miss her car, after having had one always, a new one every year. Harry, and his passion for shiny wheels. (852)

As Faulkner would put it later in *Knight's Gambit*, "one morning I stood beside the halted carriage while on all sides rushed and squawked the bright loud glittering new automobiles because the war was won and every man would be rich and at peace forever."[33] And for this utopia, "the negroes labored on."

Long ago, Richard Chase argued that "the romances of our literature, like European prose romances, are literary hybrids, unique only in their peculiar but widely differing amalgamation of novelistic and romance elements."[34] This hybridity is constitutive of the prose art of William Faulkner, and at times that generic ambivalence is projected figurally upon the narratives themselves, as here, where Surratt's amalgamated vehicle and Ethel's litter serve as indices of a broader formal and ideological crisis. Where the "world" of romance depends upon organic homologies and distinctions between kinds of being, and upon landscapes and chronotopes in which those beings can find their rightful place, the "worldless world" of modernity merges these distinct kinds of being into unfounded and progenyless monsters of appetite, speed, and abstraction. It is particularly in a work of uneven generic hybridity, like *Flags in the Dust*, where the modernity has yet to find its own idiom, that the ideological stakes are rendered in starkest clarity; here we feel most potently the antagonistic split occasioned by two competing impulses. One, manifest in the abundant textual space afforded to descriptive prose and the residual chronotopes of romance, recoils into an offensive nostalgia that the other, registered through the erasure of description and the partial establishment of new chronotopes, knows to be historically invalid. The aesthetic result is a formal disaster, as Horace Liveright reported in good faith. But the impact of that rejection on Faulkner's evolving formal compact between romance and novel was radical indeed; the next novel, written into the temporary publishers' void, would do away with Southern scenic description almost entirely.

Olfactory affect

In *The Sound and the Fury*, each of the Compson brothers suffers a peculiar olfactory wound: respectively, *eau de Parfum*, honeysuckle, and gasoline. These have formed a sort of psychic scar tissue, or ossified sense memory of a breached incestuous limit within Benjy's, Quentin's, and Jason's mental lives. When the

---

[33] Faulkner, *Knight's Gambit* (London: Chatto & Windus, 1960), 207.
[34] Richard Chase, *The American Novel and Its Traditions* [c. 1957] (Baltimore: Johns Hopkins University Press, 1980), 13–14.

pubescent Caddy is first detected by her youngest sibling to have daubed a mass-produced synthetic perfume on her person and so taken away the romantic "smell of trees" that she emanates spontaneously, his reaction is one of horrified negation: "I didn't hush." Quentin, meanwhile, is sickened by the extent to which Caddy's sexual indiscretions have become "all mixed up" with the potent aroma of honeysuckle. Most emphatic, as we shall see, is Jason's psychosomatic reaction to the reek of Caddy's escape velocity in gasoline: a crippling cephalalgia that blinkers all sense and pulverizes thought. Coming to terms with this most extreme olfactory symptom entails more than a cursory survey of Faulkner's elaborate symbolic weather-chart for this breakthrough novel; it will involve a rethinking of what exactly "consciousness" is in this text, and of how mediated it is by the systems and media that make modernity possible.

These olfactory events are occasioned or revived, in two of these three cases, by periods spent on modern forms of transportation. Quentin's honeysuckle reveries take place, first, on board an electric streetcar running between Harvard and the factory town where he meets his "little sister"; second, in Mrs Bland's car driving off to the rural picnic; and third, on the return streetcar journey back to Harvard. And Jason's gasoline-induced headaches are induced by prolonged automobile journeys in pursuit of his sexually incorrigible niece. The same cannot be said for Benjy's refrain about Caddy smelling like trees or his upset over the perfume, since Benjy never steps into anything more modern than the surrey that takes him to the graveyard every Sunday. But this should come as no surprise, as, after all, Benjy's condition collapses the very distinction between conscious and unconscious processes that defines the traumatic breach his brothers experience as odoriferous psychosomatic trouble.

What I want to establish is that, in the very writing of these olfactory disturbances, Faulkner's text implants a pattern according to which the imbrication of modern transport and traumatic scent overdetermines an event of psychic disaggregation and sensory shutdown. It is as though the aroma that evokes the absent incestuous object is nothing without its mediation in the present by technologies of speed, carburated injection, and the spreading networks of modern transportation. Situated in the fold between these two figurative domains is consciousness itself, intuited though never directly presented as the contradictory synthesis of a deeply buried sense-memory of psychic trauma, and an objective system of mass mediation and technological speed written on the surface of the earth in blacktopped roadways, tramlines, and train tracks. I deem it critical to insist that traumatic memory here takes place neither in its *locus classicus*, the domestic home, which is rather the space of repetitive scenes and rituals designed to ward off crises, nor at work or study, but in the non-places that articulate them, the essentially non-experiential zones of transit and commuting where non-purposive reverie is still allowed to take place in a world of administered functions.

But smell is, ultimately, what the new media of modernity have most signally failed to transmit; it has proved impossible to do for the closely related senses of smell and taste what had been done for visible and sonic modes of perception, namely, to transform them into information, encrypt that information, send it, and decode it at some other place and time into a new sense experience with at least some analogous relationship to the original. Odor in that sense suffers a uniquely redoubled censorship in the riot of mediation that characterizes the first half of the twentieth century: already the most denigrated of senses under conditions of bourgeois hegemony, as first Freud[35] and then Adorno[36] argued, the olfactory then fails to register at all in the wavelengths and shutter-speeds of mass mediation. It is perhaps for that reason that its stubborn persistence as a bodily capability made it singularly available as a repository and amplification chamber for affect as such in the modern. Teresa Brennan has proposed the sense of smell as the primary conductor of what she calls "the transmission of affect,"[37] and Fredric Jameson suggests that "[o]dour, the most repressed and stigmatized of senses [. . .], seems everywhere, from Baudelaire to Proust, to be a privileged vehicle for isolating affect and identifying it for a variety of dynamics."[38] Indeed, it must have appeared advantageous to modern writers to single out a sense not yet colonized by new machines of automatic inscription and reproducibility and treat it to an annexing operation on the part of literature itself—if not for narrative reasons, then precisely for the wealth of affective and impressionist intensities it will have afforded. A "disembodied body, vaporized, remaining entire in itself, yet turned into a volatile essence,"[39] odor is the writer's happy hunting ground for any affect that is separated "from its physical bearer" and torn "away from spatio-temporal coordinates."[40] Faulkner's canny distribution of three distinct olfactory "tones" across this last generation

---

[35] "The conjecture that goes deepest . . . is to the effect that, with the assumption of an erect posture by man and with the depreciation of his sense of smell, it was not only his anal erotism which threatened to fall a victim to organic repression, but the whole of his sexuality." Sigmund Freud, *Civilization and Its Discontents*, trans. James Strachey (New York: W. W. Norton, 1962), 53 n.3.

[36] "The multifarious nuances of the sense of smell embody the archetypal longing for the lower forms of existence, for direct unification with circumambient nature, with the earth and mud. Of all the senses, that of smell—which is attracted without objectifying—bears closest witness to the urge to lose oneself in and become the 'other.' When we see, we remain what we are; but when we smell, we are taken over by otherness. Hence the sense of smell is considered a disgrace in civilisation, the sign of lower social strata, lesser races and base animals." Max Horkheimer and Theodor W. Adorno, *Dialectic of Enlightenment*, trans. John Cumming (New York: Continuum, 1989), 184.

[37] Teresa Brennan, *The Transmission of Affect* (Ithaca: Cornell University Press, 2004).

[38] Fredric Jameson, *The Antinomies of Realism*, 35.

[39] Jean-Paul Sartre, *Baudelaire* (Paris: Gallimard, 1947), 201—trans. André Bleikasten and quoted in *The Ink of Melancholy*, 53.

[40] Jameson, *Antinomies of Realism*, 69; Gilles Deleuze, *Cinéma 1*, trans. Hugh Tomlinson and Barbara Habberjam (London: Athlone, 1986), 96.

of Compsons is a remarkably economical solution to a problem that could well have led to a form disaster in a text such as this. Its specific intensity is calibrated to those forms of transportation that underwrite its power precisely by making its referent (Caddy) forever absent, as we shall see. Modernity occludes the romantic referent by the power of a speed in whose wake the olfactory residues of romance are affectively kept alive.

In his satiric "obituary" for the Compson dynasty, "COMPSON 1699–1945," Faulkner frames the rise and fall of this doomed clan with references to petrochemical alienation. Ikkemotubbe grants his square mile to Jason Lycurgus Compson for passage to the "wild western land presently to be called Oklahoma: not knowing then about the oil," and President Jackson countersigns the grant "not knowing about the oil either," but this "unknown unknown," which becomes a viable concern only after the invention of the combustion engine, then knows a veritable return of the repressed: "so that one day the homeless descendants of the dispossessed would ride supine with drink and splendidly comatose above the dusty allotted harbourage of their bones in specially built scarletpainted hearses and fire-engines."[41] And then, at the far end of this compressed narrative, that slick magazine picture slapped down in front of Jason Compson's namesake by a prudish librarian, "a Cannebrière backdrop of mountains and palms and cypresses and the sea, an open powerful expensive chromiumtrimmed sports car, the woman's face hatless between a rich scarf and a seal coat, ageless and beautiful, cold serene and damned" (1134), in which Candace's original disappearance in an automobile (to South Bend, Indiana, in 1910) is fatally recapitulated in a sensational *mise-en-scène* with a Nazi staff-general in the South of France. What might the "petrochemical unconscious" of the transaction behind the Compson Domain, and Caddy's infamous eternal return as an avatar of scandal in a motor car (to be repeated upon her daughter, albeit with a difference: "whatever occupation overtook her would have arrived in no chromium Mercedes" [1141], she being prone rather to rides in "ford cars"), have to tell us about the way Quentin smells her memory in honeysuckle, and Jason tries to ward off her gasoline-drenched aroma of desertion through the heavy application of maternal camphor? Only time, and analysis, will tell. But one thing we can safely say is that, in the semiological overdetermination of these figures, one thing mercifully gets reassembled: namely the dominant olfactory affect of the preceding novel, *Flags in the Dust*, whose insistence on the "rank odor of negroes" (838) as the counterpoint to suburbia's smells of "recent varnish," "affluence and burning gasoline" (849), does nothing to exonerate its capitulation to the lowest common ideological denominator.

---

[41] Faulkner, "Appendix," *The Sound and the Fury*, in *Novels 1926–1929*, 1127.

In *The Sound and the Fury*, the "smell" of black people doesn't ring ideological alarm bells. As Benjy says, "I liked to smell Versh's house [...] *The bed smelled like T.P. I liked it*" (898, 899)—an affective value that contradicts its earlier function as a sign of discrimination. Benjy is, indeed, a kind of ideological Laundromat for sense perception, above all smell, since he can smell Damuddy's death as well as Dan the dog ("*He smell hit. He smell hit*," 946) without any attribution of value, and is himself a version of what the modern media ecology lacks, namely, a specialist olfactory medium: "*He smell what you tell him when he want to. Dont have to listen nor talk*" (944); "he cannot hear it unless he can smell it" (1011). So, the usual description of his "camera mind" manifesting a "camera-like fidelity" to the world needs to be adapted:[42] as we are about to see, what he *sees* is less faithful than what he *smells* is to the order of the Real. He is a well-nigh mechanical medium of odors that belongs, not to the white world, but to the black. Forever banished from the big house, his mother incapable of seeing him as anything but an invidious judgment upon her, Benjy dwells among the aromas of black servitude—kitchen, servants' quarters, fields—watched over by Versh, T.P. or Luster, but loved only by his disgraced sister (who does it "*like nigger women do in the pasture the ditches dark woods*,") and Dilsey herself, who fixes him a birthday cake on April 7 and takes him, hand in hand, to Easter service the next day, a walk during which it is said of the trees that border the dirt track that they feed "upon the rich and unmistakable smell of negroes in which they grew" (1101). So it is, indeed, that "Caddy smelled like trees" (909), and getting Benjy to donate to Dilsey the bottle of perfume that so upsets his olfactory sense of his sister, and commenting loftily that "'[w]e don't like perfume ourselves'" (909), can scarcely undo the semiotic equation that is set for Caddy by this aromatic destiny. Benjy will "smell hit" all already: her muddy drawers in the blooming pear tree, the same tree her daughter will descend, its roots descending into the soil of an absorbent negritude. "*She smelled like trees*": it is a racial nourishment.

A cartography of chronotopes

For all that he has no lived connection to motorized transport, Benjy Compson is granted a characteristic chronotope, which closes out the book and which we first encounter during his early "recollection" of a trip to the cemetery in 1913 or so: "I could hear Queenie's feet and the bright shapes went smooth and steady on both sides, the shadows of them flowing across Queenie's back. They went on like the bright tops of wheels. Then those on one side stopped at the tall white post where the soldier was. But on the other side they went on smooth

---

[42] See Michael Millgate, *The Achievement of William Faulkner* (New York: Random House, 1966), 98.

and steady, but a little slower" (885). This is as rich, untroubled, and hypotactic as Benjy's prose will get, and it embodies a structure of feeling made possible by a relaxed sensory acquiescence to the regular movements of a carriage pulled by a horse through the streets of town. It is the bare remnant—"the patrician (as three-year old)"[43]—of that romance chronotope opened up by the Sartoris "Getn'mun equipage" as it passed from town to plantation, and is as dependent as that one on an implicit opposition to what it is not, namely a motorcar, as Jason grumbles later on:

> I says that old rattletrap's just an eyesore, yet you'll keep it standing there in the carriage house a hundred years just so that boy can ride to the cemetery once a week. I says he's not the first fellow that'll have to do things he doesn't want to. I'd make him ride in that car like a civilized man or stay at home. What does he know about where he goes or what he goes in, and us keeping a carriage and a horse so he can take a ride on a Sunday afternoon. (1069)

Benjy's stubborn and infantile preference for the older means of conveyance contradicts his brother's deep sense of shame with regard to the antiquated "rattletrap" that has become the family's weekly spectacle of terminal obsolescence. The patrician chronotope appears doomed. Its comfort, for Benjy, lies in its repetitive regularity, stretching presumably all the way from the interment of his father in 1912 to the apocalyptic trip on Easter Sunday, April 8, 1928, when Luster takes the wrong way around the war memorial—a sixteen-year rhythmic lulling, over roughly 830 return trips.

The surrey itself is presented by Dilsey in all its fatal dilapidation: "*This thing going to fall to pieces under you all some day. Look at them wheels*" (883). But looking at the wheels is just what Benjy will do, and his sustained perceptual attention allows him to construct what is, for him, that happiest of figural entities, a simile: "They went on like the bright tops of wheels," a comparison that unites the mode of transport and the spatial field modified by it. What emerges from this chronotope of phenomenological immanence is not a description of space, but a productivity of language, a conjuration of "smooth and steady" abstract shapes where there may have been merely houses, stores, and trees—or, as it is filled in for us later, "cornice and façade [. . .], post and tree, window and doorway and signboard" (1124). This is not yet an affect (the affect comes later, when its repetition is disturbed), but what Deleuze and Guattari would call a "percept," a singular "being of sensation" that doesn't resemble anything, but which

---

[43] Richard Godden, *Fictions of Labor: William Faulkner and the South's Long Revolution* (Cambridge: Cambridge University Press, 1997), 48.

protracts its experiential intensity in such a way as to have become complicate with eternity.[44] It is out of this peculiar weave of perceptions, words, time, and eternity that a character can emerge in the first place. "Characters can only exist," they write, "and the author can only create them, because they do not perceive but have passed into the landscape and are themselves part of the compound of sensations" (169). Benjy chronotopically "passes into" the Jefferson townscape to the extent that he can assume the anachronistic, socially backward posture of a landed gentleman in a surrey: a posture that will be interpreted by everybody who sees it as the family idiot out for a ride. But the upshot is a verbal canvas for spatial abstraction, a word-painting "in which all images appear on a flat vertical plane that has no calculus for spatial relativity."[45] We are in modernism here, then, and definitively, because of the radical formal disjunctions that now obtain between the *subject* of this experience, the *objects* of this experience, and the *production* of this experience in language. The character of Benjy is an aesthetic declaration of principles, under whose new terms of engagement a "ride in a surrey" is a chronotope no longer useful to the description let alone the cognitive mapping of social space, but one whose function is simply to furnish autonomous blocs of sensation like this.

In *Flags in the Dust*, the narrator had had to resort to Marinetti-like escapades aboard an automobile to wrest from the countryside those comparable "blocs of sensation" in speed: "Earth, the unbelievable ribbon of the road, crashed beneath them and away behind into dust convolvulae: a dun moiling nausea of speed, and the roadside greenery was a tunnel rigid and streaming and unbroken" (635–36). This kind of abstraction and spatial flattening is now transposed onto Benjy's atemporal and disaffected chronotope of the surrey ride. The "bright shapes" going "smooth and steady on both sides" are no less a tunnel, and no less dependent upon a mode of transport, only the entire aesthetic ideology has been reverse engineered. An affect has given way to a percept; the nausea is gone; a sedate rhythm of animal inoccupation, *rien faire comme un bête*, has supplanted the desperate quest for human experience. The surrey shelters a futuristic mode of perception in its very anachronism, and reserves it for an autistic and illiterate "gelding" who is fated to make no literary mark upon his world beyond these words, couched for us in a preterite tense that severs it from the experience itself.

The formal decision to cede all narrative authority to successive first-person narrators for three of the book's four chapters is a decision against any intelligible description of the Southern landscape until the final chapter. If Benjy's

---

[44] Gilles Deleuze and Félix Guattari, *What is Philosophy?*, trans. Graham Burchell and High Tomlinson (London & New York: Verso, 1994), 163–200.

[45] Noel Polk, *Children of the Dark House: Text and Context in Faulkner* (Jackson, MS: University Press of Mississippi, 1996), 101.

percepts tend to abstract the environment into blocs of sensation sufficient unto themselves and absolved of all mimetic responsibility, Quentin is removed from Mississippi altogether, so that his romantic tendency to write the landscape has to be filtered through an alien topography and even stranger modes of transportation; Jason, as we shall see, is subject to episodes of acute sensory deprivation the moment he takes the wheel of that new "representational medium" or "platform for the production and potential storage of individually selected 'views,'" his automobile.[46] Only in the fourth chapter does the inveterate Southern descriptive impulse re-emerge, but it has been chastened and defamiliarized. So immersed is it now within a chronotope diametrically opposed to that of the plantation romance that it requires a new terminological category to account for it: *black epic*. For it is only on behalf of a pedestrian mass of black worshippers that this descriptive tendency is articulated, which means that it is absorbed into a "production of space" on a scale far removed from the petty bourgeois trivialities of town, and the workaday cycles of the fields; specifically it belongs to the anonymous and communal epic of black folk. The extraordinary paragraphs that tell of the Gibson family's slow walk to church on Easter Sunday are marked by an urge to depict what the rest of the text has repressed—the shape of the land, and the place of the colored folk upon it, all projected from the vantage of a "dirt road":

> On either hand the land dropped more sharply; a broad flat dotted with small cabins whose weathered roofs were on a level with the crown of the road. They were set in small grassless plots littered with broken things, bricks, planks, crockery, things of a once utilitarian value. What growth there was consisted of rank weeds and the trees were mulberries and locusts and sycamores—trees that partook also of the foul desiccation which surrounded the houses (1101).

There is, in this pedestrian chronotope of the dirt road, a sense that, although its world is stricken by some dire spiritual desolation, it is yet "a homogeneous world, and even the separation between man and world, between 'I' and 'you' cannot disturb its homogeneity."[47] To perceive here is truly to *see*, and nothing can hide from the "random and tentative sun" (1100) that shines grimly down upon these blasted particulars. It is an epic space, peopled by the anonymous, non-individuated, and impoverished:

> They emerged from the cabins and struggled up to the shaling levee to the road—men in staid, hard brown or black, with gold watch chains

---

[46] Trotter, *Literature in the First Media Age*, 233.
[47] Georg Lukács, *The Theory of the Novel*, trans. Anna Bostock (London: Merlin Press, 1971), 32.

and now and then a stick; young men in cheap violent blues or stripes and swaggering hats; women a little stiffly sibilant, and children in garments bought second hand of white people, who looked to Ben with the covertness of nocturnal animals (1101).

The old association between "negro" and "animal" is hazarded again, but with a very different ideological emphasis. The generic nocturnal animality here does not fix allegorical relations between species and "race," but fashions a link between bodies and landscape. This is a milieu to which Benjy's lumbering infancy is neither native nor alien.

I take it that the voice of this final chapter is issued in some stylistic and spiritual affinity with the ethos-cum-epos of this pedestrian chronotope, whose effective distillation is that telltale subject-predicate of the "Appendix": "They endured" (1141). That is, it is meant to stand, not as the "realist" corrective to the three preceding exercises in psychological immanence, but as an immanence all its own—an immanence of black folk who endure on roadways and in small cabins and weathered churches; the skeletal remains of the vanished Greek epos itself in an age of alienation and modernity, of motorcars and telephones and ticker tape. "As for the community," writes Lukács, "it is an organic—and therefore intrinsically meaningful—concrete totality": such pretension is exposed to ironic comeuppance in the satire of the church service itself, to be sure, where the community consumes its own mock-epic verbosity with a well-nigh gustatory fervor—"Mmmmmmmmmmmmmmmm!" (1105)—but it is the closest this novel will come to affirming a "basis" in any ethical substance whatever. The dynamic tension between realism and romance that frames the schematic narrative and stylistic ups and downs of the previous novel is displaced in *The Sound and the Fury* by an unsuspected late affirmation of the "normative childlikeness of the epic" as against its host-form's resignation to some ultimate "refusal of the immanence of being to enter into empirical life."[48] The communal trek to Easter Sunday service supplies something hitherto missing from Faulkner's art, a value not entirely vitiated by the stage theatrics that reduce Dilsey to unstoppable tears: namely, a yardstick against which to measure the decline of those avatars of the older romance chronotopes, the Compsons and Sartorises. In a sense, this allows his novel to escape the simple opposition between romance and realism, and commit his form to appearing as "something in process of becoming"[49]— four chapters undertaking to tell the same story, each inadequately.

At any rate, we can now make out the emergence of a distinctive chronotopic cartography in this work, the upper and lower extremes of whose scale are, respectively, the futuristic flatness of Benjy's abstract flowing "bright shapes"

---

[48] Lukács, *Theory of the Novel*, 71.
[49] Lukács, *Theory of the Novel*, 73.

glimpsed from an anachronistic ruling-class carriage, and the annual communitarian sigh of the oppressed as they make their way on foot over dirt roads to partake of the "opium of the masses." At one end, then, the absence of any landscape whatever, an autistic distillation of movement into sheer image ("percept"); and at the other, landscape as the canvas of the life of the folk, where what moves remains perdurably still. We need, first of all, to "emplot" this emergent cartography onto Faulkner's crystallizing sense of topography; and, second and third, to allow the two remaining chapters—Quentin's and Jason's—to fill in the middle ground, which, we shall see, is characterized by the temporalities and spatial disjunctions of mass and motorized transportation.

While the Yoknapatawpha map that Faulkner drew up as "sole owner and proprietor" in 1936 (Fig. 2.1) to accompany his next novel about Quentin Compson may not yet have been committed to paper, my sense is that by 1929 the essential contours were in place: bordered to north and south by parallel rivers, and nestled among the pine hills, Jefferson is situated alongside the perfect longitudinal stroke of the Sartoris railway line (already such a pregnant symbol in *Flags*—north to Memphis, south to Mottstown), and bisected by two utterly straight grid-line roads, at perfect right angles, off each of which other straight roads branch diagonally northwest (to Sutpen's Hundred), northeast (to McCallum's), and southeast (to Frenchman's Bend). We can leave to others the relations that may have existed between this map and the Oxford in which Faulkner dwelt.[50] What detains us here is its cartographic tension between the natural, erratic lines describing the contours of the hills, or the course of the "branch" that runs by the Compson house down to the Yoknapatawpha River, and the rigidly ruled lines that demarcate the road- and railways that open up this region to elsewhere. This graphic overlay of abstract grid-lines upon a topography given to curves and bends is an allegorical illustration of how transportation networks and channels function as "media": quartering the area, and disposing it along vectors that displace it from itself, opening it to the tides of immigration, emigration, trade, and communication that characterize capitalist modernity. "Durn that road," as Anse Bundren will complain, "keeping the folks restless and wanting to get up and go somewheres else when He aimed for them to stay put like a tree or a stand of corn."[51] Such fateful modifications of the lived environment "literally drag human beings out of the local dimension," writes Franco Moretti, "and throw them into a much larger one."[52] Any concrete "place" caught in the

---

[50] See in particular Calvin S. Brown, "Faulkner's Geography and Topography," *PMLA* 77.5 (December 1962), 652–59; and Charles S. Aiken, *William Faulkner and the Southern Landscape* (Athens, GA & London: University of Georgia Press, 2009).

[51] Faulkner, *As I Lay Dying*, in *Novels 1930–1935*, 24.

[52] Franco Moretti, *Atlas of the European Novel: 1800–1900* (London & New York: Verso, 1998), 17.

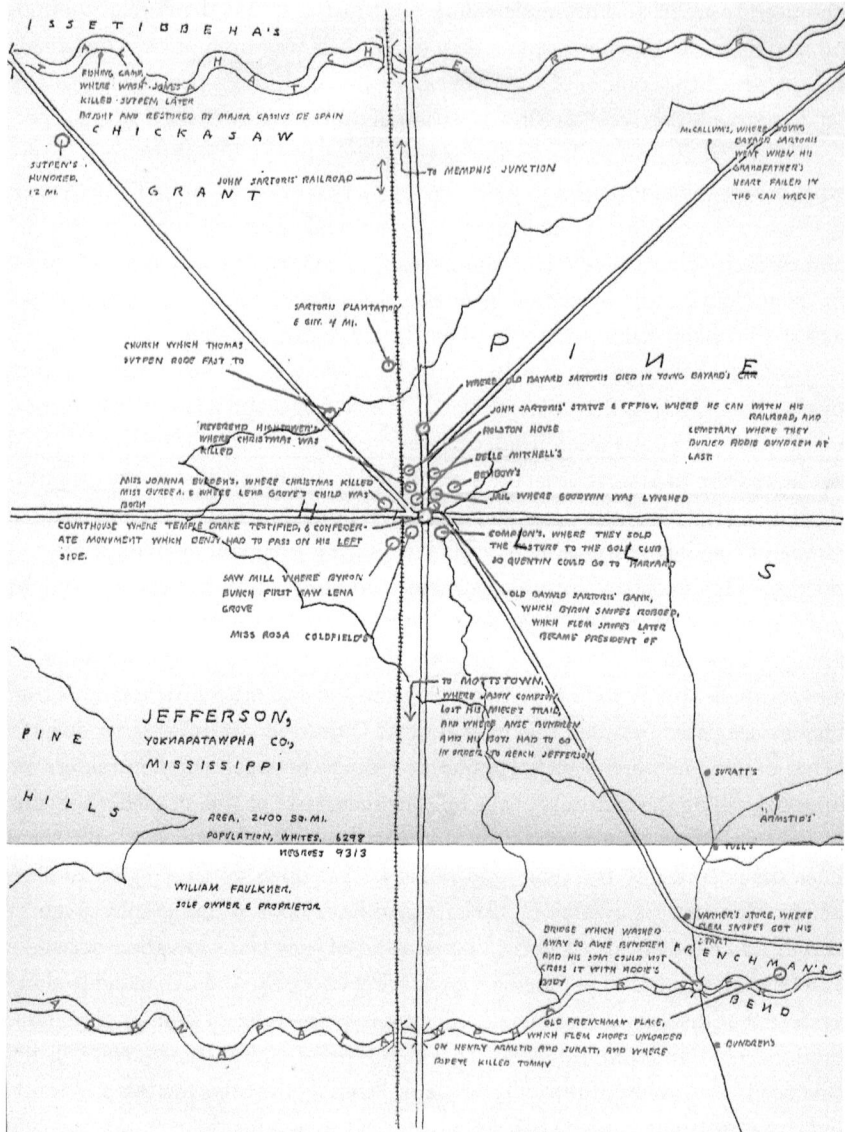

Figure 2.1 Faulkner's Map of Yoknapatawpha in 1st edition of *Absalom, Absalom!* (1936).

new national matrix of roads and railways is always and already caught in the act of becoming mere abstract "space."

What Henri Lefebvre called "representational space"—a shared, imaginary investment in the long-term inhabitation of a place—amounts to a collective symbolic appropriation of the physical environment: its transformation into local stories, memories, legends, forbidden districts, sacred places, and passionate *loci*. On the other hand, what Levebvre calls "representations of space" are those abstract projections onto real places of the rationalizing visions of planners, modelers, and architects, such that clear lines of bourgeois intellectual and economic force are driven through the dark mazes of archaic and popular representational space, much as Haussmann's boulevards finally broke apart medieval Paris.[53] My point in rehearsing these political tensions in Lefebvre's account of the production of space is to draw attention to the ways in which Faulkner's "map" of Jefferson (already implicit in *The Sound and the Fury*) dramatizes these tensions, in those violent verticals and horizontals that slash into the landscape as open-ended conduits to "America." These straight lines doubly mediate the regional locality: transmitting its messages out, and receiving others in; but by doing so, they sap the inherited richness of its representational space and flood it with imported symbolic values. Lefebvre's third conceptual category for the production of space is for us perhaps the critical one: *spatial practice*, or what I am going to call, in the literary register, the chronotope itself. For in the accumulated tensions between inherited, phenomenological, and passional investments in social space, and the slash and burn of abstract rationalization, inhabitants are still obliged to make practical sense of their world, displaying variable degrees of "competence" in distinct types of "spatial performance" as they thread it together into passable versions of coherence and collectively reproduce their environment.[54] Narrative fiction distils such everyday performances into chronotopes, and we have already glimpsed two extreme chronotopic practices that bring the prevailing antinomies of Jeffersonian space, circa 1928, into some semblance of order: Benjy's weekly absorption in a "percept" that is as close as humanly possible to purely abstract, capitalist "representations of space"; and a *black epic* pedestrianism that clings to what abstraction has left in its wake: immemorial communitarian bonds, a landscape of dust and loss, "flat and without perspective as a painted cardboard set upon the ultimate edge of the flat earth" (1102)—a traditional "representational space" suddenly exposed as flyweight and threadbare, but allied with a spatial practice that shapes the environment itself: "The earth immediately about the door was bare. It had a patina, as though from the soles of bare feet in generations, like old silver or the walls of Mexican houses which have been plastered by hand." (1081).

Faulkner draws his novelistic map of Yoknapatawpha by way of overlapping, discontinuous, and sometimes flatly contradictory chronotopes that correspond to distinct modalities of spatial practice in a lived environment going through prodigious changes—whose most distinctive signatures are the strong lines

---

[53] See Henri Lefebvre, *The Production of Space*, trans. Donald Nicholson-Smith (Oxford: Blackwell, 1992).

[54] Lefebvre, *Production of Space*, 33.

impressed like gridwork on his literal "map" of 1936. One way of conceiving the aesthetic breakthrough of *The Sound and the Fury* relative to its predecessor, then, is to appreciate the relative density, variety, and complexity of the chronotopes it puts into play to tell precisely the same underlying story of the "decline of an old Jefferson family." The essentially binary structure of *Flags*, with its monstrous grey areas and hybridities, is replaced by a fourfold chronotopic composition in depth, whose other and more potent modalities we must now turn to consider—but not before a necessary glimpse at the larger map this novel wants to draw (Fig. 2.2).

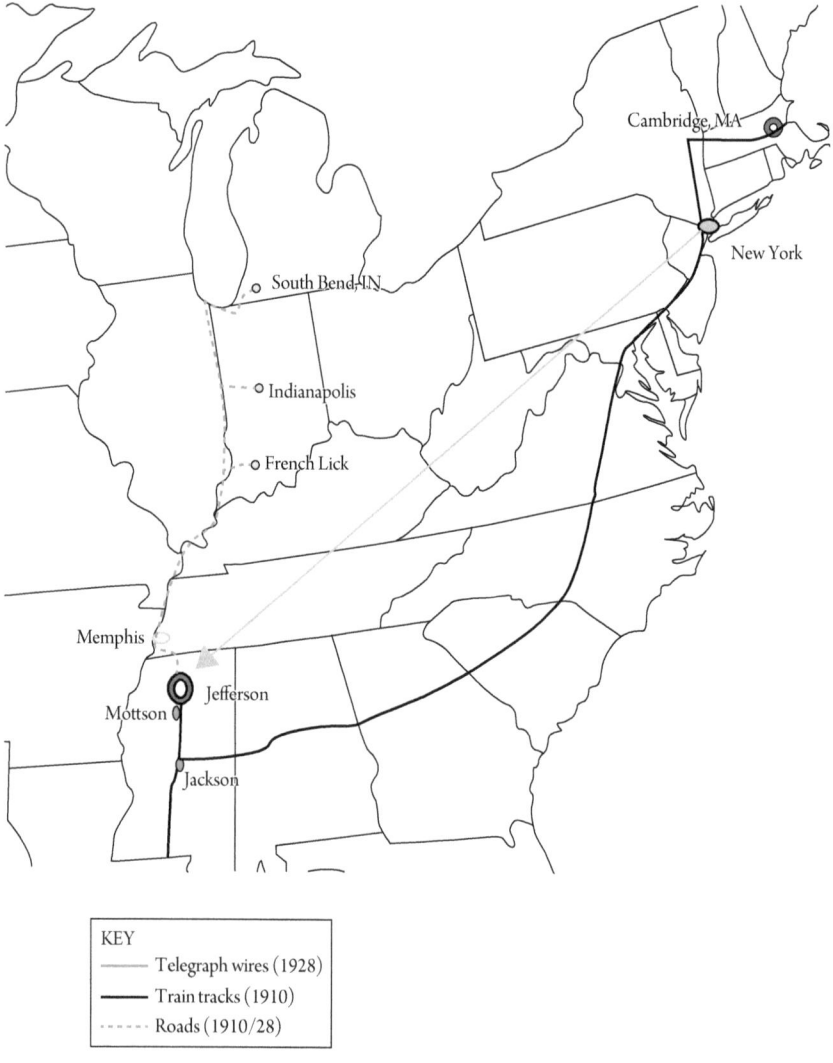

Figure 2.2 Spatial Dynamics in *The Sound and the Fury*.

If *Flags* had sought, along with so many novels of its moment, to situate its local dramas alongside the geopolitical catastrophe of the Great War, and through the recollections of Bayard and Caspey correlate the chronotopes of the region with the mechanized movements of the European front, then *The Sound and the Fury* is animated by a more ambitious *national* cartography. To be sure, French Lick, Indianapolis, and South Bend, Indiana, have only the most cursory of registrations, Jackson is the hovering institutional threat for Benjy (as it will be for Darl Bundren), Memphis is where Lorraine writes (but doesn't telephone) from and where Jason is occasionally "one of the boys" (1025), Virginia is passed through on a train, and New York is a mythic cesspit of "dam eastern jews" (1023)—none is represented spatially other than as a projection of Jeffersonian frustration. But this does not hold for the environs of Harvard University, where, as we are about to see, Faulkner takes up the descriptive impulse again in such a way as to create genuine chronotopic interference with the hometown's cartography.

Streetcar romance

Quentin Compson's last day alive is one of literature's more extraordinary for the sheer amount of movement it requires of him. Doubtless, Bloom's day ranks higher still (and there are many formal echoes of that Odyssean wanderer, not to mention his Telemachian shadow, in "June Second, 1910"), but it is often forgotten quite how exorbitant, in his fateful quest for the sublime stasis of "peaceful grottoes" (963), is Quentin's restless chronotope of perpetual motion. We forget it, thanks to the obsessively distracted nature of his ruminations on the recent past, though these, too, are "cut up" and jumbled together with a savage associationist logic that often seems closer to the atemporal suggestibility of his youngest brother (if not the stop/start nature of his frankly weird spatial trajectory itself) than to the measured transitions of his Dublin prototype. However absorbed Quentin may be in the deluge of memory occasioned by his approaching suicide, he nonetheless participates as an expert in one of modernity's more complex and demanding spatial practices, circa 1910: namely, the extensive and state-of-the-art network of trolley and interurban electric streetcar lines that threaded together the greater Boston metropolitan area. This was not simply a matter of spatial practices, trolley schedules, and the reproduction of daily life—it was the determining factor in a total transformation of Boston as a city, specifically its reification into unprecedented "rings" of suburbanization, made possible by the first mass transportation technology of the new century. While horse-drawn trolleys had served the area since the 1850s, as well as the increasingly hated steam trains, it was the rapid introduction of electrified street transportation at the end of the nineteenth century that changed the city beyond recognition:

> In the late 1880's and 1890's the electrification of street railways brought convenient transportation to at least the range of six miles from City Hall [in Boston]. The rate of building and settlement in this period became so rapid that the whole scale and plan of Greater Boston was entirely made over.[55]

The spread of middle-class affluence out to the aerated green rings and away from the industrialized core, and the concentration of working-class (and immigrant) populations nearer the old city centers, was typical of the transformed production of urban space at this time, thanks to the cheap and regular flow of electric streetcar traffic along lines embedded in roads no longer soiled by hundreds of tons of horse manure or spoiled by the choking fumes and noise of trains. This history was decisive for installing the logic of architectural reproducibility that Faulkner had already decried in *Flags*, apropos of the identikit housing of Kitson. The remarkable conformity of tens of thousands of new houses built in the Greater Boston area in the first decade of the twentieth century, to accommodate the population explosion from 200,000 to over a million in under fifty years, sprang from what Saul Bass Warner calls a "consensus of attitude" and "uniformity of behaviour" among the resituating middle class that "encouraged each man to seek and to perpetuate the new suburban environment which emphasized the pleasures of private family life, the security of a small community setting, and the enjoyments of an increased contact with nature" (153, 154).

Quentin Compson spends the greater part of his last day, then, behaving much like a new middle-class suburbanite on the weekend, taking to the tracks to distance himself from the scene of his own "industry" and take in the sights and smells of the domesticated natural environment where, hypothetically, his new shingled, three-bedroom home might stand, looking "much like those of his neighbours" (154)—in a prefiguration of that "row after row of small crowded jerrybuilt individuallyowned demiurban bungalows" that will ultimately engulf Jefferson itself.[56] Except, of course, he finds no such thing. Rather, as he pursues the outer reaches of the Greater Boston streetcar system, traversing and re-traversing the Charles River that will claim him that night, he is seeking, not suburbia, but its antithesis: a chronotope for the expression of his most

---

[55] Saul Bass Warner, *Streetcar Suburbs: The Process of Growth in Boston (1870–1900)*, 2nd ed. (Cambridge, MA: Harvard University Press, 1978), 22.

[56] Faulkner, "COMPSON 1699–1945," in David Minter, ed., *The Sound and the Fury* (New York: W. W. Norton & Co., 1994), 207.

important textual function, namely, romance. Here we face an extraordinary paradox: Faulkner has so orchestrated the elements of his fiction that it requires a complicated series of trolley and interurban car-rides around the academic bastion of Yankee supremacy to trigger the release of the Southern romantic imagination in full dress. And here, too, we need to distinguish between the trolley and the interurban as bearers of distinct chronotopic possibility for this discharge of accumulated romantic energy, a distinction that explains Quentin's curious insistence on this score. In one of the more baffling of his many exchanges, Quentin has just missed a car at the interurban stop and is unsure if another will come before noon; rather than wait emptily, however, he boards the first car that comes along, "another trolley," purely for the sake of maintaining his reverie: "Father said a man is the sum of his misfortunes," "You carry the symbol of your frustration into eternity," and so on (956, 957). But the experience is dissatisfying. "I could hear my watch whenever the car stopped, but not often they were already eating"; the lunch rush has abated, noon presides, and the flood of romance signifiers has dried up. So, "I got off and stood in my shadow and after a while a car came along and I got on and went back to the interurban station. There was a car ready to leave, and I found a seat next to the window and it started." The reverie can proceed at its proper pace and in its wonted density of associations (957), allowing Quentin to revert to the "half-baked Galahad" (961) of his interview with Sidney Head.

There is a good materialist reason for preferring the interurban over the open and relatively noisy trolley cars. Heavier and enclosed, the interurbans moved with greater speed and less canting, sliding down the center of the street in town, and then shifting to curbside for uninterrupted progress in their own right of way into the hinterlands, "without the soot, smoke, or noise of the steam railroads. To the consumer, the idea was itself electric: while interurbans travelled at two-thirds the speed of the hated railroads, they ran four to six times more frequently at half to two-thirds the fare."[57] Such electric movement, drawing its motility from neither the combustion nor the steam engine but from the city grid itself, catalyzed the capacity for commuter daydreaming like no other mode of transportation. The interurban had perfected what was already intrinsic to the trolley itself: "Trolley cars travel fast enough to produce a feeling of mental exhilaration, which is absent from or scarcely felt by passengers in horsecars." Or, as one Kentucky M.D. put it, a two-hour ride on the front seat of an open trolleycar was "the best possible cure for insomnia."[58] The unique attribute of electrified mass transport was its ability to induce a "straphanger" state of mind, belonging to neither the domestic nor industrial world, but projected

---

[57] Stephen B. Goddard, *Getting There: The Epic Struggle Between Road and Rail in the American Century* (Chicago: University of Chicago Press, 1994), 76.

[58] William D. Middleton, *The Time of the Trolley* (Waukesha, WI.: Kalmbach, 1967), 86.

inward from the extraordinary "position of having to stare at one another for minutes or even hours on end without exchanging a word," as Georg Simmel phrased it[59]—apart from the occasional "pardon me" of your neighbor wanting to alight (945).

The electric streetcar is arguably the privileged vehicle of its moment (1910 is its heyday) for the generation of affect as such: "an eternal present, [...] an element which is somehow self-sufficient, feeding on itself and perpetuating its own existence."[60] The straphanger commute, delivered over by the power of electricity to what John Dewey called an "intermediate state of existence" between the domestic and the industrial/commercial, is an atemporal breeding-ground for involuntary memories that flood the body with sudden surges of intensity.[61] Thus Quentin can use it to spin the most prodigious web of romance discourse in the novel, a discourse whose unstable grounding in shattering affects is impossible to ignore. And it is truly as if he seeks this electrical motion in order to facilitate the flow of that discourse, literally tapping into the power grid to yield a language and a scenography that, while it may be "native" to the Mississippi from which he hails, can find no better habitat on the pages of this novel than on board the Massachusetts interurbans. Romance affectivity is thus intimately allied with a spatial practice that Jefferson itself cannot afford, in 1910 or 1928: mass public transport. The Mississippi novelist, chastened by recent censure and criticism from his publisher, and inextricably tangled in the coils of a romance mythos that he can neither repudiate nor ignore, finds an outlet for that mythos where he can, and abandons his "half-baked Galahad" to it so that he can discharge his debt to the form, doubly displaced from its local habitat. It is an ingenious solution, masking the inauthentic "Southern" romance materials behind the technological form of a northeastern transport system; moreover, one that has the added benefit of allowing for the revival of a sternly repressed descriptive impulse, yielding an uncanny topographic palimpsest between Jefferson and the environs of Cambridge that is loaded with subliminal political significances.

Deposited at a distant stop near the bridge where he will welcome Little Sister Death, Quentin becomes increasingly observant of his surroundings, but in such a way that the interfusion of two times and spaces is foregrounded: "The road went into trees, where it would be shady, but June foliage in New England not much thicker than April at home. I could see a smoke stack" (962). At the far end of the interurban route, then, is the synecdoche of industry (it is Bigelow's

---

[59] Quoted in Walter Benjamin, *Illuminations*, ed. Hannah Arendt, trans. Harry Zohn (New York: Schocken Books, 1968), 191.

[60] Fredric Jameson, *Antinomies of Realism*, 36.

[61] Quoted in Werner Sollors, *Ethnic Modernism* (Cambridge, MA: Harvard University Press, 2008), 36.

mill, whose workforce is largely Italian), but also the spatial superposition of Massachusetts upon Mississippi. That complex chronotope persists during his desultory walk: "Some days in late August at home are like this, the air thin and eager like this, with something in it sad and nostalgic and familiar. Man the sum of his climatic experiences Father said. Man the sum of what have you. A problem in impure properties carried tediously to an unvarying nil: stalemate of dust and desire" (971–72). A line misremembered from *Hamlet* allows for a paternal "hauntology," a revenance of the "impure properties" of Southern gothic within the Northern light-industrial zone, carried by the medium of "dust and desire." It is here that Quentin, and we with him, can "in the descriptive element immerse." The prose luxuriates in a descriptive function elsewhere stymied and suppressed (as Michael Millgate puts it, "Quentin, in his section, is intensely aware, with the heightened sensitivity of a man about to die, of the countryside through which he walks"[62]):

> The road curved, mounting away from the water. It crossed the hill, then descended winding, carrying the eye, the mind on ahead beneath a still green tunnel, and the square cupola above the trees and the round eye of the clock but far enough. I sat down on the roadside. The grass was ankle deep, myriad. The shadows on the road were as still as if they had been put there with a stencil, with slanting pencils of sunlight. (969)
>
> We went on in the dappled shade. We came to an orchard, pink and white. It was full of bees; already we could hear them. [. . .] In the orchard the bees sounded like a wind getting up, a sound caught by a spell just under crescendo and sustained. The lane went along the wall, arched over, shattered with bloom, dissolving into trees. Sunlight slanted into it, sparse and eager. Yellow butterflies flickered along the shade like flecks of sun. (970)

Such aestheticism, pre-Raphaelite in its precosity and Impressionist in its manner, suggests a decadence that fixes Quentin's embrace of non-being as a psychic retreat into the ideal springtime of his youth. This vision is the pastoral antithesis of the dusty wasteland of "foul desiccation" in the final chapter, but the revived function of description has been hijacked by a sophomoric romanticism that will not relent until the world itself stops with it. Unsurprisingly, then, this sensitive registering apparatus, stranded between two space-times, alights upon a conspicuous anachronism: "The buggy was drawn by a white horse, his feet clopping in the thin dust; spidery wheels chattering thin and dry, moving uphill beneath a rippling shawl of leaves. [. . .] The wheels were spidery. Beneath the sag

---

[62] Michael Millgate, *The Achievement of William Faulkner* (New York: Random House, 1966), 97.

of the buggy the hooves neatly rapid like the motions of a lady doing embroidery, diminishing without progress like a figure on a treadmill being drawn rapidly offstage" (972). The arch-Faulknerian Mississippi chronotope of the surrey moving "without progress" achieves its eternal return via the extraordinary spatial saturation of the present by the past, the North by the South, in a double vision precipitated by a long, hypnagogic journey out on an electric streetcar.

Beneath this palimpsest lies a transaction. We are never allowed to forget that Quentin's time in Harvard is bought and paid for by the liquidation of Benjy's pasture, itself the penultimate shard of the original square mile of the Compson Domain, as the narrator of the "Appendix" will tell us: the "last of the property" sold "to a golf club for the ready money with which his [Jason III's] daughter Candace could have her fine wedding in April and his son Quentin could finish one year at Harvard and commit suicide the following June of 1910" (1131). Quentin frames it to himself repeatedly, this debt: his every experience and perception a guilty conjuration of that last, lost "postage stamp" of native Domain, the birthright of his youngest sibling. Which is doubtless why these two regions are, for him, in such a state of undecidable affective flux, to the extent that to take a walk in one is simultaneously to pass through the other, June becoming April, orchard pinks becoming the odoriferous blooms of honeysuckle, and a nameless Italian girl transmogrifying into the muddy-bottomed sister of his most poignant memory.

However, it takes an entirely new chronotope to instigate the moment of actual rupture in the delicate psychological membrane between these two orders of the real, between the trauma of his sister's sexuality and that of his impending self-destruction. Specifically, it takes the supreme unlikelihood, the romance "encounter," of his accidental meeting with the picnic party and their class-based absorption of him into an unrelated pleasure-seeking trajectory, to efface the border between past and present, to shatter the screen through which he has been passing back and forth ever since the streetcar had weakened it. In particular, it takes his embarkation upon that other mode of transportation, the motorcar. The Blands' car has been introduced already as an object for speculation and sarcastic comment on the journey out; it sits ominously before the drug store of the town where Quentin is arrested, "an auto, a big one" (985); but it is only once he steps aboard and submits to the onward rush of the engine that Quentin finds the edifice of narrative space-time crumbling into lacerating shards of affectivity. First revising his recent pedestrian experiences with a series of now familiar views—"We drove down the street and crossed the bridge and passed the house where the pink garment hung in the window. [...] We passed that house, and three others, and another yard where the little girl stood by the gate" (989)—the automobile then thrusts Quentin out of time altogether:

> Then we ran beside the wall, our shadows running along the wall, and after a while we passed a piece of torn newspaper lying beside the road

and I began to laugh again. I could feel it in my throat and I looked off into the trees where the afternoon slanted, thinking of afternoon and of the bird and the boys in swimming. But still I couldn't stop it and then I knew that if I tried too hard to stop I'd be crying and I thought about how I'd thought about I could not be a virgin. (989–90)

While his fellow passengers try to restrain him within the boundaries of commonsensical "reality," the affect lodged in Quentin's throat is simply too powerful a counterweight, dragging him irresistibly into the eternal present of his greatest emotional crisis, which intrudes first as a "slanting" italic mode of textual interruption, and then simply obliterates the perceptual coordinates of the Massachusetts scene. The immensely charged passage that follows, from which Quentin is jolted only by the force of Gerald Bland's fists, is an automobile flashback, unprotected by the relatively decorous intersubjective constraints of his travels on public transport, driven into sheer inwardness by the force of the vehicle's aggressively private and antisocial mode of operation. While many contemporary novels featured scenes of high-speed collisions and deaths on the road, to register their ethical complaints against the motorcar's erosion of social boundaries, Faulkner's 1929 novel prefers, in this chapter, to engineer an emotional accident that catapults its central subject into a collision with his most excruciating kernel of affective pain. Yet again, however, the deeper formal concern is with technological displacement and ideological masking. For the scene between Caddy and Quentin, the violent struggle over her virginity and his sense of honor, is strictly unwritable on its own terms, so nearly does it threaten to ravel out into melodrama and puerility; what prevents this perilous hemorrhage is the scene's mounting from within the backseat of a motorcar. Romance is reframed and relativized by the combustion engine, whose bodily affects in 1910 have no known catalogue, no named dimensions of their own, but must take refuge in reference points peculiar to each subjective pathology.

This is a significant improvement over Faulkner's earlier, simple apportioning of sheer terror to the blacks and women who accompany Bayard on his reckless automobile tours around Yoknapatawpha; as an affective discharge, the scream is without any real aesthetic dimension beyond its immediate bodily seizure and is subject to a law of diminishing returns. Reversing the polarities, Faulkner now permits a nameless affective surcharge to claim the body in such a way that he can use it as cover to acquit his narrative's deepest debt to the romantic imagination, which the automobile had hitherto precisely negated and routed. (In much the same way, he used Benjy's surrey ride to embody an aesthetic "futurism" or abstraction hitherto associated with the motorcar itself.) Moreover, he has allowed for this sudden ratcheting-up of Quentin's romance sensibilities by way of a transportational progression from streetcar to motorcar in the present: from a state of commuter distraction and alienation, permitting a more or less manageable flow of memory, to a fully privatized collapse of the phenomenological horizon, a withdrawal into "driven" phantasmatic plenitude. This coded cognitive map of the transport infrastructure of America, as Quentin is obliged to inhabit it in 1910—describing a stark difference, if not quite an antagonism, between streetcar systems and private motorcars—is profoundly historical and will be played out in another key in the next chapter as well, where the automobile again precipitates the most calamitous episodes of psychotic foreclosure.

The thirty thousand miles of tracks and $3 billion sunk in the electric railways in the USA by 1910 were facing an inevitable crisis whose most tangible form was the automobile itself. Inflation, unionization of the workforce, a decline in the immigration that fueled that workforce, chronic overcrowding at peak hours, and the constant cry for more tracks, all led to net capital investment in street railways peaking by 1905 (after fifteen years of unparalleled boom), to gross capital expenditure on these systems declining after 1907, and to an irreversible pattern of net disinvestment established by the outbreak of the Great War.[63] The credit industry and petro-capital were ready to strike:

> The tax deductibility of interest fuelled the growth and development of the commercial lending industry in the 1920s, which provided the financing necessary to underwrite the growth of home and automobile ownership. Both contributed to the housing boom and the suburban growth that followed World War I. And with accelerating suburbanization, the automobile became a more essential feature of day-to-day life, displacing transit from its historical role as the primary provider of the transportation needed to support suburban development.[64]

This historical eclipse of street-level mass transit by the motorcar, and the consequent privatization of more and more public space, is a story of the rise of oil and of its combustible form, gasoline, in the national life. But it is a story with other markers and signposts as well, not least those affecting the physical form of the vehicle poised to crush electric streetcar systems across America: "electric starters (1911), shock absorbers (1920), balloon tires (1922), the all-steel closed body (1923), power-operated windshield wipers (1923), bumpers as standard equipment (1925), and car heating (1926)"[65]—dates that fall perfectly between Quentin's chapter and Jason's, and which spell out the inevitable fact that the automobile had been thoroughly domesticated, from the open-body touring

---

[63] David W. Jones, *Mass Motorization and Mass Transit: An American History and Policy Analysis* (Bloomington, IN & Indianapolis: Indiana University Press, 2008), 33.

[64] Jones, *Mass Motorization*, 37.

[65] Jones, *Mass Motorization*, 46.

machine it was for Mrs. Bland, by the time that other Quentin jumps into the shotgun seat of a Ford car in 1928.

It is therefore no accident that, having retraced by interurban and trolley car the many miles to his Harvard room to change before committing himself to the depths, Quentin should there attempt to clean his bloodied vest with some of Shreve's supply of gasoline. The moment is critical, because it allows him to prefigure in telescopic form his brother's crippling olfactory affect, and associate it in memory with perhaps the most significant detail of Candace's courtship by and wedding to Sydney Herbert Head: "*the first car in town a girl Girl that's what Jason couldn't bear smell of gasoline making him sick then got madder than ever because a girl Girl had no sister but Benjamin Benjamin the child of my sorrowful if I'd just had a mother so I could say Mother Mother*" (1009). This collage of snippets from the long series of reveries from June Second, 1910, condenses the sequence:

> Quentin this is Herbert. My Harvard boy. Herbert will be a big brother has already promised Jason
> [. . .] *You going to drive?*
> Get in Quentin.
> *You going to drive.*
> It's her car aren't you proud of your little sister owns first auto in town Herbert his present, Louis has been giving her lessons every morning didn't you get my letter . . . At home after the first of August number Something Something Avenue South Bend Indiana
> [. . .]
> Country people poor things they *never saw an auto before* lots of them honk the horn Candace so *She wouldn't look at me* they'll get out of the way *wouldn't look at me* your father wouldn't like it if you were to injure one of them I'll declare your father will simply have to get an auto now I'm almost sorry you brought it down Herbert I've enjoyed it so much of course there's the carriage but so often when I'd like to go out Mr Compson has the darkies doing something it would be worth my head to interrupt. (948–49)

This is followed by recollections of Herbert flirting with Mrs. Compson, assuring her that the car ride has "done [her] no end of good dont you think so Quentin" and threatening to elope with her rather than Caddy in his vehicle, "I dont think Mr Compson could overtake the car" (949). Quentin's first ride in an automobile is thus the occasion on which he definitively loses his sister, not to the stock melodramatic seducer Dalton Ames, but to the vulgar Indiana man who gives her "the first auto in town" and so not only irredeemably associates her with what Old Bayard Sartoris had called "paupers" but alienates her once and for all from a Southern family still reliant for conveyance upon a carriage and all the outmoded gentility that goes with it. But her mother, Bascomb to the last, is susceptible to the siren call of the combustion engine. It is she, who will have "enjoyed it so much," who whisks Caddy off to French Lick to find a suitable bachelor for her spoiled daughter, and who settles on the car-enthusiast banker who, not pausing to look this gift horse in the mouth, will drive her away, quite literally, from the Compson Domain for good and all. And Caroline Compson will always have been the one who, at a discount, bought her that particular ticket to ride.

Quentin's tickets are all for trolleys and interurbans. His predisposition toward the one mode of transport doomed, like himself, to virtual extinction by the progress of capital in the early twentieth century marks him out as already, by 1929 when the book was released, a magnet for anachronism. Werner Sollors was more right than he knew to declare that "electric streetcars, once a prime symbol of modernity, have now assumed an aura of nostalgic quaintness after their literal disappearance from most American cities"[66]—for the fact is that by the time of the Wall Street crash, this "aura" was already fatally associated with the lines and cars that would almost all be torn from the fabric of the American city within a decade. *The Sound and the Fury* grasps this immanent nostalgia-effect of electric transit with extraordinary exactitude, and delivers it over to the character in the book most fatefully marked by the death instinct, eighteen years prior to the book's three other chapters. Unable to find a suitable material basis for his callow romanticism in the land of its origin (always already marked by the trauma of that "first car in town," and by the fruitless reactionary cynicism of the *nom du père*), Quentin discovers it instead with the well-dressed "nigger" and the woman with the hat and its "broken feather" (1007) who partake in the anonymous, and doomed, collective ritual of mass transit around Cambridge. But the remarkable thing about the streetcars as he rides them is the way the mode of perception stimulated by their chronotope feeds into and out of the stream of romance fantasy and memory it simultaneously promotes. For Quentin, the streetcar yields a truly extraordinary phenomenological intensity, of which there is no better example than in his return trip to Harvard in the evening. Here, indeed, the streetcar becomes an unparalleled affect-delivery machine:

> when we ran out of the trees I could see the twilight again, that quality of light as if time really had stopped for a while, with the sun hanging just under the horizon, and then we passed the marquee where the old man had been eating out of the sack, and the road going on under the

[66] Sollors, *Ethnic Modernism*, 36.

twilight, into twilight and the sense of water peaceful and swift beyond. Then the car went on, the draft building steadily up in the open door until it was drawing steadily through the car with the odor of summer and darkness except honeysuckle. Honeysuckle was the saddest odor of all, I think. (1007)

The olfactory note, once sounded, can spread to colonize the other senses: "The draft in the door smelled of water, a damp steady breath. [. . .] I could smell the curves of the river bend the dust and I saw the last light supine and tranquil upon the tideflats like pieces of broken mirror, then beyond them lights began in the pale clean air, trembling a little like butterflies hovering a long way off" (1007–08). The exquisite aestheticism recalled by the image of butterflies, catalyzed now by the steady propulsion of the car and the imminent embrace of the "water peaceful and swift," transmogrifies the shattered narrative world into pellets of pure bodily intensity. It is thus perfectly right that the last, and properly immortal, affect that Quentin Compson conjures out of this disastrous day should involve the projection of an aesthetic encounter upon his imminent return streetcar voyage to the appointed place. With Shreve's gasoline still rank in his nostrils, he envisages a nocturnal anagnorisis, freighted with the most melancholy pathos, between him and his roommate seated on two cars passing in opposite directions:

> *seeing on the rushing darkness only his own face no broken feather unless two of them but not two like that going to Boston the same night then my face his face for an instant across the crashing when out of the darkness two lighted windows in rigid fleeing crash gone his face and mine just I see saw did I see not goodbye the marquee empty of eating the road empty in darkness in silence the bridge arching into silence darkness sleep the water peaceful and swift not goodbye* (1009)

Apart from anything else, this is the most haunting and eloquent "streetcar affect" in all of American literature: the momentary apparition of a friendly face superimposed upon one's own reflected face in a lit car at night, from an interurban passing the other way, as one heads inexorably to the doom that even the friend's sudden realization can now, given track schedules and the speed of events, do nothing to prevent. The wonder is that it doesn't even *happen*, this super-charged anagnorisis, but arises spontaneously as an aesthetic reflux from the sheer amount of transit, the many miles clocked by a body on at least nine cars during the day. It is as if the stream of romance narrativity and the stream of sense perception have finally coalesced into a perfect current of virtual experience with nowhere to go but the ultimate terminus. Quentin's attaining this moment is perhaps his greatest achievement, a brilliant literary flare sent up over the dark night of an automobile future from the last streetcar on earth.

Jason's headache

Jason Compson, incapable of his brother's transitory epiphanies, travels a comparable number of miles on April 6, 1928, not by streetcar, but by motorcar. A champion of modern citizenship and of the level of material civilization that underwrites it, he sneers at the wasted expense of maintaining a horse and carriage and purloins his mother's investment in the hardware store where he works to purchase the vehicle that best represents his sense of that citizenship: "a thousand dollars' worth of delicate machinery" (1058), of which he is the first to admit that he "thinks too much"—"I'm not going to hammer it to pieces like it was a ford" (1060). At the same time, he speculates on cotton futures and so participates in that new and abstract, telematic citizenship of the stock market, despite his many justified misgivings about the regional tectonics and unevenness that compromise the promised freedom and equality of that national sense of belonging. In both these respects, he is a relatively beaten-down version of *Flags in the Dust*'s Harry Mitchell, a known cotton speculator (696) who identifies more with the gleaming new car in his garage than with the family disintegrating around him. Jason's spontaneous affinity with the petroleum economy is, however, ironically undercut by his seemingly genetic intolerance for the smell of gasoline itself: "*Jason couldn't bear smell of gasoline making him sick*," Quentin muses. As this Good Friday tightens around Jason's neck in coils of stress and road mileage, his mother is the one to make explicit the correlation between the cephalalgia already livid on his face by mid-afternoon and the number of trips between store and home that he has made:

> "What's the car got to do with it?" I says. "How can a car give a man a headache?"
> "You know gasoline always made you sick," she says. "Ever since you were a child. I wish you'd take some asprin." (1060)

In this section, we will ask some pointed questions about this disavowed link between distilled petroleum and Jason's headaches, and the consequent dissociation internal to his abstract sense of "being modern" in America. Specifically, we will want to know what this entails for the cognitive mapping undertaken in this chapter of *The Sound and the Fury*, the chronotope peculiar to it, and its contribution to the overall spatial architecture of the novel.

The various damages done by petroleum hydrocarbons to the human body, particularly lung damage and severe headaches, have been part of the standard literature on the topic since the beginning of the last century. The addition, in the early 1920s, of tetraethyl lead to the toxic chemical compound that fueled the U.S. automobile boom (leading, after several workers died at Standard Oil and DuPont plants, to the "leaded gas scare"), though it reduced the element of "engine knock" and improved performance, only enlarged the sensed potential for bodily harm lurking in the substance.[67] Jason Compson's problems, however, seem to date from the days of the heavier hydrocarbons, at the very end of the nineteenth century when he was still a child, well before the process of thermal cracking was developed by William Meriam Burton in 1913 to facilitate the mass production of Model T Fords on the assembly line at Highland Park. Both Quentin and his mother corroborate this deeper history of Jason's present illness, which therefore inevitably suggests some psychosomatic or aesthetic correlation between its origins and the storied vision of Caddy's "muddy drawers" in the pear tree which undergirds both Benjy's and Quentin's psychoses and tends, as well, to qualify that rather triumphalist description of Jason IV as the "first sane Compson since before Culloden" (1137). But whether or not the aversion to petroleum dates to the evening of Damuddy's death in 1898 when Jason is four years old—regardless, that is to say, of whether it clinches the origins of his olfactory affect in the quasi-incestuous *mise-en-scène* that simultaneously clinches Benjy's with trees and Quentin's with honeysuckle—we are thrust in any event outside the official history of the substance proper (which scarcely existed to develop symptoms toward, certainly not in commercial form, prior to 1905) and into its "crude" prehistory.

We may here recall how the narrator of the later "Appendix" insists on the petrochemical unconscious of the original transaction that granted the "solid square mile" of land to the "grandson of a Scottish refugee" who was the first Compson (1127)—a mutual obliviousness to the future economic value of what lies beneath bartered real estate, but which seems to have returned, deviously misplaced from its native Oklahoma, to the muddy banks of the river that snakes through the Compson Domain. There is, after all, something on the domain that seeps in crude viscosity from the pores of the earth, seeming, like toxic hydrocarbons, "to disintegrate into minute and venomous particles," "precipitating not so much a moisture as a substance partaking of the quality of thin, not quite congealed oil" (1081). Is it this crude precipitate, distilled out of the very ground itself, that permeates the mud Caddy sits in, so that young Jason,

---

[67] See http://www.nrdc.org/air/transportation/hleadgas.asp.

glancing upward at the viscid smear of it on her drawers, can then inhale it and plant the roots of his lifelong intolerance?

Quentin's repeated proprietary association of Caddy with the "*first auto in town*" is linked to Jason's gasoline sickness, and so to that younger brother's outrage that "a girl" should have usurped the supposedly masculine prerogative of motorcar ownership prior to his own seventeenth birthday. To quote the passage once more, "*the first car in town a girl Girl that's what Jason couldn't bear smell of gasoline making him sick then got madder than ever because a girl Girl*" (1009). What "Jason couldn't bear" is rendered helplessly ambivalent by the situation of that clause between two possible referents—his sister's ownership of Jefferson's first automobile, and the smell of gasoline itself, both of which, I insist, cannot be separated in the etiology of Jason's condition. The temporal loop described here implies a narrative retroactivity whereby the 1910 trauma precipitates its own germinal cause in a fantasized childhood from which gasoline would most likely have been completely absent. The event conditions its own causes; as Žižek writes, "A potentiality can be inserted into (or withdrawn from) past reality. Falling in love changes the past: it is as if I *always-already* loved you. . . . My present love causes the past which gave birth to it."[68] As it is with love, so it is with trauma. Jason has, from the moment that he realizes his own incestuous desire for Candace in the form of her 1910 touring car, a sickness for gasoline that dates back to his early childhood. It is the present position of her backside on the driver's seat of that most desirable of objects that retroactively "colours" it with a petroleum stain in 1898, such that he will *always-already* have found its smell intolerable. The sexual overtones are inescapable in the way the crass "gift" of this vehicle from Sydney Herbert Head to his sister dovetails with his "gift" to Jason of a banking job, on the promise of Caddy's fictive maidenhead; both recede to a vanishing point in Indiana, whence neither car nor job offer will be glimpsed again. Caddy's "stained" sex, first espied in 1898, will always have caused the ungovernable "stink" that motivates the retraction of these gifts—of "civilized" modernity itself—whose loss Jason can never forgive. Which means that for Jason to sit behind the wheel of an automobile in 1928 is to be drawn inexorably "back to the future" of his sister's shocking escape velocity, by motorcar, in 1910; it is to enter a psychological hall of mirrors, a labyrinth whose pungent Ariadne's thread is none other than the scent of gasoline itself.

Faulkner first introduces us to the cephalalgia that this smell induces in Jason in a scene that clearly rehearses the high stakes at play in his mediatic unconscious. Preparing to drive his niece to school, after noticing the spare tire unaffixed to the body of his vehicle, Jason accuses the girl, an offprint of his sister who bears his suicidal brother's name, of not looking "all the way naked"

---

[68] Slavoj Žižek, *Event*, Philosophy in Transit (London: Penguin, 2014), 111.

(1020); a quip that triggers a snowballing stichomythia and ends in Quentin's desperate efforts to rip the very clothes off her own back:

> Then I saw that she really was trying to tear it, to tear it right off her. By the time I got the car stopped and grabbed her hands there was about a dozen people looking. It made me so mad for a minute it kind of blinded me. (1021)

The idling engine and its implied odor, the genetic shadow of his sister about to enter the car, the threat of her nakedness, the certainty of public familial shame: all force a momentary crisis whose form is a "blinding" of Jason's sense perception. This mini-blackout, which echoes his brother's in Mrs. Bland's car and foreshadows his own more significant episode on the road later in the afternoon, has everything to do with the set of associations that defines his psychotic condition: a virulent incest taboo displaced onto the aroma of the inanimate object of his true desire, overdetermined by the fact that the latter was bought with the misappropriated capital of his own mother, whom he is thus "fucking" every time he starts the engine (as Earl Triplett more or less insinuates that afternoon). Oedipal "blinding" is the usual price paid for incestuous infractions of the family romance.

We can discern here an extraordinary effort on Faulkner's part to resituate the automobile as a figure back within the terms of that romance from which it had been ejected in *Flags in the Dust*. Whereas in that previous work the motorcar was presented as an abstract, fungible, modular, and horizontal threat to the vertical relations of the dynastic family, here Jason's tenacious faith in vehicular modernism (and faithlessness in the family as such—he "gambles everything on looking forward"[69]) is undone by the very force of his desire. The technological medium that would propel him beyond the constraints of the bounded "ethical community," and into the amoral anomie of his century, is always and already ensnared in the family plot (in multiple senses) that has robbed him of substance (literally, he gets nothing out of the liquidation of Benjy's pasture) and sentenced him to a kind of eternal return: his sister (fled north to Indiana by car) comes back with the name of his brother (fled east to Massachusetts by train) to taunt him in the Jeffersonian present with their squandered inheritance (wedding party, dowry, Harvard) in the body of a girl exactly as old as those two flights and destined to repeat the dose again, to the value of $7,000, in a Ford car. His own automobile merely immerses him deeper and deeper in the family plot whose summary negation it symbolizes. The blinding headaches are

---

[69] John T. Matthews, *William Faulkner: Seeing through the South* (Oxford: Wiley-Blackwell, 2009), 97.

inescapable symptoms of a condition he cannot articulate to himself, because to do so would be to touch the reality of his desire, and so annihilate it.

Committed in principle to a speed he cannot physically or psychologically endure, Jason is now and then obliged by the severity of his condition to delegate the execution of it to those he believes ought never to have access to it: black men—"Just turn any vehicle over to a nigger, though" (1069). His initial irritation at Luster's failure to replace his spare tire—"I feed a whole dam kitchen full of niggers to follow around after [Ben], but if I want an automobile tire changed, I have to do it myself" (1020)—is ironically amplified when he has to engage "a nigger" to fetch his car, in a stealthy attempt to avoid Earl's eagle eye.

> After about a week he got back with it.
> "Where the hell have you been?" I says. "Riding around where the wenches could see you?"
> "I come straight as I could," he says. "I had to drive clean around the square, wid all dem wagons."
> I never found a nigger yet that didn't have an airtight alibi for whatever he did. But just turn one loose in a car and he's bound to show off. I got in and went on around the square. I caught a glimpse of Earl in the door across the square.
> I went straight to the kitchen and told Dilsey to hurry up with dinner. (1044–45)

Of particular interest here is the sense in which Jason's habitual racist reflexes both express anxiety about the implicit role of automobile culture in the breakdown of racial hierarchies—a general complaint in *Flags in the Dust*, but here narrowed to a specific and blinkered ideological position—and mask a startling ellipsis in the narration of action. The paragraph break between the glimpse of Earl Triplett and the arrival in the Compson kitchen is as stark as anything in Benjy's chapter, but because it remains fully in the preterite "present" of first-person narration, its effect is not as jarring. It is a jump cut, and its result is to have evacuated descriptive prose from the narration of the trip between home and town. Indeed, the savage ellipsis reminds us that his morning journey with Quentin, interrupted by the episode of "blinding," had similarly omitted the entire journey itself, so that we had been immediately transported from the street outside the Compson house to a back street where he can "dodge the square" (1021). There, it had been the psychosexual underpinning of Jason's complex that forced the elision of space and time; here, the lingering anxiety over blacks driving powerful vehicles has the same effect. So it is again, deep in the "devilment" of defrauding his mother's accounts, when he returns to town: "I went up stairs and got the bank book out of her desk and went back to town. I went to the bank and deposited the check."

(1051). That first sentence, with its three clauses joined paratactically by simple conjunctions, equates the unmentionable time in the motorcar with a walk upstairs and retrieval of a bankbook, and collapses its chronotope into a representational void.

Here we come to the crux of Jason's chapter: its reduction of the chronotope most peculiar to it (the routine passage to and fro between the domestic sphere and the workplace) to a zero degree of textuality and the consequent erasure of any descriptive impulse whatsoever. The chronotope is thus a purely negative one, functioning presumably either as a repressive management of the mounting pain through which Jason is obliged to see the road in front of him, or as a version of the existential "commuter oblivion" that erases the repetitive experience even as it is happening and so deprives it of the very quality of experience. As Walter Benjamin memorably put it, "a generation that had gone to school in horse-drawn streetcars" was bombarded with a "tremendous development in technology" that had resulted in "a poverty of human experience in general."[70] Perhaps the most insidious of these technologies was the private automobile, which de-socialized the commute to and from work with the explosive force of its many horsepowers; though not, apparently, in the fantastic envy of the declining white landowner for the young black male, who unproblematically uses the machine to "show off" to "wenches" in his struggle with "all dem wagons" clotting the town square. Jason's anxiety about blacks behind wheels has to do with the flood of phenomenological and existential richness he suspects might characterize an experience that, for him, has been emptied of all spatio-temporal specificity.

It is a suspicion he cannot shake, and it more or less defines his contradictory détente with his mother over the issue of the carriage; as we learn on the fourth drive of the day:

> I got the car and went home. Once this morning, twice at noon, and now again, with her and having to chase all over town and having to beg them to let me eat a little of the food I am paying for. Sometimes I think what's the use of anything. With the precedent I've been set I must be crazy to keep on. And now I reckon I'll get home just in time to take a nice long drive after a basket of tomatoes or something and then have to go back to town smelling like a camphor factory so my head wont explode right off my shoulders. I keep telling her there's not a dam thing in that asprin except flour and water for imaginary invalids. I says you dont know what a headache is. I says you think I'd fool

---

[70] Walter Benjamin, "Experience and Poverty," in Rodney Livingstone and others, trans., Michael W. Jennings, Howard Eiland, and Gary Smith, eds., *Selected Writings, Vol. 2: 1927–1934* (Cambridge MA: Belknap Press of Harvard University Press, 1999), 731–32.

with that dam car at all if it depended on me. I says I can get without one I've learned to get along without lots of things but if you want to risk yourself in that old wornout surrey with a halfgrown nigger boy all right because I says God looks after Ben's kind, God knows He ought to do something for him but if you think I'm going to trust a thousand dollars' worth of delicate machinery to a halfgrown nigger or a grown one either, you'd better buy him one yourself because I says you like to ride in the car and you know you do. (1058)

I quote at length to capture a new twist to the motorcar chronotope in this chapter: its capacity, not to describe space, but to trigger a self-reflexive automobile soliloquy that has some passing resemblance to Quentin's streetcar reveries. This entire inner monologue is being thought at the wheel, and is *about* being at the wheel. What is interesting is both how the signifier "car" inevitably sounds its established Oedipal overtones (the second-person address is to Mrs. Compson; camphor, which he uses to mask the gasoline smell, is his invalid mother's smell), and returns, like a tongue to a loose tooth, to the possibility of using a black chauffeur. But these two themes of the soliloquy are exactly contradictory: Jason's resentment of the wasted money used to support surrey and driver cannot be squared with his refusal to let Luster or TP drive the family in the car. In any event, in Jason's narration of the commute, either the act of driving gets no mention and amounts to a sheer cut in space-time (a chronotope of nothing), or it stimulates this *copia* of reflexive automobility as such, as if the car were thinking through him.

Yet this pattern is rudely interrupted on the return journey to town, when he again sees a "ford coming helling toward me" with the red tie of his niece's beau at the wheel (1060). What follows is the great comic setpiece of the novel, and takes place on the roadways outside of Jefferson. The sudden re-ignition of the "Caddy theme" sparked by the sight of her daughter taking off away from home in another automobile (a perfect structural repetition of the initial trauma eighteen years previous) rewires Jason's psychological circuitry back around the disavowed kernel of incestuous desire, and takes his headache to unprecedented levels of intensity. In the chapter's first concession to the descriptive impulse (not visual, but haptic), this pain is then magnified by the execrable state of the unimproved roads around town:

I saw red. When I recognised that red tie, after all I had told her, I forgot about everything. I never thought about my head even until I came to the first forks and had to stop. Yet we spend money and spend money on roads and dam if it isn't like trying to drive over a sheet of corrugated iron roofing. I'd like to know how a man could be expected to keep up with even a wheelbarrow. (1060)

Jason "forgets everything" in another mini-blackout that prevents his way to the "forks" from being fleshed out with any descriptive detail other than the "corrugated iron roofing" with which the road surface is compared. But here, suddenly, the olfactory affect can unfurl in full dress: "So I had to stop there at the forks. Then I remembered it. It felt like somebody was inside with a hammer, beating on it. I says I've tried to keep you from being worried by her; I says far as I'm concerned, let her go to hell as fast as she pleases and the sooner the better" (1060). The intensifying cephalalgia is rooted in the undecidable relationship between the smell of gasoline and the "worry" of Caddy/Quentin's sexuality; it also declares an elective affinity with that other persistent anxiety, now roped into this second automobile soliloquy—"my people owned slaves here when you were all running little shirt tail country stores and farming land no nigger would look at on shares" (1061). This prompts an extended digression on the state of the fields around him on a (Good) Friday afternoon—"I could see three miles of land that hadn't even been broken" (1061)—and his own economic exploitation by that same parasitic laziness—"I have to work ten hours a day to support a kitchen full of niggers" (1061)—before the land itself spontaneously sends forth a "nigger" emissary who can tell him which road the Ford car took, and he drives on.

It now remains to establish the critical juxtaposition between this hollowed-out chronotope of the road and the space of the signal "event" of this Good Friday, namely the telegraph office. Note how another automobile ellipsis effects the transition:

> I stopped and returned Russell's pump and drove on to town. I went to the drugstore and got a shot and then I went to the telegraph office. It had closed at 20.21, forty points down. Forty times five dollars; buy something with that if you can. (1064)

Jason's absence from his habitual locations (home and store) between half past three and ten past five, his abject surrender in that period to the *drive* of his automotive affect, has led to a situation in which the periodic telegraphic transmissions of reports from New York to Jefferson have failed to reach their destination, and the scale of Jason's staggering losses on the cotton market is revealed all at once. Wayne Westbrook has painstakingly reconstructed these losses, stemming from the "short selling" of a contract of cotton at 12.61 cents per pound, where each point is worth $5.00: "Jason Compson's losses are breathtaking. He had sold short one cotton futures contract (month unknown) at 12.61 on the market's opening. The closing of his account late in the trading session at 20.62 means that the broker paid $10,310 to buy his contract back, or cover his short sale. The result is a stunning loss of 801 points—or $4,005," of which Jason owes $3,374.50 to the broker—"nearly half [again] the 'almost seven thousand dollars' that Quentin would steal from his room in the Compson house."[71]

Jason's knee-jerk reaction is to blame the rate of flow of information (that is, the *medium*), not his own temporary inability to access it. Under "the impression that the telegraph company would keep me informed" (1065) about the market's movements, Jason is pointedly irate at what Westbrook calls "the crude facilities for trading stocks and commodities available throughout the South," specifically "a less expensive service that quoted prices every fifteen minutes. It is this slower cheaper system that served Jefferson."[72] Less expensive than Memphis, that is, where as Jason fumes "they have it on a blackboard every ten seconds. [...] I was within sixty-seven miles of there once this afternoon" (1065). The sixty-seven miles from Memphis's continuous quotation service is (at the steady rate that Bayard Sartoris covers the miles in *Flags* in 1918) a roughly 90-minute drive: equal to the amount of time that Jason could not be reached by the telegraph agent. Taking that direct drive, instead of the fruitless, circular, and blank one he does take, would have placed him in proximity to the most advanced financial service in his region and saved him the horrendous negative yield of his short sell. Instead, his empty circulation of the unimproved roads around Jefferson nets him a loss that will only be trebled a day and a half later when Quentin reclaims eighteen years' worth of her mother's gifts to her and adds to that the sum of Jason's own private savings.

Jason is insistent that this is all a question of mediation: of the state of the roads, of the predations of "niggers" on automotive security, and of the rudimentary telegraph service offered in town, all of which put a man so far behind the "dam eastern jews" that the best he can ever hope for is to break even. But so colossal are Jason's losses (an 813-point spread as compared to a usual 32-point spread[73]), so out of all proportion to any typical (or even atypical) day of stock fluctuations, that they flout all verisimilitude. And that authorial disregard for plausibility in the matter of the novel's singular gorilla-rally on April 6, 1928, is ramified by the fact that, as anybody knowing the operations of the market would surely have been aware, no stocks were ever traded on a Good Friday, leaving us with the task of weighing up the significance of this financial high drama, this *event*, against its literal impossibility. My feeling is that we would do better to attend to Jason's feelings on the matter, which focus not on literal gain or loss but on the mechanisms whereby financial gain and loss are communicated to the Jefferson resident; on mediation as such, and indeed on money

---

[71] Wayne W. Westbrook, "Skunked on the New York Cotton Exchange: What Really Happens to Jason Compson in *The Sound and the Fury*," *The Southern Literary Journal* 41.2 (Spring 2009), 57 [53–68].

[72] Westbrook, "Skunked on the New York Cotton Exchange," 63–64.

[73] Westbrook, "Skunked on the New York Cotton Exchange," 62.

as a medium among media. For it is this latter medium in which the price of Jason's automobile, the size of his loss on the cotton market, the enormity of the booty that Quentin takes from her uncle's locked drawer; the value of Benjy's pasture, of a Harvard education, a Jefferson wedding, a golf club membership, the maintenance of a dilapidated horse and surrey; wages for black servants, the price of food and gasoline, his own clerk's wages, the cost of keeping a Memphis sex worker happy, the nickel he asks from Luster for a free pass to the traveling show, and the monthly swindle on his mother's accounts, all relate to one another as aliquot parts of a single, infinitely subdividable general equivalent.

Jason's complaint is not about this mediation of his entire world by the money form, but the speed of its circulation in Jefferson, Mississippi, relative to its velocity in more natural habitats (New York, South Bend, even Memphis). It is both as if, for Jason, "the age of finance capital has already overtaken the town of Jefferson and Jason is the man of the future," *and* as if that "overtaking" is literal and irreversible, with Jason stranded in a ditch at the side of the road.[74] What frustrates him is the impedance presented to the money medium by a locality where the roads are bad, the telegraph office offers a second-rate service, a phone call to the sheriff means less than nothing, and the structural dependency on black service retards every signal to the speed of an indifferent ambulation. In the "normal" frequency of transactions in a capitalist market, writes Marx, "Circulation sweats money from every pore."[75] In Jefferson, a general distaste for sweat prevents healthy circulation from taking place: the medium does not mediate. The exorbitant loss Jason suffers in his dealings on the market (and with his sister and niece) is less a "real" debit than a kind of fantasmatic projection of his obsession with that underlying failure, about which he cannot cease thinking. His loss is a function of the generalized inability to "keep up with a wheelbarrow" in Jefferson (1060), of the failure of money adequately to mediate value in a region where the wheels do not turn quickly enough. And just as the throb in his head is an internal impedance to the circuitry of consciousness, forcing shut-downs and recurrent blockages in the field of perception, so too Jason's monetary hoard (the $7,000 in the locked drawer) is a blockage in the circulatory system "natural" to the capitalist market that he devoutly wishes would finally sweep away the stagnant economy of Yoknapatawpha County. Whereas a true capitalist is a "rational miser," writes Marx, "throwing his money again and again into circulation" (255), Jason is a miser in the old-fashioned, irrational sense: driven by a mania for self-enrichment and characterized by ascetic, restricted consumption (consider his disgusted rejection of the traveling show), he refuses to take the mass of his fortune to market (his losses on the stock market follow from a relatively small speculative investment, as if to compound

---

[74] Matthews, *Seeing through the South*, 102.
[75] Karl Marx, *Capital, Vol. 1*, trans. Ben Fowkes (London: Penguin, 1990), 208.

his insecurities and terrify him out of circulation once and for all). His contempt for the merely human scale of market speeds in Jefferson, the resentful awe he feels for the inhuman circulatory system presided over by "dam eastern jews," have led him to withdraw the bulk of his monetary substance from circulation altogether—that is, to subtract his "message" from the very medium of capital, and so actively to thwart its accumulation.

It is worth noting that, of the original thirty stocks offered on the Dow Jones, as of October 1928, four were automobile companies, five were steel and nickel, two were utilities companies, two were aerospace firms, two were radio and phonograph corporations, and none was streetcar-related. Twenty-three years earlier, in 1905, the top corporate stock type was steam railway stock, listed at $6.55 trillion, or 31% of the total market share; street railway stock was worth $1.76 trillion, or 8.38%; and automobile stock was not visibly represented.[76] By 1910, the year that Quentin commits himself to them with such abandon, the market in streetcar stocks had become markedly bearish, due to the fact that, as a contemporary analyst observed, "the revenue of American street railways has not been charged with sums even approximating the actual costs of maintenance. This has resulted in an erroneous idea of past profits."[77] Although moved to comment that the "modern or true interurban" streetcar systems "offer excellent speculative investments" in 1910 (191), the author notes that of the "sixty companies [that] represent 2,794 miles of track" at a capitalization cost of "about $80,000 per mile," a third "failed to earn their fixed charges," a third "paid dividends [of] considerably less than 1 per cent," and a third barely rose above that level (188). The catastrophic impact of the Great War on streetcar stocks, and the unstoppable rise of automobile manufacture and stock prices, mean that Jason Compson's sense of the ways things were trending in postwar American capitalism is exact, if a little untimely, since, of course, by the time the novel featuring his various complaints against the crippled medium of market exchanges in Jefferson was published, the system centered in New York was poised to crash around his ears. The year 1927 marked a significant milestone for the automobile industry: it had become the leading industrial sector by value of product, and 55% of all American families now owned a car; but after twenty years of booming auto stock, this peak sparked a realignment of forces and a shift to monopolization, with the number of U.S. firms in the business dropping from 108 to 44 in that year alone. Two years later, in the year of the great crash, General Motors posted an after-tax profit of $248 million, and the combined sales of all U.S. automakers reached 4.5 million units domestically; but 1929 was

---

[76] See the chart in S. S. Heubner, "Scope and Functions of the Stock Market," *Stocks and the Stock Market: The Annals of the American Academy of Political and Social Science* 35.3 (May, 1910), 3.

[77] Wallace McCook Cunningham, "Electric Railway Stocks," *Stocks and the Stock Market: The Annals of the American Academy of Political and Social Science* 35.3 (May 1910), 182.

to be the last year of the great boom, as the bottom had been absorbed into three giant corporations—GM, Ford, and Chrysler (accounting for 80% of sales)—and these colossal levels of production would not be attained again until well after the end of World War II. The Depression smashed automotive affordability, and the industry shrank back to more modest proportions; small investors were wiped out.

"This is not Russia," Jason snarls to the sheriff in the next chapter (1111), and this desperate rhetorical clinging to the democratic veneer of the Republic, in the face of his own patent charlatanry, says a good deal about the underlying reasons for the imminent smash that was to make the NEP of the USSR look relatively utopian to a good number of his contemporaries. As he rides off to Mottson to reclaim his property on Easter Sunday morning like a vigilante from the Westerns, Jason thinks grimly "about rain, about the slick clay roads, himself stalled somewhere miles from town," "at the greatest possible distance from both towns" (1111–12), as the narrator heaps on the perceived adversity and has Jason come to terms with his own status as a stalled "medium," stranded at the muddy midpoint between civilizational outposts that are themselves placed somewhere between Washington and Nicaragua (where U.S. forces are deployed for "fifty thousand dollars a day," 1057). But it is this belated realization of his helpless "in-betweenness," his own medial position in the text (as the middle son), that charges Jason with the function of being its most assiduous cognitive cartographer. If he cannot describe place, he can (and must) conceive of space, and is variously to be found positioning himself in relation to a long list of spatial nodes, each imparting some gravitational pull on his person: Caddy's Indiana, the dead Quentin's Cambridge, the living Quentin's Mottson and roadside ditches, the fair's itinerant elsewhere, the golf club's adjacency, the New York of the "jews," Jackson as a desired destination for Benjy, Lorraine's Memphis, the lawmakers' Washington, the military's Nicaragua, the Bolsheviks' Russia, and so on. His is a nascent geopolitical cognitive map like few others in Faulkner's fiction, because Jason is where the world market bears down upon a consciousness that has declared itself open for business, without the courage to turn his primitive accumulation into capital proper. His *drive* is forestalled from attaining a purely capitalist immanence; it is waylaid by a romance logic that cannot be registered other than as "blindness," a serial occlusion of the sensible—"He could not see very well now," the narrator comments as Jason pulls into Mottson (1114)—which leads him inevitably back into the womb of the family, the degenerate dynasty from which the market had promised to spring him.

The "obverse reflection" of his nascent geopolitical map is a psychosexual map of his own complex, each spatial node a glittering pinprick in the night sky of his fantasy, mapping the one inescapable constellation of his sister's treacherous sex, which he has effectively pimped for eighteen years to the tune of, at the very least, $4,000.[78] In that constellation, he can forever observe the negative image of his "promised job at the heart of northern finance (Herbert Head's bank),"[79] and bear resentful witness to his permanent estrangement from it, "stalled somewhere miles from town" in a car going nowhere, "in the open air, amid a landscape in which nothing was the same except the clouds," his "tiny, fragile human body" abandoned to a "force field of destructive torrents and explosions" from within and without.[80]

There he sits in Mottson, "quietly behind the wheel of a small car, with his invisible life raveled out about him like a wornout sock" (1118). Unable to make his own way back after the absurd denouement of his chase, in a fateful capitulation to the modernized patrician stereotype against which he has fulminated so vociferously, he hires for four dollars another "nigger" to chauffeur him home. At the very same time, Luster hitches Queenie to the surrey and sets off on his inaugural ride as chauffeur of that other involuntary patrician, Benjamin Compson, to visit the family graves. In *Flags in the Dust*, these two trajectories would inevitably have come to a fateful collision; here, the "accident" is decidedly more mannered and less bluntly allegorical. In a formal inversion of the earlier traversal of the town square in Jason's motorcar—"I had to drive clean around the square, wid all dem wagons" (1044); itself a repetition of Simon Strother driving the Sartoris carriage "among the tethered wagons about the square" (545)—Luster elects to personify all of Jason's vicious stereotypes about black drivers and "show dem niggers how quality does" by parading at the reins in a square thronging with "Motors," including "Mr Jason car" (1123). Luster's "obverse reflection" of "how quality does" involves an aristocratic disdain for the established counter-clockwise flow of traffic around the monument; the sudden interruption of Benjy's futurist chronotope of "bright shapes" unleashes the full quantity of his affect—"horror; shock; agony eyeless, tongueless; just sound" (1123)—under the very proscenium of public space; and this monstrous affront to Jason's festering familial shame sends him forth from the depth of his own race-driven chronotope and excruciating olfactory affect to unleash at last what he has been itching to express for three straight days, namely violence upon a black body: "With a backhanded blow he hurled Luster aside. [...] Then he struck Luster over the head with his fist" (1123). This public double-discharge of the utter impotence and "plunging" fortunes of the once-great family is the form taken by the collision of two incompatible chronotopes.

---

[78] "Jason sells her, or at least embezzles what she has earned from the sale of herself, and hoards the profit," writes Richard Godden, *Fictions of Labor: William Faulkner and the South's Long Revolution* (Cambridge: Cambridge University Press, 1997), 48.

[79] Godden, *Fictions of Labor*, 46.

[80] Benjamin, "Experience and Poverty," 732.

3

Currents of Consciousness; or, my mother is a graphophone

And from above, thin squeaks of radio static
The captured fume of space foams in our ears—[1]

This chapter will focus principally on the soundscapes of Faulkner's two post–*Sound and the Fury* novels, particularly the complicated ways in which new sound technologies are utilized as tropological anchor-points for the redistribution of aesthetic energies within the novel as a form. The prodigious increase in social power of both broadcast and recording/playback sound devices in the 1920s and early 1930s was not only reinventing the public relationship toward media technologies and recasting the very differentiation between private and public; from the novelist's point of view, these technologies had already significantly altered the very meaning of "voice" itself—one of the form's principal technical categories—from within. Here, we ask how this subtle but irresistible infiltration of the novelistic domain of voice by new sound media might have provoked new kinds of aesthetic responsiveness and pulled the Faulknerian text in directions that opened it to unprecedented formal mutations.

One way of putting the question is to consider how it might have appeared logical for Lorine Niedecker, who had worked as a scriptwriter for radio programs airing on Madison, Wisconsin, radio station WHA in 1942, to turn her pen to an adaptation of *As I Lay Dying* a decade later.[2] Setting that great *tour de force* as a radio play twenty years after its publication, Niedecker burrowed into something unconsciously at stake in the text itself—since a radio play for voices is arguably what it already was. Given that her compositional method in this case was, as she wrote to Zukofsky, simply to "take hunks from the printed

---

[1] Hart Crane, *The Bridge*, in Langdon Hammer, ed., *Complete Poems and Selected Letters* (New York: Library of America, 2006), 54.

[2] See Lorine Niedecker, *Collected Works*, ed. Jenny Pentherby (Berkeley, CA & Los Angeles: University of California Press, 2004), 343–60.

page and plunk em down in radio," Niedecker tacitly admitted as much, for if an intermedial adaptation is just a matter of cutting and pasting, there must be something in the source material that is "adapted" to begin with.[3] Niedecker's sense of radio's poetic potential as a medium of transmitted voice rested on its constitutive blending of "the private printed page plus sound and silence."[4] Her adaptation of the only one of Faulkner's great texts to have dispensed with omniscient narration—committing itself to the multiple first-person, the weave of narrative voices in their *unitas multiplex*—plays "with multiple modes of address by employing narrators who speak directly to radio audiences, characters who speak as if privately, characters who address one another, and voices who speak collectively and in montage," and thus works in formal accord with the audacious experiments with novel form in *As I Lay Dying*.[5] It also taps into a dialectic between sound and silence that threads through that text with metaphorical potency, and runs as well through the text written and rewritten on either side of *As I Lay Dying*'s composition: *Sanctuary*. These two works, torn halves of a whole to which they do not add up, were composed at the high point of radio's astonishing success in the United States, and they can be seen variously to incorporate the lessons implicit in that medium's irresistible ascent for the form of the novel, which depends so fully upon *voice* as a technique for making continuous "connections between *narrating* and *narrative* and *narrating* and *story*."[6] If Niedecker understood the text of Faulkner's boldest formal experiment to have been shot through with the electromagnetic radiations of the radio voice, to what extent can it be demonstrated via formal analysis?

But the discussion to follow might just as well be framed by a certain inconsistency in Faulkner's own biographical relationship to the new sound media of his era. On the one hand, we learn from his daughter, Jill, that there "was not even a radio in the house, and [she] would reach her teens before her father succumbed to family pressure and allowed her to have a phonograph."[7] As Jill was born in 1933, this would make the first acquisition of a Faulkner family phonograph a post-WWII affair. On the other, we have that "not quite apocryphal" account of Faulkner's extensive immersion in jazz recordings during the composition of *Sanctuary*.[8] The author is supposed to have said that he had "worn out three

---

[3] Niedecker, *Collected Works*, 458.

[4] Jenny Pentherby, *Niedecker and the Correspondence with Zukofsky, 1931–1970* (Cambridge: Cambridge University Press, 1993), 191.

[5] Brook Houglum personal correspondence with author, February 2012.

[6] Gérard Genette, *Narrative Discourse: An Essay in Method*, trans. Jane E. Lewin (Ithaca: Cornell University Press, 1980), 32.

[7] Joesph Blotner, *Faulkner: A Biography*, one-volume edition (Jackson, MS: University Press of Mississippi, 2005), 359.

[8] Robert W. Hamblin and Charles Peek, eds., *A William Faulkner Encyclopedia* (Westport, CT: Greenwood, 1999), 261.

records of Gershwin's 'Rhapsody in Blue'" so as to "set the rhythm and jazzy tone" of a novel that, as we shall see, is infused with the electric sounds of its age.[9] Whether or not Faulkner practiced the puritanical ban his daughter later recalled, he does seem to have conceived of the domestic hearth as a sanctuary away from the medley of mechanical and electronic sounds spreading across the nation and standardizing aural responses just as Hollywood had standardized visual ones. And yet, as I will show, one can no more imagine the form taken by his novels of the early 1930s without these media thronging through them than one can conceive of *The Sound and the Fury* without new forms of transportation, or *Absalom, Absalom!* without the studio system that subsidized its production.

The Hines Hour

We begin, however, with a glimpse into these matters afforded by a significant problem of form internal to the novel written after *As I Lay Dying*. If *Light in August* can be plotted according to a generic schema, it seems clear that its ambitions are to weave into a single aesthetic substance the strands of gothic romance-cum-tragedy (the narrative of Joe Christmas), pastoral comedy (the narrative of Lena Grove and Byron Bunch), and modern irony (the narrative of Gail Hightower).[10] Such an act of generic totalization is a prodigious claim to artistic maturity in the medium of the novel; and yet, the consensus has long been that this attempt to fuse genres is found wanting, measured by a number of rigorous aesthetic criteria.[11] These failures

---

[9] Joseph Blotner, *Faulkner: A Biography*, two-volume edition (New York: Random House, 1974), 754, 1054.

[10] See here the essay by Susan V. Donaldson, "Faulkner's Pastoral, Gothic, and the Sublime," in Richard C. Moreland, ed., *A Companion to William Faulkner* (Oxford, MS & Malden, MA: Blackwell, 2007), 359–72.

[11] Although the literary world sensed immediately that the novel was Faulkner's most serious bid to date for the aesthetic prestige of the Jamesian "art novel" (and not simply a modernist prank)—George Marion O'Donnell heralded it as "a greater work than any other book William Faulkner has written"—still, John Crowe Ransom called it a "let-down," Barry Bingham complained that "the story explodes feebly in a shower of sparks," and Geoffrey Stone that it suffered from a more "tortuous construction [than] any book by Hugo or Sue"; Cleanth Brooks' judgment was summary: "The difficulty has always come with the attempt to relate the various episodes so as to show a coherent pattern of meaning." See George Marion O'Donnell, "A Mellower Light" (1932); reprinted in Nicholas Fargnoli, ed., *William Faulkner: A Literary Companion* (New York: Pegasus Books, 2008), 180; John Crowe Ransom, "Faulkner, South's Most Brilliant but Wayward Talent, Is Spent" (1935), reprinted in M. Thomas Inge, ed., *William Faulkner: The Contemporary Reviews* (Cambridge: Cambridge University Press, 1995), 121; Barry Bingham, "Faulkner Flies by Night" (1932); reprinted in Fargnoli, *William Faulkner: A Literary Companion*, 187; Geoffrey Stone, "Keeping Up with the Novelists" (1932); reprinted in Fargnoli, *William Faulkner: A Literary Companion*, 186; Cleanth Brooks, *William Faulkner: The Yoknapatawpha Country* (Baton Rouge: Louisiana State University Press, 1963), 48.

have to do explicitly with the joins, the narrative contrivances that allow the three distinct generic dimensions to come into contact with one another, and allow for transferences of energy between them. One can appreciate Faulkner's interest in establishing the ironic *topos* of Hightower's lonely house, resounding with the galloping thunder of his undead ancestor, as the medium through which the tragic and comedic strands of the narrative would be obliged to connect and come to terms. With no particular need for justification, we may take it as a given that Byron Bunch (himself a reclusive and celibate male) was in the habit of making weekly calls upon Hightower, to trade yarns and take shelter from the secular riot of town life. Similarly, it was both economical and shrewdly appropriate that Lucas Burch should enter into a business arrangement with Joe Christmas and thereby implicate the gothic and pastoral plot strands in a spatio-temporal node on the outskirts of Jefferson. The deeper formal problem would consist in contriving some convergence between Hightower's legitimate ("paid for!") sanctuary from public life and the truly exilic figure of Joe Christmas, for there would seem to be no good reason why, of all places in Jefferson to flee to upon his escape from incarceration, it might be in the ex-minister's house that Joe meets his fate. How, precisely, might the tragic and the ironic be brought into relation, thereby triggering the deeper affinities with the comic, without resorting to mere accident or happenstance and thus capitulating to the mechanics of romance?

The novel, of course, betrays considerable fretting on just this score. The nineteenth chapter is the sore spot on the face of the text where these anxieties are rehearsed and then inexpertly resolved along a double axis: first, the weakest element of the book, in Gavin Stevens's "soothing and recapitulant" theory offered to the visiting college professor; and then, in a virtual reversion to the compulsive narrative mode of *Sanctuary*, a pulp-fictional movement-image of Percy Grimm's hunt for Christmas. The point of this second line of approach is to cancel or trump the anxieties that the first surely could not settle:

> There were many reasons, opinions, as to why he [Joe] had fled to Hightower's house at the last. "Like to like," the easy, the immediate, ones said, remembering the old tales about the minister. Some believed it to have been mere chance; others said that the man had shown wisdom, since he would not have been suspected of being in the minister's house at all if someone had not seen him run across the back yard and run into the kitchen.[12]

---

[12] William Faulkner, *Light in August*, in *Novels 1930–1935*, eds. Joseph Blotner and Noel Polk (New York: Library of America, 1985), 727. Subsequent citations included in text.

This, one of the infrequent emergences of the voice of the community in the novel, is a moment of maximum danger for the novelist, who, having raised the specter of "mere chance," then has to conjure it away. That Gavin Stevens's theory does not manage that end is an understatement, amplified by the entirely insincere narrative voice (relative to the rest of the novel's elements) in which it is couched. The theory itself revolves around the dubious figure of Mrs. Hines, who (we are given to suppose), having been raised to an almost superhuman mode of sensitivity—become a "hoping machine"—upon handling Lena Grove's infant, then goes to the jailhouse where Joe is being held and "there, in the cell with him, I believe she told him about Hightower, that Hightower would save him, was going to save him" (730).

Stevens is at least perfectly consistent about the utter improbability of this sequence of events. "But of course I dont know what she told him. I dont believe that any man could reconstruct that scene" (730). No man could, of course, least of all the one responsible for the book in our hands, since the almost three-hundred-page movement building to the present moment has gone to extreme lengths to persuade us that Joe Christmas's capacity to endure a feminine duty of care is exactly nil; that his exposure to familial "hope" has been in every context lethal; that each spark of the language of salvation has been grimly extinguished in his person. The unimaginability of the scene conjured by Stevens as an explanation for Christmas's flight to Hightower's house could, of course, stand as some further mark of authorial irony, at the expense of conventional ruling-class wisdom, were it not for the fact that, in chapters fifteen and sixteen, Faulkner's most omniscient narrator had himself already laid the groundwork for this very supposition. This is the point to suggest that, planted retrospectively in an attempt to buttress Stevens's unconvincing theory, which is in turn presented as an explanation of the inexplicable climactic meeting of Christmas and Hightower, these earlier chapters (15 and 16) not only fail to paper over such cracks in the novelistic edifice, but positively exacerbate them and create the appearance of a true textual fault line that fails every stricture of novelistic form and is itself the most pressing formal embarrassment of the book. Here the schism between realism and romance rises to the surface.

Recall, briefly, how Stevens comes to describe the curious relationship between Mrs. Hines and Byron Bunch. He imagines the old woman's thirty years of limbo-like emotional arrest becoming unraveled in a single comic blow by the contact with the newborn: "Until that baby was born and she found some means by which she could stand alone, as it were, she had been like an effigy with a mechanical voice being hauled about on a cart by that fellow Bunch and made to speak when he gave the signal, as when he took her last night to tell her story to Doctor Hightower" (729). It is this last relation that strikes the discordant note. The later figure of Mrs. Hines as a "hoping machine" is, as it were, retrofitted onto its ground; prior to "hope" there had only been "a mechanical voice," but the "effigy" of a woman was still machine-like enough to be carted around and switched on or off with the automatism of a radio—a role that Bunch had assumed for himself with a kind of automatism all his own. Perhaps this latter automatism is itself a delayed rhetorical echo of one of the earliest descriptions Byron himself makes of Lucas Burch, his cryptic namesake and sexual antagonist for the duration of the novel: "He puts me in mind of one of these cars running along the street with a radio in it. You cant make out what it is saying and the car aint going anywhere in particular and when you look at it close you see that there aint even anybody in it" (425). In this case, Mrs. Hines is also a vehicle, and one like Burch's with nobody particular at the wheel, but she is a vehicle that doesn't streak past one on the street, and whose switch can be easily controlled. It is this cart-bound radio of Mrs. Hines, broadcasting a Memphis signal relayed by a Mottstown router, that (Stevens surmises) Bunch takes to play for Hightower the night before the lynching of Christmas, her grandson, in order to persuade the lapsed minister to perjure himself and offer Christmas both alibi and sanctuary.

Stevens does not generate this peculiar mechanical imagery unaided, however, and it is as an echo of the earlier descriptive prose in chapters fifteen and sixteen that his "radio" figure strives to flatten out the improbability of the whole episode. In those earlier chapters, not only is Mrs. Hines first introduced as a bodiless mechanical toy with its feet planted in the yellow press—"she was just tall enough to see over the counter, so that she didn't look like she had any body at all. It just looked like somebody had sneaked up and set a toy balloon with a face painted on it and a comic hat set on top of it, like the Katzenjammer kids in the funny paper" (660–61)—but she is specifically presented as a voice without a visible origin or a bodily ground. As she and Bunch recapitulate the back-story of Christmas's early childhood to a disbelieving Hightower, their voices meld and merge in a narrative space beyond novelistic credibility: "She speaks in the same dead, level tone [as Byron]: the two voices in monotonous strophe and antistrophe: two bodiless voices recounting dreamily something performed in a region without dimension by people without blood" (677). And again, within moments of this qualification, the narrator tries a variation of the figure: "Then she begins to speak again, without moving, almost without lip movement, as if she were a puppet and the voice that of a ventriloquist in the next room" (679).[13] Already, in a capping of this elaborate metaphorics of vocal possession and automatism, the husband himself, Eupheus Hines, has been described in comparable, if not identical terms: "He talks clearly, just a little jerkily.... His voice ceases; his tone

---

[13] It bears remarking that the first demonstration of Edison's phonograph at the Paris Academy of Sciences on March 11, 1878, was met with public accusations of "ventriloquistic charlatanry." See Count du Moncel, *The Telephone, the Microphone and the Phonograph* (1879; reprint, New York: Arno Press, 1974), 244–45.

does not drop at all. His voice just stops, exactly like when the needle is lifted from a phonograph record by the hand of someone who is not listening to the record" (673–74).

At stake in this repetitive intrusion from the domain of mechanical reproduction and electrical mediation is a cryptic authorial admission that the voices of the Hines couple, and of what they portend for *Light in August*, are not to be integrated in the organic substance of the work. Indeed, this insistent figuration of their voices as materially anchored not in a human body but in some machine or absent source, some distant undead origin only dimly related to the rounded humanistic depth of a Hightower, a Christmas, or a Lena Grove, seems to grate against the finished surfaces of the rest of the fiction. Two levels of determination are at work here, in a contradictory fusion of opposites. On the one hand, the couple is meant to speak a droning discourse of the dead: a long-interred voice, native to the turn-of-the-century milieu in which Christmas was born, that can be reanimated by no other means than the gramophonic method of mechanical storage and replay or the radiophonic method of electromagnetic dissemination through the "etheric ocean" itself.[14] They are, in that sense, just two of the "preternatural interlocutors" who, in Jeffrey Sconce's words, embodied a radically shifting social relationship to the bewildering sequence of new media technologies conducting the voice: telegraphy, telephony, phonography, and wireless.[15] On the other hand, this reconstitution of the dead voice is troped as foreign and redundant, technically current but formally alien, in a novel otherwise constituted of character voices drawn in depth; further, it is sequestered in a virtually removable couple of chapters with little narrative consequence to speak of. What speaks in and through them is an acknowledgement of formal failure and overstraining, allegorized in their figuration as foreign media embodiments.

The mediatic voices of the Hines couple both figure their formal unacceptability and strive to mask it. Of course they derive from the archaic substratum of romance; their function is to perform an eleventh-hour exposure of the foundling's parentage, to displace the theatre of operations of the novel from the open road of hazardous encounter to a closed domain of bloodlines and lineages. No matter how ironized and open to challenge this function may be, formally there is no mistaking its generic and historic provenance. But as we have seen, in Faulkner's Mississippi in 1933, romance cannot be meaningfully evoked any other way than by channeling it through the tele-technical relay stations of modern communications systems. We shall see why this is so much more completely in what follows, but the methodological implications are worth expanding upon

---

[14] See Jeffrey Sconce, *Haunted Media: Electronic Presence from Telegraphy to Television* (Durham, NC: Duke University Press, 2000).

[15] Sconce, *Haunted Media*, 10.

anew. If romance, whose undeath within the formal coils of the modern novel has been theorized by Nicholas Daly among others,[16] can best indicate its formal alienness by tropologically hijacking aspects of the modern media ecology—if figures of romance are repackaged as radios and gramophones—then we detect a prevailing transference whereby the most archaic formal and ideological layers of the modern narrative text seek expression via the newest systems of communications, systems that imperil the novel form from an altogether different direction. We will find compelling reasons, technological and philosophical, why this may have been so; but let us glance forward to the argument of the next chapter and say now that this techno-tropological layer, a subterfuge of romance, finally "explains" Christmas's taking refuge in Hightower's home, in a much more exact sense than the narrative is able to contrive. Once it is established that Joe Christmas can stand in the oncoming glare of a pair of automobile headlamps at night and watch "his body grow white out of the darkness like a Kodak print emerging from the liquid" (478), and that the hand-painted sign advertising Hightower's commercial activities from home reads: "Art Lessons/ Handpainted Xmas & Anniversary Cards/Photographs Developed" (440), then the deeper logic of Christmas's arrival at this particular door stands exposed.[17] We can leave the gothic determinations of race in this figural crux for another context; the point is to clinch a subliminal mechanism whereby media allegory becomes determinant at the level of form. What the novel cannot contain, it tropes as medially foreign—but that figuration occasions more at the level of textual effect than the narrative can possibly justify. The work of form is thus no longer fully deliberate, but emerges as an ongoing series of repercussive effects, more or less automatic, that follow from the decision to trope the romance layer technologically. Once that mechanism is in place, there is nothing to stop its automatisms from interrupting the steady flow of Jamesian ambitions with scandals of form incompatible with "a perfect narrative."

Competing Voices

No novel in the American tradition is pitched at such a cantankerous and obtuse angle to the Jamesian ideology of the novel as is *Light in August*'s great predecessor, *As I Lay Dying* (1930). *As I Lay Dying* is so openly heterogeneous

---

[16] Nicholas Daly, *Modernism, Romance, and the Fin de Siècle* (Cambridge: Cambridge University Press, 1999). See also Mark McGurl, *The Novel Art: Elevations of American Fiction after Henry James* (Princeton, NJ: Princeton University Press, 2001), 42–53; and Nancy Armstrong, *How Novels Think: The Limits of Individualism from 1719–1900* (New York: Columbia, 2005), 134–35.

[17] See on this Sascha Morrell's "Kodak Harlot Tricks of Light: Faulkner and Melville in the Darkroom of Race," in Julian Murphet and Stefan Solomon, eds., *William Faulkner in the Media Ecology* (Baton Rouge: Louisiana State University Press, 2015), 172–91.

that the truly astonishing thing is not simply that these two works should have emanated from the same author, but that they are adjacent in the unfurling of his now-canonical oeuvre. Pursuing *The Sound and the Fury*'s formal commitment to heteroclite narratorial domains to a length so extreme that no narrative work in any language to that point can match its interweaving of fifteen named voices in fifty-nine monologues, the short novel goes still further in abandoning that previous work's final recourse to an objective narrator and fully commits its discourse to the rotating, multiple first-person. Again in contradistinction to *The Sound and the Fury*'s avowedly symbolic and poetic mode of composition—in which, for instance, the sister Candace operates as the incandescent center of the elaborate fourfold structure, while the mechanics of castration oversee its various panels—*As I Lay Dying* is driven urgently forward by a compulsive narrative energy (underwritten by its ironic quest motif) that spares no time for the roving phenomenology of a Benjy or the abstract reveries of a Quentin Compson. The overriding architectural tension, indeed, is between what can only be described as a pop-cultural pseudo-romance "horizontal" momentum of action and incident and a more abstract, modernist, "vertical" dimension of inter-animating vocal ironies, whose drama is to irradiate what cannot be articulated on the level of action. This operational antinomy, between the horizontal and the vertical, lies at the structural foundation of the text and provides the coordinates on which to analyze the tension between the competitive voices that govern the narration and the quest that propels the narrative.

For now, though, it is enough to speculate that the subtraction of the objective or reliable narrator from the enunciative position, the sheer abandonment to irony in the inevitable contretemps between characterological situations and their disjunctive perspectives, spells the end of the "well-wrought urn" or art-novel—since Jamesian irony, for all its precious unspokenness and reliance on the implicit, was guaranteed by the stable position afforded by the monumental presence and gravity of his third-person prose, its assurance of some circumambient intelligence in whose capacious curtaining of the action the elusive moral Absolute lay secure. Not so for the hapless members of the Bundren clan who, unlike the Ververs or Newsomes, and unlike even the Compsons, will never know the security of an Archimedean vantage point from which their own blinkered ideas about their actions will stand framed and finalized in a stable aesthetic image. The Bundrens are cast into an all-encompassing immanence. Multiplied by fifteen, and fractured into fifty-nine shards, the first-person voice here affords, not a larger frame on the world of the text, but a smaller one. Each new narrator emerges from the given immanence, in a pattern that swallows and narrows the world on offer to a vanishing point—apart, that is, from one voice, and its amplification by another, whose peculiar functions and relations this chapter aims ultimately to elucidate.

Perhaps we may shed some initial light on that, and on the structural dynamic between a horizontal and a vertical vector more generally, by picking up the clue afforded us by the preliminary analysis of the "radio" voice of *Light in August*'s Mrs. Hines and its antagonistic gender relationship with the "gramophone" voice of her husband. It is a light that can fall to best advantage on our privileged text here, however, only by shining it through that other novel in this immediate sequence, written in first draft prior to *As I Lay Dying* but published in a greatly altered version only afterward in 1931—the notorious "sensation" novel, *Sanctuary*. There, Faulkner's narrator pauses to reflect on the public sphere as it is currently experienced acoustically in Jefferson, Mississippi, circa 1930:

> The sunny air was filled with competitive radios and phonographs in the doors of drug- and music-stores. Before these doors a throng stood all day, listening. The pieces which moved them were ballads, simple in melody and theme, of bereavement and retribution and repentance metallically sung, blurred, emphasised by static or needle—disembodied voices blaring from imitation wood cabinets or pebble-grain horn-mouths above the rapt faces, the gnarled slow hands long shaped to the imperious earth, lugubrious, harsh, and sad.[18]

What we have here is on one level, and unexceptionally, "content" in the standard sense: a descriptive overview of some specific phenomena of everyday life, delivered over a calculated hiatus within the otherwise frenzied forward momentum of this narratively driven novel.[19] On another level, of course, this passage functions at a certain altitude of generality, and it is meant to thematize an effect of modernity as it steals ever more completely over the hitherto tradition-bound and vestigially "feudal" South—namely, alienation, mechanization, the mechanical mediation and estrangement of popular ballad forms, leaving the "rapt faces" of the sharecroppers silent instead of singing. But this, too, is still content (Jameson would call it an "ideologeme"), and as such settles into a more or less comfortable textual relation with a range of extra-literary discourses, those "discourses of culture" tabulated in part by Charles Hannon and otherwise often drawn upon in the analysis of Faulkner's textual universe.[20]

---

[18] William Faulkner, *Sanctuary*, in *Novels 1930–1935*, eds. Joseph Blotner and Noel Polk (New York: Library of America, 1985), 257. Subsequent citations included in text.

[19] And it was as "content" that such material had been conscripted into *Flags in the Dust*, within spitting distance of these "drug- and music-stores," at the Beard Hotel: "a square frame building with a double veranda, from which the mournful cacophony of a cheap talking-machine came upon the afternoon," "the lugubrious reiteration of the phonograph." In *Novels 1926–1929*, 628, 629.

[20] See here Charles Hannon, *Faulkner and the Discourses of Culture* (Baton Rouge: Louisiana State University Press, 2005).

On yet a third level, however, the three sentences enact a pattern of execution, whereby two short, succinct descriptive periods are succeeded by a peculiar dilation of syntax in the third, itself operating on a distinct stylistic plane. It is here that the characteristic "Faulknerian" rhetoric establishes its theatre of operations, in a novel otherwise distinguished by its disciplined avoidance of such effects as redundancy, tautology, oxymoron, and appositive accumulation, and streamlined according to the generic and stylistic laws of efficiency proposed by the pulps. The third quoted sentence, with its very curious shifts of subject—from the ballad "pieces" to the "voices" and finally to the "hands"—rounds on the declarative minimalism of the previous two and subsumes it, amplifying it within a space of rhetorical copia. Description is shot through by narration, not in any conventional manner, but by disguising its ethical commentary as a potted fable of labor, production, and alienation. What the described scene encrypts is a sorry story about the substitution of a proper groove (that made by the human hand and plough in the dark earth) by another, artificial one (that in which the gramophone needle travels). The songs of the folk no longer rise naturally from the tillage of soil but from "imitation wood cabinets," in the form of hovering "disembodied voices." The narrative voice situates itself alongside the "competitive" radios and phonographs and becomes "blurred, emphasised," not by the mechanics of playback but by the necessity of vying with them.

In the novel as a whole, periodic eruptions of "style" in this sense (an escape valve from the "thorough and methodical study of everything on the list of the best-sellers" which Faulkner claimed to be the basis of *Sanctuary*'s composition[21]) are allegorical of the novel's antagonistic relationship toward its own raw materials, and of the origin of those materials in mechanical reproduction. "Style" is competitive, here, with everything the novel can otherwise relax into as a self-conscious instance of "best-sellerdom." It bears remembering, however, that Raymond Chandler himself described a process of autodidacticism in the vernacular rather similar to that outlined by Faulkner. "I had to learn American just like a foreign language," Chandler, born in England, wrote. "I had to study it and analyze it. As a result, when I use slang, colloquialism, snide talk or any kind of off-beat language, I do it deliberately."[22] Chandler's studied "broken-down patois" was the result of countless hours spent with cheap magazines and in speakeasies; so, as he wrote to the editor of *The Atlantic Monthly*, "when I split an infinitive, God damn it, I split it so it will stay split, and when I interrupt the velvety smoothness of my more or less literate syntax with a few sudden words of bar-room vernacular, that is done with the eyes wide open" (77).[23] Chandler's

---

[21] Quoted in Blotner, *Faulkner*, 234.

[22] Raymond Chandler, *Raymond Chandler Speaking*, eds. Dorothy Gardiner and Kathrine Sorley Walker (Berkeley, CA & Los Angeles: University of California Press, 1997), 80.

[23] See, on this dynamic, Jameson's book-length discussion in his *Raymond Chandler: The Detections of Totality* (London & New York: Verso, 2016).

attitude toward style, "the most durable thing in writing ... the most valuable investment a writer can make" (75), appears comparable to Faulkner's during the writing of *Sanctuary*:

> It is no easy trick to keep your characters and your story operating on a level which is understandable to the semi-literate public and at the same time give them some intellectual and artistic overtones which that public does not seek or demand, or, in effect, recognize, but which somehow subconsciously it accepts and likes. My theory has always been that the public will accept style provided you do not call it style either in words or by, as it were, standing off and admiring it.[24]

But here, too, the difference becomes palpable. Whereas Chandler genuinely sought a transubstantiation of the popular romance materials with which he worked, such that they were turned inside out like a glove into something velvety and fine, Faulkner preferred to exaggerate the routine and mechanical elements of popular narration until an opportunity could be seized for their dialectical negation in a reflux of literary afflatus. This latter was, for Faulkner, style as a pox on both your houses: neither a condescension to the masses nor a winking at the cognoscenti, but a nihilistic credo against reconciliation.[25] And often, as here, it was pitched into a scene already defined by the vectors of mass communications.

Radio and phonograph, despite the similarities of their means of reproduction, perform an *agon* in the soundscape whose true rules of engagement will not be properly explored until we turn to *As I Lay Dying*. In the meantime, what remains structurally critical is the narrative counterpoint between these "rapt faces" arrested by voices playing over broadcast and playback technologies and those other listeners absorbed by the following chapter's aural *punctum*—a black prisoner's dirge-like lament in song form, emanating from his jail cell, and joined on the outside after work by "a few negroes" in "natty, shoddy suits and sweat-stained overalls," singing "in chorus with the murderer" (258). The convict is scant hours away from his execution in literal terms, but in Faulkner's typical *hysteron proteron* reversal of present and future tenses, this

---

[24] Letter to Bernice Baumgarten, April 16, 1951, in *Selected Letters of Raymond Chandler*, ed. Frank McShane (New York: Delta Press, 1987), 269.

[25] Peter Lurie writes that "Faulkner sought to present readers with both the narrative pleasure they knew from popular cultural forms and a commentary on them." See *Vision's Immanence* (Baltimore: Johns Hopkins University Press, 2004), 62. My point is that the stylistic "commentary" is immanently adversarial, and isn't even commentary; it is a vertical resistance to the horizontal momentum of informational transaction.

distance is bridged such that the voice heard in the town square is already a post-mortem one.

> [W]hite people slowed and stopped in the leafed darkness that was almost summer, to listen to those who were sure to die and him who was already dead singing about heaven and being tired; or perhaps in the interval between songs a rich, sourceless voice coming out of the high darkness where the ragged shadow of the heaven-tree which snooded the street lamp at the corner fretted and mourned: 'Fo days mo! Den dey ghy stroy de bes ba'ytone singer in nawth Mississippi!'" (258)

The exercise in parallelism is revelatory.[26] What arrests attention in both scenes, via the always open ears in a public space, are the disembodied voices of the deathless, the undead—the baritone lament of the condemned man whom we never see beyond a flat silhouette; the reedy tenor ballads abstracted from all body by technology itself.

The figural relationship between these scenes of public audition is clinched by the persistent, cryptic figure of a corpse. The black murderer and singer of spirituals is himself always "already dead"—both socially in Orlando Patterson's sense, and legally in the terms of the Yoknapatawpha Circuit Court—a living corpse coffined in one of the novels' three powerful *topoi* of imprisonment: the Old Frenchman place, the jailhouse, and Miss Reba's. On the other hand, the "rapt faces" held in thrall to the blaring "disembodied voices" on a Saturday are provided with an objective correlative for their nameless, alienated affect when they return to the scene on Monday: "All day long a knot of them stood about the door to the undertaker's parlor," where they can see the body of Tommy lying "on a wooden table, barefoot, in overalls" (257).[27] This orphaned corpse is a figural correlative of the "lugubrious, harsh, and sad" industrialized soundscape constructed by the phonographs and radios, just as the condemned baritone is himself the embodiment of the prodigious collective affect spread by his voice.

If that were not enough, this entire set of relations between sonic experience and cadaver is taken to scabrous, satirical lengths in the later sequence concerning the wake of the gambler, Red. There, at a nightclub called The Grotto, an orchestra plays music "sultry, evocative; filled with movement of feet, the voluptuous hysteria of muscles warming the scent of flesh, of the blood" (340) in a space whose central exhibit is the coffin of Red, "black, with silver fittings" (347). The proprietor quashes the mourners' requests for Red's favorite jazz tunes, like "I Can't Give You Anything but Love," terrified that with everyone already "all ginned up

---

[26] Erich Nunn is right to call it a juxtaposition in "'Don't Play No Blues': Race, Music, and Mourning in Faulkner's *Sanctuary*," *The Faulkner Journal* 22.4 (Spring 2009), 79.

[27] This structural relation is analyzed in Nunn, "'Don't Play No Blues'," 81–82.

on free whisky, they'll start dancing" (348). His suggestion of the hymn "Nearer, My God, to Thee" is supposed to prevent getting "them all to dancing," but by the time the "cornetist rose and played In That Haven of Rest in solo" (349), it is clear that the jazz sensibility informing the performance style of this "orchestra from a downtown hotel" (348) has already had the inevitable effect: the entire scene is "drowned in a sudden pandemonium of chairs and screams" (351). Before long, the coffin itself has been upended, the corpse jostled, and the plug of wax masking Popeye's bullet-hole dislodged. Three scenes thus engineer an obscure relation between a boxed-in corpse and the collective experience of musical audition in a manner that cannot possibly be accidental; Faulkner's narrator is working overtime metaphorically to establish a kind of "living death" in contemporary melody and harmony that might have some material bearing on the destinies of voice itself in an altered, electrified soundscape.

To get at that complex, we must first take a detour through *Sanctuary*'s dense and distributed soundscape and the dynamics of its presentation. It will have escaped few readers of this novel that its "natural" soundscape appears afflicted by a "second-natural" overlay of jazzy, mechanical, and electrical sound effects. From the inaugural three notes of an unseen bird in the woods around the Old Frenchman place, we are given to hear the stricken world of *Sanctuary* as through a phonograph horn in a market square; the bird sings "three bars in monotonous repetition" a sound "meaningless and profound ... out of which a moment later came the sound of an automobile passing along a road and dying away" (181). The same sonic fold between repetitious birdsong and the intrusive sound of a motor car is repeated twice more (182, 183), underscoring the degree to which the romantic sound par excellence, and privileged trope for the unfettered voice of poetic utterance, is here consonant with the sounds of a modern media ecology. That Horace himself is referred to by Popeye as a "bird out front" of the house (184) cryptically reprises his role in *Flags in the Dust*, where he played the romantic poet manqué, and suggests that the book he holds as a talisman—"the kind that people read. Some people do" (182)—may just as well be a volume of Keats or Shelley. The inveterate romanticism that Horace represents (among other things, he is an etiolated avatar of that Chandlerian "man of honor" who "down these mean streets ... must go"[28]), and will be severely punished for, is gestured at satirically in this "monotonous repetition" of an unseen bird's accompaniment to his inadvertent stumbling upon the scene of the crime.

The thrice-told tale of what happens at the Old Frenchman place, and indeed the novel as a whole, is usually addressed in terms of its excessive visuality.[29]

---

[28] Chandler, *The Simple Art of Murder* (London: Vintage, 1988), 16.
[29] See, for instance, Richard Gray, *The Life of William Faulkner: A Critical Biography* (Oxford: Blackwell, 1994), 171–73; Greg Forter, "Faulkner, Trauma, and the Uses of Crime Fiction," in Mooreland, ed., *Companion to William Faulkner*, 388–92; Peter Lurie, *Vision's Immanence*, 39–42.

And yet, what most impresses is neither the "blonde running" of Temple's distress, nor the meticulously mapped floor-plan, but the extent to which those "dirty yellowish clay marbles" (208) or "clots of phlegm" (187) that are the old man's cataracted eyes seem to project a caul upon the very dominion of the visible. That he is "deef" (210) as well does not seem to prevent the audible spectrum from registering its variable impressions on the textual apparatus. From the "voices—a word; now and then a laugh" (215) to which Temple is hyper-sensitively attuned throughout her ordeal, to the meat that "hissed and spluttered in the skillet" (216), the "crackle" of the mattress and its "faint dry whisper of shucks" (227), from which vantage point she and Tommy are obliged, not to *see* the drunken brawling of the men in the other room, but to *hear* it in acute detail, down to the enigmatic "dry, light sounds like billiard balls" (228) of Gowan Stevens's teeth being knocked together,[30] and the fateful choking, snoring and moaning of Stevens himself (234)—the entire episode is framed according to a nocturnal inversion of the daytime relations between sight and sound. "Face to face," we read, "their voices were like shadows upon two close blank walls" (220): the narrative voice is invested in this inversion, in which an acoustic horror subsumes the visual throughout the dying of daylight. Sounds are separated from known bodies, rendered quasi-autonomous and malevolent in a way the "stamped tin" visual quality of Popeye could only faintly evoke. That absurd figure, so generative of Chandlerian similes—"like a modernist lampstand" (183), "like the face of a wax doll set too near a hot fire and forgotten" (182)—is always "as though seen by electric light" (181), poached as it is from the artificial glare of pulp fiction and gangster film: "a right pretty little man, even if he aint no John Gilbert" (336). But his backlit blackness is also a catlike silence, and greatly more troubling at night: "She did not see Popeye at all when he entered," but then, inevitably, "without having heard, felt, the door open," there he was—shifted far down the Platonic spectrum of sense, lower than sight and lower even than hearing, into that most powerful affective dimension of smell, which Freud characterized as that from which, in primitive hominid intercourse, all civilizational processes have historically striven upwards since *Homo erectus*.[31] Popeye's *punctum* is olfactory: "the brilliantine which [he] used on his hair," for Temple (234); or, "He smells black, Benbow thought; he smells like that black stuff that ran out of Bovary's mouth and down upon her bridal veil when they raised her head" (184), a figure in which race, abjection, and literariness are hopelessly confounded.

---

[30] Edwin T. Arnold and Dawn Trouard, *Reading Faulkner: Sanctuary* (Jackson; MS: University Press of Mississippi, 1996), 79.

[31] See the notorious footnote in Sigmund Freud, *Civilization and its Discontents*, trans. James Strachey (New York: W. W. Norton, 1961), 46–47.

Popeye's instantiation of a certain sonic void is preserved into the day, where it balloons into an act on the cusp of an aesthetic sound barrier—rape by corncob constituting what Faulkner called "the most horrific idea I could think of," strictly unrepresentable, yet somehow symptomatic of "what a person in Mississippi would believe to be current trends," albeit "a little more than they had been getting; stronger and rawer—more brutal."[32] It cannot be written: thanks to a bar of internalized censorship, it is a paradigmatic "absent event," as characterized in our introduction, and must therefore imprint itself negatively. The novel presents the breach of this representational sound barrier through an inversion of sound and silence:

> it was as though sound and silence had become inverted. She could hear silence in a thick rustling as he moved toward her through it, thrusting it aside, and she began to say Something is going to happen to me. She was saying it to the old man with the yellow clots for eyes. "Something is happening to me!" she screamed at him, sitting in his chair in the sunlight, his hands crossed on the top of the stick. "I told you it was!" she screamed, voiding the words like hot silent bubbles into the bright silence about them until he turned his head and the two phlegm-clots above her where she lay tossing and thrashing on the rough, sunny boards. "I told you! I told you all the time!" (140)

Whose voice is this? If it is the narrator's, then that generally impersonal source of narrative information has suffered a sea-change. Although the anaphoric anchoring of the prose in the repeated pronoun "she" correlates it with the dominant narrative voice, certain deformations of the short-sentence form loosen its hold on the text. For one thing, the descriptive discourse has been irradiated by metaphorical color: silence has become a "bright" and movable element whose disturbance results in "thick rustling"; words are "hot silent bubbles"; eyes are "phlegm-clots." For another, Temple's reported speech, both emergent and quoted, is drawn into the elaboration of larger periods around it, and not allocated freestanding paragraphs as per the usual format of novelistic speech. And further, while the novel's usual temporal relation between narrative discourse and incident is businesslike, indicative and "isomorphic," here we have entered into a strange and paradoxical temporality where both nothing and everything is happening—the pronoun "something" that Temple reaches for to denominate her rape is also a narrative "nothing," since we have no way (at this point in the text) of filling it in with any content. If it is not the narrator's voice, then neither is it the voice of Temple, who speaks in a much more idiomatic

---

[32] Quoted in Blotner, *Faulkner*, 233–34.

language of youth and feminine distraction. Rather, it would appear to have been generated out of some intense exposure of the narrator's usually clipped and disaffected tone to the excruciating affect of Temple's experience—a stylistic compromise hovering on the brink of an event, a "something," it cannot name.

To whom is it addressed? Diegetically, Temple's cries do have an addressee; the question is whether the passage itself, in its "free indirect" stylistic compromise, does as well. As a figure of the *deus absconditus*, the old man functions allegorically as an avatar of the Big Other, that regulative virtual authority woven collectively out of the social matrix of human intercourse, but installed in each individual as an ultimate court of appeal—the apotheosis of a living ethical community to Whom all language is ultimately addressed.[33] But in this scenario, the Big Other neither sees nor hears; two of His three pillars of authority have collapsed: the Imaginary of the visual (He cannot see or recognize the subject); the Real of the audible (He cannot hear the subject's direct appeal from the traumatic place of her own violation). We might say that cinema and recorded/broadcast sound have deprived the Big Other of His primary organs of perception. All that is left is the Symbolic itself, thrust into an unimaginable, inaudible space whose architectonic is warped by a trauma it cannot name. Language here emerges into an impure relationship with itself, such that the "silence" of the symbolic order assumes the sonic qualities of the Real, turned inside out by the rape's namelessness. This is the oxymoronic vacuum in which Popeye moves in two-dimensional fatality, "silence in a thick rustling," "thrusting it aside" to open the void of representation around which the entire novel turns in cyclonic movements. The void itself, as it were, enters and takes hold of Temple, who while "voiding the words like hot silent bubbles into the bright silence about them," is having done to her that unmentionable "Something" that her ejaculations draw back from a future tense into the present continuous and then thrust into the past: "is going to happen," "is happening," "I told you it was!"

This truly remarkable passage is the climax of the long, frenzied opening act of the novel, and assumes the same sort of relation to the mechanical ticking-off of the narrative chronology that precedes it as the third sentence does to the two previous, indicative ones in the quoted paragraph on radios and phonographs, above. Since the prose is forbidden by its structure from telling us what is happening, the passage concerning the crisis of an event refashions itself into a desperate expression of literary style. Only in belated retrospect, and in the context of a forensic reconstruction (376), will the "Something" come properly to light, almost 240 pages later. Here, at the very moment of its taking place, style commandeers the narrative voice and draws it vertically away from the "stream

---

[33] Jacques Lacan, *The Seminar of Jacques Lacan, Book II: The Ego in Freud's Theory and in the Technique of Psychoanalysis, 1954–1955*, ed. Jacques-Alain Miller, trans. Sylvana Tomaselli (Cambridge: Cambridge University Press, 1988), 235–47.

of event," toward the placeless vantage-point of the literary Big Other, Who, blinded by cinema and deafened by radio and phonography, still warms His hands over the dwindling fires of the Symbolic. At this moment, what is at stake in *Sanctuary*'s self-conflicted narrative voice becomes starkly clear: it is patiently awaiting those moments when what Chandler called the "trick" of keeping "your characters and your story operating on a level which is understandable to the semi-literate public" no longer has to be played; when it can drop the pretense and get back to those "intellectual and artistic overtones which that public does not seek or demand" that we call *style*—only without Chandler's sense of uplift and public service. Because these periods are not addressed to any public at all; they are addressed to the literary Big Other, to the fading status of literature as the sanctioned source of an entire ethical order of things.

The novel's schizophrenic narrative voice, alternating between sullen stretches of monosyllabic narration and sudden purple efflorescences of "style," is fascinated by the dialectical play between silence and sound that secretly attends the plot. Nowhere does this sonic fascination achieve such exalted elaboration as in the structural "repeat" of Temple's trapped night at the Old Frenchman place, represented by her extended incarceration at Miss Reba's in Memphis. Here again, the visual is ruthlessly subordinated to an acoustic dominant, to the extent that our entire image of the place is assembled from fragments of ambivalent aural information, taken by the extremely sensitive sound recording apparatus that Temple has become—and I will force the issue by relating this situation to that of the auditor of a typical radio drama of the early 1930s. There are few passages in modern literature ("Sirens" in *Ulysses* comes to mind) so committed to the symbolic registration of sound, to the virtual exclusion of visible data. Given that Temple's eyes focus "into black pinheads at every sound on the stairs" (337), and that so much happens in a diaphanous gloom of shuttered interiority behind wooden walls, it is no surprise that the acoustic signals are relatively strong and clear. Miss Reba's two dogs conduct a sonic composition unlike any in American letters, their "wheezy, flatulent sounds" (277) modulating into "vicious falsetto" snarling (278), their "claws clicking on the metal strips which bound the carpet to the stairs" (279) when they are not "sniffing and whining outside the door" (279) or coming "up the stairs in a furious scrabble" (285). It is only when their stillness lasts more than a second that Temple "could almost see them crouching there in the dark" (285).

Temple is an ideal radio auditor, able to transform well-directed sound effects into visual hallucinations, but that is because her Memphis training in the art of listening has been exhaustive. She "could hear the rhythmic splash-splash of the washing board somewhere" (279); the window shades make "faint rasping sounds. Temple began to hear a clock" (281); when she is not "listening to the secret whisper of her blood" (282), she finds that she is "hearing her watch; had been hearing it for some time" (285). Soon enough, all of this incessant sounding of the Real congeals into a malevolent white noise of lost signal clarity: "she began to hear a hundred conflicting sounds in a single converging threat" (281), we read, as we do of her discovery "that the house was full of noises, seeping into the room muffled and indistinguishable, as though from a distance" (285). Or again: "The house was full of sounds. Indistinguishable, remote, they came to her with a quality of awakening, resurgence, as though the house itself had been asleep, rousing itself with dark" (287), that very darkness being "full of the sound of the city" (285)—car engines, a "grind of gears," the very "sound of traffic—motor horns, trolleys" (277), out of which modern soundscapes are made. And yet, within this "indistinguishable" white noise, Temple has been trained to locate discrete signals:

> She could distinguish voices now from below stairs. She had been hearing them for some time, lying in the room's musty isolation. Later a mechanical piano began to play. Now and then she heard automobile brakes in the street beneath the window; once two voices quarrelling bitterly came up and beneath the shade. (288)

This amounts to a technical mastery of sorts, over the babble and hiss of indiscriminate media noise. Temple separates one kind of sound from another, holds them apart in time and space thanks to the operation of some internal filter or adjustable microphone. She is learning to map her world acoustically in three dimensions. But all this is of no consequence because, yet again (with an air of the eternal return), Popeye is spliced into this space as a sonic void, an embodiment of silence: "Temple neither saw nor heard her door when it opened. She just happened to look toward it after how long she did not know, and saw Popeye standing there, his hat slanted across his face. Still without making any sound he entered and shut the door and shot the bolt and came toward the bed" (289). Personification of the "absent event" that Temple can no more name than the novel can, Popeye appears or "abrupts" into the feminine place he has always already "voided," not with the phallus but with pieces of disposable equipment. That he finally, in the fit of his latest assault, makes "a high whinnying sound like a horse" (289) displaces him entirely from the realm of the human, as does the later speculation that he "went off and got fixed up with one of these glands, these monkey glands" (357). With no proper place in the Symbolic Order, Popeye's few sounds do not invalidate his preternatural silence so much as they confirm it by lapsing out of sense altogether.

In any event, when in this same room Temple is finally prompted by Horace to put into language the first phase of her passion, what manifests itself is the wish to cancel or "invert" the real or "void" of her sex. Temple's recounting of her violation partakes of an asymptotic logic that approaches the event without ever reaching it. Locating her ear-witness account back on the night before the assault occurs, Temple tells of the immense efforts of her imaginary to ward off the inevitable by trying "to make like I was a boy" (328), so that she could "show them" the phallus and put an end to the melodramatic crisis with a comic *dénouement*. This retroactive filling in of the void that she has become is then succeeded by the prosthetic desire of "fastening myself up some way" (329) in a medieval chastity belt bristling with "long sharp spikes" that she could "jab . . . all the way through him" (329) in a pre-emptive, *hysteron proteron* inversion of sexual roles. Back then, as she puts it, "I didn't know it was going to be just the other way" (329). In open defiance of narrative chronology, the fantastic logic of inversion has gripped the voice from within. What follows is its apotheosis. As Popeye's hand gropes "inside the top of my knickers," approaching "where my insides begin," those same "insides started bubbling" and all of a sudden she is evacuated from the world of the living—"I was crying because I was dead [. . . and] because they had put shucks in the coffin where I was dead" (330). Temple has joined the ranks of the living-dead negro murderer, Tommy, laid out in the undertaker's parlor, and Red in his richly lined box. From within her own coffin, Temple first reduces Popeye to "a little black thing like a nigger boy" (331), and then

> the little black man got littler and littler and I was saying Now. You see now. I'm a man now. Then I thought about being a man, and as soon as I thought it, it happened. It made a kind of plopping sound, like blowing a little rubber tube wrong-side outward. It felt cold, like the inside of your mouth when you hold it open. I could feel it (331).

"Something is happening to me!" Temple's extraordinary narrative management of the rape, adhering strictly to the bar of censorship that makes it a void in the text's symbolic space, literally inverts all of its terms, blows the "little rubber tube wrong-side outward," in order to demonstrate both the degree to which fantasy is shaped by the trauma that it compensates for and the power of the imaginary over the monstrous real that it bears within.

For Horace, however, the lesson is in the first instance moral and sentimental, a romantic fable of evil and innocence. Retreating to his house, he takes up a photograph of the incestuously desired Little Belle, which suddenly "appear[s] to breathe in his palms in a shallow bath of highlight" (333)—as if Temple's story is best understood filtered through the industrialized romance of contemporary moving pictures, where it would be projected soon enough anyway, in Stephen Roberts's 1933 Paramount production of *The Story of Temple Drake*. But the affective depth-charge of what he has just heard is too contaminating, too surcharged with the trauma of an event that has no established place on the imaginary screens of present-day romance. Indeed, the only way this event can be felt in its truth is through a deformation of the symbolic, which is then precisely what happens. Following him into the house is what the narrator calls the "voice of the night" (332), or a little piece of the traumatized acoustic imagination developed in Temple through her ordeal; "he knew suddenly that it was the friction of the earth on its axis, approaching that moment when it must decide to turn on or to remain forever still" (333). His ears now tingling to the vocal nihilism of all things, he is ready to regurgitate the little kernel of the real in Temple's imaginary inversion of her "void":

> he gave over and plunged forward and struck the lavatory and leaned upon his braced arms while the shucks set up a terrific uproar beneath her thighs. Lying with her head lifted slightly, her chin depressed like a figure lifted down from a crucifix, she watched something black and furious go roaring out of her pale body. She was bound naked on her back on a flat car moving at speed through a black tunnel, the blackness streaming in rigid threads overhead, a roar of iron wheels in her ears. The car shot bodily from the tunnel in a long upward slant, the darkness overhead now shredded with parallel attenuations of living fire, toward a crescendo like a held breath, an interval in which she would swing faintly and lazily in nothingness filled with pale, myriad points of light. Far beneath her she could hear the faint, furious uproar of the shucks. (333)

The second major crescendo of style in the novel, this passage begins with one of the great transitional jump cuts in all Faulkner, mid-sentence, from Horace retching over a toilet to Temple back on the bed during the long night at the Old Frenchman Place, underlining the scrambling of focalization wrought by the intensity of affect here. What follows is a synthetic syntax pertaining to a meta-character, not Horace, not Temple, but both and neither, an abstract triangulation of narrative voice strung out between them and the omniscient narrator who is once again freed from the mechanics of storytelling. Such a voice presents a particularly rich opportunity for "sliding to an identification with represented subject positions; and hence the contamination of authorial discourse by other voices: by inflections of represented discourse, folds within the fabric of the text."[34]

In this complex voice, the absent event is giddily displaced and condensed, subjected to rules of metaphor and simile that owe a good deal to the Freudian dreamwork. What Temple "sees" is the very same pronoun that "is [always already] happening" to her, only now in the process of being voided from her physically: "*something* black and furious go[ing] roaring out of her pale body."

---

[34] John Frow, *Character and Person* (Oxford: Oxford University Press, 2014), 180.

Popeye, the incarnation of "black" in this fiction, is expelled like a "nigger boy" (331) or baby from the same hole that he has torn in the textual space, become Temple's child in a "roar" that is helplessly confounded with that of the train that got Temple in her predicament to begin with: "a roar of iron wheels."

Here the text touches upon the existential limit already breached in Horace's "voice of the night." It is a limit touched again, later, when Horace reels from the lynching and immolation of Lee Goodwin in an atmosphere of hell that the narrator cannot better describe than by evoking its uncanny inversion of the standard relations between silence and sound:

> from the central mass of fire there came no sound at all. . . . Horace couldn't hear them. He couldn't hear the man who had got burned screaming. He couldn't hear the fire, though it still swirled upward unabated, as though it were living upon itself, and soundless: a voice of fury like in a dream, roaring silently out of a peaceful void. (384)

With this, the text completes its baroque tropological circuit of a certain "voice of fury" that paradoxically roars "silently out of a peaceful void." A novel that begins with three "monotonous" repetitive notes of Mississippi birdsong, and culminates in a Parisian soundscape of Massenet, Scriabin, and Berlioz—a gradation from late romantic to early atonal music—having meanwhile touched upon commercial ballads, dirge-like spirituals, and hectic jazz, not to mention a dizzying range of urban and everyday acoustics, is just as concerned with an encompassing "silence" whose *locus classicus* is the "void" torn in the text by its central, unrepresentable event. One of its chief formal concerns is to establish a technics of style whereby these sounds and that silence are sutured to one another in a narrative voice capable of "inverting" one into the other, a voice whose "roaring" and "silence" can loop on a Möbius strip. But it is also deeply concerned with the establishment of a prototypical *hysteron proteron* effect, an inversion of the usual sequence of before and after, whose most uncanny material source in the media ecology of 1930 was the radio itself, of which Adorno noted that its electromagnetic propagation vastly outstrips the speed of sound. Recalling an unnerving experience of listening to a radio in Kronberg—to a Berlin station broadcasting the live song of a nightingale, also in Kronberg (just feet away from Adorno)—and hearing the radio sound before the "live" ones of the actual bird, Adorno remarked the "astonishing results which may influence the 'expression' of the 'radio voice' by giving it a touch of unreality and witchcraft. . . . one of the essentials of that voice."[35] *Hysteron proteron*: in radio you hear the "effect" before you hear its "cause."

---

[35] Theodor W. Adorno, *Current of Music: Elements of a Radio Theory*, trans. and ed. Robert Hullot-Kentor (Cambridge: Polity, 2009), 74.

Before more fully establishing the material basis of these kinds of effects in the circumambient radio waves that, in 1930, were allowing "voices from the void" to speak in the most intimate spaces of the individual on a national level, and thereby redefining the "regional," it is worth quickly reviewing what *Sanctuary* has tried to teach us about the torsions internal to literary voice in that year. First, as a novel, it has knowingly capitulated to both the narrative and the stylistic economies of the pulps: a plot as lurid and sensational as could be conceived in the cynical rush to some hypothetical lowest common denominator of popular taste,[36] and an abundance of what one reviewer called "the short sentence used as understatement ... familiar from Hemingway and Lardner," but positively *de rigeur* in the *Black Mask* school of writing.[37] Second, however, in reflexive critique of just that inaugural formal decision, the novel then allegorizes the stakes of its own composition by (a) building into its text plentiful figurations of the new forces putting the form's cultural authority at risk—radios, phonographs, telephones, player pianos, jazz bands, magazines, newspapers, fast cars, and so on—and (b) insisting on the relationship between that ambient noise and the underlying silencing death drive that results in the literal cadavers of the anonymous black murderer, Tommy, and Red, and the coffined, "living dead" self-image of Temple at her most critical point as a narrator; not to mention the cremated body of Lee Goodwin himself. Third, as we have seen repeatedly, the novel further strives to "manage" its own fall into pop-romance sensationalism by recurring to intermittent stretches of prose with no narrative or descriptive purpose, whose sole function is to protest the dominant short-sentence form by sublating it in a new, dilating discursive atmosphere. And fourth, figurally, the symptomatic device of *hysteron proteron* orchestrates many of these stylistic flourishes, thereby articulating their logic with that of the sonic media ecology of the day.

Here is where we must pose the question of voice. What we are given to read over the length of the text is a stylistic oscillation between two narrative voices: (1) the lean and economical, streamlined syntax of Hammett-like preterite indicativeness ("He looked at her. ... He was in bed. ... He rose to his elbow. ... She came and looked down at him," 305), and (2) the kind of baroque syntactic constructions we have been attending to here. In the social world drawn by the novel, the town square's soundscape is allegorically orchestrated by the "disembodied voices" of mechanical and electronic reproduction, and by the mourning songs of the living dead; it is from this mechanized, melancholic

---

[36] Alan Reynolds Thompson remarked in the *Bookman* (April 1931): "Those who play the game of exploiting the *frisson nouveau* find that its stakes are continually rising; each must raise his predecessor's ante. Mr. Faulkner has evidently determined not to be a piker." See Inge, *Contemporary Reviews*, 59.

[37] Philip E. Wheelwright in *The Symposium*, 2 (April 1931); see Inge, *Contemporary Reviews*, 62.

space that the stylistic brevity of the first voice is addressed. But within and against this flattened voice is lodged the "void" of what cannot be represented in it, the absent event that the reader is asked to construct out of the belated evidence provided in the trial. Given that this "void" is the very location of the sensation itself, and of Temple's excessively fascinating sex ("I saw her. She was some baby. Jeez. I wouldn't have used no cob," as one drummer puts it, 383), it presents a vulnerable, reversible spot on the surface of the narrative, where the second voice can establish its theatre of operations. This other voice then tries to do to the first voice what Temple tries, imaginatively, to do to her fascinating "it": turn it "wrong-side outward." The second voice thus takes the same material made available through the first voice, but subjects it to the defamiliarization of its rules of engagement, much as the Freudian dreamwork subjects the daytime experiences of the subject to the alien formalizations of the Unconscious in order to make palpable the inexpressible wishes of the latent dream thoughts in the manifest dream content.

Above all, this second voice deranges the very categories of person and identity, cause and effect, that stabilize the narrative coordinates of the first voice. The intersubjective panic that associates the novel's first great stylistic crescendo with the blind and deaf addressee of the old man feeds into the second crescendo's radical elision of the distinction between Horace and Temple; the moment of astonishing indistinction ("he gave over and plunged forward and struck the lavatory and leaned upon his braced arms while the shucks set up a terrific uproar beneath her thighs," 333) prepares us to read the rest of that great paragraph as a voice shot through with multiple characteristics and affective intensities. The passage belongs as much to Horace as it does to Temple, and to the narrator as much as to either. The third-person pronoun "she" refers to her fantasy, to his fantasy of her fantasy, and to the narrator's conjuring of both psychic intensities, in a manner that cannot be arbitrated. The text here fashions a discursive space where the legalistic ascription of certain actions to given agents, which defines the bullet-point prose of the marketplace, is drawn inside-out at its most sensitive spot. It has tapped into a zone of affective interanimation (the vomiting and the anticipation of rape forming a strange loop) where spatial and gendered distances are obviated in a stylistic frequency that threads them together on a singular trajectory: "the darkness overhead now shredded with parallel attenuations of living fire, toward a crescendo like a held breath" (333). The "voice of fury" roaring "silently out of a peaceful void" radiates upward and outward, away from the story's sensational crime, turning its dominant style inside out at the moments when genuine affective intensity strains against the vocal limits of popular romance. This "voice of fury" functions like that rubbery apotropaic extrusion that Temple "plops" out of her own depths. Its wish is retroactively to ward off and protest the many crimes being perpetrated against literary taste by the host form, "basely conceived" to make money. Its appeal is to an unresponsive Big Other: a radio signal sent far out past the curvature of the earth, to a "nothingness filled with pale, myriad points of light" (333), "cauterised out of the old and tragic flank of the world" (331–32), some "shadowy world upon whose scarred flanks the old wounds whirl onward at dizzy speed into darkness lurking with new disasters" (283)—where the literary Auditor awaits the distress signal sent up from the scene of literature's rape by a new media ecology. This is Literature, in the midst of its violation by new media voices, lodging its pointless complaint.

"Since December 28, 1895," Kittler remarks, "there has been one infallible criterion for high literature: it cannot be filmed."[38] *Sanctuary* is, in most of its component parts, eminently filmable, woven of a narrative voice that Stanley Aronowitz would characterize in terms of its literalness, which is to say, relatively, an "abandonment of subjectivity in the work. In place of interiority, which presupposed the individual who was distinguished from the objects outside of her- or himself by consciousness [. . .], literalism dissolves the subject-object split into object relations."[39] The voice that carries the bulk of *Sanctuary*'s narrative pursues such literalism into a Hemingwayesque techno-stylistics of the object-world, adapted in its grammatical as well as its syntactical substance to the simple subject-predicate relations that govern a utilitarian, exploitable cosmos. The text is, in that regard, signally unprotected by the prophylactics of "high literary" unfilmability; it, too, becomes exploitable and openly remediable within the various transferences that are making "the power of the written word subordinate to another power, a more glittering, a grosser power" in the cinema.[40] And yet, as spectators of the exploitation movie *The Story of Temple Drake* (1931) were well aware (however it may have served as a *cause célèbre* for the tightening of industry censorship), there was something "unfilmable" at the very center of the sensational melodrama itself: the lowest literature "cannot be filmed" either. This strange overlap between what "cannot be filmed" in high literary aesthetics and in exploitation fiction and film is the occasion for a veritable "silence" or "void" at the heart of the material; this is the uncanny point at which the novel's curious second voice materializes, at those moments when the text draws closest to it. This second voice is the eruption into the novel of a "high literary" style that cannot be filmed, in Kittler's sense—its extremely complex and contradictory weave of multiple tenses, inverted subject positions, *hysteron proteron* figures, palimpsestic characters, and impossible and fantasmatic points of view, mark it out as non-remediable style.

---

[38] Friedrich Kittler, *Discourse Networks 1800/1900*, trans. Michael Metteer, with Chris Cullen (Stanford, CA: Stanford University Press, 1990), 248.

[39] Stanley Aronowitz, *Dead Artists, Live Theories, and Other Cultural Problems* (London: Routledge, 1994), 54.

[40] F. Scott Fitzgerald, *The Crack-Up with Other Pieces and Stories* (London: Penguin, 1965), 49.

One final point concerns the framing of this entire complex within the specific sexual hiatus whose parameters coincide with the opening and closing of the text: Horace's temporary abandonment of the domesticated conjugal knot. The ten-year exposure of the incurable romantic to the real of marital cohabitation (rendered into metaphor for Horace in the drip and reek of Belle's weekly supply of shrimp) results in a flight back to the narcissistic temptations of pre-Oedipal incestuous desire. But what Horace discovers in this hysterical traversal of the borderlands separating the imaginary (incest) from the symbolic (paternity) is the excruciating real of sound in which Temple throbs and waits, and which, as feminine, has assumed the qualities of a force that cuts through the "Borromean Knot" that holds these three orders together-and-apart: electricity. "It was as though femininity were a current running through a wire along which a certain number of identical bulbs were hung" (262), Horace thinks; no matter where you are, there it is, a current pumped indifferently into every domestic interior through wires that threaded the continent, blinking out into millions of identical bulbs, and millions of other appliances too—particularly sonic ones, phonographs and radios alike. The masculine recoil from a feminized electrical current of voice has a mediatic unconscious.

Furnishing an electrical soundscape

Charles Hannon has discussed the transformation in electrical power supply taking place in Faulkner's Oxford, Mississippi, around 1935–36, as he was writing his masterpiece *Absalom, Absalom!*[41] Faulkner worked at the local university power plant in 1929, while he was writing *As I Lay Dying*, and purchased a dilapidated house in need of serious repair in that same year; Hannon argues persuasively that electricity and its supply would have been at the forefront of Faulkner's consciousness in the mid-1930s, around the time that the Tennessee Valley Authority offered to buy out the local station and absorb it and the rest of Lafayette County into the regional grid. But earlier still, even as he was writing his *tour de force* "to the hum of the powerhouse dynamo,"[42] this question of electrical energy, its supply and distribution, and the new kinds of appliances it was powering at the time had percolated into his fictional maps of Yoknapatawpha County. As we shall see, *As I Lay Dying* stands tall as an allegory of the uncanny impact of electromagnetic and electrical voices on the technical resources of the novel as a form. But in order to assume the dense weave of allegorical meanings that it does, the novel had first to take cognizance of what was happening to

---

[41] See Charles Hannon, "Topologies of Discourse in Faulkner," in John T. Matthews, ed., *Faulkner in Context* (Cambridge: Cambridge University Press, 2015), 91–99.

[42] Blotner, *Faulkner*, 249.

the now rather older medium of phonography under the onslaught of radio and electrification—which is to say, its subsumption into an electrical grid, as phonography was absorbed into the electric media, much as electricity was subsuming the cinematic apparatus at the same time, and layering it over with sounds. This is a story of convergence around the universal fact and availability, unevenly developed and distributed, of electricity in the late 1920s and early 1930s.

Still, electricity in its raw state was far too immaterial and inhuman a force with which to grapple objectively as an author, let alone (at another level) to legitimate a new sonic hegemony in the language of corporate PR. The uncanny technical operations whereby sound waves could be converted into and out of electronic pulses, via ingenious feats of engineering in amplification and transmission, were strictly unthinkable on a popular level, nor could they be directly "represented" in fictional form. Given how relatively recently modern culture had been transformed by the mechanical successes of motion photography, phonography, and typewriting, there could be no question of simply subsuming that barely accepted mechanical media system within another, electrical and convergent one, without the meliorative tactics of "remediation." As Bolter and Grusin put it, new media cannot survive the economic and ideological trials of mass acceptance (let alone literary critique) without a kind of systemic homage and deference to the media that already enjoy widespread approval. Each "medium or constellation of media," they write, "responds to, redeploys, competes with, and reforms other media" (55); and it does so with particular delicacy at the moment of emergence, in order to stabilize the frames of reference in which it is understood. If it was already the case that, as Lisa Gitelman writes, mechanical phonography had obtruded onto a well-established mediatic space and "abruptly called its commonsensical parameters into question, begging a mutual redefinition of print, speech, and public," while at the same time appearing as "part of an ongoing industrialization of communication" that the literary monopoly was already well attuned to,[43] then the same kinds of observations could be made, but amplified, regarding the moment of 1922, when the RCA monopoly began seriously to refashion the nascent "commonsensical parameters" of phonography itself, electrifying its *modus operandi* and situating it within a spectrum of new electronic acoustics.

We will follow a few threads through the revolutionary media history of the 1910s and '20s, insofar as that history touches upon the reproduction of sound and its domestication (since that is what the novel's formal preoccupation with "voice" would be most sensitive to). The first of these concerns the kinds of casings or "boxes" that were to house the electrical sounds of the radio age. It was, after all, as *furniture* that the domesticated appliances of vocal reproduction were

---

[43] Lisa Gitelman, *Always Already New: Media, History and the Data of Culture* (Cambridge, MA: MIT Press, 2006), 13.

obliged to pose in the period's imagination generally, and this in two stages: first, in the market-sensitive dissimulation of the apparatus of the mechanical phonograph in the high years of that industry's mass success; second, the continuation of that same process during the protracted period of conversion from mechanical sound reproduction to electrical methods. The overriding imperative of the first stage of phonography's consolidation as a domestic appliance was to disguise "the phonographic apparatus itself, eliding the mechanical functioning of the machine and focusing consumer attention and interest instead on the sounds it produced"; and it did so above all by "incorporating" the phonograph "into furniture."[44] It is as furniture that we tend to glimpse the acoustic apparatus in *Sanctuary*: Miss Reba's standing "mechanical piano" (288, 313),[45] the new telephone installed in Horace's room over which he hears "across a remote blaring of victrola or radio music, a man's voice" (318), and that latter machine itself, imagined by Horace, looming bulky and immobile with the full solidity of drugstore furnishing: "Against Horace's ear the radio or the victrola performed a reedy arpeggio of saxophones. Obscene, facile, they seemed to be quarrelling with one another like two dextrous monkeys in a cage. He could hear the gross breathing of the man at the other end of the wire" (318). Here again, as in the town square, an *a priori* antagonism is projected onto the very sounds the machine is amplifying, where the jazzy reed instruments, having been reduced to wave frequencies, "quarrel" with animal ferocity—in what is almost surely an inter-textual reverberation of Stevens's "Squiggling like saxophones"[46]—and where the "victrola or radio" disjunction is repeated, inverted, in order to underscore an abiding antagonism. The point is that what makes possible the near light-speed transmission of that "reedy arpeggio," first through the amplification system of a Victrola or radio, and thence through the earpiece of Horace's new telephone, is of course electricity itself. The new acoustic media system that allowed for such diffusion depended on electrical modes of encoding, amplification, transmission, decoding, and reproducing sound, such that telephony, a newly converted phonograph industry, radio, and eventually sound film all constitute moments, distinct applications, in a single, coordinated *electrical-acoustic apparatus*.[47] But given that we are positioned in the middle of a momentous process of conversion, this electrical remediation of the mechanical cannot be

---

[44] Steve Wurtzler, *Electric Sounds: Technological Change and the Rise of Corporate Mass Media* (New York: Columbia University Press, 2007), eBook edition, loc. 2726 of 9211.

[45] This device was hailed as the harbinger of a new "musical democracy," its revolutionary impact defined in terms of the fact that it "allowed anyone to 'play' music skillfully without effort." See Craig H. Roell, *The Piano in America, 1890–1940* (Chapel Hill, NC: University of North Carolina Press, 1989), 102.

[46] Wallace Stevens, "A High-Toned Old Christian Woman," *Collected Poetry and Prose* (New York: Library of America, 1997), 47.

[47] Wurtzler, *Electric Sounds*, loc. 141 of 9211, and ff.

understood in isolation from the medium it was in the act of supplanting, from within identical casings and housings, as furniture.

In "The Curves of the Needle," Theodor Adorno commented that the "transformation of the piano from a musical instrument into a piece of furniture—which Max Weber accurately perceived—is recurring in the case of the gramophone but in an extraordinarily more rapid fashion."[48] Steve Wurtzler concurs that from 1906 onward, changing designs for the Victrola "folded the reproducing horn on itself and enclosed it—as well as the turntable, sound box, and tone arm—within a cabinet that contained the entire machine. The phonograph became a piece of furniture."[49] The vice-president of Victor attributed this decisive modification to the gendering of the middle-class "parlor": "it was my opinion that ladies did not like the mechanical-looking things in their parlors."[50] This feminization of the look of the appliance was coeval with a wholesale rethinking of the protocols that governed the use of the device, including even the "technical protocols of the medium, like the hardness of recording surfaces and the design of recording styli," which had "emerged partly in response to the timbre of women's voices, which proved tricky to record well."[51] These transformations rapidly altered the social and cultural meaning of the devices, veiling the "mechanical being" and factory-made technical materiality of the equipment in pompous nineteenth-century costumes. For Adorno, enclosing the Victrola's horn in imitation or genuine wood was a disavowal of the very machinery that gave it voice; while the horns were still external, their "brassiness" at least indicated the fact of machine production, but in "better social circles ... they were quickly muffled into the colored masses or wood chalices."[52] That muffling was intended to physically resemble nothing so much as a kind of upright wooden sarcophagus on legs, sometimes done up in "Sheraton" or "Queen Anne" garb, but always heavy, somber, dark-wooden cabinets into which the horn was discreetly tucked away behind L-shaped storage doors. Columbia's response was to replicate the pomposity in a 1907 cabinet-model, internal-horn graphophone "eventually called the 'Grafonola,'" which "mimicked the physical appearance of an upright piano," but this sold poorly. "Columbia next produced an alternative 'library-table style' more consistent with the Victrola's transformation of the phonograph into a piece of furniture"[53]—in this case a portable sewing machine plus horn. It is thanks to such a gendered cultural transformation, from

---

[48] Theodor Adorno, "Curves of the Needle," in Richard Leppert, ed., Susan H. Gillespie, trans., *Essays on Music* (Berkeley, CA & Los Angeles: University of California Press, 2002), 273.

[49] Wurtzler, *Electric Sounds*, loc. 2637 of 9211.

[50] Leon Douglass, quoted in Tim Gracyk, "Leon F. Douglass, Inventor and Victor's First Vice President," *Victrola and 78 Journal* 8 (Spring 1996), available at www.gracyk.com/leon.shtml.

[51] Gitelman, *Always Already New*, 15.

[52] Adorno, "Curves of the Needle," 273.

[53] Wurtzler, *Electric Sounds*, loc. 2656 of 9211.

a "mechanical-looking thing" to a wood-cased item of respectable furniture in which the obtrusive technical elements are stowed and obscured, that the second Mrs. Bundren in *As I Lay Dying* can finally appear carrying a graphophone, one of "them that shuts up like a hand-grip, with a handle and all, so a fellow can carry it with him wherever he wants."[54]

But radio, too, required a domestication of its outrageously inhuman electronic apparatus, in a process accelerated by the already advanced evolution of phonograph design. For the first decade and a half of its astonishing social proliferation, radio consisted of a congeries of parts that had to be purchased separately and assembled at home. Dry cells and storage batteries, vacuum tubes, antenna wire, insulators, lightning arrestors, ground wire, tuning apparatus, microphones, headphones, all were required, along with a knowledge of circuit diagrams, electronics and the vagaries of the ionosphere. The resultant contraption, once assembled, was "a complicated maze of wires and controls which confuse women and discourage their use of it."[55] Such "[a]malgams of unadorned and undisguised components and wires [...] were distinctly unattractive, banished by some women to the attic, basement or garage, tolerated by others only because of their novelty."[56] Though sales were astronomical and uptake ubiquitous, this gendering of radio's domestic place would require extensive rethinking in the later 1920s, as the medium shifted from a relatively narrowcast or "DX"-seeking device to a proper broadcast instrument. As Steven Connor sums it up, "During the teens of the century and the early 1920s, radio listeners [...] had often built their own apparatus, which needed to be carefully maintained. Once the designs of radio had stabilized and been commercialized, the radio set, often disguised as a piece of furniture, was merely a way station through which sounds and voices could pass on their way to the listener."[57] Domesticated radios had a tendency to lie flat in conventional, horizontal sarcophagus form; nor is the coffin an outrageous comparison for these newly contrived pieces of modern furniture, given that the mass-produced phenomenon of the "disembodied voice," played out in the variable fortunes of phonography and radio in the period and conducted by the resonant organic substance of wood, was inseparable from anxieties about its qualitative "death"—its alienation from organic life as such, despite carrying all the correct wavelengths of voice. But two kinds of voice lay dying in these wooden caskets.

---

[54] William Faulkner, *As I Lay Dying*, in *Novels 1930–1935*, eds. Joseph Blotner and Noel Polk (New York: Library of America, 1985), 176. Subsequent citations included in text.

[55] Radio Press Service, cited in "Women and Wireless," *Literary Digest* (December 15, 1925), 25.

[56] Susan Douglas, *Listening In: Radio and the American Imagination* (Minneapolis, MN: University of Minnesota Press, 2004), 69.

[57] Steven Connor, "I Switch Off: Beckett and the Ordeals of Radio," in Debra Rae Cohen, Michael Coyle, and Jane Lewty, eds., *Broadcasting Modernism* (Gainesville, FL: University Press of Florida, 2013), 277–78.

In the gramophone, phonograph, or graphophone, human voices migrated from living lips to fixed grooves in wax and shellac, thereby becoming susceptible to infinite replay outside the domain of presence. In Friedrich Kittler's terms, the phonographic voice is *"posthum schon zu Lebzeiten"* (posthumous in its own lifetime), which, as Thomas Y. Levin remarks, puts it squarely in the domain of writing "because to write [...] is to invoke a techne that will continue even during one's radical absence (i.e., one's death)."[58] But this is a very distinct kind of writing, in that such inscription seems to preserve the unfathomable material secrets of one's own voice, that incalculable complex of color, accent, intonation, timbre, lisp, and stutter over which one has no control, and which invariably strikes one as foreign and distasteful upon playback.[59] No doubt this recorded voice neutrally stores these details in an accurate facsimile of one's own; it captures me in my innermost being as a speaking subject—but it does so in a manner that I cannot help finding uncanny and unpleasant. The recorded voice is the "death mask" of my living one. And to encounter it in playback is to be confronted by my own specter, the lifenessness of my life. This machine that writes the voice, automatically and in its real, also preserves it beyond death, as a living death. Maurice Renard, in 1907, wrote: "How terrible it is to hear this copper throat and its sounds from beyond the grave! It is more than a photographic, or I had better say cinematographic, something; it is the voice itself, the living voice, still alive among carrion, skeletons, nothingness."[60] In Kittler's version of the consequences, "Once technological media guarantee the similarity of the dead to stored data by turning them into the latter's mechanical product, the boundaries of the body, death and lust, leave the most indelible traces."[61] Driving death like a wedge into the humanist voice-as-presence, the graphophone exposes the machine that speaks as the human itself, already undead, already revenant; and henceforth to inscribe its name into a novel is to dismantle from within the symbolic hierarchies on which that form is predicated.

What, then, of the radio voice? When it first rose to national prominence in the post-WWI years, the most striking of its technical properties was its similarity to the gramophonic voice. Adorno, in his 1939 contribution to the Princeton Radio Research Program, insisted that radio and phonograph were technically "akin" in their qualitative sound, and that both were "steps in the

---

[58] Kittler quoted in Thomas Y. Levin, "Tones from out of Nowhere: Rudolf Pfenninger and the Archaeology of Synthetic Sound," in Wendy Hui Kyong Chun and Thomas Keenan, eds., *New Media, Old Media: A History and Theory Reader* (New York & London: Routledge, 2006), 47.

[59] Benjamin wrote: "Experiments have proved that a man does not recognize ... his own voice on the phonograph." *Illuminations*, trans. Harry Zohn (New York: Schocken Books, 1968), 137. This anticipated Malraux's famous anecdote along the same lines by some twenty years.

[60] Quoted in Friedrich Kittler, *Gramophone, Film, Typewriter*, trans. Geoffrey Winthrop-Young and Michael Wutz (Stanford CA: Stanford University Press, 1999), 53.

[61] Kittler, *Gramophone, Film, Typewriter*, 55.

mechanization of musical production. They are often both combined not merely as far as the sets are concerned, but also as far as the actual performance is concerned."[62] The technical compatibility of the two sounds fomented one of the critical realizations of the era: that radio could equally sustain a live or a phonographically recorded music performance, with no perceptible loss in quality or in the effect of liveness it generated as a medium. So it was that the director of the Berlin Radio Station, Dr. Hans Flesch, instituted the policy in the early 1930s of playing nothing but pre-recorded phonographic records rather than live music over the air. It was Adorno's conviction that this policy was highly advisable, in its tendency to "break the spell of immediacy" that hovered over the radio voice: it was that illusion of presence, here and now, of the radio voice that Adorno particularly wanted to discredit for its implicit authoritarian tendencies.[63] By inserting a recorded phonographic signal into the intimation of presence broached by the radio voice, it was hoped, the artificiality of the phenomenon could be crystallized, if not perceived. Indeed, phenomenologically, there was no difference between the experience of a live and a recorded performance over the wireless: "technical acoustic conditions of radio may make good sense of the shortcomings of a phonograph record. In particular, you do not hear the scratchings of the needle over the radio, though you do hear it when you play the phonograph in your room" (77–78). Kittler's remarks are comparable:

> Broadcasting of weightless material came about for the purpose of mass transmission of records: in 1921 in the United States, in 1922 in Great Britain, and in 1923 in the German Reich. "The uniting of radio with phonograph that constitutes the average radio program yields a very special pattern quite superior in power to the combination of radio and telegraph press that yields our news and weather programs." Whereas Morse signs are much too discrete and binary to be a symbolic code for radio waves, the continuous low frequencies of records are ideal for the amplitude and frequency modulations known as broadcasting.[64]

The fullest social extension of radio happened not for informational reasons, but above all for the purpose of transmitting musical recordings more broadly than the phonograph might. The technical specifications of this growing amity and compatibility, which cut to the heart of many of the forecast profit margins of the phonograph record distributors, are complex. Edison's early phonograph, geared toward the higher end of the frequency range, had not been especially tolerant of these "continuous low frequencies." It was only the work of

---

[62] Adorno, *Current of Music*, 75, 77.
[63] Adorno, *Current of Music*, 78.
[64] Kittler, *Gramophone, Film, Typewriter*, 94.

Bell Laboratories (inventors of the graphophone) that finally, in 1924, delivered the technology over to the electronic age by introducing electromagnetic cutting amplifiers for recording and an electromagnetic pickup for replaying. "In the same year, Siemens presented the recording studios of the media conglomerates with equally electric ribbon microphones, as a result of which grooves were finally able to store frequencies ranging from 100 bass hertz to 5 kilohertz overtones, thus rising to the level of medium-wave transmitters."[65] The rapid pace of technological development at the time, above all electrification, ensured that commercial convergence rather than divergence between the phonograph and the radio voice was the rule.

Following a slump after the introduction of broadcast radio in 1920, phonograph recordings again increased sales with the release of the new electrical machines in the mid-1920s: Columbia's Vivatonal and Brunswick's Panatrope phonographs.[66] Electrical-process recording transformed the tinny recordings of the mechanical age of the device into new and higher-fidelity sound: deeper frequencies, "more sound" as the marketing departments put it, "and greater control in performing sound reproduction."[67] Moreover, and most germane here, the transformation of the phonograph player into an electrical appliance allowed for the most remarkable technical convergence of all—the combined phonograph-radio machines in which the electrical current powered both the turntable and the radio receiver, and the horn could be moved from one source to the other with a single switch. As we shall see, this fitting into furniture of the two most important, if strangely antagonistic, audio technologies of the age augurs something in the order of a "reconciliation under duress" with significant repercussions across the cultural terrain: not least the economic dimension at stake here, according to which the phonographic element is effectively subsumed by its radio protégé. 1929 is the watershed year in which "the two most popular sales lines for Victor were the combined radio and phonograph consoles and portable Victrola devices. As the 1930s began, the phonograph increasingly became an adjunct to the domestic radio receiver rather than a separate and distinct domestic entertainment device."[68] Wurtzler is clear about the reasons for this: "The technological convergence of radio and phonograph embodied in combined machines was literalized in the economic realm when, in 1929, RCA acquired the Victor company. Victor, for decades the leader in disk-model phonographs, became a subsidiary of the radio industry giant, itself formed only a decade earlier as a patent-holding company."[69]

---

[65] Kittler, *Gramophone, Film, Typewriter*, 98.
[66] Wurtzler, *Electric Sounds*, loc. 994 of 9211.
[67] Wurtzler, *Electric Sounds*, loc. 970 of 9211.
[68] Wurtzler, *Electric Sounds*, loc. 967 of 9211.
[69] Wurtzler, *Electric Sounds*, loc. 975 of 9211.

However, this convergence carried with it a sizable threat; that threat resided on the fault line of gender difference, where suddenly the electrically synchronized voices of the phonograph and the radio stood revealed as antagonistic and irreconcilable after all. Even as it made greater and greater technical sense, and was broadly in line with the non-auratic direction in which most cultural production now moved, the growing tendency to broadcast pre-recorded materials rather than live ones nonetheless stimulated a tremendous amount of cultural and ideological resistance. Flesch himself was assailed for "mechanizing" the radio experience, and his policy increasingly discredited. In the United States, where the spatial reach of the new broadcast networks was greater than anywhere on earth at the time, such reactive discrediting of the practice took punitive forms. In August 1928, the Federal Radio Commission ruled against Chicago station WCRW for playing too much recorded music and reduced the station's power from 500 to 100 watts. In the United States, indeed, so pervasive was the reaction that "prior to the early 1940s, the broadcast of recorded music on phonograph disks occurred only on avant-garde radio stations, and even then only by way of exception. Otherwise, all radio music presented performances of live vocal and instrumental music from either the studio or the concert hall. Radio, in other words, most of all staked its claim on the degree of its achieved ability to reproduce live music as natural sound, ostensibly every bit as immediately alive in the home as if the radio mechanism itself was transparent in transmission and played no part at all in the sound."[70]

Such anxiety had everything to do with a dawning realization that, although technically compatible and increasingly convergent, phonography and radio nevertheless played distinct gender roles in the media unconscious of modernity: phonography was masculine; radio, feminine. Recall the "talking machine" voices of the old Hines couple in *Light in August*, and specifically how Eupheus Hines is troped as *gramophonic*, while his spouse is rendered metaphorically *radiophonic* and placed explicitly outside the physical lines that inscribe the phonographic voice on disk or wax cylinder. This openly gendered differentiation has a point of purchase in the reality of technological mediation. Thomas Levin has provided an account of how those very lines, under the inspection of artists and visionaries such as László Moholy-Nagy, provoked a call for "a scientific examination of the tiny inscriptions in the grooves of the phonograph in order to learn exactly what graphic forms corresponded to which acoustic phenomena. Through magnification [...] one could discover the general formal logic that governed the relation of the acoustic to the graphematic, master it, and then be able to produce marks that, once reduced to the appropriate size and inscribed onto the record surface, would literally be acoustic writing."[71] That is,

---

[70] Robert Hullot-Kentor, "Introduction," in Adorno, *Current of Music*, 18–19.

[71] Thomas Y. Levin, "Tones from out of Nowhere: Rudolf Pfenninger and the Archaeology of Synthetic Sound," *Grey Room* 12 (Summer, 2003), 55 [32–79].

due to the indelible material trace that makes phonographic playback possible, the material surface of the inscription was available for symbolic inspection and mastery, allowing for entirely new, artificial voices and tones via a "groove-script alphabet," as Moholy-Nagy called it. The origin of synthetic sound in this microscopic attention to phonographic grooves demands serious theoretical attention and suggests a clear demarcation between the often conflated phonographic and radio voices of modernity. In any event, "the fugitive sounds captured by the phonograph meant what they did because of the ways they might resemble and—particularly—because of the ways they had to be distinguished from the only other snare [for acoustic phenomena] available: inscriptions made on paper."[72] Where phonographic inscription was in principle available for symbolic inspection, a masculine medium relying on the familiar literary trappings of stylus and engraving, the fully electronic media, and above all radio, could claim no such affinity with writing or any alphabet: post-symbolic in essence, radio conjured an anxiously feminine media mystique, despite (or better, because of) the romance of its early exponents as young men questing for an elusive vibration. Radio was Mrs. Hines to phonography's Eupheus: a voice plucked from the air, evanescent and immaterial, riding invisible waves and untethered to any groove or mirror in things, requiring the exhaustive efforts of heroized DX knights, braving the ionosphere on the promise of a sibilant whisper.

It is fitting that a married couple should serve to allegorize this split, since it was in the private home that these two media were first driven into an irreconcilable knot and then falsely assimilated into a technological apotheosis. In the space of the home the phonograph revealed its compensatory and utopian dimension: "It is the bourgeois family that gathers around the gramophone in order to enjoy the music that it itself—as was already the case in the feudal household—is unable to perform." While it may thus exacerbate the ineluctable processes of cultural alienation in modernity, the phonograph also, continues Adorno, "belongs to the pregnant stillness of individuals," and moreover carries with it an unpredictable archival function whose ends are "admittedly unknown."[73] The social authority of the gramophone diminishes in direct ratio to its incorporation within the private domicile and its rituals, where it becomes endowed instead with an air of withdrawal and connoisseurship. But inversely, as Adorno was (somewhat woodenly) to put it in his own English,

> the authority of radio becomes greater the more it addresses the listener in his privacy. [. . .] The isolated listener definitely feels overwhelmed by the might of the personal voice of an anonymous organization. [. . . T]he deeper this voice is involved within his own privacy, the more it

---

[72] Gitelman, *Always Already New*, 25.
[73] Adorno, "Curves of the Needle," 272.

appears to pour out of the cells of his intimate life; the more he gets the impression that his own cupboard, his own phonograph, his own bedroom speaks to him in a personal way, devoid of the intermediary stages of the printed word; the more perfectly he is ready to accept wholesale whatever he hears. It is just this privacy which fosters the authority of the radio voice and helps to hide it by making it no longer appear to come from outside.[74]

The radio voice's emanation from deep within the private sanctuary of the alienated individual, amidst the movables of her boudoir, or the fittings of his den, allowed it to sink so deep into the creases of intimacy that it appeared indistinguishable from the innermost cellular level of his or her being. Its authority was then on the order of an impulse, a vocal uncanny, that is *"in me more than me"*[75]—lodged within the very furnishings of the subject's protected world. It thus occupies a structural place not unlike that of the Goethean "Mother's Voice" whose spectral presence had underwritten an entire discourse network of literary hegemony; only, as Franco Berardi points out, in this new dispensation, the underwriting is that of capital. Thanks to "the capture of feminine nervous and physical energies by the machinery of global exploitation, mothers are less and less the source of language"; from the advent of radio onward, mothers "are replaced by linguistic machines that are constantly talking and showing. The connective generation is learning language in a framework where the relation between language learning and the affective body tends to be less and less relevant."[76] While phonography certainly partook of the circulation of commodities peculiar to the capitalist accumulation cycle (in particular, the marketing and sale of recorded cylinders and disks), playback in that medium was in the hands of the listener: dependent on mood, available time, and the size of a collection. It tended toward a "repetitive intensity," as Gitelman remarks, "reminiscent of the literacy practices surrounding devotional texts [...] or literacy in situations of particular scarcity," obeying a logic of "repetition and continual reconsumption, rewind and replay."[77] This again seems to locate the phonograph closer to literature than to radio, whose streaming constancy of voice and music, though it could not be commodified in the same way, nevertheless brought it closer to capitalism's cultural nerve center in the continuous present: a universally embedded desiring machine, whispering exhortations like an evil step-mother in the collective ear of the masses, not from the outside but from within.

---

[74] Adorno, *Current of Music*, 70.
[75] See Slavoj Žižek, *The Plague of Fantasies* (London & New York: Verso, 1997), 8.
[76] Franco "Bifo" Berardi, *The Uprising: On Poetry and Finance* (Los Angeles: Semiotext(e), 2012), 107.
[77] Gitelman, *Always Already New*, 67–68.

Radio was haunted, in a way that the increasingly legible modulations of phonograph grooves were not. "Already in 1920," writes Laurence Rickels, "Edison was convinced that there just had to be a radio frequency between the long and the short of the waves which, once he contained it and gave it an on/off gadget switch, would put through the direct connection to the world of the dead."[78] Edison's testimony, in an interview with one B. C. Forbes, concerned a quantum theory of the human "personality" as the immortal propagating wave-particles of a pluralized soul. "These units, if they are as tiny as I believe them to be, would pass through a wall of stone or concrete almost as easily as they would pass through the air."[79] Jeffrey Sconce remarks: "Like many other occult stories inspired by wireless phenomena, Edison's vision of the soul attempted to come to terms with the unnerving empirical evidence of radio, a technology that provided an almost daily reminder of the tenuous link between bodies and consciousness."[80] Moreover, Sconce's journey through the "haunted" landscape of early twentieth-century electronic media insists repeatedly that this "unnerving empirical evidence" was universally troped as feminine and given over to feminine powers of induction and mediumship. "Communication with the spirit world required more than a mere telegraph, be it electromagnetic, celestial, or otherwise. Spiritual contact also depended on the equally enigmatic technology of the 'medium,' a complex receiver who channelled the mysteries of spiritual electricity through the circuitry of another unfathomable entity in nineteenth-century science—the female body" (44). Radio waves, borne on the impalpable substance of the air itself, became conflated with the Spiritualist figure of an "etheric ocean" in which the souls of the dead swam eternally. What bound the scattered subjects of a vast American landmass thanks to networked simultaneous transmission (allowing, for instance, almost twenty-three million to tune in to President Coolidge's inauguration in 1925), also inserted between and among them this "ocean" of trapped souls in an enveloping ether. The radio voice was troubled by this "voice from the void" that accompanied it at its innermost uncanny point, the node where "liveness" and absolute deadness intersected. The afterlife of this purchase in the American imagination, on the experiments of J. Gilbert Wright, Mark Dyne, Attile von Szalay, Friedrich Jürgernson and Konstantin Raudive, is too well known to require any substantive reflection. Nineteenth-century Spiritualism and late modern paranormal science meet in the sense that "Each new communications technology seems to evoke [...] the nervous

---

[78] Laurence A. Rickels, "Resistance in Theory," in Barbara Cohen et al., eds., *Material Events: Paul de Man and the Afterlife of Theory* (Minneapolis: University of Minnesota Press, 2001), 164.

[79] B. C. Forbes, "Edison Working on How to Communicate with the Next World," *American Magazine* (October 1920), 9–11.

[80] Jeffrey Sconce, *Haunted Media: Electronic Presence from Telegraphy to Television* (Durham, NC & London: Duke University Press, 2000), 82.

ambivalence of wireless, a simultaneous desire and dread of actually making such extraordinary forms of contact."[81]

In his sensation novel, *Sanctuary*, written self-consciously for money and as a kind of self-sacrificial gesture toward the marketplace of serial fictions, repetitive functions, styleless style, and the lowest common denominators of sex, violence, and detection, Faulkner turns repeatedly to the variable figure of mechanized technologies of sound. In what is inevitably a rather unstable and fluctuating structural dynamism, the figure of the death-filled box that makes song extends from a literal coffin in whose somber presence an orchestra is obliged to reiterate dance patterns that eventually tumble the corpse out of its housing, to a wooden rural jailhouse cell in which an "already dead" and never seen man sings bluesy spirituals, and finally to the town square whose commercial shopfronts are converted into stands for "imitation wood cabinets or pebble-grain hornmouths," self-repudiating amplification points for distant broadcast signals or worn record grooves relaying deathless "ballads" themselves not a long way off, musically, from the condemned man's dirges. What becomes furniture, in a world of mechanical reproduction, also houses death, and amplifies a bodiless voice. That much seems clear from the figural matrix through which Faulkner saw fit to project and manage his own anxieties about the mechanization of novel writing. But he does not yet approach the urgent question of how this might affect the intimate spaces of the family home; in no episode in *Sanctuary* does the sepulchral furniture of radio or phonograph do more than blare down a telephone wire into anything like a domestic space—the whole of *Sanctuary* is projected into the suspension of marital relations between Horace and Belle. What remains to be analyzed, and worked through, is what this box full of dead song and dead voice would usher into the realm of the domestic and of the family as such, since it is here that the true test of novelistic method and narrative voice would be posed.

Voices from the air

Now we turn to Faulkner's supreme fictional allegory, *As I Lay Dying*, in order to determine how its form may have been shaped and reshaped by this circumambient pressure from the air itself, and its agitation by bodiless voices speaking out of its midst. We here take up one of the perennial problems of writing about this novella, finely phrased by Eric Sundquist:

> [I]n the absence of a controlling narrator the characters, who as narrators themselves participate in the dissolution of the book's integrity

[81] Sconce, *Haunted Media*, 83.

and yet by that very act define and maintain its fragile form, do indeed, as Darl says, "sound as though they [are] speaking out of the air about your head" and appear to be acting in a virtual vacuum—the vacuum left both by the "author" who is not, as it were, present and by the integrated form that we as a consequence imagine would be there if he were.[82]

This is bound up with that other "vacuum created by Addie's death" (32), the death of the Mother, which assumes a disproportionate significance in light of Kittler's theoretical extrapolations from the putative Goethean "Mother's Voice" whose primary orality underwrote an entire romance discourse network.[83] But Sundquist clinches what is at stake in this briefest of Faulkner's major fictions, by probing the "fragility" of its form in relation to the dissociated vocal qualities of its constituent elements: those fifty-nine chapters in first-person monologue, each of them broadcast from a point equidistant to all the others and engulfed by nothingness, "almost inside a vacuum" as Faulkner himself put it.[84] And we will ask how far this "vacuum," sapping the organic integrity of the novel form, might be related to the contemporary sense that radio was not only powered by vacuum tubes but had "opened up a void" in the media ecology of 1930—specifically a void between speaker and listener, presence and absence, body and language.[85] Moreover, the correlative question must also be posed relative to a medium whose larger destiny was to stitch the national fabric into a single garment, about the tendency of these dissociated narrative voices to "escape the gabble of idiolects to move into a shared, communal field of verbal expression, a not always harmonious choir of living voices," since critics have felt that, too, to be a formal consequence of the novel's initial separation into discrete vocal channels or currents of consciousness.[86]

In any event, the first question concerns how *As I Lay Dying* works to rethink and reformulate the emergent threats of mechanically reproduced "disembodied voices" to the novelist's art. I want to argue that this novel—written hard on the heels of *Sanctuary*—takes its predecessor's media problematic and raises it to a

---

[82] Eric Sundquist, *Faulkner: The House Divided* (Baltimore and London: Johns Hopkins University Press, 1983), 32.

[83] David E. Wellbery, "Foreword," in Friedrich Kittler, *Discourse Networks 1800/1900* (Stanford, CA: Stanford University Press, 1990), xxiii.

[84] Quoted in Frederick L. Gwynn and Joseph Blotner, eds., *Faulkner in the University: Class Conferences at the University of Virginia, 1957–1958* (New York: Vintage, 1965), 113–14.

[85] Debra Rae Cohen, Michael Coyle, and Jane Lewty, "Introduction," in Cohen, Coyle, and Lewty, eds., *Broadcasting Modernism* (Gainesville, FL: University Press of Florida, 2009), 3.

[86] Stephen M. Ross, *Fiction's Inexhaustible Voice: Speech and Writing in Faulkner* (Athens, GA & London: University of Georgia Press, 1989), 113.

new level of abstraction. Rather than again using the new mechanical media of voice as "figures" of a disintegrating social fabric, it projects their internal relations onto the overarching structural principle of the novel itself. Faulkner thus constructs what is properly an allegory of antagonistic media relations, designed with the usual "selfish gene" of its own medial propagation at heart. At the same time, however, *As I Lay Dying* yields some disturbing and remarkable results as a diagnostic of the inner decomposition and reconfiguration of the family as such, and its reconstitution by the new media ecology. The cornerstone of this allegorical operation is an aggressively promoted conception of "the road," a horizontal principle that functions as the x-axis of the text's imaginary coordination.

In the previous chapter, we explored the transforming social space of the South in the 1920s, the expansion and improvement of its transportation infrastructure, in order to shed light on some of the ways in which Faulkner's period chronotopes operated to increase, radically, the number of kinds and speeds of mobility across the imaginary landscape of Yoknapatawpha. Paved, gravel, and dirt roadways, new train lines, an efflorescence of automobiles, private and commercial flight paths, telegraph and telephone wires, and the stimulus of the World War on the velocities of movement in as sleepy a backwater as rural Mississippi—Faulkner's work in the late 1920s and early 1930s responded to these overlapping networks of transport through a range of narrative, stylistic and figurative techniques. Here, however, opening the stable doors to radio and phonography, and their disseminated networks, has apparently multiplied the implicit pathways of modernity, now moving at near-light speed, by the number of radio stations broadcasting signals through the very air of the region; not only the literal roads and tracks crisscrossing the Mississippi terrain but these electrical agitations of the ether, electromagnetic pulses penetrating every last recess of social space by the power of fifty kilowatts, themselves stand exposed as so many intangible routes from the city to the country, from the North to the South, from the national corporations to the regional substations and cramped local homesteads. The "competitive radios and phonographs" resounding in the public air of Jefferson, Mississippi, are either receiving the broadcasts of powerful Memphis transmitters (most of these by 1930 participants in one or other of the large networks—NBC Blue and Red, MBS, and CBS), or playing recordings of songs written and recorded in New York, Chicago, or London, or doing both at once. The "throng" attuned to these electrified analog signals, their "rapt faces" and "gnarled slow hands," are simultaneously present and absent to their own experience, shot through with sounds neither here nor there but uncannily both, leaving the men's bodies behind while taking their persons elsewhere, to a sonic utopia. It is as though the sounds are roads to a nowhere into which the men are immediately hurled, gone, before the eyes have had a chance to explain to the mind the dislocation and dispossession at stake. Verbal description lags behind this light-speed evacuation of human presence by the ghostly, disembodied sounds of electric mediation, this "information superhighway" of the 1920s.

Which may be one reason why William Faulkner began his supreme allegory of the media revolution with a powerful meditation on the familial dispossession inflicted by the road itself: "Durn that road. [...] A-laying there, right up to my door, where every bad luck that comes and goes is bound to find it" (24). Anse Bundren's great soliloquy on being "flouted by a road" (26) sits at the basis of *As I Lay Dying*'s conception. Not only do these well-nigh metaphysical misgivings haunt the family's progress along the damaged roadways of the flooded county with a kind of theological impedance, but the sawing and adzing of Cash's "carpenter notions" will somehow box this "durn road" into a funerary conveyance for the mother who has not ceased even in death to say "Get up and move then" (24–25). What is more, the "longways"-inflected eyes of Darl will discover strange frequencies vibrating in and around that coffin: ethereal thoroughfares of the spirit, currents of consciousness, packing him as full of voices as *Absalom*'s Quentin Compson, and readying him for the final train ride downriver into the sanatorium netherworld. It is, of course, to Jefferson that this agitating road will lead the Bundren family, upon the mother's dying wish, to that scene of the very "competitive radios and phonographs" that *Sanctuary*, sitting stagnant in the publisher's galley racks, had already delineated: Jefferson, where Addie's only kin are the dead, and where she will be exchanged for a woman, a second "Mrs. Bundren" possessed of a graphophone "shut up like a hand-grip" (176).

It makes some sense to focus briefly on that final swap. Herein is embedded something concrete about the allegory I have offered to elaborate, since this deft spousal transaction of Anse's crystallizes the links between sound reproduction technologies, "furniture," death-in-life, and the manner in which gender is at stake in that complex. Cash's painstaking labors render a well-crafted funereal box that will resonate with the great monologue of Addie in the fortieth chapter, one of literature's most precise assaults on the ideological edifice of the family. The second Mrs. Bundren's "grip"-graphophone, on the other hand, re-establishes the nuclear family around the mechanical repetition of "new records" in "the mail order" (177). *As I Lay Dying* ends with a bitterly ironic vision of familial harmony, a figure of inclusive disjunction where the graphophone is privileged:

> And then I see that the grip she was carrying was one of them little graphophones. It was for a fact, all shut up as pretty as a picture, and everytime a new record would come from the mail order and us setting in the house in the winter, listening to it, I would think what a shame Darl couldn't be to enjoy it too. But it is better so for him. This world is not his world; this life his life. (177–78)

The family bound by the graphophone is bound in the same breath by the death of a Mother and a determinate exclusion of the second-eldest son. There is more to this scene that meets the ear. In what follows I propose to show that Darl's "other-worldliness" has little do with the inscription machine of the graphophone and rather more to do with electric mediation and the age of the wireless, and that it is this latter mediation that has secretly orchestrated a whole range of effects within the text and established the very parameters of its form.

In substituting the weird radio sounds of Addie's restless unfulfillment and "already dead" biopolitical positioning within Southern rural patriarchal culture, for the second Mrs. Bundren's fold-up graphophone and its small-town utopia, Anse is interring what we could call a "radio corpse" in order to purchase at discount an idyllic modern scene of techno-familial convergence.[87] Reacting to the broader national shift toward an electrified radio economy of sounds, Anse exchanges the spook for the worn grooves. What is immortal in the one Mrs. Bundren, her passionate haunting of the margins of a patriarchal capitalist economy with the evidence of its innermost symbolic "lack," is to be swapped for a properly mortal and pliant technology, a submissive machine of a woman, onto which the mail-order stream of wax cylinder recordings can be loaded within a domestic space no longer vibrating to uncanny radio radiation.

Why, then, does Addie's casketed corpse begin to behave like a radio? It is well to remember in this context that the advent of Spiritualism and of the table-rapping phenomenon that swept America on the heels of the invention of the telegraph a few generations before the radio craze, required not only conductive female bodies (such as the Fox sisters) but an apt physical domicile to channel the chorus of undead voices. In her book, *Modern American Spiritualism* (1870), Emma Hardinge noted that the architectural structure of the Fox cottage was itself a vital contributing factor to the phenomenon of spiritual telegraphy that shook the nation: the wood-frame house was "particularly suited to their [the dead's] purpose from the fact of its *being charged with the aura requisite to make it a battery for the working of the telegraph*."[88] That a house, and within it a woman, could be so charged was a core principle of Spiritualist belief: here and there, certain buildings become spiritual batteries enabling an electromagnetic flow between the higher vibrations of the spirit world and the sublunary frequencies

---

[87] This concept is developed by Daniel Tiffany in relation to Ezra Pound's poetics and politics; see his *Radio Corpse: Imagism and the Cryptaesthetic of Ezra Pound* (Cambridge, MA: Harvard University Press, 1998).

[88] Emma Hardinge, *Modern American Spiritualism: A Twenty Years' Record of the Communion between Earth and the World of Spirits*, 2nd ed. (New York: By the Author, 1870), 29. Emphasis in original.

of the body. The female medium is a conduit within a conduit, a sensitive body nestled inside the architectural antenna of the domicile, through which messages from the dead can be heard. Before they can enter that sensitive body, these voices must first enter the house:

> Tilting a little down the hill, as our house does, a breeze draws through the hall all the time, upslanting. A feather dropped near the front door will rise and brush along the ceiling, slanting backward, until it reaches the down-turning current at the back door: so with voices. As you enter the hall, they sound as though they were speaking out of the air about your head. (14)

Not copper coils wound to pick up radio frequencies, but a spartan wooden frame structure, supplies the Bundren family with its electromagnetic receiver.[89] Here, as they enter, voices are immediately detached from themselves, dislocated by a gradient breeze, "as though they were speaking out of the air." In a novel so concerned with the technical specificities of voice, and preoccupied with the formal and ideological meanings of vocal carriers, such a statement immediately confers upon the Bundren residence a paradigmatic quality. For the house interpolates an "upslanting" dissociation between body and resonance. As a resonator, the house also becomes a transmitter; its aura, predicated on the inaugural "tilt" of the builder's noncompliance with the immaterial "spirit-level" as well as with his tool, throngs with spiritual signal interference.

We are on similar terrain here to that sketched in a 1935 report from Mason, Ohio, about mysterious signals emanating from the farms surrounding a newly installed five-thousand-watt transmitter: "An ordinary waterspout at the corner of a farmhouse hums the strains of a symphony, or declaims a dramatic bit from a play. A tin roof, next door, makes political speeches, or bursts into song. Inquire among the farmers, and nearly all will tell you of hearing these mysterious, ghostly voices issuing from inanimate things."[90] The rural farmyards and houses of America were subjected to the invisible throng of radio waves throughout the 1930s in ways that led to surreal derangements of the usual relations between objects and noises, bodies and voices. Their homes, on the fringes of a rapidly urbanizing modern economy, were conducting the frequencies of a

---

[89] Here it is worth noting that Jay Watson reads this passage as illustrative of another media phenomenon of the period, early sound film, with its conquest of synchronization. See Watson, "The Unsynchable William Faulkner: Faulknerian Voice and Early Sound Film," in Julian Murphet and Stefan Solomon, eds., *William Faulkner in the Media Ecology* (Baton Rouge: Louisiana State University Press, 2015), 103–05.

[90] Alden Armagnac, "Weird Electrical Freaks Traced to Runaway Radio Waves," *Popular Science Monthly* (June 1935), 21.

medium fast reinventing itself for an age of domestic broadcast consumption. The domestic, like the regional, was being turned inside out.[91]

Consider the further implications of vocal transitivity in the following two-part description of that "spiritual" chorus raised just outside the house in an attempt to steer Addie's mortal soul heavenward. First:

> Whitfield begins. His voice is bigger than him. It's like they are not the same. It's like he is one, and his voice is one, swimming on two horses side by side across the ford and coming into the house, the mud-splashed one and the one that never even got wet, triumphant and sad. Somebody in the house begins to cry. It sounds like her eyes and her voice were turned back inside her, listening. (59)

As the minister enters the house he is delaminated into two distinct layers: himself and his voice, metaphorized into adjacent riders splashing through a ford, one filthy, the other exempt from mortal soil. The house is a site where voice meets voice as quasi-autonomous, depersonalized, yet spiritual agents, sprung from their physical bodies. The singing broadens and expands, and shifts gender roles:

> Whitfield stops at last. The women sing again. In the thick air it's like their voices come out of the air, flowing together and on in the sad, comforting tunes. When they cease it's like they hadn't gone away. It's like they had just disappeared into the air and when we moved we would loose them again out of the air around us, sad and comforting. (59)

More than a space of acoustic delamination, the house is also a sonic environment in which, though sounds and voices "cease," they nevertheless do not die. Rather, voices, having been alienated from the carapace of bodies, vanish into air pockets that can be dislodged, the way a receiver plucks audible signals from electromagnetic radiation.

The sounds of Cash's labour on the coffin in these strange environs, where voices speak "out of the air" rather than of mouths, bear consideration:

> Cash labours about the trestles, moving back and forth, lifting and placing the planks with long clattering reverberations in the dead air as though he were lifting and dropping them at the bottom of an invisible

---

[91] Scott Romine discusses the dialectics of regionality and nationality in radio and other media, in a later context, in his *The Real South: Southern Narrative in the Age of Cultural Reproduction* (Baton Rouge: Louisiana State University Press, 2008).

well, the sounds ceasing without departing, as if any movement might dislodge them from the immediate air in reverberant repetition. (49)

The voice telling us this is called "Darl," the voice in this text best attuned to what he here calls the noises lodged in "the immediate air in reverberant repetition." Chez Bundren abstracts sounds to a zone between silence and white noise where "reverberations" are trapped visibly, as if in amber, decocted as so many waveforms imprinted on the "dead air": "The air smells like sulphur. Upon the impalpable plane of it their shadows form as upon a wall, as though like sound they had not gone very far away in falling but had merely congealed for a moment, immediate and musing" (49). Sounds congeal like shadows on the sulphurous plane of dead air. Become "immediate," these sounds lose their mediacy of "personhood," and in their projection upon the "impalpable" wall of air, they mount a case for autonomy at the very time that they call out for a medium.

Arresting here is the way that sound waves, petrified in space, manifest themselves in the visual field: reified as silhouettes, "shadows" of bodies from which they have been separated, like the vampire's assistant in Dreyer's *Vampyr* (1932). This insistence on the congelation of sonic frequencies into visual arabesques and friezes, which we have already seen at play in *Sanctuary*'s stricken acoustical world, connects to a broader concern in *As I Lay Dying* with the reification of action into visual phenomena, and more broadly still with Faulkner's ongoing preoccupation with the impossibility of narrating events and the necessity of a kind of baffled oxymoronic compromise in the face of them. So, for instance, Jewel and the horse "stand in rigid terrific hiatus," (9) Cash's face has a "a rapt, dynamic immobility above his tireless elbow" (49) and the sign for New Hope "wheels up like a motionless hand" (69)—but the dynamism of the immobile is already implicit in the sonic reverberations trapped in the "dead air" of the Bundren house, since waveforms connote propagation, while their inscription within the visible field denotes stasis and arrest. But all this is perfectly appropriate, since the air here is indeed "dead," infected as by a kind of creeping paralysis by the "dying" of the book's title, which is described for us very precisely as a bronze "casting" of some incessant cessation:

> It is like a casting of fading bronze upon the pillow, the hands alone still with any semblance of life: a curled, gnarled alertness; a spent yet alert quality from which weariness, exhaustion, travail has not yet departed, as though they doubted even yet the actuality of rest, guarding with horned and penurious alertness the cessation which they know cannot last. (34)

In what was to become a typical Faulknerian construction, in paradox heaped upon paradox, the qualities that persist *beyond* the moment of bodily "rest" are the very qualities—"weariness, exhaustion, travail"—that tend *toward* eternal rest and to the cessation of all movement. In this syntactical economy, the "semblance of life" carried beyond the actuality of death is not that of liveliness, but of deathliness: in the living corpse ("She has been dead these ten days," remarks Peabody, 29), what persists of life is the stubborn alertness of a being-toward-death. This immortal dimension of the human, which perceives all "cessation" as a mere narrative ruse and illusion, casts its doubts upon death not from the robust vantage-point of some *élan vital*, but from the Beckettian purview of "exhaustion" itself.[92] Not life but "weariness" outlives death.

This is what Lacan identifies as the "death drive": "the path toward death is nothing other than what is called *jouissance*."[93] Why should this "immortal" weariness, this exhaustion beyond the very boundary between life and death, be equated with *jouissance*? Because it functions as a surplus within the biopolitical economy of farm labor, an excessive stain of work—like calloused palms and suntanned forearms—that persists beyond the body's passage into death; a "semblance of life" that manifests itself as a kind of indefinite repetition of what wore it out. As Lacan writes, "what interests us qua repetition, and which is registered with a dialectic of *jouissance*, is properly speaking what goes against life. It is at the level of repetition that Freud sees himself constrained, in some way, by virtue of the very structure of discourse, to spell out the death instinct."[94] In Slavoj Žižek's helpful revisitation of this territory, he tells of "the 'infinity' (undeadness, excess of life) in the very core of our being, the strange 'immortality' whose Freudian name is the death drive."[95] Addie's hands give it material shape, a gesture against life.

This undead, "exhausted" quality of the death drive, its "curled, gnarled alertness," is also what survives in the voice as such. Just as the sounds of Cash's labors, and of the singing voices that enter the Bundren house, are separated from their sources and preserved in a sonic death-mask, so too the "spent yet alert" properties of Addie's living corpse are simultaneously of and not of her body; they belong as much to the inhuman sphere of repetition, of labor and seriality, associated with Lacanian *jouissance*. No less a characterization is worthy of the voice itself. Mladen Dolar comments, apropos of its alleged "metaphysics of presence," that the "voice may well be the key to the presence of the present and to an unalloyed interiority, but it conceals in its bosom that inaudible object voice which disrupts both."[96] It is this uncanny dimension of the

---

[92] And on Beckett's immortal exhaustion, see Gilles Deleuze, "The Exhausted," in Daniel W. Smith and Michael A. Greco, trans., *Essays Critical and Clinical* (Minneapolis: University of Minnesota Press, 1997), 152–74.

[93] Jacques Lacan, *The Seminar of Jacques Lacan, Book XVII*, trans. Russell Grigg (New York & London: W. W. Norton, 2007), 18.

[94] Lacan, *The Seminar of Jacques Lacan, Book XVII*, 45.

[95] Slavoj Žižek, *In Defence of Lost Causes* (London & New York: Verso, 2009), 344.

[96] Mladen Dolar, *A Voice and Nothing More* (Cambridge, MA: MIT Press, 2007), 42.

voice, as an impossible and quasi-alien "object" in the precincts of thought, that "introduces a scission, a rupture in the middle of full presence, and refers to a void—but a void which is not simply a lack, an empty space; it is a void in which the voice comes to resonate" (42). In order to enter into this dimension, the voice needs to stop making sense and decouple itself from meaning; "only when it becomes divorced from meaning can [the voice] appear as the pivotal object of drive" in the Lacanian sense.[97] The dominant function of voice is that desire-driven and sanctioned quest for signification that governs the channels of social communication. But the flip side of this intercourse is as important, if often unacknowledged: "The object voice [. . .] is the by-product of this operation, its side-result that the drive gets hold of, circling around it, coming back to the same place in a movement of repetition" (72).

In order to conceive the voice as the object of the drive, we must divorce it from empirical voices that can be heard. Inside the heard voice is another voice; an aphonic voice, as it were. It is this insistent dimension of the voice that is related to the death drive, for by being everywhere and nowhere, this "object voice" haunts all voices with an implicit Babel, what Lacan calls a "*lalangue*," in which the "voice of the signifier" becomes a "vehicle of enjoyment" through "the infinity of sound reverberations and puns which form the texture of the unconscious."[98] The autopoetic free play of sonic repetitions, echoes, puns, and rhymes that holds together the "aesthetic dimension" of poetic artifacts is precisely language's death drive; it is where the voice as an object obtrudes into the mechanisms of sense with an aphonic excess that persists beyond the message-driven significance of this or that utterance in its moment of composition.

It is also where voices go once decoupled from their bodies, transformed via analog processes of waveform interaction in the electromagnetic sphere or microgroove inscription on wax or shellac, into disembodied, ghostly, mechanical adjuncts of the "voice as presence." What continues to compel about Faulkner's uncanny descriptions of voices "speaking out of the air," and of sounds congealed into shadows cast on the vaporous white wall of nonsense outside the Bundren house, is how pregnant they are with this sense of the "object voice." Taking up its vector from the persistence in the house's "dying" mother of a corporeal excess, an "undeath" of "weariness," this attention to the object voice meditates on that worn-out persistence within all voices of what will not cease to sound, of what inscribes itself invisibly but materially in the air itself: "When they cease it's like they hadn't gone away. It's like they had just disappeared into the air and when we moved we would loose them again out of the air around us, sad and comforting" (59). Voices, too, we are led to believe, have a "horned and penurious alertness." But in order to propagate itself, this uncanny object voice

---

[97] Dolar, *A Voice and Nothing More*, 71.
[98] Lacan, *The Seminar of Jacques Lacan, Book XVII*, 158.

will require some instrument or mechanism to "loose [it] again out of the air around us"—an antenna or a stylus, and beyond that a medium, with which to fathom this aphonic voice and render it intelligible once more.

Animal magnetism

The name of that instrument, as we have already surmised, is "Darl," with his eyes attuned to the longways cast of the land and, beyond even that, "his eyes gone further than the food and the lamp, full of the land dug out of his skull and the holes filled with distance beyond the land" (18). Darl, after all, is the one to whom it falls to bring the description of Addie's "exhausted" body into voice (34), and who serves more generally as the "voice among voices," charged with the ostensibly authorial capacity to divine events and thoughts transpiring anywhere on the bandwidth of the Bundren family. It is Darl who most assuredly raises the formal issue of voice; in so many senses, everything hinges on what we are to make of his mediatory hub through which frequencies pass and transmigrate, hopping between stations, opening up vexing extrinsic questions of telepathy, clairvoyance, and Spiritualism. For Cleanth Brooks, the position of Darl's voice in the novel is clear: "it is very likely that Darl will appear to be the representative intelligence of the novel and the mouthpiece of the author" due to the "poetry" of his language and the revulsion he displays toward the burial journey quest.[99] Olga Vickery remarks Darl's ability to "penetrate the minds of others" and "expose, with merciless accuracy, the secret thoughts and motives of others."[100] For Calvin Bedient, Darl's monologues "belong to the family itself," his "clairvoyance" of their secrets so "attentive and catholic" that it partakes of the automatisms of "photographic film."[101] André Bleikasten raises Darl to the novel's center of perception; he "stages the show," as the "setting of the book is invented in his look, created through his words."[102] Eric Sundquist's centrifugal sense that the novel is woven of voices "that seem utterly severed from the peculiar bodily selves that ostensibly produce them" is notionally resisted, as he puts it, by the intermittent centripetality of Darl's "hallucination and clairvoyance," which "tempts us to identify him with the omniscient author"; but this itself is undone by the ultimate disembodiment betokened by the "link between

---

[99] Cleanth Brooks, *The Yoknapatawpha Country* (New Haven: Yale University Press, 1963), 144–45.

[100] Olga W. Vickery, *The Novels of William Faulkner: An Interpretation* (Baton Rouge: Louisiana State University Press, 1959).

[101] Calvin Bedient, "Pride and Nakedness: As I Lay Dying," *Modern Language Quarterly* 29 (1968), 71, 70.

[102] André Bleikasten, *Faulkner's* As I Lay Dying, rev. and enlarged ed., trans. Roger Little (Bloomington: Indiana University Press, 1973), 114.

omniscience and madness" that Darl also makes.[103] As he puts it, "Darl's intense consciousness, like that of an omniscient author-narrator, defines a self whose identity risks being lost in the act of becoming saturated with the ability to be connected to other minds" (35). Stephen Ross's more detailed analysis shows that the "surface of mimetic voice" that governs the textual operations of *As I Lay Dying* is undercut by "hints of an augmenting authorial voice" within "the cluster of voices weaving their self-referring discourse around the dying Addie."[104]

In that case, the weird sense that Darl's voice is distributed between its own approved and nominated zone (under the most frequent chapter rubric, "Darl") and other zones named otherwise is explained away as the interference of the authorial voice within the bricolage of first-person voices through which this text is articulated. It just happens that "the author" privileges Darl's voice as his native habitat, but then ranges out beyond the strict borders of that voice in order to inscribe its presence elsewhere. For instance, the vernacular voice of Vardaman, a young child, is generally conveyed with heavy accents of Hill Country dialect—"Then hit want. Hit hadn't happened then. Hit was a-layin right there on the ground. And now she's gittin ready to cook hit" (38). Vardaman speaks in simple clauses and a stripped-down vocabulary of a few dozen words; at least, that is, until the end of his first and longest chapter, when, lingering over the dis-apparition of Jewel's horse, the child's linguistic competence is suddenly supplemented and shepherded by an altogether distinct stylistic power:

> It is as though the dark were resolving him out of his integrity, into an unrelated scattering of components—snuffings and stampings; smells of cooling flesh and ammoniac hair; an illusion of a coordinated whole of splotched hide and strong bones within which, detached and secret and familiar, an *is* different from my *is*. I see him dissolve—legs, a rolling eye, a gaudy splotching like cold flames—and float upon the dark in fading solution; all one yet neither; all either yet none. I can see hearing coil toward him, caressing, shaping his hard shape—fetlock, hip, shoulder and head; smell and sound. I am not afraid. (38)

By the time we reach the first person singular pronoun in this remarkable passage, we are no longer advised to refer it to Vardaman at all, but, since Darl is later to pose the cognate question—"Because if I had one, it is *was*. And if it is *was*, it can't be *is*. Can it?" (65)—the "I" who here equivocates between two

---

[103] Eric J. Sundquist, *Faulkner: A House Divided* (Baltimore: Johns Hopkins University Press, 1985), 34, 35.

[104] Stephen M. Ross, *Fiction's Inexhaustible Voice: Speech and Writing in Faulkner* (Athens, GA & London: University of Georgia Press, 1989), 116.

present participles of the verb "to be" should, at least in part, be assigned to Darl. What seems to be happening here is that inside the voice named Vardaman, the voice of Darl is worming, dissociating the identity of that voice from itself, and allowing a complex, alloyed "I" to speak where the text is telling us a simple identity stands. This is precisely how Vernon Tull comes to think of those curious land-filled eyes that epitomize what is "queer" about Darl: "It's like he had got into the inside of you, someway. Like somehow you was looking at yourself and your doings outen his eyes" (81). "Eyes" are taken as an analog for "voice" insofar as this latter is what we are given to read in the text: sounds are petrified into visual waveforms and suspended as friezes on the summer air; or, in Lacanian terms, Darl's "object gaze" is confounded with his "object voice" in the way other characters are obliged to register what is "awry" in his look. It is also what is awry in his voice, which is not where it should properly be, but displaced into "yourself" as a voice, occupying it in such a way as to allow you to "hear" yourself at a second remove—as an object.

It is much the same near the end of Dewey Dell's second monologue, where a similarly simple and vernacular voice is interrupted by the sentence, "The dead air shapes the dead earth in the dead darkness, further away than seeing shapes the dead earth" (42), in which the somber vocal repetitions associate a rhythmic and textural density with death itself. Or again, even as imperturbable a characterological speech zone as that of the laconic carpenter Cash, with its clipped syntax, club-footed conjugations, and backwoods grammar, seems susceptible here and there to these migratory interpolations, as when, meditating on Darl's insanity or otherwise, it transmogrifies from one style into another mid-sentence: "But I aint so sho that ere a man has the right to say what is crazy and what aint. It's like there was a fellow in every man that's done a-past the sanity or the insanity, that watches the sane and the insane doings of that man with the same horror and the same astonishment" (161). That last sentence breaks around the caesura of the comma into two distinct vocal modes, the first thronging with contractions and colloquialisms, the second reaching into polysyllabic existentialism while still formatted grammatically to the relatively simple constructions for which Cash is mostly responsible. Jewel, Darl's arch-enemy, to whom is given only two paragraphs of narration in the novel, seems immune; and Anse, the novel's greatest egotist, who has only two further brief chapters beyond his great expostulation on the road, cannot truly be said to narrate at all. But the logic of the way in which the family is constructed as a narrative chorus dictates that into each member's voice must creep the stealthy stylistic signature of the vocal dominant, Darl.

Brooks's conclusion is therefore perfectly arguable, but it leaves unasked the far more interesting question of why and how these complex stylistic tranferences take place. For after all, it is not merely that Darl's style—its "poetry," complex metaphorics, multi-clausal hypotactic constructions, erudite vocabulary, occasional flouting of grammatical proprieties to make a point—invades and subverts the styles of his siblings, it is that he is the privileged medium through which a kind of "telepathy" is allowed to operate within the narrative. Recall the night that Darl is responsible for memorializing, on which Jewel's non-arrival from his nocturnal piecework out on Lon Quick's field suddenly announces itself to the four siblings as an emergency, a crisis: "But now it was like we had all—and by a kind of telepathic agreement of admitted fear—flung the whole thing back like covers on the bed and we were all sitting bolt upright in our nakedness" (87). This "telepathic agreement," which allows Darl and Dewey Dell to speak "without the words" (18), is the medium of Darl's clairvoyance, allowing for his spontaneous intuition of his sister's pregnancy. Darl's telepathic powers of divination stretch to include the motivations of his nemesis, giving him insights into Jewel's approach to horse buying. His "prophetic and preternatural vision," in Brooks's words, is nonetheless ill-served by a reduction of it to the role of representing the "artistic temperament" in a text whose insistence on the curious qualities of the "object voice" is as marked as this one.[105] Rampton's equivalent remarks about Darl's alienation from his family by virtue of his "aesthetic stance ... on experience," Minter's on the character's "philosophic and poetic" disposition, or Singal's on Darl's "Modernist artist" credentials whose speech "often sounds so much like Faulknerian rhetoric," all miss the mark hit by Irving Howe's apt description of Darl's "somewhat disembodied consciousness [that] is not that of an external observer but, so to speak, of the family itself: the secret hovering Bundren voice."[106] Darl's simultaneous clairvoyance and stylistic transference as a disembodied consciousness brings to light some of the submerged media unconscious of the Bundren "object" voice.

For if, as we have argued, there is a demonstrable sense in which the Bundren domicile is presented in conventional "radio" terms—a wooden shell in which a voice resonates, but also where a strange dissociation takes place between the two kinds of voice implicit in each voice, and where these voices can be heard speaking "out of the air"—and if furthermore there seems to be a particular dynamic at play between the "broadcasting" and "reception" of voices in a pre- or supra-vocal sense among the family members who inhabit this home—then Darl's function in the midst of all this traffic of voices stands sharply revealed as a kind of transmitter/receiver, an ideally dialogical radio power that goes by the shorthand of telepathy and insanity. The key passage in this context concerns

---

[105] Brooks, *The Yoknapatawpha Country*, 146.

[106] See respectively David Rampton, *William Faulkner: A Literary Life* (Houndmills & New York: Palgrave Macmillan, 2008), 56; David Minter, *William Faulkner: His Life and Work* (Baltimore & London: Johns Hopkins University Press, 1980), 118; Daniel J. Singal, *William Faulkner: The Making of a Modernist* (Chapel Hill, NC & London: University of North Carolina Press, 1997), 149; and Irving Howe, *William Faulkner: A Critical Study*, 2nd ed. (New York: Vintage, 1952), 179.

the moment when Darl and Vardaman tune in to what the dead mother is saying from her Cash-built coffin:

> She was under the apple tree and Darl and I go across the moon and the cat jumps down and runs and we can hear her inside the wood.
> "Hear?" Darl says. "Put your ear close."
> I put my ear close and I can hear her. Only I cant tell what she is saying.
> "What is she saying, Darl?" I say. "Who is she talking to?"
> "She's talking to God," Darl says. "She is calling on Him to help her." (144)

When Diana York Blaine registers her complaint against the chorus of male critical approval of Cash's "heroic" fashioning of Addie's coffin, she does so ironically enough in terms that give the game away: "After all," Blaine chides us, "he is making her not a stereo cabinet but a coffin"; but can we be so sure?[107] The box of the coffin, now revealed as precisely a kind of portable stereo, carries within itself this uncanny capacity for restless if indeterminate speech: voices carry, speech rustles, in the woodwork. Out of the air, but conducted by paneling and joints "on the bevel," this speech is the object voice incarnate, and Vardaman's inability to decipher it speaks volumes: he can hear her but he cannot "tell what she is saying." There is a voice, it is speaking and yet not speaking, always more and more beneath the threshold of sense, stammering "neither really *in* language nor *outside* it," as Barthes wrote once, the voice become a "foreigner in [its] own language," in Deleuze's formulation, since although it is recognizable as "hers" (it carries her intonations, pitch, and tone) it does not avail itself of meaning.[108]

Cash, the carpenter of this unique communicating vessel, has prepared for this moment of uncanny audition by explaining his choice of the beveled seam for a coffin. Although in beds, "where people lie down all the time, the joints and seams are made sideways, because the stress is sideways," this principle cannot hold for a mortuary casket. "The animal magnetism of a dead body makes the stress come slanting, so the seams and joins of a coffin are made on the bevel" (53). "Animal magnetism" is a term belonging to mesmerism and subsequently to the Spiritualist tradition—the hypothesis of a vital fluid, possessed of magnetic force, and producing electricity as it comes into contact with the vital fluids of other bodies. It is this substance that mesmerism "attracted" outside of consciousness, and which led to speculative beliefs about a spirit world afloat in the "etheric ocean," into which privileged female mediums could tap thanks to techniques borrowed from (first) telegraphy and (then) radio. So pervasive were theories of animal magnetism even in the most advanced circles that when Samuel Morse sought funding from the

---

[107] Diana York Blaine, "The Abjection of Addie and Other Myths of the Maternal in *As I Lay Dying*," in Linda Wagner-Martin, ed., *William Faulkner: Six Decades of Criticism* (East Lansing, MI: Michigan State University Press, 2002), 89.

[108] Roland Barthes, *The Rustle of Language*, trans. Richard Howard (Berkeley, CA & Los Angeles: University of California Press, 1989), 76; Gilles Deleuze, "He Stuttered," in *Essays Critical and Clinical*, 110.

U.S. Congress in 1838 for his telegraph line, the chair of that congressional committee noted that "[i]t would require a scientific analysis to determine how far the magnetism of mesmerism was analogous to the magnetism to be employed in telegraphs."[109] A century later, when the same magnetism was generating the truly uncanny acoustic effects of radio, the belief was still current in the deep South. Cash is the only character in the novel who deliberately cuts the Gordian knot of the text's abiding structural binary opposition—between vertical, "up-and-down" lines of force and horizontal, "long ways" lines of force—by forcing a diagonal into it: the bevel cut that is most suitable to a coffin, since it is what respects the "slanting" stress of a dead body's animal magnetism. Cash understands "talking machines." His desire for a graphophone is of a piece with the deliberate labor he expends crafting his mother's coffin, and the concrete-insulated leg with which he grounds its electrical energy: both envisage motherhood and domestic space as matters of "disembodied voices" and wooden cabinets.

Darl turns his ears to this voice and hears more than the *lalangue* that Vardaman hears. The news that his mother is "talking to God," that she is "calling on Him to help her," not only forces the uncanny spectral object voice into the vicinity of sense, it trebles the figurative matrix of media via which the voice itself is being conducted. Now not only gramophony and radio but telephony as well comes into play as a possible channel and transmitter of the dead mother's voice; the stereo cabinet has been fitted with a spiritual telephone booth, with a direct connection to the Almighty. The voice droning "inside the wood" is doing so according to a suggested triplication of techniques: needle-groove amplification, wire-conducted electromagnetic signals, and wireless electromagnetic waves. Vibrating with all this currency of consciousness, the furniture-like wooden box is rendered mediatically ambivalent in the very act of becoming audible to the youngest son, whose habits of intellectual abstraction are all resolutely metaphorical and preoccupied with the visual. The dialogue continues:

"What does she want Him to do?" I say.

"She wants Him to hide her away from the sight of man," Darl says.

"Why does she want to hide her away from the sight of man, Darl?"

"So she can lay down her life," Darl says.

"Why does she want to lay down her life, Darl?"

"Listen," Darl says. We hear her. We hear her turn over on her side. "Listen," Darl says.

"She's turned over," I say. "She's looking at me through the wood."

"Yes," Darl says.

"How can she see through the wood, Darl?" (144)

---

[109] Quoted in Jeffrey Sconce, *Haunted Media*, 34–35.

This begins as a catechism of sorts, in which one interlocutor, Vardaman, reiterates the last phrases of the other as questions, with the addition of the single, phatic, syllable of his name, "Darl." The subject of the catechism is the desire of the dead mother to be removed from the field of the visible, a desire decrypted by Darl from the audible rustling of her voice in the box. Yet when enjoined to "listen," Vardaman himself can hear only the turning of his mother's eyes toward him and their X-ray penetration of the wood to hold him in the full horror of their gaze. The object voice is insistently translated into the object gaze by his habits of thought; only Darl can hear and dwell within the object voice as such. It is Darl who must be present to rejoin the object voice with its "human" freight of meaning, since there is something so awry about his own gaze, which seems to drift off all vertical presences and meander along the "road" of mediation.

Materialities of the voice

The fortunes of the dead mother's voice in *As I Lay Dying* raise in the most pregnant terms the "Oedipus complex" as such. Oedipus, certainly, was to have been marked by blindness as well as lameness, but by no means by deafness, since it was his uncloseable ears that had admitted the acousmatic object voices of the oracle and Sphinx in the first place, and all our woe. Freud makes little of this sensory orientation of his famous "complex," this privileging of ear over eye, yet in his recommendation of underlying reasons for the capacity of Sophocles' play to move even a modern audience, he suggests that there "must be something which makes a voice within us ready to recognize the compelling force of destiny" in the drama. This inner voice, mirroring that of the oracle, as that of the Sphinx, is for Freud the very proof of the Oedipus complex as a scientific hypothesis of "universal validity." The "curse" of the oracle's object voice belongs *a priori* to "all of us," laid upon us "before our birth," though for the most part we "live in ignorance" of its whispered promptings and injunctions.[110] At the bedrock of the modern subject is this obscure voice, this looping reiteration of a dual command to murder one's father and have "sexual relations" with one's mother.

Darl's "feelings" for his mother are infamously neutral on the level of the body; he allows her coffin to go adrift on the flood, lights a fire to immolate the decomposing corpse at Gillespie's farm, and otherwise seeks to separate himself and Jewel from the mourning work her death objectively requires of them.

---

[110] Sigmund Freud, *The Interpretation of Dreams*, ed. and trans. James Strachey (London: Penguin, 1991), 363–65.

However, on the level of the disembodied voice, he is her privileged medium and interpreter. But this relationship is not exactly "emotional," either, since it cannot be framed as a named, narratable feeling; rather, it resides at an affective and unclassifiable distance from what can be represented or cleanly stated. Since Darl "functions out of a perfect detachment that is the source of his exactingly objective vision," it is possible to say that his narration of her death "has the power of a passion based not on empathy but on its absence, on an indiscriminate wonder," or affect.[111] It amounts to an Oedipal wish, converted into a death drive. His voice, even as it threads the rapidly atomizing family unit into some semblance of telepathic accord, is profoundly resonant with his mother's "inhuman" anathematization of patriarchy, family, and the Symbolic Order as such. As voice, he penetrates her indeed, so that she begins (like Dewey Dell's sexual fantasy) "to part and open upon the alone, and the process of coming alone is terrible" (41), since what it incestuously engenders is "*the outraged entrails of events*" in "*the womb of time*" (107).

Darl's vocal penetration and impregnation of his mother's posthumous condition, which results in the great event of Addie's monologue, has perhaps a mediatic prehistory. "Darl has a little spy-glass he got in France at the war," he tells us in infantile third-person. "In it it had a woman and a pig with two backs and no face" (172). Addie, who has been subject to animal metamorphoses in the forms of fish and horse, now appears in the spy-glass of Darl's porcine Oedipal imaginary, where she makes the beast with two backs with him. More important is the sudden revelation that Anse's grousing about the road's making Darl "full of the land" has implied all along his second son's conscription and relocation to the front in the Great War, and presumably his being damaged there beyond all psychological repair. And here we are obliged to consider this radical displacement within the terms of a radio imaginary, too, for that war like no other reinforced standing "oceanic associations between wireless, separation, and death."

> Families that had never sent children to Europe suddenly found their sons [...] going overseas, possibly never to return. [...] The only contact families had with their children during this traumatic period was through a precarious relay of wireless and telegraphy. [...] The trauma of war [...] inspired many tales of clairvoyance, ghostly combat, and soldiers speaking from beyond the grave.[112]

---

[111] Donald Kartiganer "'By It I Would Stand or Fall': Life and Death in *As I Lay Dying*," in Mooreland, ed., *Companion to William Faulkner*, 439. Kartiganer interprets Darl's presence in the novel as an incarnation of the death drive itself, an agent of "the residue of inanimacy that survives in life not as an intimation of immortality but of the death we all harbor," 439.

[112] Jeffrey Sconce, *Haunted Media*, 74.

One of these, *Thy Son Liveth: Messages from a Soldier to his Mother*, concerned "a young American wireless enthusiast sent to France [who] dies in battle, but then communicates with his mother through the wireless set left idle in his room at home" (74). Such intimate contact, across immense distances, was to have associated the very medium of radio with "another void of modernity, the barren expanses of what came to be called 'No-Man's Land'" (75), which is where John Limon has asked us, slyly, to situate the true significance of Addie's monologue.[113] Moreover, Limon's sense that the transference of militant Western Front nihilism from the veteran Darl to the mother Addie—which allows the novel to "incorporate muddy undead formlessness into its form" (362)—can be better supported by a material insistence that Darl's "clairvoyance" was the result of some traumatized, transatlantic electromagnetic recalibration of his Oedipus complex.

Consider in this respect the telegraphic trauma that binds together the otherwise fatuous jingoism of "Shall Not Perish" (1943), where Faulkner thinks again about the mediation of martial death in the Great War in the context of World War II. A telegraph—"a little scrap of paper not even big enough to start a fire with, that didn't even need a stamp on the envelope"[114]—brings the news of Pete Grimes's death, rocking his mother's world; a newspaper brings news of the death of that "ay-viator," "Major de Spain's Boy" (103). But this only brings back more vividly the absent Pete, and in language that directly recapitulates the prose of Darl, the nine-year-old narrator reflects:

> it's like, since nobody can tell us exactly where he was when he stopped being *is*, instead of just becoming *was* at some single spot on the earth where the people who loved him could weight him down with a stone, Pete still *is* everywhere about the earth, one among all the fighters forever, *was* or *is* either. So Mother and Father and I don't need a little wooden box to catch the voices of them that saw the courage and the sacrifice. (104)

There is that "little wooden box" once more, correlating two distinct but related senses: coffin and radio. At one level, we are being told clichéd things about the immortality of the Corps, not the corpse; but at another, the grammatical bafflement of tense and the intuited ubiquity of Pete's being in the world radiate uncannily with the radio imaginary that sustained intercontinental relations between mothers and sons in the first truly global conflict. Sconce points out how "wireless suggested that one's consciousness might someday be free to

---

[113] John Limon, "Addie in No-Man's Land," in William Faulkner, *As I Lay Dying*, ed. Michael Gorra, Norton Critical Edition (New York: W. W. Norton & Co., 2010), 348–62.

[114] Faulkner, *Collected Stories*, 101–02.

encircle the earth in a form of electronic omniscience," precisely what is being said here of the undead Pete.[115] As with any number of "soldiers speaking from beyond the grave" in popular stories at the time, Pete doesn't have to lie in a "wooden box" for his Mother and Father to "catch the voices" that carry on the air interminably all around them—his just one more soul rising from "a watery grave in the Atlantic or from the trenches along the Siegfried line [...] evaporated into the flowing ether, perhaps to be retrieved by wireless or perhaps to wander forever" (75).

In *As I Lay Dying*, it is the mother who requires a wooden box, a sounding-board cut on the bevel according to the principles of animal magnetism by an eldest son obsessed with "talking machines," in order that the undead veteran second son, Darl, who "sits at the supper table with his eyes gone further than the food and the lamp, full of the land dug out of his skull and the holes filled with distance beyond the land" (18), can continue to receive her narrowcast messages. "The nihilists say it is the end," Peabody remarks (29); what he neglects to add is that they never stop saying it. The transatlantic electromagnetic mediation of Addie and Darl's death-driven Oedipal scenario by telegraphy a decade or so before is maintained in an emergent radio economy of voices across an even vaster distance, between the living and the dead. Now it is the dead mother who must speak, and the veteran survivor who must tune in to her Nietzschean signals so that he can in turn broadcast them within a novel of which he has become the staticky, intermittent vestige of the form's oldest mode of omniscience—the narratorial—reduced to mere "hints of an augmenting authorial voice" amidst a rotating first-person.[116]

Allegory: network

The revolution in cultural norms and values precipitated by the launch of radio broadcasting in North America on May 20, 1920, was unprecedented. Though it had been initially conceived as a wireless version of point-to-point telephony and appealed commercially to the proliferating amateur enthusiasts of DXing, radio's reinvention as a point-to-mass broadcasting apparatus sealed its fate as a major industry of the first half of the twentieth century. Beginning in the Northeast and Midwest, the wildfire spread of broadcasting towers and stations reached the South as early as February 1922, when stations in Montgomery, Alabama, Kansas City, Missouri, and Jefferson City, Missouri, were licensed to begin broadcasting. By the end of that year, there were multiple stations in Memphis, St Louis and Atlanta, dozens across the South; nationwide, more

---

[115] Sconce, *Haunted Media*, 63.
[116] Ross, *Fiction's Interminable Voice*, 120.

than a million radio sets were in use. Memphis, Tennessee, was the southern epicenter of radio broadcasting, and by the end of the decade, that city alone accommodated ten stations; Nashville's WSM began broadcasting the world's longest-running radio show, the "WSN Barn Dance" (later the "Grand Ole Opry") in 1925. Meanwhile, Mississippi, slower and sleepier than its northern neighbor, saw the licensing of KFNG, WDBT, and WCBH in 1924, with several others following in subsequent years.

For all this local distribution of broadcasting licenses, however, the trend was inevitably toward national standardization. The centralized commercial networks—NBC (Blue and Red) and CBS—specialized in nationwide syndication of programs broadcast from New York that benefited from state-of-the-art production values and the performances of celebrities whose fame was burnished by the magazines. As befit the monopolistic complexion of the Radio Corporation of America, the net result was the world's first truly mass public, hooked to the regular supply of near-identical, serialized aural products. Parochial regionalism was broken up by the seemingly immediate propagation of signals from the very centre of cultural capital. Since "listeners prefer[ed] national programs to local ones by a ratio of nearly nine to one, audiences tuned [their] sets to network stations for most of [the four to five hours a day they listened]. Across the country, millions and millions of listeners heard the same programs for hours each day."[117] This process was not uncontested, and "educators and labor organizations, corporate interests, amateur operators and government" all took part in what was a national debate around the social purpose of a medium with such unprecedented reach into the most intimate recesses of life. But despite early speculation that the driver of radio's propagation would be the instantaneous transmission of fine music and educational uplift, the economic and regulatory environment fostered by the electrical monopolies (AT&T, Westinghouse, RKO) created a situation in which "entertainment" tended to supplant education in the interests of a reliable rate of profit. As what Tom Gunning would call the "heightened astonishment" of radio's early years gradually faded "into understanding" and habituation dulled the nation's wondrous attention to the technology,[118] as the "cacophonous public forum in which anyone could take part" of unregulated broadcasting and amateur interference was restrained in the wake of the *Titanic* disaster,[119] and as the outlandish technicality of the medium was encased in the acceptable vestments of furniture, the medium was domesticated in the most

---

[117] Bruce Lenthall, *Radio's America: The Great Depression and the Rise of Modern Mass Culture* (Chicago & London: University of Chicago Press, 2007), 13.

[118] Tom Gunning, "Renewing Old Technologies: Astonishment, Second Nature, and the Uncanny in Technology from the Previous Turn-of-the-Century," in David Thorburn and Henry Jenkins, eds., *Rethinking Media Change: The Aesthetics of Transition* (Cambridge, MA: MIT Press, 2003), 42, 45.

[119] John Durham Peters, *Speaking Into the Air: A History of the Idea of Communication* (Chicago: University of Chicago Press, 1999), 208.

radical of senses, transformed from a speculative (and quasi-spiritual) search engine to a delivery platform for capitalist ideology and advertising.

This crystallized for a sustained moment of transition (1925–1930) in a complex tension between local, regional, and national modes of radio address, with "independent stations featur[ing] locally produced programs with local talent," while the centralized New York–based broadcasting interests of the networks "standardiz[ed] the broadcast day so that listeners tuning between stations often heard the same chain program."[120] As Wurtzler puts it, the "differences between local and national, between rural and urban, and between the immigrant and the native-born provided a focus both to how sound technology was imagined and how it was materially grafted onto social relations."[121] But the material unevenness between a rallying of local and rural specificities and the corporate interests invested in the incorporation of the national population in a single consuming body was too stark. Monopoly capitalism in 1930, despite the Great Depression it had engendered, was an irresistible force:

> U.S. broadcasting was shaped by multiple, overlapping, and mutually reinforcing determinants. These included the conservative manner in which radio was constructed as an entertainment device, a series of economic arrangements largely orchestrated by powerful electrical and communications corporations, and federal radio regulation that ultimately served the interests of corporate broadcasting control and radio spatially conceived as a national mode of address.[122]

So what had been, for one exhilarating, protracted moment in media history, a genuine collective sense that *the medium was the message* (one enthusiast reported "it is not the *substance* of communication without wires, but the *fact* of it that enthrals"[123]), was steadily converted into a mediatic unconscious: the erasure of the medium as an object of attention, and the supra-egoic installation of a *network*, a "system for binding together a national audience, even against its own will" on the basis of the fact that the "medium was now an increasingly familiar, convenient, and wholly unremarkable presence in the home, less a bridge to the 'unknown' that a machine echoing (or, more ominously, orchestrating) the structure of daily life."[124]

An irresistible medium of mass-produced mass-consumption was precisely how the first wave of cultural critics among America's public intellectuals

---

[120] Susan Douglas, *Listening In*, 57.
[121] Wurtzler, *Electric Sounds*, loc. 425 of 9211.
[122] Wurtzler, *Electric Sounds*, loc. 854 of 9211.
[123] Susan Douglas, *Listening In*, 73.
[124] Jeffrey Sconce, *Haunted Media*, 109, 105.

heralded network radio: a concentration of cultural authority in a few hands, disseminating "uniform programs and messages to a mass public" where distinctive regional cultures had previously been the norm.[125] In Michelle Hilmes's adaptation of this situation to the one explored by Benedict Anderson in relation to print capitalism, the result was an "imagined community" at the level of nationality, whose utopian dimension was the felt simultaneity of a sense of unity and mutual understanding. "As the nation found a voice through radio," she writes, "the 'imagined community' of the twentieth-century United States began to take shape" through a rhetoric of physical connection, geographical coverage, grounding in the family circle, naturalized technology, and the pervasiveness of commercial interests.[126] What this portended for the parochial distinctiveness of small towns, let alone the rural hinterlands, was obvious as early as 1924 to one astute observer:

> Look at a map of the United States . . . and try to conjure up a picture of what radio broadcasting will eventually mean to the hundreds of little towns that are set down in type so small that it can hardly be read. How unrelated they seem! . . . These little towns, these unmarked homes in vast countries seem disconnected. . . . If these little towns and villages so remote from one another, so nationally related and yet physically so unrelated, could be made to acquire a sense of intimacy, if they could be brought into direct contact with each other! [. . .] This is exactly what radio is bringing about.[127]

Exactly, provided we explain that such "intimacy" under the conditions of network broadcasting is thoroughly mediated by the private interests that effect these electromagnetic hookups and contacts for purposes of gain.

That all of this should have cast its shadow on Faulkner during the writing of *As I Lay Dying* and *Sanctuary* is hardly surprising. For a writer whose aesthetic ideology was so sensitively attuned to the successive colonizations of public and private space across the American South, there is no question but that this seismic cultural transformation served as a powerful illustration of just those tendencies at the turn of the 1930s. Yet Faulkner was not one of those "popular" writers of pulp fiction treated in Sconce's wonderful book; not for him the sensationalist science-fictions of his contemporaries. Rather, what we have been attending to is the more surreptitious logic whereby this electrical colonization of the soundscape filtered into his verbal art at the technical, tropological, and

---

[125] Bruce Lenthall, *Radio's America*, 13.

[126] Michelle Hilmes, *Radio Voices: American Broadcasting, 1922–1952* (Minneapolis, MN & London: University of Minnesota Press, 1997), 13.

[127] Waldemar Kaempffert, "The Social Destiny of Radio," *Forum* 71 (June 1924), 771.

allegorical levels. Above all, it has appeared that the technical dimension of narrative *voice* was the formal element most extensively modified by the vocal transmigrations and uncanniness of the radio voice and its compatible accompaniment, the phonographic voice. It now remains finally to correlate the full extent of our potted media history here with the extraordinary formal ingenuities of *As I Lay Dying*. In *Sanctuary* we noted the warping of a popular, radio-inflected narrative style around a constitutive void where sound and silence were inverted, and concomitant eruptions of "high modernistic" stylistics in response to the "competitive" electrical sounds on the marketplace. In this sister text we have instead wanted to stress the allegorical proclivities of a form deprived of any omniscient narratorial vantage point, and whose component monologues both fall apart into uncorrelated corpuscles and gesture weakly at a higher-order harmonics. It only remains to suggest of *what*, exactly, this allegory might have been allegorical to begin with, and what the place of romance may have been in it.

Here it is critical to emphasize that the coming of network broadcasting exposed the dialectical character of the first phase of radio's stabilization as a national medium. For the suppression of the technicality of the device in the late 1920s, its streamlining as a domestic appliance, was simultaneously a suppression of what Adorno had called the "spook" in the machine:

> The haunting factor in radio is not the newness of the mechanical tool, or the overpowering of man by the machine. It is only the remnants of the pre-technical concept of authenticity haunting an art technique basically opposed to it. When these remnants are driven out, the "spook" in radio will be finished.[128]

But whereas Adorno was attuned to the residual concept of "authenticity" in radio's hegemonic period of the high-fidelity late 1930s, his observations could well be adapted to the transitional period of the late 1920s, with one archaeological variation. Not "authenticity" but precisely *mystery* and *magic* were the pre-technical keywords of an earlier moment when radio became popular and proliferated. Associations with Spiritualism, the ether, trapped souls, "telepathy, séances and angelic visitations,"[129] endowed radio with a sense of "black magic"; "inherently magical" in its instrumentalization of invisible and inaudible waves, radio was for a long time surrounded by a "melodramatic rhetoric" that "enhanced that sense of magic."[130] Douglas's observation that "when the radio boom first

---

[128] Adorno, *Current of Music*, 91.

[129] John Durham Peters, *Speaking into the Air: A History of the Idea of Communication* (Chicago & London: University of Chicago Press, 1999), 206.

[130] Susan Douglas, *Listening In*, 47, 48.

swept through America in the 1920s, the word *miracle* was used repeatedly to try to convey the revolutionary, and mystical, properties of the device" (28) is of a piece with her generic classification of this rhetoric as "romantic"—not just in the vulgar sense of a national love affair with the medium, but very precisely as a generic categorization of the discourse that surrounded it. Radio, the most modern of media, was heralded atavistically as a mode of access to pre-modern thrills and adventures in other worlds, its ostensible irrationality in lockstep with its origins in engineering and physics.

The subsumption of local licensing and DX-fishing into a new "metaphor of blanketing and [the] inescapable sense of electronic presence"[131] that network broadcasting occasioned was the historical transformation that revealed its own recent past *as* an episode of romance. Retroactively, "the spreading commercialization of unilateral broadcasting, and the exiling of amateur transmitters to the hinterlands of the spectrum" (106) conferred upon those quixotic figures the sense of knight-errantry that we today cannot separate from their obsessions with a new and complex electrical technology. And, I add, it did so instantly: retroactive romanticism was a spontaneous ideological effect of the inevitable demise of this "class" of techno-warriors crushed beneath the heels of the homogenizing bourgeoisie.

As I Lay Dying's formal concern with a mode of discursive "telepathy" between distinctly nominated speech zones, and its outrageous central performance of a posthumous narrative voice, underscore its deeper affinity with the species of contemporary romance just outlined. Its ongoing interest in the separability of voices and bodies, in the fashioning of a wooden casket cut to the specifications of "animal magnetism," and in certain sounds being emitted by the corpse from within that casket, take further its formal and thematic interest in radio romanticism. Moreover, the structuring opposition, coordinated on the one hand by the vectors of Anse's "lengthways" roads, and his "up-and-down ways" modes of vertical implantation, and on the other by the crux formed by Addie's "words go straight up in a thin line" and her "how terribly doing goes along the earth" (117), suggests a simplified romance cosmology that is lit up by the speculative and ambivalent presence of radio as both a "vertical" (voices from the air) and "horizontal" (the imposition of a blanketing network) medium. Finally, the satirical "exchange," of a dead mother radiating uncanny noises from her bevel-cut box for a new mother gripping a graphophone, which caps off the Bundrens' quest, can be read as a figural engagement with the "competitive" voices of radios and phonographs already fleshed out in the Jefferson town square in *Sanctuary*.

If the turn of the decade marked one decisive phase of the demise of the radio "spook," even as it made available a new mode of romantic nostalgia for the

---

[131] Sconce, *Haunted Media*, 109.

recent past, then we can begin to speculate about the allegorical form itself. For at the molar narrative level, the final "exchange" between two mothers clinches a pervasive allegorical logic threaded throughout the text. Inasmuch as *As I Lay Dying*'s quest concerns the outrageously protracted interment of one Mrs. Bundren, and the acquisition of a new one, it arguably functions as an allegory of the protracted social moment of radio romance, and its inevitable surcease. The quest to bury the radio corpse does not prevent that corpse from speaking, and we can surely recognize in Darl, who gets "into the inside of you, someway" (81), a belated avatar of the quixotic DX fisher, whose deviant Oedipus complex has equipped him with the requisite spiritual antennae to receive the messages of a dead mother with whom, in France, he had already hypothetically established electromagnetic contact. If she is replaced by a woman with a graphophone, then on the literal level we are being driven backward in media time, since in 1930 that technology is already dead; and yet, the seamless cohesion of the family unit around this mechanized talking machine surely suggests the instauration of a new media dominant whose ability to prosper will have depended upon the proper burial of broadcast radio's "supernatural" prehistory, and the exile of those "amateur transmitters" who had interfered with the instauration of centralized entertainment capital. The graphophone is an anachronistic mask for the broadcast pacification of the public and the stabilization of gender norms within the family. Addie's and Darl's fates, as allegorical figures of the radio romance, are sealed by the historical inevitability of the twentieth century's enduring media legacy: the network as an inescapable matrix of corporate interests threading through the most intimate fibers of the family and the individual. Cash's eulogy is precise: "everytime a new record would come from the mail order and us setting in the house in the winter, listening to it, I would think what a shame Darl couldn't be to enjoy it too. But it is better so for him. This world is not his world; this life his life" (177–78). Whether it is a hit record or a top-rating NBC program is less important in this context than the affirmation that Darl's "world" of radio romance is definitively "not" this world, and his uncanny death-in-life "not" this life of standardized consumption. All of this may well strike the reader as a preposterous misreading, and at the level of mere asseveration it is, of course, radically insufficient. But that it is a *strong* misreading, at the very least, may finally be attested by a return to our analysis of the function of voice in the novel as a whole. For here, in the play of vocal strategies that sustain the compelling forward narrative drive of the text, we may see that the terms of this allegory are replicated in the technical substratum itself.

We can make a first-order distinction between the novel's fifteen narrative voices according to the tenses they employ. Here the Bundren family is distinguished from the guest narrators—neighbors Vernon and Cora Tull, Doc Peabody, the Rev. Whitfield, the farmers Samson and Henry Armstid, Moseley the pharmacist, and Skeet MacGowan the soda-jerk—on the basis of temporal proximity. While there is a near-perfect (and for Faulkner highly unusual) "agreement" between the substance of the sequence of narrations and the consecutive events of story time (with one or two exceptions in "flash-back"), there is a marked difference in relative degrees of temporal distance. Broadly speaking, as narrators, the Bundrens tend to be less distanced in time than the outsiders are from the disastrous course of events that attend their actions. Consider Cora's comment that "It was the sweetest thing I ever saw" (16), which puts her wholly inaccurate assessment of Darl's filial piety in a tense of deep retrospection; or Samson's transitional "So next morning I never went down there" (76), which again adopts a conventional preterite, as does Armstid's "Along towards nine oclock it begun to get hot" (125) and "Or that's what I thought then" (129)—generally, these guest narrators open up a significant temporal gap between their *situations d'énonciation* and the events and things they describe. The deictics that populate their discourse—"I ever," "next morning," "down there," "I thought then"—all allow us clearly to distinguish the temporal plane to which they refer, either to the "now" of narration, or the "then" of the story.

In contradistinction to that distance (which is not strictly upheld, as we know from some of Tull's present-tense contributions), we can say that the Bundren narrators tend to situate their "time of enunciation" much closer to the action and often explicitly in it, thanks to their frequent use of the present tense. In Vardaman's paratactic impressionism—"Pa walks around. His shadow does. The saw sounds like it is asleep" (43)—Dewey Dell's ecstatic periods of swollen immanence—"I feel the darkness rushing past my breast, past the cow; I begin to rush upon the darkness but the cow stops me and the darkness rushes on upon the sweet blast of her morning breath" (41)—and Jewel's one-off venting of spleen in mostly subjunctive clauses, but also sentences from which the primary verb is removed, leaving the present participles standing in stark immediacy—"And now them others sitting there, like buzzards. Waiting, fanning themselves" (11)—we learn to track variable qualities of the present tense. These voices inhabit phenomenologically distinctive "nows," and their presents are bound by different logics and even metaphysics. "My mother is a fish" (54) tells us something radically different from "It's not that I wouldn't and will not it's that it is too soon too soon too soon" (78), which is distinct from "Sawing and knocking, and keeping the air always moving" (11). These modalities of the present are different again from the odd vocal tense of the paterfamilias, who employs a vernacular idiom in which it is sometimes hard to distinguish past from present; like Samson, who tends to write the past tense of the verb "to say" as "says" (which is also indifferent to person), Anse prefers to speak in an undecidable, mildly iterative or aphoristic tense: "'Yonder,' Cash says, jerking his head toward the lane" (68), "And Darl sitting there on the plank seat" (68), "It's a hard country on a man" (71), "Sometimes I wonder why" (71) "Durn that road" (24). But there is no mistaking the temporal situation of his self-referring shifters which, when they appear, prove the tense as present and even open up a rare futurity: "But now I can get them teeth. That will be a comfort" (71).

Strangely, Vardaman's voice shifts from its established present tense to a classical narrative preterite during the flood scene (100–01), so that a brief return to the present must be indicated in italics (100) before reverting again to the present tense in future monologues, albeit with the new capacity to introduce retrospection within the frame of the present (151–52). Dewey Dell, too, breaks from the hold of the present into conventional past tense once the family reaches Jefferson (174–75); it is as if her voice, silent for some hundred pages, has been projected out of the immediacy of the events by the colonization of her narrative arc by MacGowan and Moseley. And this slippage into the preterite has been prepared for all along by the one (living) Bundren who only ever speaks from a temporal vantage point that sequesters the violence and fatigue to which his body is subjected by the story. Cash's present tense is reserved for his subjective reflections. The man in love with talking machines and playback has his strictly narrative speech "canned" by the simple past tense of "I made it on the bevel" (53), "It wasn't on a balance" (111), and "So we sent up the street, toward the square" (158). His infrequent present-tense periods are reserved for personal judgments: "I dont reckon nothing excuses setting fire to a man's barn" (158), "it's better to build a tight chicken coop than a shoddy courthouse" (158), and "I aint so sho that ere a man has the right to say what is crazy and what aint" (161). This very alternation—between a settled past tense in which his terrible bodily tribulations are never alluded to and an opinionated and apophthegmic present—is precisely what gives Cash's voice its imperturbable distance from events; it is that distance that then comes dramatically into focus in the throwaway line "He set that way all the time we was in front of Mrs. Bundren's house, hearing the music" (159) and in his climactic, iterative periods about "everytime a new record would come from the mail order" (177).

The relatively conventional temporality of Cash's narrative voice is then radicalized in the post-mortem *énonciation* of Addie Bundren herself, who executes the closest thing the family has to a sustained classical *récit*. This is a narrative voice in which we feel the absolute distance between the two planes of its composition—between the story material "whose events are already over and done with before the telling of it can begin,"[132] and the time of the narration, which here assumes a merely speculative location in time and tends toward an infinite distance from its content. Addie never speaks a sentence in the present tense. Unlike Cash, even when she voices a judgment or belief, it is couched in the inexorable past: "That was when I learned that words are no good [. . .]. I knew that fear was invented by someone that never had the fear" (115). That

---

[132] Fredric Jameson, *The Antinomies of Realism* (London & New York: Verso, 2013), 9.

the story she is called upon to tell bears some not-too-distant affinities with one of American literature's most hallowed texts further ramifies the sense of predestination implicit in the temporal severance between the situation of enunciation and the *énoncé*.

> While I waited for him in the woods, waiting for him before he saw me, I would think of him as dressed in sin. I would think of him as thinking of me as dressed also in sin, he the more beautiful since the garment which he had exchanged for sin was sanctified. I would think of the sin as garments which we would remove in order to shape and coerce the terrible blood to the forlorn echo of the dead word high in the air. (118)

Readers of these sentences cannot possibly *not* hear the intertext of *The Scarlet Letter*, with its *in medias res* exploration of the consequences of a similar series of trysts between a hypocritical preacher and a married woman; when we realize that the fruit of this union is named "Jewel" as an echo to the "Pearl" of that other text, we must surely grasp the nameless "dead word high in the air" as Hawthorne's, whose "forlorn echo" is then felt as a determining instance ("shap[ing] and coerc[ing] the terrible blood") within the preterition of this voice's implacable *récit*. This literary redoubling of the temporal gap between "what happens" to Addie and her telling of it, and indeed the radicalization of that gap in the conceit of her posthumous speech, gives her voice a complexion within the novel that any contemporary reader might have recognized as "radiophonic." Horace McCoy's *They Shoot Horses, Don't They?* (1935) and James M. Cain's *The Postman Always Rings Twice* (1934) share with Faulkner's book this conceit of a (legally) dead narrating instance—a coincidence with the rise of radio culture that cannot have been mere happenstance. "Both pulp or hard-boiled detective stories and *film noir* are indeed structurally distinguished by the fundamental fact of the *voice-over*, which signals in advance the closure of events to be narrated just as surely as it marks the operative presence of an essentially radio aesthetic which has no equivalent in the earlier novel."[133] The same can be said for Addie's pivotal monologue in *As I Lay Dying*; the "dead word high in the air" is as much radio's as it is Hawthorne's, or God's.

The dialectical obverse of the posthumous voice of the *récit* is Darl's unbroken immersion in the present tense. And nowhere else do we feel to the same degree what Genette calls the "'live' running commentary" on the preposterous sequence of events as in these meticulously composed periods of first-person immanence.[134] That is, although the structural implication of the "voice-over" as

---

[133] Fredric Jameson, "The Synoptic Chandler," in Joan Copjec, ed., *Shades of Noir* (London & New York: Verso, 1993), 36.

[134] Genette, *Narrative Discourse*, 216.

a radio aesthetic is best exemplified by the resolute narrative closure of Addie's *récit*, it is with Darl that we are most conspicuously abandoned to the unique vocal qualities of radio's "liveness" as a medium. Here what Genette has to say about the relatively rare literary phenomenon of narrative in the present tense: "Radio or television reporting is obviously the most perfectly live form of this kind of narrative, where the narrating follows so closely on the action that it can be considered practically simultaneous, whence the use of the present tense."[135] For that same reason, however, the frequency of such a narrative voice in fiction is historically low prior to radio's saturation of the narrative imagination at the end of the 1920s.[136]

In Darl's chapters, the first-person-singular pronoun almost always appears only to specify his own reported acts of speech within the frame of the story ("I say" is its most frequent form of appearance, *passim*); by and large, his narration concerns the environment ("The air smells like sulphur," 49), the general action ("the wagon sheers crosswise, poised on the crest of the ford as the log strikes it," 98), and, most abundantly, the actions of his fellow actors ("He flows upward in a stooping swirl like the lash of a whip," 9; "she sits on the seat beside Vardaman and sets the parcel on her lap," 67). His voice is thus preoccupied to an extraordinary extent with the third person, and it is this that gives it the true quality of a "live" running commentary on events, since the suppression of the first person over a sustained period allows for a certain "depersonalization" of the voice and its immersion in the field of action. Apart from rare exceptions (e.g., "I can see," 67, 98, 148, 149, 155; "I know," 98, "I reach," 149) Darl's descriptions and narrations in the present tense are issued in a tone of almost fastidious objectivity, from which the accents of an interested observer and the vagaries of subjective perception are excluded, and where the merest hint of a subjunctive is subjugated in advance. Indeed, the exceptions prove the rule: the rare pockets of past-tense retrospection, as in the memory of drinking from the bucket late at night (8), the dislocating switches into italicized past tense (97), or the extended *récit* about Jewel's nocturnal travails (83–89), function as relativizing interpolations of a subjective preterite within the governing simultaneity of Darl's "objective" broadcasts. Like any classical radio reporter, Darl subtracts the first-person-singular pronoun from his account of proceedings so his narrative may appear inexorable, accurate, finished, despite the isotopy and isochrony of the embedded present tense. Even the descriptions grounded in

---

[135] Genette, *Narrative Discourse*, 216, n.9.

[136] The first person is a stalking horse for the conventional third-person preterite in the history of the novel, from the days of Richardson at least; but it is really not until Dostoevsky's *Notes from the Underground* (1864) and after that Joyce's Molly soliloquy in *Ulysses* (1922) that the first-person present-tense narrative attains sound footing. The novelty of Darl's voice in *As I Lay Dying*, technically, is that it is narrating things that are happening isochronically with the narrative itself in the field of action, and not in a private chamber.

his own bodily experience are rendered absolute by grammatical fiat, tilting into the first person plural: "It has a chill, scouring quality, as though the earth under us were in motion too" (107), "We watch through the dissolving proscenium of the doorway" (149). There is even the occasional sense of a live correction or qualification of the voice's public commitments to record: "Lon Quick could look even at a cloudy sky and tell the time to ten minutes. Big Lon I mean, not little Lon" (108).

One of the prototypical broadcasts in the history of network radio, Herbert Morrison's coverage of the arrival of the Hindenburg zeppelin in Lakehurst, New Jersey, for Chicago station WLS on May 6, 1937, encapsulates the logic of this mode of address. An experienced announcer of live musical broadcasts and of natural disasters (including a large Midwestern flood), Morrison's professional commentary was, ironically, in this case not broadcast live but recorded for subsequent network use: "It's practically standing still now. They've dropped ropes out of the nose of the ship, and they've been taken a hold of down on the field by a number of men. It's starting to rain again; it's—the rain has slacked up a little bit. The back motors of the ship are just holding it just, just enough to keep it from—It burst into flames!" Such is the essence of "live," running commentary, even when it is not live. But Morrison could have learned a thing or two about radio professionalism from Darl Bundren. Where Morrison's diction is full of contractions and his grammar wrong-footed by the unfolding of events, Darl remains imperturbably exact, his voice never slipping into the affective excess of Morrison ("It's fire—and it's crashing! It's crashing terrible! Oh, my, get out of the way, please! It's burning and bursting into flames, and the—and it's falling on the mooring—"): "Overhead the flames sound like thunder; across us rushes a cool draft: there is no heat at all in it yet, and a handful of chaff lifts suddenly and sucks swiftly along the stall where a horse is screaming" (147). Not for the cool and collected commentary of Darl Bundren is the latent cry—Oh, the equinity!

When Orson Welles used the Halloween broadcast of his "Mercury Theatre on the Air" show in 1938 to raise the stakes of broadcasting to a new level of reflexivity, it was the already established convention of live emergency interruptions to standard musical programing that proved the most logical point of entry into a national audience's recently trained habits of reception. "Ladies and gentlemen, this is the most terrifying thing I have ever witnessed .... Wait a minute! Someone's crawling. Someone or ... something. I can see peering out of that black hole two luminous disks ... are they eyes? It might be a face. It might be ... good heavens, something's wriggling out of the shadow like a gray snake. Now it's another one, and another one, and another one. They look like tentacles to me..." Tongue-in-cheek sensationalism aside, this radio voice of irrefutable testimony is grounded as much in the use of present-tense first-person as it is in the social and technical institution of the apparatus itself; a dual grounding tested and certified by Morrison's broadcast a year and a half earlier. Since network broadcasting has no interlocutor, since its reportorial voice is issued in a context of unanswerable monologism, the grammatical tense and person serve to underscore the established form of what will inevitably be nominated as the radio age's new "omniscient narrator."

The emergence of this new narrative voice of incontestable authority in the media ecology of the 1930s, thanks to radio's tendency, even when using pre-recorded disks, to make its acousmatic voices "appear more objective and infallible than a live voice,"[137] altered at a stroke the inherited rules of literary narration, as any cursory inspection of the narrative styles of contemporary *noir* and pulp fictions will attest. Another study would be required to track its propagation in the domain of serious literature, but as an indication it is worth considering the fabled "Camera Eye" and "Newsreel" sections of Dos Passos's *USA* trilogy, not as remediations of a cinematic narrativity, but as a kind of collage-surrealistic deformation of the primary mode of radio address. This can be noted above all in those sections' tendency to weave in and out of a present tense nowhere else evident in the trilogy's great mass of text: "admits he threw bomb policewoman buys drink after one loses on wheat" (*NR* 14: 205), "the Chautaqua Lecturer wants his dinner and quarrels with his wife" (*CE* 24: 239), "Paris comes into the room in the servantgirl's eyes" (*CE* 39: 620), "syndicated wage-earners seize opportunity to threaten employers unprepared for change" (*NR* 36: 621). This scrambled use of radio journalism's present tense serves high literature by way of a double function, combining an abundance of social cliché incorporated as "found text," and the thrills of immediacy that the preterite lacks by contrast. Given that network radio was, to paraphrase Adorno, a "symptom of an entire network of social processes,"[138] it was inevitable that its voice, borne by "a sort of mechanization of human sense organs,"[139] would bleed into literary discourse at a technical as well as a tropological level; since live broadcasting was precisely what literature could not manage itself, its envious and competitive striving for cultural authority could hardly take place without some explicit engagement with those very qualities.

Our reading of Darl's narrative voice as a mode of live commentary, however, opens up a contradiction in the allegory itself. If, at one level, Darl is a quixotic remnant of a romantic radio past that must be conjured away from the rational grid of a new national network, at another he is a carrier of the new sorts of signal that will standardize and spread that very network. As a characterological *figure*, Darl is already anachronistic in 1929, a romantic throwback; but as a *voice*, he is mimicking precisely the most innovative and

---

[137] Adorno, *Current of Music*, 47.
[138] David Jenemann, *Adorno in America* (Minneapolis: University of Minnesota Press, 2007), 54.
[139] Adorno, *Current of Music*, 48.

irresistible forces of technical modernity: broadcast simultaneous commentary. It is just this tension and inner contradiction that makes the allegory so powerful, and we can see a version of the same internal paradox played out at the level of diction and idiom. Whereas all of the other narrators are obliged to present their "speech" (the question of whether or not it is "inner speech" is a vexed one) in visible approximations of dialectal accentuation, Darl's voice is almost wholly unmarked by the colloquialisms and accent of his region. What Stephen Ross calls the "eye dialect" of printed conventions for the specificities of local speech patterns is used by Faulkner to transcribe the variable idiolects of poor white farmers, small-town shopkeepers, members of the professions, and tradespeople, allowing for a bravura display of the resources of "mimetic speech" to flesh out the first (named) Yoknapatawpha novel's living community of spoken English.[140] But just as Darl's voice is situated at a narratological place "closer" to the action that any other narrator, so too his diction is located "further" than any other narrator from his region, or indeed, his nation. Darl is, of course, the epicenter of what Ross calls the text's "richly metaphoric digression[s], and philosophically charged speculation[s] burdened by Latinate diction and convoluted syntax" (111). We have already stipulated that, insofar as these tendencies affect other narratorial zones, this should be understood as a projection of Darl's mobile and "clairvoyant" voice into the voices of other members of his family. Now it must be insisted that this "infection" of the discourse by Darl's voice consists in a "de-regionalization" of the text's otherwise meticulously presented mimetic speech; indeed, it partakes of an abstraction from region fully consonant with what we have assessed as network radio's subsumption of local and regional cultures within a coercive "imagined community" at the level of the nation, but broadcast almost exclusively from the concentration of "modernity" in the Northeast. While the text's abundant polyphony, its rotation of narrators marked by distinctive idiolects, at one level performs a dialogical cross-section of a certain rural locale, at another level it is as if that regional dialogism is itself put into uneven "dialogue" with the regionless monologism of a type of speech that radio was busy installing as the privileged "omniscient narrative" voice of the period.

Darl here appears as a personification of Faulkner's fitful commitment to the aesthetic creeds of "modernism" as what tends to negate or displace "provincial culture with its small towns, its agriculture, its still living religion, its implicit norms of conduct"[141]—but this, too, in a dual sense. On the one

---

[140] Ross, *Fiction's Interminable Voice*, 111.

[141] Hugh Kenner, "Faulkner and the Avant-Garde," in Evans Harrington and Ann J. Abadie, eds., *Faulkner, Modernism, and Film: Faulkner and Yoknapatawpha, 1978* (Jackson, MS: University Press of Mississippi, 1979), 190.

hand, as a radio voice of live, simultaneous broadcasting, Darl's discourse belongs to the metropolitan centers of media monopoly and provincial subsumption; but on the other, as *style*, it belongs as much to the "international tradition" manifest in the works of Joyce, Pound, Eliot, and Beckett, since in Darl's prose we attend to a programmatically "depersonalized" vocal mechanism capable of periods that at least track and "mimic" those novel literary modes of voice:

> How do our lives ravel out into the no-wind, no-sound, the weary gestures wearily recapitulant: echoes of old compulsions with no-hand on no-strings: in sunset we fall into furious attitudes, dead gestures of dolls. (139)

This famous sentence, divided up by two colons that perform a logic of appositive predication, is surely a self-conscious (and perhaps self-mocking) bid for recognition in the cloisters of international modernism, where Faulkner's oratorical "garrulousness" broke too many of those hallowed proscriptions against rhetoric and excess made in the name of "the well-wrought artefact, the tireless revision, the skilled reader, the habitual reader, in an economy of typescripts, numbered pages, typographic cues for which a speaking voice has no equivalent, etymologies, dictionaries."[142] To be sure, in this instance, the bid is framed in relation to a national exemplar, that of Eugene O'Neill's much-lampooned *Strange Interlude*, with its too-frequent recourse to the melancholy introspective aside: "Round and round ... thoughts ... damn pests! ... mosquitoes of the soul ... whine, sting, suck one's blood ...," "What is she thinking? ... we sit together in silence, thinking ... thoughts that never know the other's thoughts ...," "Oh, God, so deaf and dumb and blind! ... teach me to be resigned to be an atom!"[143] But elsewhere, the calling card is delivered by a hand more evidently disciplined by the stylistic lingua franca of a prose modernist cadre more cosmopolitan than nationalist:

> The sun, an hour above the horizon, is poised like a bloody egg upon a crest of thunderheads; the light has turned copper: in the eye portentous, in the nose sulphurous, smelling of lightning. (27)

The initial non-restrictive adjectival clause here has dropped its relative pronoun *and* verb form, giving its dependency a terse, appositive ring that reverberates with "modernist" values. Next, the metaphorical intensity of "bloody egg" and "crest" accumulates semantic energy just at the point where a semicolon

---

[142] Kenner, "Faulkner and the Avant-Garde," 186.

[143] Eugene O'Neill, *Strange Interlude*, in Travis Bogard, ed., *Complete Plays: 1920–1931*, Vol. 2 (New York: Library of America, 1988), 679, 760, 811.

introduces a cut, whose paratactic sequel, a new clause about the light, shifts the tense into the past perfect. The colon that follows then introduces in short sequence three further relative clauses using a "zero" relative pronoun and omitting all the dependent verbs apart from the present-participle form of "to smell," which closes the sentence with its modulation to a new sensory register. Plentiful other examples could be adduced to demonstrate the degree to which Darl's narrative discourse is saturated by aesthetic considerations that have nothing to do with the "mimetic voice" and have as little to do with the engaging immediacies of the radio voice's "live" commentary. When this tendency to aesthetic autonomy from within the present-tense narration is considered in relation to the relative absence of dialectal markers and tonalities, we are obliged to conclude that, just as Darl's voice is abstracted from regionalism by the neutral and impersonal tone of a "networked" broadcaster, so too is it abstracted from the very freight of content itself by an intermittent "modernist" autotelism at the level of style. In Bedient's words, "the language gets in the way of the reality it describes, or better, the language here secretly flouts and overcomes reality, achieving a proud independency."[144] For Martin Green, Faulkner's rhetoric tends to manifest its stylistic excesses "*in vacuo*," leaving a fathomless "gap between it and the writer," let alone the first-person narrator.[145] That gap is the space of modernism; but the very same gap was open to radiophonic exploitation as well. As Adorno put it in a comment with the most profound consequences for a reading of *As I Lay Dying*, the "'broke' farmer is consoled by the radio-instilled belief that Toscanini is playing for him and him alone, and that an order of things that allows him to hear Toscanini compensates for farm products, or that even though he is ploughing under cotton, radio is giving him culture."[146] Darl is the text's strategy for having it both ways at once: his voice is what "plays" as a compensation for the narrative ruination of a familial economic unit predicated on the land. But he is also what must be separated from that very unit, since the "order of things" to which he gives voice is incompatible with the figure he assumes in the narrative.

The stereotypical critical concern with what tend to be called lapses in "verisimilitude" latent in the way Faulkner depicts poor Southern white rural speech as shot through with patches of Latinate eloquence and epiphanic euphony—let alone having Darl compare the apparition of Addie's coffin on Gillespie's sawhorses to a "cubistic bug" (147)—is a fundamental misunderstanding of the way Darl's "speech zone" works within the text. Cleanth Brooks's typical comment about the way "these interior monologues use words and expressions which we

---

[144] Bedient, "Pride and Nakedness: *As I Lay Dying*," 75–76.

[145] Martin Green, *Re-Appraisals: Some Commonsense Readings in American Literature* (New York: W. W. Norton & Co., 1965), 174.

[146] Adorno, quoted in Jenemann, *Adorno in America*, 78.

feel are beyond their education and background,"[147] founders on any reading of the novel that is attuned to the thorough depersonalization of Darl Bundren as a function of new media developments. Radio, let alone mobilization for war in France, is what allows alien "words and expressions" to circulate in "interior monologies" hitherto shaped, in "education and background," only by local conditions. Modernism is what squares the circle by exploiting these discursive disjunctures and anachronisms as a seedbed for untold formal and aesthetic novelties. Faulkner's interest in these ideological and idiomatic dissonances can be said to proceed both from his inconsistent affiliation with international modernism as a movement, and from his "naturalistic" concern with the ways in which modern communications have usurped regionalism from within. His allegory in *As I Lay Dying* is precisely "about" the overdetermined ways in which a distinctive Yoknapatawpha "voice" is being doubly erased, doubly subsumed, by modernist universalism and by nationalist broadcast corporations at once: the critical irony being that modernist "resistance" to monolithic mass-cultural forms participates in a comparable tactic of abstraction.

This is the place, at last, categorically to refute any assertion that a "*communal discourse*" supervenes over the various individual voices of the text, such that "*As I Lay Dying* depicts a community of voices more than a series of isolated souls."[148] It depicts neither, but rather a series of overlapping schisms in the substance of a "living language," engendered by mutations of the media ecology. The schism between local dialect and networked uniformity plays out in the dissonance and interference patterns generated by a constant formal movement between Darl and the other narrators, both within and between named chapters. The forced break between the suppressed "radio romance" of DX fishing and the new era of coast-to-coast broadcast programming is felt in the qualitative split between the "Spiritualist" Darl–Addie dyad and the centripetal material energies drawing the rest of the family to Jefferson. The break between "naturalist" local representationality and modernist universalism is endemic to the novel's acute ambivalence about dialectal verisimilitude and passages of sheer "formalist" musicality. The net result is less a "shared, communal field of verbal expression, a not always harmonic choir of living voices," than it is a dynamic figure of the "network" itself: a volatile and self-contradictory media dialectic whose genetic origins in capitalist universality render otiose any thought of an Archimedean vantage point or any "omniscient narrator" who is not radically thrown into the buckling field of immanence itself, like a log bobbing and rearing up on the electromagnetic currents of consciousness that radio had exposed as the medium of capitalism itself.

---

[147] Cleanth Brooks, *William Faulkner: The Yoknapatawpha Country* (New Haven & London: Yale University Press, 1963), 141–66.

[148] Ross, *Fiction's Interminable Voice*, 125.

4

The Negative Plate; or, *Absalom, Absalom!* and the camera's voice

> *I prefer silence to sound, and the image produced by words occurs in silence. That is, the thunder and the music of the prose take place in silence.*[1]

News that stays news

Absalom, Absalom! is the greatest work of literary art to be subsidized by those new corporate forms of patronage, the Hollywood studio system and magazine capital. Faulkner worked intermittently on the novel between early 1934 and mid-1936, a period during which, among other things, he also worked on *Sutter's Gold* (July 1935), *Wooden Crosses/Road to Glory* (Fox, December 1935), *A Banjo on My Knee* (Fox, March, 1936), and at least some of *Slave Ship/The Last Slaver* (Fox, September 1936), as well as roughly twenty short stories for the magazines (including his Hollywood story "Golden Land" and the entirety of what would become *The Unvanquished*), and that additional novel written as a "respite" from *Absalom*'s "inchoate" state of composition, *Pylon*.[2] The checks from *The Post*, Universal, and Fox paid the bills—$9,000 for the *Unvanquished* stories alone (that "pulp series" of "trash," as Faulkner described them[3]), and $1,000 per week on a week-by-week basis from the studios, to a total of eight weeks. This in a national economy where $1,000 represented an average family's annual income in 1935. Thomas McHaney is right to say that Faulkner's salary at Fox was "dizzyingly high when contrasted with the economy of

---

[1] William Faulkner in *The Paris Review—The Art of Fiction* No. 12, William Faulkner (Spring, 1956), at http://www.theparisreview.org/interviews/4954/the-art-of-fiction-no-12-william-faulkner.

[2] Joseph Blotner and Noel Polk, "Note on the Texts," in Faulkner, *Novels 1930–1935* (New York: Library of America, 1985), 1025.

[3] Quoted in Joseph Blotner, *Faulkner: A Biography* (Jackson, MS: University Press of Mississippi, 2005), 335.

Mississippi"[4]—a hired farmhand might have expected to earn $216 in a calendar year in the mid-1930s; a steelworker, $423—but perhaps more to the point, and to focus only on the studios, the discrepancy between this exorbitant rate of pay and the material returns expected from it by the brass is staggering in the context of an economic depression. Four motion pictures worked on, only one of which credited Faulkner as a co-writer (though his dialogue was wholly omitted), and one as a "story" contributor, while one appeared with no credit, and one went unproduced. Speculative capital was the name of the Hollywood game.

In what follows, we will examine *Absalom, Absalom!* on its own aesthetic terms for symptoms of its medial unconscious; however, it cannot be altogether contained in a sacred grove of textual autonomy. If it is the case that other modes and regimes of writing not only subsidized the production over 26 months of this great novel but were constantly both impeding its progress and managing the creative stresses of its difficult aesthetic realization, then these coeval texts—screenplays, treatments, short stories, reviews—can usefully be considered as "adjunctive or incremental to the design." It is possible to read them not merely as irritating economic distractions or as a "relief" from the herculean formal labours of the *chef d'oeuvre*, but—since they somehow got Faulkner to that moment on March 30, 1935, when he could scrawl *Absalom, Absalom!* at the top of a blank sheet of paper and write the whole stalled thing through again, in more or less its present form—as tributary formal processes in their own right. Indeed, if we stretch the frame a little wider still, and admit Faulkner's subsequent novel, *If I Forget Thee, Jerusalem*, as part of an integrated sequence whose central bulk is *Absalom, Absalom!* (if not necessarily, with Richard Godden, as that work's "coda" and palpable intertext[5]), then veritable patterns of a medial nature emerge that require some attention.

For what then appears is the fact that, uniquely in Faulkner's work, the major novels published on either side of *Absalom* feature central characters whose economic occupation is the same as his own, even as *The Unvanquished* is as close as Faulkner ever came to a book-length capitulation to what Melville had called "altogether writ[ing] the *other* way," the kind that simply pays.[6] As Carolyn Porter has put it, this "approximate novel" appears to have siphoned off Faulkner's own "romantic attachment to the cavalier legends passed down in his own family," thus allowing him to face the labors of *Absalom* unencumbered by the overlay

---

[4] Thomas L. McHaney, "Faulkner's Genre Experiments," in Richard C. Moreland, ed., *A Companion to William Faulkner* (Oxford: Blackwell, 2007), 336.

[5] Richard Godden, with Pamela Knights, "Forget Jerusalem, Go to Hollywood—'To Die. Yes. To die?' (A Coda to *Absalom, Absalom!*)," in Godden, *Fictions of Labor: William Faulkner and the South's Long Revolution* (Cambridge: Cambridge University Press, 1997), 179–234.

[6] Herman Melville, letter to Hawthorne, June, 1851.

of what Mark McGurl calls "simple romantic entertainments."[7] Meanwhile, like Faulkner himself, the Reporter and Harry Wilburne are writers (one professional, the other amateur) of *text that pays* in the modern media system, and their placement in novels on either side of the great work they "supported" brings to light the figure I will call their brother-avatar in it: Quentin himself, first proposed by Rosa Coldfield in terms they could well have understood.

> So maybe you will enter the literary profession as so many Southern gentlemen and gentlewomen too are doing now and maybe some day you will remember this and write about it. You will be married then I expect and perhaps your wife will want a new gown or a new chair for the house and you can write this and submit it to the magazines.[8]

If we see this sequence of works as a protracted metacommentary, within the art-novel form, upon its own straitened conditions and means of production in the mid-1930s, reflecting in great depth on the altered circumstances of literary economics brought about by the new media and their function within the general division of labor and the Depression itself, then we can begin to understand how *Absalom, Absalom!* is permeated by the evolving machinery of this allegory. And since Mark McGurl has already conclusively demonstrated the dialectical formal and class relations between *The Unvanquished* and *Absalom*,[9] it will suffice here to see how *Pylon*, by drawing off some of the medial resentment informing *Absalom*'s composition and focusing the hypothetical "class consciousness" of the supposedly proletarianized writer, prepares for an extended analysis of its magnificent successor along comparable lines.

Pylon is bookended by scenes that dramatize the objective situation of writing in the modern media ecology in openly agonistic terms. If "literature" still persists as the aspirational *telos* of the Reporter's vocation, his labor is subject to an industrial regime openly inimical to its realization, as he is brutally reminded by his editor after a rambling pitch that never quite arrives at an angle: "The people who own this paper or who direct its policies or anyway who pay the salaries ... have no Lewises or Hemingways or even Tchekovs on the staff: one very good reason doubtless being that they do not want them, since what they want is not

---

[7] Carolyn Porter, *Seeing and Being: The Plight of the Participant Observer in Emerson, James, Adams, and Faulkner* (Middletown, CT: Wesleyan University Press, 1981), 219; Mark McGurl, *The Novel Art: Elevations of American Fiction after Henry James* (Princeton, NJ: Princeton University Press, 2001), 147.

[8] William Faulkner, *Absalom, Absalom!*, in *Novels 1936–1940* (New York: Library of America, 1990), 7.

[9] Mark McGurl, *The Novel Art*, 146–157.

fiction, not even Nobel Prize fiction, but news."[10] But this professional insistence on the generic and discursive proprieties of the media system is ironically qualified by the editor's frequenting of the country club, his golf clubs gleaming like "obstetrical shapes" (833) in the back of his roadster and the "sum of money it represented" (834), his jacket "which unmistakably represented money" (833), and the fat wallet from which he either does or does not dispense the "jack" to keep his worker on what amounts to a 24/7 work regimen; and by the contrast of all this with the precarious rental gothic of his employee, his cheap room filled with "objects which possessed that quality of veteran prostitutes: of being overlaid by the ghosts of so many anonymous proprietors that even the present titleholder held merely rights but no actual possession" (836)—a material association between himself and those "rented cunts" he finds himself musing on in sympathetic reverie along Grandlieu Street (815). It is also a thinly veiled reference to the "orthodox prostitution" of which Faulkner was at this time accusing himself in reference to his story series for the *Post*.[11] The difference between literature and news is a class difference; it has something to do with the fact that the editor possesses, while the reporter rents and is rented, locked into one of those "ranked coffincubicles of dead tail; the Great American in one billion printings slavepostchained and scribblescrawled: annotations of eternal electrodeitch and bottomhope" (818). His status as a member of the waged precariat, which he protests by the compound interest of these verbose deposits in his mental account, is confirmed by the number of times he is fired and rehired in a forty-eight-hour period.

News, here, is what does *not* stay news, but is reified into undeviating headlines:

> the stilldamp neat row of boxes which in the paper's natural order had no scarehead, containing, since there was nothing new in them since time began, likewise no alarm:—that crosssection out of timespace as though of a lightray caught by a speed lens for a second's fraction between infinity and furious and trivial dust:
> FARMERS REFUSE BANKERS DENY
> STRIKERS DEMAND   PRESIDENT'S YACHT
> ACREAGE REDUCTION   QUINTUPLETS GAIN
> EX-SENATOR RENAUD CELEBRATES TENTH
> ANNIVERSARY AS RESTAURATEUR   (825–26)

Such is that "fragile web of ink and paper, assertive, proclamative; profound and irrevocable if only in the sense of being profoundly and irrevocably

---

[10] Faulkner, *Pylon*, in *Novels 1930–1935* (New York: Library of America, 1985), 808.
[11] Faulkner, *Selected Letters*, ed. Joseph Blotner (New York: Vintage, 1978), 85.

unimportant—the dead instant's fruit of forty tons of machinery and an entire nation's antic delusion" (850)—that the fixed and variable capital invested by "the people who own this paper" is supposed to yield. And just as the now open, now hidden class struggle between editor and reporter is contested over this "dead instant's fruit" of an entire means of mediatic production, so that other scene of class confrontation played out in the Feinman Airport Superintendent's office ("a place like a board room in a bank," 876) comes to a head around a mimeographed event program.

The Reporter has already performed for us something of the figurative importance of this apparently inconsequential piece of printed material, and his own ontological relationship to it, by first taking out of his pocket and reading "the pamphlet program of yesterday… opening it at the second fading imprint of the mimeograph" (itself remediated on this page of the novel, 871), and then evoking for us its mental image: "he could see the program again, the faint mimeographed letters beating and pulsing against his cringing eyeballs" (873). In the Reporter's mental processes (the locus of the labor power he sells), printed type demonstrates its Imaginary capabilities within the Symbolic. While it is the purpose of mass-produced copy to conjure a mass hallucination (of types, "identical from day to day—the bankers the farmers the strikers, the foolish the unlucky and the merely criminal," 918), in the Reporter this only goes halfway, since as a waged employee of this process he cannot escape the materiality of the Symbolic itself, those "faint mimeographed letters" throbbing on the inside of his eyelids like muscle fatigue—another lesson in how "rapidly and firmly capitalist production [seizes] the vital forces of the people at their very roots."[12] But this is merely a preparation for the broader meaning of the program's place in *Pylon*, its use as an industrial weapon against the value of labor power itself.

The death of a principal participant in the air show, Frank Burnham, whose name is printed twice on the mimeographed précis of Friday's events, means that the investors in the spectacle are now "advertising something they cant produce. They feel that Frank's name should come off the program" (879). The committee chairman goes further, addressing the airmen: "You contestants are the real benefactors of these printed programs. Not us.… We had these programs printed at considerable expense … printed in good faith that what we guaranteed in them would be performed" (879). A new edition, not just striking through Burnham's name but expunging it completely, will be issued at the "considerable expense," this time, of the contestants themselves, assembled like "the delegation from the shops" before "the mill-owners" (876) who have unilaterally decided to tax the prize money at the rate of 2.5% to cover printing costs. So it is that a disposable program, which must, like the "news," match text to fact,

---

[12] Karl Marx, *Capital, Vol. 1*, trans. Ben Fowkes (London: Penguin, 1990), 380.

serves as the potential flashpoint of a class antagonism that never fully matures, since the "strike" that Jiggs feels to be imminent is dissipated into that romance escape valve already treated in our first chapter ("it isn't the money..."): class consciousness usurped by a genetic and suicidal race chivalry in the skies.

Nevertheless, the episode foments a deep associative link between the Reporter's status as waged "precarian" of the mass media and the pilots' proto-class consciousness, whose fulcrum is what Derrida called the "paper machine."[13] Doubtless it is this association, which allows us to break from the Reporter's focalization to enter the super's office though he remains outside, that also enables him to say with perfect symptomatology, and accurately predicting the industrial outcome, that "I may not know airplanes but I know sewage board Jews!" (924) The capitalist-as-Jew, presiding over the news industry as it does over the new airport, and over the Hollywood studios and the magazines along with them, crystallizes in Faulkner's imagination as the stereotypical racial *point de caption* of a new integrated cultural economy. Print capitalism, reeking from the leaky "sewage" of civic corruption, is here a Jewish cabal. When Feinman finally speaks, it is to a familiar tune: "Aint we promised these folks out there [...] a series of races? Aint they paying their money in here to see them? And aint it the more airplanes they will have to look at the better they will think they got for the money?" (929–30) For "races" put "stories" or "movies"; for "airplanes" substitute "chases" or "girls." The monstrous Jew-capitalist spells out explicitly the form that culture must take in the golden land of the lowest common denominator; capital flocks to media and technologies that deliver bigger bang for your buck. Literature cedes to flybills, posters, newspapers and programs.

Which is why, in the final scene, we return with a crash to the agon between news and literature as it had been established in the early sequence with the editor. From the moment that the Reporter sits down—"and racked the note form into the typewriter and began to fill it in, carefully—the neat convenient flimsy scrap of paper which by a few marks became transposed into an implement sharper than steel and more enduring than stone" (916)—to forge the receipt for Ord's ship, the allegorical tension has been mounting: what will all this tragicomic experience have amounted to at the level of our protagonist's craft? What will it elicit as text? Will he, after all, transfigure the three-day Calvary of Roger Shumann into something befitting its mythic and romantic scope, or will he accede to the industrial discipline of his workplace and type up some serviceable copy? It is a question voiced by Faulkner himself in his contemporary review of the airman-writer Jimmy Collins's *Test Pilot*: "I had expected," he wrote of this text, "hoped, that it would be a kind of new trend, a literature or blundering at

---

[13] Jacques Derrida, *Paper Machine*, trans. Rachel Bowlby (Stanford, CA: Stanford University Press, 2005).

self-expression ... of this whole new business of speed" (188); instead, he found only "a kind of sentimental journalese [...] you have seen it before a hundred times and it has been phrased just that way in ten thousand newspaper columns and magazines. But then, Collins was a newspaper writer" (189). And so in *Pylon* we arrive finally at the Promethean scene of writing itself, having been ushered from the "noisy sphere" of its circulation, "where everything takes place on the surface and in full view of everyone," and "into the hidden abode of production"—but only, inevitably, once the event has already passed.[14] Here is that "astonishing amount of savagely defaced and torn copy which littered the adjacent floor" (990), "all the sheets, whole and in fragments" (991), which a bright copyboy happens upon in the news office the next morning and painstakingly reassembles into "sentences and paragraphs which he believed to be not only news but the beginning of literature" (991). This is literature at long last, so stimulating in its allegorical substantives ("Last Checkered Flag," "Last Pylon") and personifications ("Death"), that the boy dreams lyrically of finishing it himself, like Charles Foster Kane with Jed Leland's review. But of course, the fatuous detritus of failed romance that we are then given to read is only the draft *rejectimenta*, mere prelude to the actual submitted copy, this latter scrawled over with the direct address to the editor, "*I guess this is what you want you bastard*"—a terse unpublishable squib that amounts to an ambivalent resignation letter.

Literature has here coiled up into a savagely condensed satire of its objective position within the new media ecology: an entire novel's ponderous quest (not unrelated to that of the journalist Thomson in *Citizen Kane*) for good copy is throttled into twelve lines of bitter negation, a final acquiescence to the bottom-line cynicism that keeps the paper alive. Obliged to toss off another handful of stories in the immediate aftermath of finishing *Pylon*, and just before resuming work on *Absalom*, Faulkner wrote to Hal Smith:

> I cannot and will not go on like this. I believe I have got enough fair literature in me yet to deserve reasonable freedom from bourgeoise [sic] material petty impediments and compulsion, without having to quit writing and go to the moving pictures every two years.[15]

Pylon already says much the same thing. But before we can ask how its satire of the media system's erosions of literary autonomy is resumed in the next major work, we need briefly to account for *Pylon*'s ruminations on another medium, namely photography.

---

[14] Marx, *Capital, Vol. 1*, 279.

[15] Quoted in Joseph Blotner, *Faulkner: A Biography*, one-volume edition (Jackson, MS: University Press of Mississippi, 2005), 345.

When the Reporter returns to the newspaper office to forge his note of receipt, we are treated to a Marxian metaphor of the machine factory process: "now the whole building began to tremble to the remote travail of the presses; now about the copydesk the six or seven men, coatless and collarless, in their green eyeshades like a uniform, seemed to concentrate toward a subterranean crisis, like so many puny humans conducting the lyingin of a mastodon" (915). The subterranean travails of the forty-ton rotary presses will have concerned, in New Valois in 1935, the reproduction not simply of print but of photographic images like the one the photographer at lakeside takes of Shumann's final moments, and of the advertisers' illustrated material that the editor threatens to tear out of the paper "with my own hands" if he learns that the sacked Reporter has landed a job with any of their firms (826). *The Saturday Evening Post*, publishing the "Unvanquished" stories while *Pylon* goes to press, runs its lavishly illustrated issues off the same machines. These presses are, like all since the collotype revolution of the 1880s, photomechanical in nature, freely able to blend symbolic type and reproduced photographs on the same page, on a mass basis.[16] It is impossible to conceive of a modern newspaper or magazine surviving on any other basis; this implies, though, that photography as a chemical process has stealthily infiltrated the very material underpinning of the discourse network of the Enlightenment—i.e., printing itself. Why should this matter? Because the interposition of "subterranean" photomechanical processes between the labor of writing and the moment of publication amounts to a disavowed crisis of cognition and control in the very notion of authorship. This is allegorized in the text of *Pylon* by the complicated and only fitfully realized pseudo-couple of the Reporter and photographer, who are finally brought into a working relationship at the moment of tragic climax. While the Reporter goes through the first phase of his convulsive shock, the photographer describes his own affective reaction to the crash: "Only Jesus, I near vomited into the box while I was changing plates" (937). Striving to account for this robust cynicism and philistinism, the Reporter speculates on the very qualities of a photographic psychology: "perhaps it was the bilious aspect of an inverted world seen through a hooded lens or emerging in grimacing and attitudinal miniature from stinking trays in a celibate and stygian cell lighted by a red lamp" (933). This intimate knowledge of the labor of photographic development is an essential component of the working writer's contemporary trade, since there is nothing that he can write that, if it is to reach a public readership, will not have passed through a photomechanical remediation, a stygian episode in the red-light district of the cultural economy, whence

---

[16] See Helena E. Wright, "Photography in the Printing Press: the photomechanical revolution," *Presenting Pictures*, ed. Bernard Finn (London: Science Museum, 2004), 21–42; and Gerry Beegan, *The Mass Image: a social history of photomechanical reproduction in Victorian London* (London: Palgrave Macmillan, 2008).

it will be "pitilessly dragged out onto the street by advertisements and subjected to the brutal heteronomies of economic chaos. This is the hard schooling of its new form."[17]

Picture writing

Faulkner knew it: "I imagine as long as people will continue to read novels, people will continue to write them, or vice versa; unless of course the pictorial magazines and comic strips finally atrophy man's capacity to read, and literature really is on its way back to the picture writing in the Neanderthal cave."[18] The pressure from the "brutal heteronomies" of illustrated print capitalism upon the novel form was extreme, and its consequences were defensively felt as regressive. But it is not as though pictures, images, were somehow alien to the novel's more pristine work; Faulkner also admitted that, "With me, a story usually begins with a single idea or memory or mental picture. The writing of the story is simply a matter of working up to that moment." (Ibid.) Picture writing is ineluctable. It is difficult to say where the words end and pictures begin, and vice versa. What that means for literature is difficult to say in a competitive media environment, but already in 1897 Stephane Mallarmé had responded to a survey on photographic book illustrations with an emphatic "no": "all that a book evokes must take place in the reader's mind; but, if you use photography, why not go straight to the cinematograph, whose unreeling (unfolding) will replace, images and text, many a volume, advantageously."[19]

Pylon makes the case that, circa 1935, writing can no longer be written as if it existed in the autonomous domain created for it by a centuries-long, uncontested media monopoly, but must take into account the radical implications for its form represented by a set of new material relations with images. The material basis of modern culture is not at all what it was for Goethe, which is to say, literature as a universally legislating archive; it is a system of media in which "actual conjunctions of words and images" are the norm rather than the exception. As W. J. T. Mitchell puts it, in these media "one encounters a concrete set of empirical givens, an image-text structure" that cannot but alter the coordinates through which writers of text approach their craft.[20] Indeed, although Gilles Deleuze is correct at the upper limit of theoretical reflection to propose

---

[17] Walter Benjamin, *One-Way Street and Other Writings*, trans. Edmund Jephcott and Kingsley Shorter (London & New York: Verso, 1985), 62.

[18] Faulkner, *Paris Review*.

[19] Mallarmé, quoted in Christophe Wall-Romana, *Cinepoetry: Imaginary Cinemas in French Poetry* (New York: Fordham University Press, 2013), 61–62.

[20] W. J. T. Mitchell, *Picture Theory* (Chicago & London: University of Chicago Press, 1994), 90.

that there "is no link that could move from the visible to the statement, or from the statement to the visible," his further qualification that "there is a continual relinking which takes place over the irrational break or crack" gains further salience in the context of a media ecology where precisely this sort of "relinking" is not an incidental but a programmatic and institutional norm of the day.[21]

We have already seen something of the extent to which an acute sensitivity to photomechanical reproduction may have characterized literary production in the age of illustrated magazines. Johanna Drucker has written that with "graphics as an interface between producer and consumer," the very idea of the paper page as a platform for literary dissemination had changed radically.[22] Much as Derrida once proposed, circa 1935, paper is "a multimedia," being able to *get to work like a multimedia*" on the basis of new technologies where word and image are routinely blended.[23] In what follows, we will briefly consider two further contemporary linkages between text and image—the photographic essay and the talking picture—before undertaking a demonstration of *Absalom*'s status as a novel shot through with a formal awareness of that "image-text structure" that was henceforth ineluctable and perhaps the most promising basis for any aesthetic elaboration in prose. After all, it would appear to have been at this precise moment in literary history that the literary world finally and irrevocably learned that writing itself, "in its physical, graphic form, is an inseparable suturing of the visual and the verbal, the 'imagetext' incarnate."[24] And nowhere more ambitiously than in *Absalom, Absalom!*

To make sense of these new linkages, however, we need to distinguish them from an older and once hegemonic one. Friedrich Kittler has written: "As long as the book was responsible for all serial data flows, words quivered with sensuality and memory. It was the passion of all reading to hallucinate meaning between lines and letters: the visible and audible world of Romantic poetics. And the passion of all writing was (in the words of E. T. A. Hoffmann) the poet's desire to 'describe' the hallucinated 'picture in your mind with all its vivid colors, the light and the shade,' in order to 'strike' the 'gentle reader' 'like an electric shock.'"[25] Mallarmé said much the same thing fifty years later. Dedicated simultaneously to conjuring *and* describing the passionately hallucinated mental

---

[21] Gilles Deleuze, *Foucault*, ed. and trans. Seán Hand (London & New York: Continuum, 1999), 55.

[22] Johanna Drucker, *The Visible Word: Experimental Typography and Modern Art, 1909–1923* (Chicago: University of Chicago Press, 1994), 94.

[23] Jacques Derrida, *Paper Machine*, trans. Rachel Bowlby (Stanford, CA: Stanford University Press, 2005), 43, 47.

[24] Mitchell, *Picture Theory*, 95.

[25] Friedrich Kittler, *Gramophone, Film, Typewriter*, trans. Geoffrey Winthrop-Young and Michael Wutz (Stanford, CA: Stanford University Press, 1999), 10. He is quoting from Hoffmann's "The Sandman" (1816), first translated into English by John Oxenford and C. A. Feiling in their *Tales from the German* (London: Chapman and Hall, 1844).

image, romantic literature undertook its electroshock audio-visual tautologies thanks to literature's authoritative causal chain, circa 1800, which led back from printed words to the signed manuscript, which in turn had emerged from the author's "inner voice," which was itself ultimately underwritten by the Mother's Voice. If romantic reading was "an exercise in scriptographically or typographically induced verbal hallucinations, whereby linguistic signs were commuted into sounds and images,"[26] then that was due to a "primary orality" which provided the phonocentric and imaginary linchpin to literature's dispersive means of production. Romantic writers "understood language as a form of originary orality, a transcendental inner voice superior and anterior to any form of written language."[27] The ultimate source of this inner voice was a Mother whose feminine proximity to nature grounded literacy in the spontaneous overflowing of Being itself. "Romanticism is the discursive production of the mother as the source of discursive production."[28] In Kittler's analysis, this fixing of the dangerously disseminated literary sign by an anchor dropped ever deeper into embodiment and maternal vocality explains the hermeneutic model of interpretation itself. Nor are these phonocentric figures simply the illegitimate tools of Western metaphysics; they are material properties of a stabilized discourse network. "Primary orality, the Mother, the self-presence of the origin: these are not merely sublimations or philosophical hallucinations, they are discursive facts, nodal points in a positive and empirical discursive network."[29]

The unraveling of that network under the impetus of machines that recorded real sounds and durably registered the impress of light's reflective traces jolted those figures out of synch with text's new destinies. Kittler remarks that photography's most radical effect on romantic literature consisted in the affirmation of its material *channel*, as opposed to its imaginary special effects. Storage was the key. "If novels succeeded in giving rise to *lanterna magica* images in solitary readers, in principle these inner images still could not be stored."[30] Photography's material channel, photosensitive chemical compounds on a flat surface (metal sheets, glass plates, paper, celluloid), ended romantic literature's subsumptive symbolic monopoly over visual data, arrogating to itself for a century and a half thereafter all primary rights over visual information by virtue of its self-evident recording of it. "Photographs have the kind of authority over imagination today," Walter Lippmann wrote in 1922, "which the printed word had yesterday,

---

[26] Joseph Tabbi and Michael Wutz, eds., *Reading Matters: Narrative in the New Media Ecology* (Ithaca, NY: Cornell University Press, 1997), 99.

[27] Geoffrey Winthrop-Young and Michael Wutz, "Translator's Introduction: Friedrich Kittler and Media Discourse Analysis," in Kittler, *Gramophone, Film, Typewriter*, xxiv.

[28] David E. Wellbery, "Foreword," in Friedrich Kittler, *Discourse Networks 1800/1900* (Stanford, CA: Stanford University Press, 1990), xxiii.

[29] Wellbery, "Foreword," xxiii.

[30] Kittler, *Optical Media*, trans. Anthony Enns (Cambridge: Polity, 2010), 118.

and the spoken word before that. They seem utterly real. They come, we imagine, directly to us without human meddling, and they are the most effortless food for the mind conceivable."[31] Meanwhile, the technical separation of voice from the paper monopoly of literature had been made possible by the new recording and playback mechanisms considered in the previous chapter. The radical differentiation of acoustics, optics and text occasioned by the new media system not only made the "phantasms" of human voices and physiognomies materially perceptible and storable, but, in the absence of any synthetic *Gesamtmedia*, also made it impossible to effect passages between their channels. As Rilke sought desperately for "a way to establish the connection so urgently needed between the different provinces now so strangely separated from one another,"[32] the visible specters and audible spooks went their several ways, well apart from the linear tracks of type which, thanks to the typewriter, no longer borrowed authority from the inspirited handwriting of the male genius, and could affirm its own channel—in the poetics of *Un coup de dés* and the "Calligrammes" of Apollinaire, on to *The Waste Land*, cummings and beyond. Michael Davidson notes that the "modernist typographic renaissance," which "permitted poets to utilize the range of the typewriter keyboard," "began as an attempt to stave off such ephemerality as was manifest in commercial publishing and advertising."[33] More radically, "Once imaginary effects and real inscription have been renounced, what remains are the rituals of the symbolic," as Kittler puts it. "Since December 28, 1895, there has been one infallible criterion for high literature: it cannot be filmed."[34]

So, even if, once "memories and dreams, the dead and ghosts, become technically reproducible, readers and writers no longer need the powers of hallucination"; even if our "realm of the dead has withdrawn from the books in which it resided for so long" and taken up residence on photosensitive and phonographic surfaces;[35] there remained a serious synchronization problem, an analogue of which we can see being played out in the domain of motion picture production at the end of the 1920s. For the material fact remained that the proliferating photo-spectral "onion skins" of moving persons,[36] and their acousmatic voices

---

[31] Walter Lippmann, *Public Opinion* (New York: W. W. Norton, 1922), 37.

[32] Rainer Maria Rilke, "Primal Sound," in Carl Niemeyer, trans., *Primal Sound and other prose pieces* (Cummington, MA: Cummington Press, 1948), archived at http://layoftheland.net/archive/art4639-2013/weeks1-5/RILKE_SOUND.pdf.

[33] Michael Davidson, *Ghostlier Demarcations: Modern Poetry and the Material Word* (Berkeley, CA & Los Angeles: University of California Press, 1997), 29, 13.

[34] Kittler, *Discourse Networks*, 248.

[35] Kittler, *Gramophone*, 10.

[36] "Honoré de Balzac metaphorically proposed that a thin layer of skin is taken with each photograph." Carol Mavor, *Black and Blue: The Bruising Passion of* Camera Lucida, La Jetée, Sans soleil, *and* Hiroshima mon amour (Durham, NC: Duke University Press, 2012), 40. See also Andrew Herschberger, "Introduction," Douglas Prince, *Epidermis: The Poetry of Skin* (Manchester, NH: Maple Seed Press, 2010).

on record and wireless, shared no common ground or channel until the various experiments with sound synchronization had attained acceptable industrial triage in *The Jazz Singer* (1927) and thereafter. It was the procedure of "goat-glanding"—the synthetic supplementation of the silent filmstrip by a phonograph or an optical soundtrack—that finally closed the circle and allowed photographs to speak in voices that were, so to speak, in time.[37] As Mieke Bal has written, this moment "opened the possibility of a new engagement between language and image. [. . .] Neither literature nor visual art nor a simple combination of the two, but a fundamentally different art [emerged] in which language and image were inextricably intertwined[. . .]. From that position, cinema was able to cast doubt on the essentialism that sought to separate the media."[38]

However poor in technical quality, however corrosive of the established aesthetic lingua franca of the international silent film, however subject to errors of focus and synchronization, and however mixed in media and uptake for the next five years, sound film realized the original Edisonian fantasy of a recorded moving image played in lockstep with the sound that belonged to it.[39] "Orality, aurality, and visuality would huddle together under one potential umbrella of marvellous future technology," as Lisa Gitelman paraphrases that inaugurating fantasy, further noting that "when Edison filed his first motion picture patent caveat [. . .] in October 1888, he claimed an invention that 'does for the eye what the phonograph does for the ear.' His 'kinetoscope' would locate the common denominator of vision and hearing, just as the phonograph had located the common denominator of sound and text."[40] That common denominator was electricity, of course, hooked up to two entirely distinct mechanical recording and playback media in such a way that their discontinuous signals could be experienced, even if purely artificially, as a perceptual unity. "The voice and the image can only appear as cut apart, they cannot consummate their reunion in a forever lost mythic unity. The talking film is but a jerry-rigged assemblage, and perhaps in this condition it finds its greatness," Michel Chion rightly observes.[41] But this

---

[37] On goat-glanding, see Tim Armstrong, *Modernism, Technology, and the Body: A Cultural Study* (Cambridge: Cambridge University Press, 1998), 221–47; and Laura Marcus, *The Tenth Muse: Writing about Cinema in the Modernist Period* (Oxford: Oxford University Press, 2010), 406.

[38] Mieke Bal, "Phantom Sentences," in Robert S. Kawashima, Gilles Philippe, and Thelma Sowlet, eds., *Phantom Sentences: Essays in linguistics and literature presented to Ann Banfield* (Bern: Peter Lang, 2008), 26.

[39] See, on the resistance to sound cinema, Michael North, "*Close Up*: International Modernism's Struggle with Sound," in *Camera Works: Photography and the Twentieth-Century Word* (Oxford: Oxford University Press, 2005), 83–105.

[40] Lisa Gitelman, *Scripts, Grooves, and Writing Machines: Representing Technology in the Edison Era* (Stanford, CA: Stanford University Press, 1999), 87.

[41] Michel Chion, *The Voice in Cinema*, trans. Claudia Gorbman (New York: Columbia University Press, 1999), 150–51.

greatness can never be the same as that of romantic literature's, prior to its Fall into the differentiated data streams of gramophone, film, and typewriter.

Given the relative success of its new "secondary orality," or what I prefer to call its *technorality*, Hollywood's remaining problem concerned what its moving images should have been supposed to say, a question unanswerable within the industrial conditions of "deaf cinema."[42] The answer would be found in what was left of that once supreme medium, literature. And now it really was a medium, visible for the first time in history as such—"script, instead of continuing to be a translation from the mother's mouth, has become an irreducible medium among media," and so for hire, like any other, to the highest bidder.[43] What remained of literature—novelists, poets, and dramatists reeling from what Fitzgerald would call the "rankling indignity [of] seeing the power of the written word subordinate to another power, a more glittering, a grosser power"[44]—was conscripted as a noble suture, a surgical seam for stitching the goat's testes of recorded sound onto the speechless photographic images of cinema and tightening the ligature via dialogue. Its expert surgeons were available thanks to the economic crash of 1929. A generation of writers was now adrift on the free market due to the collapse in the trade of printed books, and the invulnerable profit margin of the talkies. "Peanuts," as Saul Warner knew, were all you needed to pay for the goat's nuts of literature, to suture picture and voice on the big screen.[45]

If the cinema performed one epochal linkage between word and image in the 1930s—realized in two new mechanical storage/playback technologies, and sutured by literature's devolution into "typewriting" (not incidentally, Faulkner wrote all of his screen treatments, dialogue patches, and full screenplays directly on his typewriter)—then another contemporary genre deserves attention for effecting the linkage in a more unsettling manner. Three canonical photo-essayistic texts warrant particular attention: *Let Us Now Praise Famous Men* (1941), the collaborative venture of James Agee and Walker Evans; the more "proletarian-heroic" *You Have Seen Their Faces* (1937), with text by Erskine Caldwell and photo-images by Margaret Bourke-White; and the lesser-known *12 Million Black Voices* (1941), written polemically by Richard Wright and using photographs assembled by Edwin Rosskam. The culmination of a decade-long trend, these three volumes instantiated for William Stott a "documentary

---

[42] The characterization is Chion's, in his *Voice in Cinema*, 3, 95.

[43] Friedrich Kittler, *Discourse Networks*, 199.

[44] F. Scott Fitzgerald, *The Crack-Up: with Other Pieces and Stories* (London: Penguin, 1965), 49.

[45] "By then I had heard about Jack Warner boasting how he has the best writer in the country under hire for peanuts." Faulkner's reaction was to carry a knife and fantasize about cutting up William Herndon, "the agent who got me the contract." Any reader of Faulkner knows where he might have applied the blade. See the interview with Albert I. Bezzerides, "Bill and Buzz: Fellow Scenarists," in Louis Daniel Brodsky, *William Faulkner: Life Glimpses* (Austin, TX: University of Texas Press, 1990), 78.

synthesis" of what Alain Badiou has called the twentieth century's "passion for the Real" in literary and pictorial form.[46] In Michael Denning's paraphrase of Stott's pioneering work, the synthesis "reoriented cultural history and criticism by changing the objects of study, making photography, and particularly the photographs of the Farm Security Administration, the central depression genre, and by turning critical debate to the formal and political issues raised by documentary: the problematic of capturing the 'real,' the desire for the objectivity and immediacy of 'experience,' the dangers of manipulation and propaganda."[47] For Denning himself, however, this entire period's fascination with photography and its purported "social realism," when linked to prose, arose in the first place from a much more fundamental crisis: "the documentary impulse itself was less a triumph of realism than a sign of the failures of narrative imagination. [. . .] The knowable communities and settled social relations that provide the underpinning for realist narrative were themselves in crisis. The documentary impulse was a peculiarly modernist solution to this crisis" (119)—modernist above all in its collage-like insistence on stark juxtapositions and medial interfusions. In this context the photograph, re-mediated as a half-tone image in the pages of Wright's book, or, like Evans's, glossily packaged up front in full photogravure, compensates for the inevitable failure of narrative thinking to encompass the totality of human suffering and exploitation caused by the Great Depression. Where narrative falters and collapses, or reverts to exhausted stereotypes, photography reifies the face of suffering into indexical masks—loci of pure affective intensity that compensate for the unraveling and inadequacy of narrative textures. It is the irresolvable tension between the two, what Agee called their co-equality, that obviates any easy "realist" closure: "The photographs are not illustrative. They, and the text, are co-equal, mutually independent, and fully collaborative."[48] For W. J. T. Mitchell, this "aggressively modernist experimental deviation" from the conventional "discursive or narrative suturing" of the mixed medium of the photographic essay, speaks to a "hopelessly compromised and *impure* representational practice" that might well be thought of as constitutive of modernism in general. [49] In his reading of this open co-independence, what results from such an aggressive division of labor is "an ethics of form imposed on the reader/viewer in the structural division of the photos and text. Our labor as beholders is as divided as that of Agee and Evans, and we find ourselves drawn, as they were, into a vortex of collaboration and resistance" (300).

[46] See William Stott, *Documentary Expression and Thirties America* (Chicago: University of Chicago Press, 1986); and Alain Badiou, *The Century*, trans. Alberto Toscano (Cambridge: Polity, 2007), 48–57.

[47] Michael Denning, *The Cultural Front: The Laboring of American Culture in the Twentieth Century* (London & New York: Verso, 1998), 119.

[48] Walker Evans in James Agee and Walker Evans, *Let Us Now Praise Famous Men* (Boston: Mariner Books, 2001), 10.

[49] Mitchell, *Picture Theory*, 94.

I will resist the temptation to force a premature identification of this "vortex" with that of the "now two now four" Quentin–Shreve/Henry–Charles tornado that drives the later narrative engine of *Absalom, Absalom!*—but not before a fitting proof that Faulkner's text was far from being only incidentally coeval with Agee's and Evans's perplexing "ethics of form." For in the very first note in the first appendix to their great photo-essay, heading a list of suggested intertexts and cognate documents including Dovzhenko's *Aerograd* [*Frontier*] (1935), Sleepy John Estes's "New Salty Dog," and "Road maps and contour maps of the middle south," we find the signal promotion of none other than that "[d]etail of gesture, landscape, costume, air, action, mystery, and incident throughout the writings of William Faulkner."[50] Which is to say that Agee and Evans had understood their form as always already implicated with that of Faulkner's literary modernism, a modernism analyzable through a congeries of textual detail, both narrative and descriptive, but contained within a verbal machinery predominantly oral in nature, "written with reading aloud in mind" (11).

Talking pictures

Not many modernist novelists can have been so bold as to cast in the role of dominant narrator a fully fledged romantic poet. The move seems almost too schematic and facile, the prank of a sophomore; yet Faulkner was committed. Rosa Coldfield, fount of so much of *Absalom*'s narrative raw material, of which the others are tributary, is incapable of mediating it other than (in, perhaps, some tactical remounting of Joyce's experiment with Gerty in "Nausicaa") in the spoiled and overripe idiom of that "poetry" long ago issued under her name in the local newspaper. Rosa

> established (if not affirmed) herself as the town's and the county's poetess laureate by issuing to the stern and meagre subscription list of the county newspaper poems, ode eulogy and epitaph, out of some bitter and implacable reserve of undefeat (8).

It is as a romantic poet—published at age nineteen in the year of Tennyson's *Enoch Arden* and the tail-end of Dickinson's miraculous four-year blossoming of inspiration, who, as her father starved himself to inglorious death, "was accumulating her first folio in which the lost cause's unregenerate vanquished were name by name embalmed" (8)—that Miss Rosa approaches Quentin with what is

---

[50] Agee and Evans, *Let Us Now Praise Famous Men*, 399.

immediately understood to be a matter of generational literary transmission and thus of the anxiety of influence: "you can write this and submit it to the magazines" (7). Aware of her quarry, and of the altered circumstances of literary production since she first entered the market in 1864, the "undefeated" ghost of romance seeks to pass it forward to a coming young professional whose future domestic economy is (hypothetically) hooked up to the modern economy of letters.

It is then, per Kittler's argument, just as any romantic poet would have it: the ululating prose, lyrical to a pre-Raphaelite fault, dissolves of its own nature into sheer image, again and again:

> talking in that grim haggard amazed voice until at last listening would renege and hearing-sense self-confound and the long-dead object of her impotent yet indomitable frustration would appear, as though by outraged recapitulation evoked, quiet inattentive and harmless, out of the biding and dreamy and victorious dust. (5)

The visible world of romantic poetics seems duly "hallucinated" by an auditor whose listening "reneges" only to give way immediately to a visual image, "the voice not ceasing but vanishing into and then out of the long intervals like a stream, [...] and the ghost mused with shadowy docility as if it were the voice which he haunted where a more fortunate one would have had a house" (6). Sutpen is first and last a ghost, not unlike those agitated into speech by electromagnetic waves, that haunts a voice, and emerges as an image on that voice's "stream." The question concerns what kind of image this is, in a specifically mediatic sense: mental hallucination, or something else, something materially implicated in the post-romantic media ecology itself?

Given that it becomes increasingly difficult to disentangle the primary orality of the storyteller (be it Rosa or Mr. Compson or the Quentin–Shreve dyad) from the evocation of visual images in the hypothetical consciousness of some meta-Quentin, it is as if the narrative stream of words asks to be read on three levels simultaneously: (1) as sheer romance storytelling; (2) as verbal descriptions of the images evoked by that storytelling (which is to say a kind of psychological ekphrasis); and (3) as the return into discourse of that ekphrasis such that it again becomes an element in the stream of narration. The question of medial specificity concerns stage (2) here: does the ekphrastic description of evoked images conform to Hoffman's tautological romantic paradigm ("the poet's desire to 'describe' the hallucinated 'picture in your mind with all its vivid colors, the light and the shade,'" in Kittler's paraphrase[51]), or does it rather concern an image different in material kind from the stream of enabling utterance?

---

[51] Kittler, *Gramophone, Film, Typewriter*, 10.

Before proceeding to substantiate my reasoning, I will begin by claiming that the second alternative is the correct one and that, given this, it is crucial to appreciate that there can no longer be any question of *redundancy*—the transformation of discourse into picture and back again is here a properly dialectical one, involving a passage through the negative, whereby something critical happens to the genre and the ideological space it appears to inhabit. Indeed, something of the highest importance is taking place that interrupts the perfect tautology of romance "hallucination" and substitutes for it a tropological negation of the negation that *appears* to be doing the work of reduplication, but in fact alienates it at the root.

Rosa's voice discovers in Quentin its appropriate channel. Irresistibly tuned in, Quentin suffers the uncanny experience of becoming something like a radio set, "his very body [...] an empty hall echoing with sonorous defeated names; he was not a being, an entity, he was a commonwealth. He was a barracks filled with stubborn back-looking ghosts" (9). Better than any crude nineteen-year-old's "ode eulogy and epitaph" rolled off the local paper's presses in 1864, Quentin's resonant body is a fitting medium for those "unregenerate vanquished [...] name by name embalmed," since in him they somehow still *move* as images, not in the virtual theatre of romantic "hallucination," but really and materially. "Out of quiet thunderclap he would abrupt" (6), thanks to a voice "undefeated" after forty-five years of romance's immolation on the pyre of both military conquest and technological progress. But there is an intriguing mathematics to this visual abruption in Quentin of the storied dead, quite "as though in inverse ratio to the vanishing voice, the invoked ghost of the man whom she could neither forgive nor revenge herself upon began to assume a quality almost of solidity, permanence" (10). The voice triggers a multimedia transcoding, its auditory signal modulated, by inverse ratio, into a visual one. Sutpen becomes an image in Quentin thanks to some "common denominator of vision and hearing," like the kinetoscope of Edison's dreams that is now, in the 1930s, as these words are actually being written, an established reality on the cinema screen at last. For that exact contextual reason, the common denominator must not have any basis in romantic hallucination; there is a strong separation of the image-capacitor from the vanished milieu of its discursive location. As Quentin will say very precisely: "No. If I had been there I could not have seen it this plain" (158). The image is experienced in "inverse ratio" to the stream of language that claims, but travesties, indexical links (for although Rosa's romance is "not only divorced from, but irrevocably excommunicated from, all reality" (159), her voice claims the innumerable rhetorical advantages of "having been there"—what Quentin will call "the molecularity of having seen, felt, remembered" (210)) to that "it" which Quentin now proclaims to see more clearly than he would have had he been there himself. A palpable image has been emancipated from the deluge of disreputable genre discourse that Rosa offers as proof of her connection to the stream of event. Something has survived the carnage of romance.

That Rosa is spinning an openly romantic yarn can scarcely be contradicted; her terms are flagrant. Her antihero is labeled a "demon," an "ogre," a "djinn," and "Bluebeard" himself. Her story will turn, by way of various supplements and overlays, on matters of incest, spurned lovers, fratricide, bigamy, renunciation, delayed recognition, disownments, returns of the repressed, and a hopelessly miscegenated dynastic plot. There will be fatal gunshots on thresholds, sabers valiantly drawn, murder by scythe, a Caribbean escapade, a subdued rebellion, the hunting of a French architect, bastards and prostitutes, war, weddings, and wrestling matches by firelight. At least one contributory narrator will be obliged to complain of a "limit even to irony beyond which it became either just vicious but not fatal horseplay or harmless coincidence" (220), and "that it was nonsense, it could not be true; that such coincidences only happened in books" (262). So grotesque a tapestry of perdurable romance tropes and the privileged *topoi* of Southern gothicism has scarcely ever been conceived: the triumph and climax of all superannuated narrative devices and figures, a cathartic hemorrhaging of the accumulated clichés of centuries of plantation mythos and the apologetics of romance. And yet, the voice ultimately responsible for putting this monstrous and illegitimate material into motion, and for nurturing it into a rancid potboiler over forty-five years of "undefeat," has discovered in Quentin the "kinetoscopic" means of eating her cake and having it too. For in Quentin, this material, carried as voice into his channel, becomes, not a romance hallucinogen, but images of a new order of things. Specifically, it becomes photography.

> Quentin seemed to see them, the four of them arranged into the conventional family group of the period, with formal and lifeless decorum, and seen now as the fading and ancient photograph itself would have been seen enlarged and hung on the wall behind and above the voice and of whose presence there the voice's owner was not even aware [...]—a picture, a group which even to Quentin had a quality strange, contradictory, and bizarre; not quite comprehensible not (even to twenty) quite right (10–11).

Not quite right, but somehow perfectly conventional and full of "formal and lifeless decorum": the subjunctive image projected, "resolved" out of the voice, "behind and above it," hangs on the wall like a "fading and ancient" photographic group portrait, unbeknownst to the "voice's owner" herself. The entire novel will revolve around that "not quite right," but notice how explicitly the prose is soliciting our credence in a multimedia demonstration where a voice is transposed into a photographic image, and where the passage from one to the other concerns a leap from orator to "hearer."

"Inside the heard voice is an unheard voice," writes Mladen Dolar, "an aphonic voice, as it were."[52] This strange "object voice" within the communicating one "does not coincide with any existing thing, although it is always evoked only by bits of materiality, attached to them as an invisible, inaudible appendage, yet not amalgamated with them: it is both evoked and covered, enveloped by them" (74). Quentin's inhabited act of audition seems automatically to have separated the impermissible words themselves (rendered inaudible to the young writer by virtue of a canon of proscriptions soon to be issued against romantic slither[53]) from their sustaining "object" dimension, the *voice as such*, which drones with truth and becomes visible as a photographic emanation. In Quentin, "listening reneges" in order to become a picture show on the basis of a "self-confounding" of "hearing-sense" (5).

Technically, what this novel is doing, both for us and for the cinematic institution it secretly shadows, is affirming a material contact between voice and image, formed by its own typeset letters and spaces, such that voice is transmuted into image by virtue of printed text, but *athwart* the logic of romance. For this is not one of those allegories of romantic reading in which "a hallucinatory process [. . .] turns words into a real and visible world."[54] The voice here is Real (a radio ghost), and the "world" it allows Quentin to see is visible, but not in that sense. Quentin's vision of the conjured ghosts is always and already photographic, just as his audition of them is radiophonic or phonographic. It has nothing whatsoever to do with the semantics of discourse (or interpretation), and everything to do with the object voice that these new media make properly audible for the first time in history. "It is more than a photographic, or I had better say cinematographic, something," wrote Maurice Renard in 1907 of the recorded voice, two years prior to Quentin's hearing-not-listening; "it is the voice itself, the living voice, still alive among carrion, skeletons, nothingness."[55] Abruptly demoting the linguistic element of oral communication to a dispensable scaffolding, this apprehension of the voice is ecstatically understood in the dimension of cinematography. The sound technologies of modernity disclose the inner truth of the object voice as photographic.

Nor is it simply a matter of *not having been there*, but rather, of not listening to "it" now either—allowing the voice to "walk out of" its own talking (145), and into a purely "objectal" state. Quentin's sustained act of "not listening but hearing" is authorized by the always-already-heard quality of the whole discourse, its overheated compaction of romance conventions, "formal and lifeless" in themselves, but somehow warming the object voice that is "evoked and covered" by

---

[52] Mladen Dolar, *A Voice and Nothing More* (Cambridge, MA: MIT Press, 2007), 73.
[53] In March 1913, by Ezra Pound: "A Few Don'ts by an Imagiste," *Poetry* (March 1913).
[54] Kittler, *Gramophone, Film, Typewriter*, 50.
[55] Quoted in Kittler, *Gramophone, Film, Typewriter*, 53.

those "few old mouth-to-mouth tales" from which everything is woven (83). "*So they will have told you doubtless already how*" (111). Indeed:

> *But you were not listening, because you knew it all already, had learned, absorbed it already without the medium of speech somehow from having been born and living beside it, with it, as children will and do* (176).

If it all sounds rather like the Mother whose pre-linguistic, choric presence is the source of all romantic literary creation, that is no accident. Only it is now the desiccated childless "Aunt" who somehow manages to embody this primary orality after the event, to which one has precisely no need to listen. Rather, one must only *hear* her, tune into that obscure, "objectal" quality of her voice in which the lurid romance is both canceled and preserved. The medium of speech is needed *after* the "knowing it all already" has been duly registered. For what it does is engender the moment that "it" staggers into view as so many hauntological photographic images, precious not for their narrative qualities, but for their affective and evidentiary ones.

Récit vs. affect

Fredric Jameson accounts for the qualitative break in Conrad's *Lord Jim* between the high aesthetic seriousness of the *Patna* episode and the "light reading and romance" of the Patusan section—"a virtual paradigm of romance as such"—in terms of a residual textual heterogeneity as yet unstabilized by modernist canons of form, and as the expression within the novel of an institutional schism in culture itself between its "high" and mass forms.[56] In media terms, this can also be decoded as the stamping onto the novel's form of a structural separation in cultural space between the prestige of the printed book and the rise of mass media institutions that thrived on Patusan-like materials to propagate their hold on the human sensory apparatus. This instance of a text still undecided about what to do with the increasingly embarrassing romance that undergirds its very narrative substance has the clear advantage of promoting a working solution: sequestration, and the internal division of authorial labor. Just so much of the text will function at a level of high aesthetic originality and tension; the rest will rip along as a good romance should. No such option was available to Faulkner, however, for whom the now established examples of Joyce, Hemingway, and Dos Passos had forever closed the door upon such mixed modes and pragmatisms. Henceforth the formal solution to what is,

---

[56] Fredric Jameson, *The Political Unconscious: Narrative as a Socially Symbolic Act* (Ithaca, NY: Cornell University Press, 1981), 206–07.

nevertheless, an enduring dilemma—managed by Joyce through the machinery of satire—could not be pursued by way of sectional distributions, but must be worked through systematically with a profound sensitivity to the immanence of the entire text; unless, as already intimated, there is a case to be made for considering the generic division of labor that Faulkner managed temporally in his weekly alternations between studio work, magazine work, and novel work, in this very light. Even so, *Absalom* itself makes no bones about its scandalous accommodation of romance tropes, narrative patterns, scenes, and situations—an excessive generic capitulation noted by every contemporary reviewer, and which marks this text out in many ways as comparable to *Lord Jim*'s fragmented generic constitution. What needs to be decided is the nature of the aesthetic "management program" employed to turn this outrageous dependency on the very "tyranny of the affects" that serious modern literature had put behind it into another, and highly successful, occasion for the performative modernization of the art-novel form itself.[57]

Clearly, the exhaustive use of embodied storytelling in *Absalom* is, as it was in previous novels, a key to grasping the nature of its management of romance; but before we can re-join this interest in Conradian recitation to our now established genitive relation between the "object voice" and the photographic image, we might pause to consider some other formal tensions implicit in this structural preference against omniscient narration. Hugh Kenner described Faulkner's consistent projection into modern textual forms of his irrecusable "love of many words, superfluous if we examine them one by one but defensible as contributing to a copiousness, a garrulousness, a quality of psychic overflowing he discerned in the tradition of oral storytelling and prized above any satisfactions to be obtained from erasure, paring, spareness."[58] This strategic disappointment of the modernist canon against rhetoric and redundancy is also a flouting of the new assumptions surrounding "written literature [...] which has accepted and come to terms with its status as writing, in fact as writing for a printing press, and envisions a reader silent before printed pages" (186). Indeed, the case is fairly put that Faulkner goes well beyond Conrad in his genuine aesthetic regard for the rhythms of oral speech, placing us, as we read, in the position of auditors prompted by the proliferation of shifters and deictic markers to perform our situated proximity to an embodied narrator; "to pretend as listeners" that we do not "confront anonymously the anonymity of print" (187). Only of course, we are doing just that; there is no storyteller present, and the common fund

---

[57] Ezra Pound specified romance's "tyranny of affects" as the great obstacle to new literary work, in *Selected Prose 1909–1965*, ed. William Cookson (New York: New Directions, 1973), 360.

[58] Hugh Kenner, "Faulkner and the Avant-Garde," in Evans Harrington and Ann J. Abadie, eds., *Faulkner, Modernism, and Film: Faulkner and Yoknapatawpha, 1978* (Jackson, MS: University Press of Mississippi, 1979), 185.

of knowledge assumed by the narrator has to be cobbled together on the fly through attentive close reading, lest we are forever kept outside the circle that the text so irresistibly invites us to join.

In these ways and others, Faulkner's verbal art seeks, within the anonymity of print, to reinvent the closed village circle of the storyteller as evoked by Walter Benjamin.[59] Here we threaten to revert, as Forster put it, to something predating picture writing: we are transformed "from readers into listeners, to whom 'a' voice speaks, the voice of the tribal narrator, squatting in the middle of the cave."[60] Moreover, Faulkner doubles down on the most powerful genetic strands of the romance mode, namely its orchestration by the narrative form of the *récit* as such. The narrative temporality of that ur-form is inevitably double: on the one hand, the material content of the tale, "whose events are already over and done with before the telling of it can begin";[61] on the other, the present of our own audition, whose lived contours the deixis teasingly fleshes out: "Yes—tomorrow. Now I must go to bed. Goodnight."[62] In his recent account of the struggle of aesthetic sensibilities and valences that constituted realism as a narrative mode, Fredric Jameson marks the persistence of that "ultimate source and paradigm of all storytelling,"[63] the *récit*, within the transvaluative aesthetic protocols of nineteenth-century realism. Here, in tension with the rise of everyday life and modern routine as objects of novelistic attention—"*the kind of narrative pleasure compatible with the new regularity of bourgeois life*"[64]—the *récit* endured with a vestigial romantic sense of the evental moment, the irrevocable mark, the completed action, all presided over by an air of destiny and fate. Thus the "deeper philosophical content of this narrative form [of the *récit*] might also be evoked as the narrative preterite, the mark of irrevocable time, of the event that has happened once and for all."[65] As such, the *récit* unquestionably shaped the evolution of the novel form at the most intimate level of its narrative genetics, since even the most ambitious nineteenth-century novel seems to spring fully formed from some archetypal "individual who looks back, all passion spent," some narrator who "has mastered the world and tells a civilized company of listeners about a series of events which can now be composed and named."[66]

---

[59] Walter Benjamin, *Illuminations*, ed. Hannah Arendt, trans. Harry Zohn (New York: Schocken Books, 1968), 83–110.

[60] E. M. Forster, *Aspects of the Novel* (London: Edward Arnold, 1927), 27.

[61] Fredric Jameson, *The Antinomies of Realism* (London & New York: Verso, 2013), 9.

[62] Henry James, *The Turn of the Screw and Other Stories*, ed. T. J. Lutig (Oxford: Oxford University Press, 1998), 118.

[63] Jameson, *Political Unconscious*, 105.

[64] Franco Moretti, "Serious Century," in Moretti, ed., *The Novel, Volume I: History, Geography, and Culture* (Princeton, NJ: Princeton University Press, 2006), 381.

[65] Jameson, *Antinomies*, 21.

[66] Jonathan Culler, *Structuralist Poetics* (Ithaca, NY: Cornell University Press, 1975), 195.

Into this predestined, orally sanctioned, romantic continuum of fatal time there arrives the shock of some pure textual immanence—related in the final instance to Kenner's writing "which has accepted and come to terms with its status as writing"[67]—or what Jameson calls "impulses of scenic elaboration, description and above all affective investment, which allow [realism] to develop towards a scenic present which in reality, but secretly, abhors the other temporalities which constitute the force of the tale or récit" (11). The generic compromise represented by the great realist novel consists in a plot-scaffolding of romantic temporality whose purpose is to engineer moments of sheer phenomenological immanence that cancel time altogether. These distended moments outside narrative continuity are related to unnamed affective states, bodily intensities that have no designated place on the map of romance. In contrast to the "named emotions" of love, honor, loyalty, despair, these new bodily affects and sensations have to be constructed on the spot, out of a language that, because it can never name the experience in question, is committed to an asymptotic nominalism, an experimental casting about "on a sliding scale of the incremental" (42) for tones, notes, vibrations, shades which, rightly assembled, will not touch or name the thing itself, but rather, precipitate its verbal transfiguration into a well-nigh visual constellation: proof perfect that it existed, without having reified it with a "local habitation and a name." One of the highest achievements of the printed book as a form was, then, to have liberated language (from within the license permitted by an extended *récit*) to present the unpresentable by way of an audio-visual separation of powers. As Jameson analyzes the frenzy of the perceptual in the prose of Zola—"a tremendous fermenting and bubbling pullulation in which the simplicity of words and names is unsettled to the point of an ecstatic dizziness by the visual multiplicity of the things themselves" (54)—the end result is nothing less than peeling away the visual from the verbal: "the realm of the visual begins to separate from that of the verbal and conceptual and to float away in a new kind of autonomy. Precisely this autonomy will create the space for affect" (55). It is a moment of tremendous critical force, and it allows us to take up the discussion of Faulkner's masterpiece with new direction and vigor.

Jameson's account of realism is predicated on our awareness of the subsequent phase of modernism in which the "system of the récit and of chronological temporality and narrative" (73)—where the newer phenomenological intensities are still threaded throughout realism—rapidly disintegrates and the "space for affect" spreads to incorporate, hypothetically, the entire work. The routing of the "system of the récit" certainly seems to have been an ideological constant in the modernists' wars of position against their forebears (though whether it was

---

[67] Kenner, "Faulkner and the Avant-Garde," 185.

ever fully realized is a pertinent question), and the relative expansion of affect's space in the prose narrative is an indubitable feature of the modern novel. But we can now add to this analysis the speculation that the war against romance in modern aesthetics is decodable as a struggle, allegorically carried out within the individual texts themselves, between a verbal level of known narratological signifiers and invariable functions, and some "visual" transposition of all that into an affective realm tied to the verbal level without ever being reducible to it. While this struggle took place within the terms of a détente throughout the period of realism, in the modern proper the stakes were raised prodigiously: imagism is but one name for that "visual" domain liberated from within the kingdom of the signifier where affectivity as such was allowed to prosper in a "new kind of autonomy."

This way of conceiving the aesthetic antagonism at work in *Absalom* seems preferable to Kenner's more conventional opposition between an oral regionalism and a cosmopolitan avant-gardism whose meridian is Stein's Paris: "folk material imitated, synthesized, by the devices of the twentieth-century avant-garde."[68] For this transcoding of that high modernist tension into something constitutive of the realist moment—the romance DNA of the *récit* coexisting with the emergence of a properly modern and "visual" affectivity—precisely specifies what is at work in this great text, without yet accounting for the peculiar dynamic in which it is couched here, and which will fully distinguish it from any readily identifiable realism. Indeed, it is to be hoped that by identifying this latent dynamic, we will contribute to a still evolving and always provisional and situational theory of modernism itself.

The mediatic unconscious

What, then, if the story just told could be recounted in another register, such that the hiving-off of a semi-autonomous "realm of the visual" from a verbal infrastructure built out of romantic cell tissues is seen simultaneously in media-historical terms? Would it not then appear that this momentous freeing up a "space of affect" from within the straitjacket of narrativity is precisely coeval with that Kittlerian partition of the data-streams of modernity into a Symbolic (type-written and -set print), an Imaginary (the photographic), and a Real (the phonographic)? This would give the hard-won affective dimension of a text the added function of allegorizing, from within the text, that medium's historical bleeding-out of Imaginary and Real qualities in the age of Edison. And if that were a plausible case, then something of the highest methodological importance

---

[68] Kenner, "Faulkner and the Avant-Garde," 195.

could at once be settled, and that is the radical distinction between the routine "hallucinations" of a romantic regime of reading (in which, remember, "novels succeeded in giving rise to *lanterna magica* images in solitary readers") and this apparently very similar relationship between a romance narrativity and a semi-autonomous "visuality" of affect. For in this latter case, what immediately becomes apparent is that the "visual" domain of affect is *not* a redoubled, Imaginary expression of the selfsame romance content in the story, but quite distinctly the winning of a realm of freedom from within the prescriptions of narrative closure—a negation rather than a continuation by other means of material now felt to be "abhorrent" to the continuous present of affect. That is to say that the mediatic unconscious of the progressive victory of "affect" over "récit" in the modern prose narrative entails a well-nigh ontological antagonism between the visuality of the one and the textuality of the other, which the text is obliged to allegorize on its own terms, as a now open, now subliminal figural war over the means of novelistic production. With this we touch again upon the resistance to suture in the photo-essay of Agee and Evans, the allegorical *agon* between Reporter and photographer in *Pylon*'s scenes of multimedia *reportage*, and the problems of goat-glanding in sound cinema—in modernism the "imagetext" erupts into palpable formal antagonisms, just at the points where industrial rationalization insists most heavily upon problem-free synchronization.

What we had wanted to understand more fully was how the voice of Rosa Coldfield, the romance poet, might have given rise to photographic pictures and moving ghosts in her elective amanuensis Quentin's (and our own, performative) sustained audition. Now we may hazard some answers to that question, and to the associated one of why an hiatus of forty-five years should have lapsed between the first publication of these romance figures and ideologemes in the local subscription newspaper and this final delivery of the material to the young "Southern gentleman" most likely to work them up for a magazine. Something is clearly at stake in this belated transmission, and if we peremptorily name "photomechanical printing processes" as the most decisive alteration in the literary means of production to have taken place between 1864 and 1909—shattering the old romance habits of readerly "hallucination" by the bold stroke of incorporated photographic images (like the scandalous one of Hightower in *Light in August* that makes him look like "Satan in the old prints," 448)—it is because the novel, in context, seems to request it. Just as in *Pylon* the Reporter must constantly be sensitive to the admixture of his textual romances with the photographer's "inverted world seen through a hooded lens or emerging [...] from stinking trays in a celibate and stygian cell lighted by a red lamp" (*Pylon*, 933), so, too, Rosa must find the appropriate photographic psychology upon which to graft her "outraged recapitulation." The reason for this is quite clear: her tales have become mediatically inaudible ("But Quentin was not listening," 142), mere verbiage and rhetoric stapled together by clichés and cliff-hangers. The "system of the récit" that she embodies to the point of being its sclerotic apotheosis has so far depleted its "tyranny of affects" that it seems to emerge "out of another world almost—the queer archaic sheet of ancient good notepaper written over with the neat faded cramped script which [...] he did not recognize as revealing a character cold, implacable, and even ruthless" (7). This voice insistently "vanishes" on the instant of audition, because in 1909 its content is perfectly incapable of making any affective impact whatsoever; the ruthlessness of its appeal is predicated on its desperate self-consciousness as a spent narratological force. What it seeks is an escape velocity from within the crypt of an entire Goethean discourse network—"*beside a shuttered and unsleeping candle she embalmed the War and its heritage of suffering and injustice and sorrow [...] embalming blotting from the breathable air the poisonous secret effluvium*" (140)— through a photographic vector personified in the eldest Compson brother of the second generation since the demon first made his Satanic print upon her own sensitive recording apparatus: "*bat-like image of his own torment cast by the fierce demoniac lantern up from beneath the earth's crust and hence in retrograde, reverse; from abysmal and chaotic dark to eternal and abysmal dark*" (142). The trick will be to transpose this doubly negated, romantic-hallucinated *lanterna magica* Sutpen-affect onto a modern photographic plate and so perpetuate the material for a new media ecology.

Photographic affect

The problem with Rosa's unsublated romance material is that the stomach of 1909 will not hold it, being "too strong" for the cooler digestive tracts of the modern. Photography appears as a way out of the dilemma: the negating flash of an instant in which thousands of words will congeal into a single picture and then vanish again. We will recall the striking language of "All the Dead Pilots":

> The courage, the recklessness, call it what you will, is the flash, the instant of sublimation; then flick! the old darkness again. That's why. It's too strong for a steady diet. And if it were a steady diet, it would not be a flash, a glare. And so, being momentary, it can be preserved and prolonged only on paper: a picture, a few written words that any match, a minute and harmless flame that any child can engender, can obliterate in an instant. (531)

The point is to interrupt the "steady diet," or what Gertrude Stein would call the "steady pounding," of Rosa's too verbose incantations with just such a flash and a glare, in order to render momentary, and thus properly affective once more, what has lost all affective potentiality. Paper may still serve as the material support for the hoary "old mouth-to-mouth tales" from which this superannuated storyteller will weave her fatalistic *récit*, just as it did when her poems were first published to an indifferent world (the ruined world of romance); only now, the momentary glare of the photograph will have transfigured their empty sentimental gestures and melodramatic formulae into an instant's piercing intensity.

Rosa knows precisely what an affect is and how it works on the body; her problem is that she lacks the up-to-date mediatic means to make one palpable. As she says, something irrevocable happens to the body, after which the challenge is to render it communicable via cultural means:

> *You see? There are some things which happen to us which the intelligence and the senses refuse just as the stomach sometimes refuses what the palate has accepted but which digestion cannot compass—occurrences which stop us dead as though by some impalpable intervention, like a sheet of glass through which we watch all subsequent events transpire as though in a soundless vacuum, and fade, vanish; are gone, leaving us immobile, impotent, helpless; fixed, until we can die. That was I.* (125)

Here is the strong echo of the photo-sensitive voice that frames the story of "All the Dead Pilots," with its breathless evocation of "some dim and threatful apotheosis of the race seen for an instant in the glare of a thunderclap and then forever gone."[69] We can construe the *"sheet of glass"* and the *"soundless vacuum,"* behind and within which the intervening occurrence of an event obliges "us" to wait out all posterity in a series of fading images, in terms familiar not only from Jameson's account of affect, but from collodion wet plate photography too—its exposure of the negative print onto a glass plate, and the hushed laboratory quiet of its further development into printed images. And it is then no great leap to arrive at a notion of this *"immobile . . . fixed"* rictus in which the post-eventual subject is held, that does justice to the photographic genealogy of the figure here rehearsed in quick time. *"You see?"* These strange *"things"* that happen to us, embalming us within and outside the currents of time (the way, though too slowly now, Rosa's own poems will do for the War dead), do so imperceptibly—for they do not fall within the romantic distribution of the sensible. Rather, they "stop us dead" with their own perception of us: this undead romantic subject is the fixed and helpless fossilization of a narrative being pursuant to the "impalpable" touch of an event. *"That was I."* The grammar is exact: that which persists through the rising and falling away of a succession of phenomenological intensities, as a sort of abstract and stunned adhesion to an event that never perceptibly happened, "that was I." And *that* is affect. It all seems both consistently

---

[69] Faulkner, *Collected Stories* (London: Vintage, 1995), 511.

illustrative of, and perversely excessive in its commitment to, Faulkner's later credo about the "aim of every artist" being "to arrest motion, which is life, by artificial means and hold it fixed so that 100 years later when a stranger looks at it, it moves again since it is life"[70]—a credo which we need to keep juxtaposed in our minds with the famous statement by Henry Fox Talbot on the photographic miracle: "we may receive on paper the fleeting shadow, arrest it there and in the space of a single minute fix it there so firmly as to be no more capable of change."[71]

What ruptures the romance "stream of event" is a "crystallized instant" of affectivity that blooms as a photographic figure. Rosa's self-metaphorization here, as a "fixed" image on the obverse of a glass plate inside a *camera obscura*, comes on the heels of one of *Absalom*'s great narrative ellipses, the death of Charles Bon:

> *You see, I never saw him. I never even saw him dead. I heard an echo, but not the shot; I saw a closed door but did not enter it. [. . .] One day he was not. Then he was. Then he was not. It was too short, too fast, too quick; six hours of a summer afternoon saw it all—a space too short to leave even the imprint of a body on a mattress, and blood can come from anywhere—if there was blood, since I never saw him. [. . .] No, there had been no shot. That sound was merely the sharp and final clap-to of a door between us and all that was, all that might have been—a retroactive severance of the stream of event: a forever crystallised instant in imponderable time accomplished by three weak yet indomitable women which, preceding the accomplished fact which we declined, refused, robbed the brother of the prey, reft the murderer of a victim for his very bullet.* (124, 126, 131)

This is one of two cardinal narratological absences of the novel, approached asymptotically via a narrative stutter which, the closer it comes to naming the event, "fixing" it, the more wildly it strives to negate it, via outright denial and the alibi of *non habeas corpus*. "*I never saw him*," the alibi repetitiously runs, and "*there had been no shot*": it is a strange way to tell the death of the ambiguous New Orleans suitor, himself a kind of dandified avatar of Joe Christmas. Just as Rosa, having been touched by the event, is held in a helpless affective trance, so too the event itself—the gunshot that ends a dynasty in an instant—does not "happen," but is only echoed in a lackluster facsimile of itself. If we missed it, that is because, by becoming "*a retroactive severance of the stream of event*," the event breaks anachronistically from narrativity and becomes its own self-sufficient

---

[70] Faulkner, *Paris Review*.

[71] Henry Talbot, "Some Account of the Art of Photogenic Drawing" (1831), reproduced in Beaumont Newhall, *Photography: Essays and Images* (London: Secker & Warburg, 1980), 28.

cause, leaving it *"a forever crystallized instant in imponderable time"*—an affect, or a photographic plate.

It is as a photograph seeking development at last that we are to understand Charles Bon, and his death, in the narration of Rosa Coldfield to Quentin Compson. This is one effect of the retroaction of which Rosa speaks. Inasmuch as he is adduced affectively as a "forever crystallized instant," Charles folds back photographically into the narrative stream where he functions as a "shadowy" *actant*. The refrain "I never saw him" serves as an alibi in more senses than one, since it is a disavowal that charges the following parenthesis with the paradoxical function of analepsis and prolepsis at once: "*(I never saw him. I never even saw him dead. I heard a name, I saw a photograph, I helped to make a grave: and that was all)*" (121). Proleptically, obviously the moment looks forward to the moment we have already considered. Analeptically, it is a vital and vulnerable moment in the narrative logic of the novel, since it gestures explicitly toward that magazine urtext or proto-narrative whence many of its governing energies are derived—the short story "Evangeline," which centrally features the enigma of an exchanged photographic image, white for black.

At the heart of "Evangeline" is a photograph, given by Judith Sutpen, of herself, to Charles Bon in exchange for an engagement ring (not unlike Thomas Sutpen's inaugural swap of the hundred acres of "Indian" land for "a stereopticon"[72]). This photographic troth, plighted against the oncoming crisis of civil war, and carried with Bon through the four years of battle, reappears on the day of his death— dead from the "last shot" of the war (591)—when, laid in the room prepared for him by his widow Judith, she "locked the door upon herself and her dead husband and the picture" (601). There follows an inscrutable "pounding noise," after which she emerges and categorically refuses a place for the photograph in the casket in which Bon will be interred, before taking a poker and beating the lock of the metal case that holds the portrait "to where it wouldn't never open again." (601) This is a mystery that is solved only after the Sutpen mansion goes up in flames and the narrator retrieves the surviving case from the ashes, breaking it open to reveal not Judith's portrait but "the smooth, oval, unblemished face, the mouth rich, full, a little loose, the hot, slumberous, secretive eyes, the inklike hair with its faint but unmistakable wiriness—all the ineradicable and tragic stamp of negro blood" that coursed through the body of Bon's unnamed New Orleans wife (608). The substitution of one photograph for another, white wife for black, is never narratively explained in "Evangeline"; what matters is its evidentiary function in explaining Henry's murder of Charles Bon (for a miscegenating bigamist), but also its amphibious status as sole indexical survivor of the failed dynastic experiment. Yes, it is a case of simple substitution, but the substitution retroactively disturbs

---

[72] Faulkner, *Uncollected Stories*, ed. Joseph Blotner (New York: Random House, 1979), 583.

the romance of cliché out of which the narrative is self-mockingly woven: maidens leaning on columns, red roses pinned in hair, unrequited ghosts, silver cases. Into this all too familiar generic space obtrudes a palpable "othering," whose locus is the photograph. Pressed into a locket and sealed shut for forty years, it is as if the snapped "white face" of Judith has developed of its own accord into a negative, a "black face" in which the unmentionable, the unnarrativizable truth is finally disclosed. It is a classic case of those "failures of narrative imagination" of which Michael Denning has charged the realist impulse of 1930s documentarism—where photography seals a gap in the narrative substance, papering over a genuine crisis in totalization.[73] Here the ekphrastic photograph exceeds narrative logic in an uncanny development, stimulating a train of speculation that its evidentiary function fails to satisfy; it is therefore not enough to say, as Katherine Henninger does, that the story "turns on a simple mystery, solved by an unproblematic photographic 'truth,'" for (in Hegelian terms, as we shall see) if the photograph is what preserves the True, then that True is internally bifurcated, self-negating—the *narrative* photograph is insistently of a blonde white woman, while the *retrieved* and affectively suturing photograph is palpably of a Negro.[74]

We will have occasion, shortly, to return to this tantalizing racial reversibility allegorized through a photographic substitution. In the meantime, back on the pages of *Absalom*, our speculation concerns the photographic ontology of Bon himself, who bears photographs in all his (unnarratable) death scenes. We are told: "*we had no corpse; we even had no murderer . . . who came and crashed a door and cried his crime and vanished, who for the fact that he was still alive was just that much more shadowy than the abstraction that we had nailed into a box*" (126). Charles Bon drains away into the status of a two-dimensional image in a *camera obscura*: an abstraction in a box. Indeed, he is only ever a photograph in this prose, and perhaps a virtual one at that.

> *I dont know even now if I was ever aware that I had seen nothing of his face but that photograph, that shadow, that picture in a young girl's bedroom: a picture casual and framed upon a littered dressing table yet bowered and dressed (or so I thought) with all the maiden and invisible lily-roses, because even before I saw the photograph I could have recognized, nay described, the very face. But I never saw it.* (121–22)

Charles Bon is, for Rosa, the nominal site upon which a photographic virtuality erects its specious and seductive kingdom of the déjà-vu. "*June gave substance*

---

[73] Denning, *Cultural Front*, 119.

[74] Katherine R. Henninger, "Faulkner, Photography, and a Regional Ethics of Form," in Joseph R. Urgo and Ann J. Abadie, eds., *Faulkner and Material Culture, Faulkner & Yoknapatawpha, 2004* (Jackson, MS: University Press of Mississippi, 2007), 134.

to that shadow with a name emerging from Ellen's vain and garrulous folly, that shape without even a face yet because I had not even seen the photograph then, reflected in the secret and bemused gaze of a young girl" (121)—but does she ever literally "see" the photograph that insists on imprinting itself, mechanically, in a mental substance scooped out by these "obverse reflections" of desire and dream, relayed between mother and daughter? Bon's photographic image is suspended in a liquid element of the "not-yet," a latency too dangerous to develop. It is as though all of space is a photosensitive surface primed for the faintest touch of his passing, but never to be processed. The "shadow with a name" leaves its negative impress everywhere on the Sutpen estate, in "*the nooky seat which held invisible imprint of his absent thighs just as the obliterating sand, the million finger-nerves of frond and leaf, the very sun and moony constellations which had looked down at him, the circumambient air, held somewhere yet his foot, his passing shape, his face, his speaking voice, his name: Charles Bon*" (122–23); and in the dark house itself, "*where he had been but a shape, a shadow: not of a man, a being, but of some esoteric piece of furniture—vase or chair or desk*" (124).

No wonder, then, that Bon's enigmatic lack of presence leads Rosa to fantasize about the ultimate fantasy machine, which will later be called the movies, and still later, television: "*if I were God I would invent out of this seething turmoil we call progress something (a machine perhaps) which would adorn the barren mirror altars of every plain girl who breathes with such as this—which is so little since we want so little—this pictured face. It would not even need a skull behind it; almost anonymous, it would only need vague inference of some walking flesh and blood desired by someone else even if only in some shadow-realm of make-believe.*" (122) Judith Sensibar is right to claim that "We never know what Bon looks like—his features, hair color, his eyes. These are facts and they don't interest Rosa. All she cares about are how and why photographs work as they do upon the spectator's imagination."[75] Charles is always and already photographic, "a picture, an image," who "appeared almost phoenix-like, full-sprung from no childhood, born of no woman and impervious to time and, vanished, leaving no bones nor dust anywhere" (61). The Bon "photograph" exists as a projection of that "machine" which Rosa patents in her fancy—it is the affective *point de caption* of a tissue of romance ideologemes that cannot find release within a romance discourse network. They have slipped their traces and transposed their ideological burden onto a media technology that belongs to the twentieth, not the nineteenth, century. Hooked up to a machine that services desire through mechanically reproduced facial images, Rosa's "plain girl" is the very prototype of Hollywood's female "fans" who "read the fan magazines, wrote letters to their

---

[75] Judith L. Sensibar, "Faulkner's Real and Imaginary Photos of Desire," in Doreen Fowler and An J. Abadie, eds., *Faulkner and Popular Culture: Faulkner and Yoknapatawpha 1988* (Jackson, MS: University Press of Mississippi, 1990), 129.

idols, and knew the film plots by heart,"[76] leading to that feedback loop of which Siegfried Kracauer wrote: "Sensational film hits and life usually correspond to each other because the Little Miss Typists model themselves after the examples they see on the screen."[77] In "The Leg," Davy, who inexplicably encounters his own image as lewd matinee idol,[78] is a prefiguration of that extraordinary rupture with the "long-standing patriarchal economy of vision" betokened by Valentino "as a figure and function of female spectatorship," enjoying a "precarious status as both cult of consumption and manifestation of an alternative public sphere."[79] Indeed, even Mr. Compson cannot resist a little anachronistic flirtation with the cinematic romance of the figure: "a man a little older than his actual years and enclosed and surrounded by a sort of Scythian glitter [. . .] he seems to have withdrawn into a mere spectator, passive, a little sardonic, and completely enigmatic. He seems to hover, shadowy, almost substanceless, a little behind and above" (77)—much like that photographic group portrait that Quentin first sees conjured out of the stream of Rosa's interminable voice.

Amphibologies of the photogram

All of which now prepares us to engage again the notorious photograph of Bon's New Orleans wife, and the passage it makes from the spare fabric of "Evangeline" to the ornate tapestry of *Absalom*. Insofar as this novel is an effort of unsparing aesthetic labor to transfigure that disposable magazine fare into Literature, it is worth recalling here Rosa's first, ironic overture to Quentin the potential magazine scribe. Her ultimate quarry is not Quentin, of course, who will take it all with him to the bottom of the Charles River within a year, but Faulkner himself, who has already, in 1932, sought to place "it" in the magazines. Moreover, it is Faulkner who was simultaneously engaged in the submissive task of making romance function again, with words, on the big screen, and who would soon, with Dudley Murphy, consider adapting *Absalom* itself into a risible screen romance. The multimedia travails of all "this," as it is transposed from those "few old mouth-to-mouth tales" (83) into magazine story, novel, and finally screen treatment, are already latent in its promissory donation here, Rosa to Quentin. In "Evangeline," the first of those magazine efforts—which was promptly

---

[76] Lary May, *Screening Out the Past: The Birth of Mass Culture and the Motion Picture Industry* (Chicago: University of Chicago Press, 1983), 164.

[77] Siegfried Kracauer, *The Mass Ornament: Weimar Essays*, trans. Thomas Y. Levin (Cambridge, MA: Harvard University Press, 1995), 292.

[78] In Sensibar's summary, in this early (1925) tale, "a photograph created by a jealous lover's ghost drives his girlfriend mad, nearly causes his rival's murder, incites the girl's brother to murder, and causes the brother's death." See "Faulkner's Real and Imaginary Photos of Desire," 114.

[79] Hansen, *Babel and Babylon*, 248, 253.

rejected by the *Post* and the *Woman's Home Companion* in 1931—the primary oral bearer of the narrative material is no shabby-genteel old white woman, but what Blotner calls a "gnomelike mulatto woman named Raby."[80] And just as this curious racial reversal from the oral original subtly informs the generic transformation from magazine schlock into mature modernist masterpiece, so too, as we have seen, that early story turns on a very strange racial substitution at the level of photographic image.

So much is preserved in *Absalom*, except the reversibility is now properly hysterical. The first time we hear of the notorious photograph in the novel, it is, as Mr. Compson recalls, found with Bon, "on whose dead body four years later Judith was to find the photograph of the other woman and the child" (74). Any doubts about the racial complexion of this "other woman" are briskly settled shortly afterward, with the direct reference to "the picture of the octoroon mistress and the little boy" (78). But this is substantially challenged when Rosa later describes the portrait as being of Judith herself: "*And how I saw that what she held in that lax and negligent hand was the photograph, the picture of herself in its metal case which she had given him, held casual and forgotten against her flank as any interrupted pastime book*" (118). Once again, as per "Evangeline," the narrative discourse seems to want to insist upon the photograph's being, not of the woman now known simply as "the octoroon mistress," but of the white intended herself, although there is of course no corroboration of that hypothesis via visual examination. A few pages later, some of this specificity has fallen away, and Judith is found "*standing before that closed door which I was not to enter* [...] *with the photograph hanging at her side and her face absolutely calm*" (124). The subclause that acts as a predicate of the object noun "the photograph" is subtracted, and we are left in an indeterminate position vis-à-vis this "proof" of nothing at all. Note how, in the next, penultimate mention of the photograph, the object noun shifts strategically from the picture itself to the case that houses it: "when they brought Bon's body in and Judith took from his pocket the metal case she had given him with her picture in it" (288), which is a kind of suspense device, clearing a perfect epistemological vacuum into which the headlong reanimation of events precipitated by Quentin and Shreve's dialogue can then rush; and Shreve squares the circle with predictable presumption:

> and the Aunt Rosa comes boiling out that afternoon and finds Judith standing without a tear before the closed door, holding the metal case she had given him with her picture in it but that didn't have her picture in it now but that of the octoroon and the kid. And your old man wouldn't know about that too: why the black son of a bitch should have

[80] Blotner, *Faulkner*, 279.

taken her picture out and put the octoroon's picture in, so he invented a reason for it. But I know. And you know too. (295)

The mystery of "Evangeline" is rehearsed only to be unsolved, or solved purely within the jagged narrative imaginary that the photograph was otherwise meant to suture. What arrests us here, beyond the sudden racist invective, is the sheer willfulness of the "solution" hazarded. Into the yawning gap between Mr. Compson's and Rosa's versions of photographic verity, Shreve inserts the deliberative substitution at which "Evangeline" only gestured implicitly. This restaging of events accepts both "pictures" (black-face and white-face) in an accelerated overlapping development of one out of the other—with once again "black" trumping white, the octoroon's image displacing Judith's face. However, in this case the ekphrastic photograph does not supplement the narrative and paper over its gaps; instead, it is produced from *within* the coils of the narrative romance now at full heat—a romance at this stage fully seasoned by the competing figures of bigamy, incest, and miscegenation. Only when the last of these pennies is allowed to drop can the mystery of the photograph be hastily resolved, developed logically out of the figure of racial mixing and amphibology itself. And it can only be resolved "doubly," as a figure oscillating between two racial codes and colors, a positive and a negative print.

It is as if the nameless "octoroon mistress" had this function above all to assume in the novel. For what is at stake in her, as a character and as a fate, is the capacity of developing, within the "white" image of a face, its unnerving and destabilizing "black" ur-image. The very epithet "octoroon" stages this dynamic implicitly with its lexical computation of racial complexion; as though, seen through the scrim of a suitable ideological filter, the "seven eighths" of whiteness carried by her blood might all of a sudden disappear behind a "polarized" glare-block, and allow the definitive "one eighth" to stand forth. But photography provides a much clearer tropology within which to elaborate this elusive racial contagion. And it is as a photograph, we must remember, that she is summoned into being in the first place, by Bon himself, as Mr. Compson recreates his expert seduction and education of the young Henry in the ways of decadent "morganatic" ceremonies and mulatto courtesans. The entire passage, stretching over pages, deserves the fullest attention, as Faulkner's mature novelistic art seizes hold of the photographic process as the privileged means of access to a figure, like Joe Christmas's, suspended "between" racial essences.

> So I can imagine him [Bon], the way he did it [told Henry about the mistress]: the way in which he took the innocent and negative plate of Henry's provincial soul and intellect and exposed it by slow degrees to this esoteric milieu, building gradually toward the picture which he desired it to retain, accept. (91)

Here the figure is out in the open, and it is immensely generative in context. Running with the conceit, Mr. Compson intuits that the beauty of the photographic method lies in its obtuse angle to discourse, its unarguable visual impression on the "negative plate": "I can see him corrupting Henry gradually into the purlieus of elegance, with no foreword, nor forewarning, the postulation to come after the fact, exposing Henry slowly to the surface aspect" (91). Pressing the button so that the shutter lifts and the light steals in, Bon "exposes" the provincial boy to a rapid series of impressions of what Pound called the "cinematographic" surfaces of modern city life,[81] registered in the prose as a parataxis of independent clauses: "the architecture a little curious," "the inference of great and easy wealth," "the flash and glitter of a myriad carriage wheels," and "the mentor, the man" himself at the center of this gaudy spectacle. This transitive mental photography allows its agent to sit back and watch the technical effects as they register automatically: "watching him with that cold and catlike inscrutable calculation, watching the picture resolve and become fixed" (91).

And then, just as abruptly it is declared, "'But that's not it. That's just the base, the foundation. It can belong to anyone,'" as though a cheap picture postcard had become confused with truth, necessitating a curious superposition of silent cinematic dumb-show on the same image: "a dialogue without words, speech, which would fix and then remove without obliterating one line the picture, this background, leaving the background, the plate prepared and innocent again: the plate docile, with that puritan's humility toward anything which is a matter of sense rather than logic" (91–92). At this point, the photographic figure is working very hard indeed to compass the full effect of "corruption" understood as a predilection towards racial intermixture; it is becoming also something akin to Freud's "mystic writing pad" with its two layers of waxy, erasable surface and deep, clayish indelibility. By this stage, like Freud's unconscious, the "plate" on which all this dazzling exposure is having its impact has itself become a desiring machine, with affinities to Rosa's invention of the same—a virtual cinema of rapid impressions driven by a hunger for more, a nascent addiction to photography. "[W]aiting for the next picture which the mentor, the corruptor, intended for it: that next picture, following the fixation and acceptance of which the mentor would say again . . . 'But even this is not it'" (92). At which point, it is time to slow down, as Bon proceeds to do: "he (Bon) would be talking now, lazily, almost cryptically, stroking onto the plate himself now the picture which he wanted there; I can imagine how he did it—the calculation, the surgeon's alertness and cold detachment, the exposures brief, so brief as to be cryptic, almost staccato, the plate unaware of what the complete picture would show, scarce-seen yet ineradicable" (92). Here, cinema has indeed supplanted mere photography,

---

[81] Ezra Pound, Review of Jean Cocteau, *Poésies 1917–1920* (Editions de la Sirène, Paris), *The Dial* 70 (January 1921), 110.

as the individual photograms recede into temporal unconsciousness and the "plate" surrenders to the "cryptic" and "staccato" "yet ineradicable" contributions to that elusive "complete picture" now well on the way to development.

There follows another cascade of metonymies—"a trap, a riding horse standing before a closed and curiously monastic doorway," "a façade shuttered and blank, drowsing in steamy morning sunlight," and finally the great revelation itself, "a row of faces like a bazaar of flowers, the supreme apotheosis of chattlery, of human flesh bred of the two races for that sale" (92–93). It has been toward this "corridor of doomed and tragic flower faces," of the "two races," that the photographic process has been leading all along, in such a way as to extinguish all resistance in advance, via sheer shutter speed: "this seen by Henry quickly, exposed quickly and then removed," "that brief, before Henry had time to know what he had seen, but now slowing: now would come the instant for which Bon had built" (93).

It is an extraordinary elaboration of a figure, all geared towards the image of the "octoroon mistress" herself—distilled from this photographic exuberance and excess as the very inner principle of its imaginary, but whom, of course, Henry never "sees" outside of this extravagant verbal cinema. She whose image is destined to appear in that place reserved for the "proper" portrait of the white betrothed is first conjured into being through the application of a photographic process that does not "fix" her directly on to the "negative plate" of Henry's fancy, but evokes her laterally through a tantalizing metonymic forest of signs and duplications. Just so, we have no way of knowing whether Rosa ever sees a photograph of the Bon whom she avowedly "never saw"; but we are apprised of a certain "machine" that generates photographic images out of some pregnant "negative plate" of the white Southern imagination.

What matters most here is that every passage through this medium, of the "negative plate" of a Sutpen or a Coldfield mind, seems to leave behind it some unwanted mark, a supplementary trace, that haunts the "positive image" yielded of the mistress and ultimately of Bon himself. "Have you forgot that this woman, this child, are niggers? You, Henry Sutpen of Sutpen's Hundred in Mississippi?" as Bon asks with his final trump card, a card that will fatally come to affect his own substance too (98). No, there is that in the complex technological nature of Henry's image of her, and of Rosa's image of Bon, which preserves such knowledge deep in the mediatic unconscious: a "negative" print from which the glamorous romantic one is cast, a black face serving as the origin of the white one the imaginary grasps as its own.[82] Such is the Real of the negative plate, its ineluctable inscription with the antagonistic knot of slavery out of which the

---

[82] For an excellent discussion of the figure of the photographic negative in Faulkner's fiction, see Sascha Morrell, "Kodak Harlot Tricks of Light: Faulkner and Melville in the Darkroom of Race," in Solomon and Murphet, eds., *William Faulkner in the Media Ecology*, 172–93.

entire florid Imaginary of Southern romance is ultimately derived. Here lies the unstated fountainhead of that final apocalyptic and anachronistic vision of a future in which "I who regard you will also have sprung from the loins of African kings" (311), since every face classified as "white" within the distribution of the visible in the South, and in America at large, is so on the basis of those countless "black loins" whose labour (in both senses of the term) sustains them in their imaginary whiteness.[83]

As Joel Williamson once wrote, "the fact was that numbers of mulatto children were constantly appearing. Particularly during late slavery, apparently whole plantation communities fell into a morass of interracial sexuality as men of the master class spawned one child after another with their female slaves."[84] Whatever the status of this mytheme as history, there is no doubt that it sustains the fantasy of *Absalom, Absalom!*, which is in turn sustained tropologically by a complex transference of biological metaphors into photographic ones, or what I am going to call a figuration of *photogenetics*: where sex is fashioned forth as a "machine" of images, in which black becomes white and vice versa, and where the very capacity to imagine a "mulatto" seems to turn on a rigorous photographic pedagogy, so that the "supreme apotheosis of chattlery, of human flesh bred of the two races for ... sale"—the "octoroon mistress" herself—must take the form of a virtual photograph. Charles's intention is to "progress" from that negative to the positive print of a "wife," replacing the octoroon "mistress" to whom he is wed with the white "betrothed" whom he will never wed. His failure consists, partly, in his inability to negate the negation fully, his clinging to the negative print even as the positive one is developing to the extent that, upon his death, the positive portrait of Judith will "regress" into that of the New Orleans mulatta, who registers, first and last, photographically.

And that is for more reasons than one, but principally because she herself is, within Faulkner's infamous economics of repetition and doubling, already a duplication or off-print of that older "negative," Sutpen's first, Haitian wife. For any distinct image of this more doubtful character (sometimes called Eulalia, but on no reliable authority), we must depend principally upon Sutpen's own account, mediated in turn by Colonel Compson, Mr. Compson, and his son, Quentin. In that narrative echo chamber, we are thrown back almost entirely upon the grammatical and syntactic resources of *negation* to sense her at all. Sutpen is wont to refer, when he mentions her directly, to that "one very factor which would destroy the entire plan and design which I had been working toward" (226), the "fact" that "rendered it impossible that this woman and child

---

[83] Richard Godden, *Fictions of Labor*, 115–78.

[84] Joel Williamson, *A Rage for Order: Black-White Relations in the American South since Emancipation* (Oxford: Oxford University Press, 1986), 27–28.

be incorporated in my design" (218); her very being contaminated by a "misrepresentation" that "voided ... the central motivation of his entire design" (217). The woman is the locus of an insensible but inexorable negativity; she is touched by a nameless "fact" or "factor" that corrupts absolutely the wellsprings of Sutpen's fantastic auto-commission, to render anew in his own hands and name the image of the great Tidewater "white house" that had stamped his own bumpkin's "negative plate" with such an indelible impression. She is by his lights only "incidentally of course, a wife" (218), conscripted as a necessary but disposable device within the unfurling of the dynastic plot, and yet her "incident" functions narratologically much more potently than the adverb allows, since it harbors within it that subliminal "factor" which by 1901 had already assumed a pregnant genetic meaning: "a gene or other agent that is transmitted from parent to offspring and influences or determines a hereditary character."[85] If this is not yet Sutpen's meaning, it is already implicitly Mr. Compson's, and certainly it becomes Quentin's and Shreve's, since by the book's terminus, this "factor" will have overwhelmed all other explanatory devices to fill the epistemological ellipsis into which Henry's shooting of Bon structurally falls. And here again, her function is precisely allegorical of the larger textual and narratological method that surrounds her, since she is the object of what her parents "deliberately withheld from" Sutpen, "the one fact which I have reason to know they were aware would have caused me to decline the entire matter" (141)—she who is the occasion of so much narrative ellipsis is the subject of a most critical epistemological evasion in turn.

In our only proper glimpse of her, again through the multiple filters of Compson and Sutpen romance, what is again striking is the degree to which the narrative voice strains to adduce her, not as a being extended in time, but as a visual forestalling of that subsequent history which would flow in tragic inevitability from its having being seen:

> the girl just emerging for a second of the telling, in a single word almost, so that Grandfather said it was like he had just seen her too for a second by the flash of one of the muskets—a bent face, a single cheek, a chin for an instant beyond a curtain of fallen hair, a white slender arm raised, a delicate hand clutching a ramrod, and that was all. (206)

Lit in flamboyant chiaroscuro by the conflagrations of Haitian revolt, a flash of musket-shot and flicker of cane-fire, the woman is fixed as an image thanks to a nocturnal ground of blackness against which she can stand metonymized as "a white slender arm raised" in the night. She is, prior to this, only "a shadow that

---

[85] Oxford English Dictionary. Factor, *n.*, 7.b.

almost emerged for a moment and then faded again but not completely away," (204), "just that shadow which could load a musket but could not have been trusted to fire one" (205); beyond the arrested profile she is nothing at all, sheer negation: "and that was all. No more detail and information," as Mr. Compson puts it. An enigmatic shade emerging into one brilliant, fixed "white" image before returning to darkness, the Haitian girl who carries that troubling "factor" is apprehended as a photographic trace. And just as that other photograph, of the "octoroon mistress," appears in order to paper over a narrative ellipse, so too this galvanizing moment of vision, mounted and framed by "a word," is positioned at the cusp of the greatest narrative hole in the novel—that ellipse within an ellipse that is Sutpen's single-handed "quelling" of the Haitian uprising.

We need to pay particular attention to this great subsidence of narrative materials, and we need especially to think about it in relation to our verbal "photograph" of that feminine negative of Sutpen's design:

> No more detail and information about that [the woman, the girl] than about how he got from the field, his overseeing, into the besieged house when the niggers rushed at him with their machetes, than how he got from the rotting cabin in Virginia to the fields he oversaw: and this, Grandfather said, more incredible to him than the getting there from Virginia because that did infer time, a space the getting across which did indicate something of leisureliness since time is longer than any distance, while the other, the getting from the fields into the barricaded house, seemed to have occurred with a sort of violent abrogation which must have been almost as short as his telling about it—a very condensation of time which was the gauge of its own violence, and he telling it in that pleasant faintly forensic anecdotal manner apparently just as he remembered it. (206)

We are here at the very navel of *Absalom, Absalom!*, staring into a puckered fold of skin upon skin, layered over some unmentionable umbilical orifice; the site of an originary rupture between the text and its conditions of historical possibility. If the book itself is structured in the main according to the formal principle of suppression—ellipsis—followed by subsequent revisitation and gap-filling ("and I reckon Grandfather was saying 'Wait wait for God's sake wait' about like you are until he finally did stop and back up and start all over again with at least some regard for cause and effect even if none for logical sequence and continuity," 204), then here is its embryonic and self-allegorizing figuration in the narrative itself: Sutpen's symptomatic silence with regard to his passage to Haiti, and in Haiti, his passage from the fields to the house on the night of the uprising. It is as though this compacted double occlusion, a "violent abrogation" of narrative responsibility, ripples upwards and outwards and informs the narrative economy of the entire text.

It is critical to discern just where and at what points these elisions are made. The arrival in Haiti happens hard on the heels of the momentous "primal scene" at the big house in Tidewater, while the latter ellipse is precipitated by the brief "photo" of the planter's daughter who will marry Sutpen and give birth to his first child. In both cases, what is especially relevant is that this allegorization of ellipsis as a narrative device is projected upon a purely fantasmatic screen: Haiti had no French plantations in 1820. But it was precisely where the anachronistic romantic imagination went to convert its idealist aspirations into the "deliverables" of material property.[86] A romance passage, no longer narratable thanks to a political event of the first order, now must be transfigured into vivid and disconnected photographic affects that show, with a pure symptomatology, their debt to a "negative plate" with no purchase on the prose of romance.

The negative plate

Faulkner's extraordinary elaborations of this figure point to a persistent slippage and evasion at the very core of our prevailing theorizations of the photographic image. The return of an indexical language of the "molecularity" of the material touch of some sensible matter on a sensitive surface may well aid us in our reflections on the historicity of photographic materials, but only by way of a denial. As Jessica Evans summarizes the basic case for Peircean indexicality, "the photograph, unlike a drawing or computer-generated image, is ... physically or causally linked to its referent, being the result of an optical redistribution of light rays emanating from an object on to light-sensitive materials."[87] Exactly so, and nobody should therefore make the epistemological error of seeing the photographic sign as a "representation" of the object as such; rather, the photograph is concrete evidence of there having been an object in the first place, an object in the time of light, capable of reflecting enough luminosity to mark the photochemical surface of the film. But herein, precisely, lie the conundrum and the theoretical dilemma persistently kept out of the frame. For whereas it

---

[86] "The greed of those who came to make quick fortunes in Saint-Domingue and then return to France ended up making all experience, even amatory, subordinate to the lure of money and property. [... S]omething happens to romance when we turn to those places where everything was allowed because thousands were enslaved, where the fact of slavery—the conversion of person into thing for the ends of capital—turned all previous orders upside down. If racial mixing threatened to contaminate, the masters had to conjure purity out of phantasmal impurity." Joan Dayan, *Haiti, History, and the Gods* (Berkeley, CA & Los Angeles: University of California Press, 1998), 197, 190.

[87] Jessica Evans, "Introduction to Part 1," in Evans and Stuart Hall, eds., *Visual Culture: The Reader* (London: Sage Publications, 1999), 13.

is commonplace to speak of the rhetorical disposition, the denotative and connotative codes, the ambiguities of semiological capture according to cultural context, the horizon of viewership, and the social construction of the visible itself, what is never acknowledged is that the avowed "object" linked indexically to the visible photographic image as its referent is itself, precisely, another photographic image. Virtually every photograph that is not a Polaroid is already a photograph of another photograph.

This is to be taken literally. Since Henry Fox Talbot's invention of the Calotype process in 1841, the technical protocol of photographic print-taking has been predominantly a composite one. For Daguerre (and Niépce before him), of course, photography had been a process of direct "sun writing"—imprints left latent on iodized silver plates, and chemically conjured forth by the agency of quicksilver. The English Talbot, who speculated romantically about the photographic "pencil of Nature," actually took a very distinct approach that put Nature at a qualified distance. In the Calotype, "a piece of paper was brushed with weak salt solution, dried, then brushed with a weak silver nitrate solution, dried, making silver chloride in the paper. This made it sensitive to light, and the paper was now ready for exposure. This might take half an hour, giving a print-out image." But this was not yet the end; within a year, a modification ensued—Talbot "added gallic acid, the paper became more sensitive to light, and it was no longer necessary to expose until the image became visible. With further treatment of gallic acid and silver nitrate, the latent image would be developed." It was this latent image, the "negative"—said Talbot, "the paper when removed is often perfectly blank but when kept in the dark the picture begins to appear spontaneously, and keeps improving for several minutes"—that could then be placed on top of more photo paper and allowed to develop, into a "positive" print, in natural sunlight.[88] Friedrich Kittler spells out the critical difference at stake between the two processes: "With Daguerre's process, the recording and fixing of the image always produced a positive reproduction of the lighting conditions. Experiments with negative reproductions failed because of their irreversibility. Talbot resolved this problem by always photographing the negative again just as it had been produced itself in order to obtain as many positive copies as he wanted."[89] Two far-reaching effects followed from this passage of the photographic image through its own negative: the capabilities for magnification and miniaturization, and the limitless number of potential copies. It is this latter possibility that made the greatest impact, and Kittler evokes Hegel to valorize the point: "in a series first of originals, second of negatives, and third of negatives of a negative, photography became a mass medium. For Hegel, the negation of a negation was supposed to be anything but a return to the first position, but mass media are based on

[88] http://www.rleggat.com/photohistory/history/calotype.htm.
[89] Friedrich Kittler, *Optical Media*, trans. Anthony Enns (Cambridge: Polity Press, 2010), 133–34.

precisely this oscillation" (134). With the advent of collodion photography in 1851, the intermediary stage of a negative print (now on glass), allowing multiple positive prints (along with the direct positive, ambrotype and ferrotype, collodion prints), was standardized. Photography has, since that time and until digital processing, been preeminently a process of double negatives: photographing already photographed negative prints.

Why, then, is the theorization of photography so silent on this particular score? Not only silent, but positively disavowing, as in Barthes's defiant claim in *Camera Lucida* that it "is a mistake to associate Photography, by reason of its technical origins, with the notion of a dark passage (*camera obscura*). It is *camera lucida* that we should say (such was the name of that apparatus, anterior to Photography, which permitted drawing an object through a prism, one eye on the model, the other on the paper)."[90] Capitalizing the process, idealizing it, at the same time that he resituates its essence in a pre-mechanical device (anterior even to Daguerre's "sun writing" apparatus), Barthes is at least open in his repudiation of the "technical origins" that dictate a detour through the darkroom. Other photographic theorists have been less confessional. Even Walter Benjamin, so sensitive to the material effects of the medium, was captivated by the demystificatory effect of photographic reproduction on the "aura" of the traditional work of art to the extent that he overlooked the singular aura of that material basis of photographic reproduction itself—the negative, which he nowhere mentions. Rosalind Krauss, who likes to speak of the photograph as indexical icon—"Every photograph is the result of a physical imprint transferred by light reflections onto a sensitive surface. The photograph is thus a type of icon, or visual likeness, which bears an indexical relationship to its object"—symptomatically represses the vital point that the "object" every positive print "relates to" iconically is not the profilmic one, but the negative print itself; she mentions negatives only in relation to a certain trend in Surrealist photo-practice.[91] Going back to Bazin's case for photographic realism, recall his insistence that "For the first time, between the originating object and its reproduction there intervenes only the instrumentality of a nonliving agent. For the first time, an image of the world is formed automatically, without the creative intervention of man."[92] We need only to hint here that, in the post-Talbot universe, the necessary intervention of re-photographing the negative plate, in carefully controlled conditions, and according to specific criteria about scale, size, and number, is anything but "automatic" in that naïve sense. Stanley Cavell's development of

---

[90] Roland Barthes, *Camera Lucida*, trans. Richard Howard (London: Vintage, 2000), 106.

[91] Rosalind Krauss, *The Originality of the Avant-Garde and Other Myths* (Cambridge, MA: MIT Press, 1986), 203, 101.

[92] André Bazin, *What is Cinema?* Vol. 1, trans. High Gray (Berkeley, CA & Los Angeles: University of California Press, 1968), 13.

Bazin's ontology into a claim that photography is a species of "automatic world projection" merely perpetuates a willed ignorance of the highly skilled technical knowledge and fixed capital required to transform any "snapped" exposure into a photograph proper.[93] Even in D. N. Rodowick's digital-era work, photography is still presented as *"a process of mechanically recording an image through the automatic registration of reflected light on a photosensitive surface. This image is analogical, defined as a transformation of substance isomorphic with the originating image regardless of scale."*[94]

In all these cases and many others, there is a systematic avoidance of the messy duplication, the double negation of almost all photographic "lucidity" to date: the reality that every positive print we view has been exposed *only* to the light reflected off a negative plate, which is in turn the *only* isomorphic record of the "originating image" as such. Or, to put this another way, the "time" preserved in any positive photographic image (like the time of the *récit*) is implicitly and essentially double: there is the time of the "original" exposure, and the time of the secondary exposure to the negative "original." Two times of light, only the latter of which is properly "there" in the positive print; the record of the first exposure, typically stored away in photographic archives, rarely sees the light of day, and even then usually only to be re-photographed. The photograph's uncanny rapprochement of temporal positions (that of our viewing of it, and that of the exposure) is effectively haunted by another, invisible, unmentionable moment—one that literally *is* the "past" moment we witness (exposure to the negative print) but which we spontaneously push back into the originating exposure to the pro-filmic object, and forget about in its unromantic intermediary technicality. This is the vanishing mediator par excellence, this re-photographing of the negative plate, without which there can be no positive image at all, but which appears never to have provoked a single photographic theorist or critic into elaborating as a true source of photographic meaning. For unlike the moment at which the photochemical surface of film is exposed to the light reflected off a pro-filmic scene, this latter moment is effectively an "any-moment-whatever"—an undeterminable instant in a photographic studio, not subject to all the random contingency of a location shoot, but subject to a rigorous quality control. No wonder it vanishes from cognition, since it has no apparent determinacy in space or time; it appears to thought as sheerly abstract and general—whereas it is precisely the very condition of what we see. Which is why, for all his forceful adaptation of the Derridean "supplement" to insert the photographic record within "a dynamic play of differences … that refuses to settle

---

[93] Stanley Cavell, *The World Viewed: Reflections on the Ontology of Film* (Cambridge, MA: Harvard University Press, 1979), 72.

[94] D. N. Rodowick, *The Virtual Life of Film* (Cambridge, MA: Harvard University Press, 2007), 31; emphasis in original.

at any of the available poles of identification," Geoffrey Batchen, too, misses the most radical opportunity offered by the medium itself to do precisely that.[95]

In this collective disavowal of the "negation of the negation," there is a more symptomatic problem at stake, one with tenacious links to an anti-Hegelian disposition in the humanities that would prefer not to think in the outrageous figures and tropologies of the dialectic—even when the "technical origins" of a whole subsector of cultural practice seemed to recommend no method more thoroughly. It is such an assumption that has tacitly guided our current exploration of photographic figures in the mature fiction of William Faulkner, since as we have seen, that fiction allows us to glimpse the extraordinary social logic of photography as a process of "positive" racial figuration via a technique of double negation—as if, in Faulkner's house of fiction in the 1930s, there had to be reserved a special chamber, a darkroom or Dark House, in which to fix the negative print of American race relations and re-photograph it; and as if the compulsive logic of the fiction was to advert to this darkroom above all else, never to disavow what it meant to see "black" as the negative of "white" and vice versa. We have seen just how lively the metaphor of photographic negation is in this literary space, above all in *Absalom, Absalom!*, which, perhaps more than any other text in history, subjects its law of narrative articulation to a Hegelian amphibology of tropes, clustering around the "dark passage" of the *camera obscura*—a darkroom become a dark house, raised by dark hands to enframe a white *imago*, which will come undone thanks to the material recrudescence of the black trace of its first exposure to the fortunes of propagation.

But now we need to ponder the ultimate relation of that figural amphibology and double negation to the media history we have been proposing throughout, and to the specific destiny of literature—the medium of printed matter—within it. How does the negative plate, which I now propose as the figurative kernel of the colonel's transfigured romance, inform that broader historical narrative, and affect the manner in which the depleted romance materials conduct their affective charge into a modern media ecology? In Faulkner's novels of this period, prior to *Absalom, Absalom!*, we detect traces of the photo-aesthetic as it develops into something—a metaphor, a vortex of transpositions—capable of connecting with Quentin's figure (in *The Sound and the Fury*) of the racial "obverse reflection" and saying something never before thought about the crucible of race in the United States. I will pursue here a tentative hypothesis that Quentin's figure of the "obverse reflection" was to cross-pollinate with the evolving figure of photography's negative "hauntology" in such a way as to germinate an utterly unique and complex figure of racial "development" as such. In order to observe this complex figure in its emergence, we need only return to the oddly broken

---

[95] Geoffrey Batchen, *Burning with Desire: The Conception of Photography* (Cambridge, MA: MIT Press, 1999), 202.

narrative surface of the text of *Light in August*, and to the "unreconstructible" reasons behind Joe Christmas's final appearance at the door of the Reverend Hightower. When Joe Christmas stands naked in the oncoming glare of a pair of automobile headlamps on the night before his murder of Joanna Burden, and watches "his body grow white out of the darkness like a Kodak print emerging from the liquid,"[96] it is already clear that his racial ambivalence and ambiguity is being troped photographically, and in the most explicit terms. This apparent racial "whiteness," so unequivocal in narrative statement, is troubled figurally by its passage through the "double negation" of photographic development, for any print "emerging from the liquid" of a stop bath or a fixer is, first of all, a negative print—that is, a print in which white is seen as black, black as white. It is this print that must then be "bleached" to remove the developed negative image from the film, revealing a latent positive image that is then printed through a second exposure to light, and a second developer. What Christmas sees when he looks down at his own whiteness is then, undecidably, either of these two self-negating moments. Either his body is black and prints itself negatively as white, or it is white and appears as such in the image after the "bleaching" and re-development of a negative print. The photographic figure has meshed perfectly with the very tortured racial uncertainty of Christmas's reflections; it is itself an "obverse reflection" of the truth that cannot appear unmediated.

And that series of reflections must, in some further mediated capacity, prepare us for the otherwise anomalous fact that the hand-painted sign advertising the Reverend Hightower's commercial activities from home reads: "Art Lessons/Handpainted Xmas & Anniversary Cards/Photographs Developed."[97] Nowhere does this hint attain to any further explicit embellishment; it appears as a possibly random "effect of the real," unless we rouse ourselves to connect the latent dots and understand that nothing other than this public service of photographic development is what yields the deeper figural logic behind Christmas's ultimate arrival at this particular Jefferson door. For this is the house in which the ultimate inscription of the Christmas body into a racial absolute will be violently made, via knife-blade and outrage. It is where that indeterminate "whiteness" of his denuded body is redeveloped into a Kodak "darkness" that will know no further amphibology: the obverse of the obverse reflection is a destiny in race in which, much as Quentin's ruminations are haunted by the same trope, castration deals the final hand. The hand that "develops" Christmas into a fixed racial image—Percy Grimm's—is also the hand that strips him of the very outrageous "white" member that emerges into salient relief in the light of the onrushing automobile headlamps: "He looked straight into the headlights as it shot past. From it a woman's shrill voice flew back,

---

[96] Faulkner, *Light in August*, in *Novels 1930–1935*, 478.
[97] Faulkner, *Light in August*, 440.

shrieking. 'White bastards!' he shouted, 'That's not the first of your bitches that ever saw .'" (478). The unstable and unvoiced image of the black/white phallus as such, the locus of every anxiety raised in the novel, remains photographically reversible until the very moment that it is cut away, so that "from out the slashed garments about his hips and loins the pent black blood seemed to rush like a released breath" (743). Blackness ("black blood") is finally "forced" as the inner truth of an image cut short in its infinite tropological redevelopment, from white to black and back again, by the Grimm hand of a pre-emptive fate. "Finally," as an entry on photographic development puts it, "the film is fixed, washed, dried and cut."[98]

Faulkner's emergent intuition that racial salience in the United States, and perhaps specifically in the South, is less a cut-and-dried phenomenon than a reversible and inherently dialectical process or development, is, I think, clarified by his partial adaptation of a photographic figure to its representation in *Light in August*. Consider, too, the remarkable build-up to Christmas's murder of Joanna Burden, his lover, while he reels on the day after his night-time "exposure" as a Kodak print, a build-up that keeps insisting on the social life of "pictures," reified images on paper and celluloid, that marks the stations of his cross. He first reads a magazine "of that type whose covers bear either pictures of young women in underclothes or pictures of men in the act of shooting one another with pistols." (479–80) Later, "at seven o'clock," he passes "people, white and black, going toward the square and the picture show" (482). Still later (but actually earlier) in a flashback concerning Joe's approach to a nocturnal rendezvous on horseback, we read this: "It—the horse and the rider—had a strange, dreamy effect, like a moving picture in slow motion as it galloped steady and flagging up the street and toward the old corner where he used to wait, less urgent perhaps but not less eager, and more young" (553). And, upon arriving at his destination, and being called a "Beale Street Playboy," the narrator divagates: "Beale Street, that three or four Memphis city blocks in comparison with which Harlem is a movie set" (556). There is little question that, from the moment he is represented as a Kodak print, Joe is haunted by figures of photography and the mass-mediation of imagetexts, pinioned by an industrial conscription of his image in sensational and lurid forms. "Developed" on the one hand by this industrialized hall of mirrors, and on the other by the Grimm hand of racial overdetermination, Joe meanwhile absorbs back into his self-representation the full panoply of these mediated spectral accompaniments. In a novel that cannot stabilize its restless romantic genealogy without recourse to figures of, and transposed devices from, the newer media ecology, this photographic *mise en abyme* is obliged to stand for "self-consciousness" as such: so that we end up with a prose of the self (an

---

[98] http://en.wikipedia.org/wiki/Photographic_processing.

objectivized "stream of consciousness") mediated through the stuttering and unfluid concatenation of still images, "like a moving picture in slow motion," in which the once-buried photogram is now discernible and a "dreamy effect" of temporal pixelation steals over the naturalistic landscape—yet another anarchronistic affect of romance discharged atemporally from within the prose of the mechanized world.[99]

At any rate, it now seems timely to establish the insistent tropological association of the negative plate with the notion of genetic transmission in *Absalom* as a making of miniature replicas, iconic tokens of the selfsame Sutpen facial pattern. His "face exactly like the [driver] negro's save for the teeth" (18), his two legitimate children "two replicas of his face in miniature" (16), Clytie and Judith, "the two Sutpen faces [...] looking down through the square entrance to the loft" (24), and so on. The Sutpen face is threaded throughout the text, layered on any number of bodies (male or female, black or white). Sutpen's genetic "factor" prints off an indefinite number of casts in the flesh and skin of others—exactly the way a negative plate provides for the off-printing of innumerable miniature icons, "emerging," as it were, "in grimacing and attitudinal miniature from stinking trays in a celibate and stygian cell lighted by a red lamp."[100] The only exception to this iron rule of photogenetic transmission is, of course, Bon himself, whose visage is never described and already so innately photographic that nobody thinks to call it a Sutpen. He is the photogenetic trace become hyperreal, with all the ontological precarity of the photogram in the filmstrip, orphaned to the limitless succession of sheer temporal becoming conceived of in a "snapshot view of transition":[101] "other children had been made by fathers and mothers where he had been created new when he began to remember, new again when he came to the point where his carcass quit being a baby and became a boy, new again when he quit being a boy and became a man" (252). Bon is always *just that much different* in each successive recasting, as Gertrude Stein would say of the photographic ontology of her modern *écriture*. Declaring her literary aesthetic to be in line with the "period of the cinema and series production," Stein insisted that just as in a motion picture "no two pictures are exactly alike each one is just that much different than the one before," her prose involved "no repetition," since each sentence would begin again the presentation of a topic, a person, who was perpetually "just that much different from" the way it was and will be.[102] So it is with Charles Bon.

---

[99] Here I take inspiration from the method of Garrett Stewart's pioneering analyses in *Between Film and Screen: Modernism and Photo-Synthesis* (Chicago: University of Chicago Press, 1996).

[100] Faulkner, *Pylon*, in *Novels 1930--1935*, 933.

[101] Henri Bergson, *Creative Evolution* (New York: Dover, 1998), 302.

[102] Gertrude Stein, "Portraits and Repetition," in *Gertrude Stein: Writings 1934-1946* (New York: The Library of America, 1998), 294-95.

In this he is much like his mistress, who

> would not grow from one metamorphosis—dissolution or adultery—to the next carrying along with her all the old accumulated rubbish-years which we call memory, the recognizable I, but changing from phase to phase ... carrying nothing of what was into what is, leaving nothing of what is behind but eliding complete and intact and unresisting into the next avatar as the overblown rose or magnolia elides from one rich June to the next, leaving no bones, no substance (162–63).

Which leaves their son, Charles Etienne Saint-Valery Bon, to clinch the cinematic metaphorization very precisely indeed:

> there followed something like a year composed of a succession of periods of utter immobility like a broken cinema film, which the white-colored man who had married her spent on his back recovering from the mauling he had received [...], broken by other periods, intervals, of furious and incomprehensible and apparently reasonless moving, progression—a maelstrom of faces and bodies through which the man thrust (170–71).

The Bon family group portrait is unthinkable within the terms of wet plate photography; the photogenetics have leapfrogged into a cinematic dispensation so radical that it literally dissociates each member's "self" into so many immobile photograms strung together on what Bergson called "a becoming, abstract, uniform and invisible, situated at the back of the apparatus of knowledge, in order to imitate what there is that is characteristic in this becoming itself."[103]

Charles Bon's face is never "seen" in the prose other than as an undescribed photographic image, but on Shreve's account, when Bon himself sees a Sutpen face, he half-claims it as his own. Henry's appearance at Ole Miss provokes the following speculated interior speech: "one part of him said *My brow my skull my jaw my hands* and the other said *Wait*" (258). Shortly thereafter, his reflection that this common genetic factor is something that Henry "*could see in my face in his turn if he but knew to look*" is replaced by another one: "*there, just behind a little, obscured a little by that alien blood whose admixing was necessary in order that he exist is the face of the man who shaped us both out of that blind chancy darkness which we call the future*" (261). But Shreve's innocence of the trope of photogenetics renders this quaint. Rather, what this hypothetical first

---

[103] Henri Bergson, *Creative Evolution*, 306.

encounter must trigger for us is a dawning awareness that the "blind chancy darkness" out of which the Sutpen face is cast, and re-cast, is Bon's *own* suppressed image—the negative plate he represents. Child as father to the man, and grandfather to the second son conceived as his positive print: behind Henry and Sutpen both is this negative ur-image in starkest retrograde. Bon, the negative plate, cannot for that reason be framed within the family portrait of the clan whose dynastic shape he (negatively) convokes. Confronting the paternal image of which he is supposed, narratively, to have been just one of many off-prints, he at last "saw face to face the man who might be his father, and nothing happened—no shock, no hot communicated flesh that speech would have been too slow even to impede—nothing" (264). A photogenetic ontology is incapable of communicating through flesh. Begotten as he is upon the supercharged photographic allure of a "white slender arm raised" in the imaginary musket-flash and cane-fire of a Haitian sugar rebellion, Bon's melodramatic moment of recognition fizzles out in the generalized denial of the negative plate. Romance scenographies are torn and scattered by the logic of the "broken cinema film."

It is symptomatic in this regard that our first introduction to the photographic trope in the novel concerns a Sutpen family portrait, "the four of them arranged into the conventional family group of the period, with formal and lifeless decorum, and seen now as the fading and ancient photograph itself would have been seen" (10–11); and that, to close off the trope's abundant transformative work in the intervening pages, its last appearance should concern, again, a Sutpen family portrait:

> Not two of them in a New England college sitting-room but one in a Mississippi library sixty years ago, with holly and mistletoe in vases on the mantel or thrust behind, crowning and garlanding with the season and time the pictures on the walls, and a sprig or two decorating the photograph, the group—mother and two children—on the desk behind which the father sat when the son entered. (243)

With Father cropped from the frame and deposited in palpable patriarchal plenitude behind the table on which the proprietary picture of his all-white dependents now sits framed and garlanded, the son (Henry) will "recall later how he had seen through the window beyond his father's head the sister and the lover in the garden" (243)—thereby seeing simultaneously his own photographic image alongside his sister, and his "negative plate" (Bon) just beyond the glass window and the Sutpen face, doing to Judith what he most wants to do himself, just as the fateful news of their genetic complication is finally delivered. But if the first photograph is a projection of the "object voice" of Rosa sitting in her shuttered dark room, this last one is the projection of a confabulation in a darkened New England sitting-room, where "two of them" have been melded into "one" and displaced into a "Mississippi library" which, like Jay Gatsby's, is more about the photographic "show" of cultural sophistication than the actual consumption of literature. Quentin and Shreve are themselves subsumed within a photographic logic and filiated to the Sutpen ur-image who is not Sutpen but Bon himself.[104] Freud wrote with fascination of the "procedure by means of which [Francis] Galton produced family portraits: namely by projecting two images on to a single plate, so that certain features common to both are emphasized, while those which fail to fit in with on another cancel one another out and are indistinct in the picture."[105] So here, the Harvard roommates are superimposed onto a single plate, which notoriously allows them, in the time-traveling dimension of a narrativity they have in turn contracted from Rosa Coldfield, to become Henry and Bon interchangeably (see Fig. 4.1).

Even if he will never carry it out, it is to Quentin, ultimately, that the task must fall of synthesizing the photo-syntheses and committing to paper, to print, his reconstruction out of the now innumerable affect-photographs of the story that has been entrusted to him. The "commonwealth" or verbal "barracks" that he started as has become a photo gallery or, better, composite Sutpen portrait, of which the proto-eugenicist Galton had written: "A composite portrait represents the picture that would rise before the mind's eye of a man who had the gift of pictorial imagination in an exalted degree. But the imaginative power even of the highest artists is far from precise, and is so apt to be biased by special cases that may have struck their fancies, that no two artists agree in any of their typical forms" (134). Quentin's dilemma, and proposed technical salvation, could not more starkly have been expressed.

On the other hand, a corollary development of this practice in the early twentieth century is suggestive of Quentin's very self-image as a "barracks," since Stanislav Ignacy Witkiewicz's (aka Witkacy's) well-known photograph *Multiple Self-Portrait*, using multiple exposures of his own image on a single plate, is perhaps the most striking single illustration of that figure (see Fig. 4.2).

---

[104] Here I cannot resist speculating that the infamous eight-month delay in Sutpen's return to the Hundred after Bon's burial might well be construed as his "negative" or "retrograde" pregnancy, or un-gestation, with the image that, in dialectical truth, had rather brought about his own patriarchal identity and image in the world.

[105] Sigmund Freud, *The Interpretation of Dreams*, trans. James Strachey, Penguin Freud Library, Vol. 4 (London: Penguin, 1991), 400. Galton himself put it this way: "Those of [the composite's] outlines are sharpest and darkest that are common to the largest number of the components; the purely individual peculiarities leave little or no visible trace." Francis Galton, "Composite Portraits, made by combining those of many different persons into a single resultant figure," *Journal of the Anthropological Institute of Great Britain and Ireland* 8 (1879), 134.

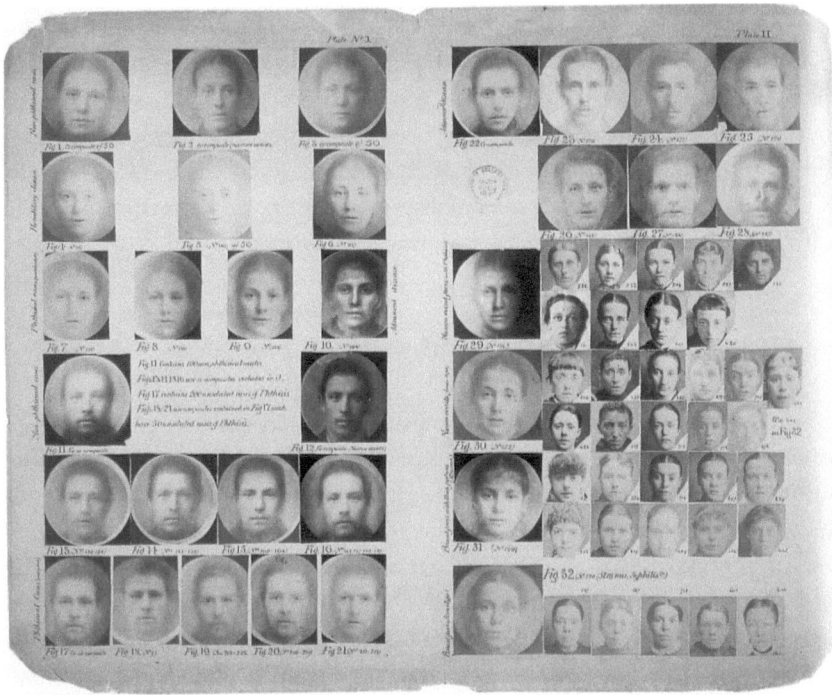

Figure 4.1 Francis Galton, «Composite-Fotografie». © Francis Galton. Source: Der Neue Mensch. Obsessionen des 20. Jahrhunderts, hrsg. von Nicola Lepp/Martin Roth/Klaus Vogel, Katalog zur Ausstellung im Deutschen Hygiene-Museum Dresden vom 22. April bis 8. August 1999, Ostfildern/Ruit 1999, S. 124.

Figure 4.2 Stanislav Ignacy Witkiewicz, *Multiple Self-Portrait in Mirrors* (1915–17). Source: Stanisław Ignacy Witkiewicz—Portret wielokrotny—Google Art Project.jpg.

What we have learned in the meantime is that the composite family portrait that Quentin is charged with putting into literary form has, at its ontogenetic root, a negative plate, whose "darkest" commonalty "to the largest number of the components" assumes the name of Charles Bon. If indeed he enjoys the "gift of pictorial imagination in an exalted degree," Quentin will nevertheless have to learn how to enact its passage through the negative plate.

Quentin Compson, *scriptor*

It is good to remind ourselves of Quentin's status in the text of *Absalom*, as privileged writer-to-be, the figure entrusted with the hard task of formal resolution; as Faulkner himself put it, "Quentin Compson, of Sound & Fury, tells it, or ties it together."[106] How can we begin to draw to a close our discussion of what is at stake in this monumental act of transmission from one, exhausted media paradigm (that of literature's monopoly in romance) to another, ascendant cinematic one, and thereby make allegorical sense of Quentin's quest to tie it all together in prose? We have seen how the romance "donor" of the voluminous material laces it with cryptic, proleptic signs of its *"blind chancy darkness"* in a media future predicated on photography; and we have seen how Quentin "exposes" it as so many ghostly images projected on a glass plate or wall. But it surely cannot be supposed that all of Rosa's absurdly overripe narration in the form of the *récit* could somehow be gathered up into a new media form that would make "hearing it" redundant. If "listening reneges," *hearing persists*, alongside the "silent" moving images cast upon the glass plate of a proto-cinematic new century's audition. And indeed, the very modernism of the text in our hands turns upon this simultaneous, and deeply anachronistic, act of synchronization.

Some methodological light can be shed by Roland Barthes's concept of the "post-meaning": "It is not a question of recovering a pre-meaning, an origin of the world, of facts, anterior to meaning, but rather to imagine a post-meaning: one must traverse, as though the length of an initiatic way, the whole meaning, in order to extenuate it, to exempt it."[107] What I am reaching for is a sense of Quentin's authorial responsibilities that correlates to this account of an exhaustive and ineluctable "traversal" of romance, resulting in in an "extenuation" of its very form in some new, imaginary "post-meaning." Quentin is not going back before Rosa's narration; he is not in quest of worldly origins. Rather, he wants to create an exemption of its materials, an obtuse narratological metalepsis, such that what Genette calls that figure's "deliberate transgression of the threshold of embedding" occurs at a point

---

[106] Faulkner, *Selected Letters*, 78.
[107] Roland Barthes, *Roland Barthes*, trans. Richard Howard (New York: Hill and Wang, 2010), 87.

where media boundaries are also transgressed.[108] Some further specification of this problem can be attained through reference to Barthes's account of the "third meaning" that he finds himself obliged to read off the photographic stills of Eisenstein films: a third order of sense reducible neither to the immediate denotational content of the image nor to its conscription within the symbolic or "obvious meaning" created by narrative ordering. The so-called third meaning intrudes into this closed semiotic space, but only once the full plenitude of signifier and signified has been traversed. Barthes's language is temporally exact: "Is that all? No, for I still cannot detach myself from the image. I read, I receive (and probably even first and foremost) a third meaning—evident, erratic, obstinate."[109] This unwonted supplement, "that my intellection cannot succeed in absorbing," "appears to extend outside culture, knowledge, information" (54–55), which is to say, *beyond the horizon of a given discourse network*. Such an obtuse supplement appears, as it were, at the very limits posed by a system of media, and obtrudes into that *"blind chancy darkness"* where it dissolves and another system assumes cultural hegemony.

It is crucial, then, that Rosa should lard her garish tale with photographic figures, and that her belated commentator Mr. Compson should follow suit, since photography was, historically, the means of technical reproducibility that both seemed to confirm and extend the romance hallucinogen of the Goethean discourse network, and which heralded the radically mechanical and "post-human" media system of the twentieth century. Photography, that is, functioned simultaneously as an extension of the world of romance (recall Talbot's romantic apologia for a method of inscription that essentially required no machinery) and as its death-knell. For a thinker like Kittler, the decisive media revolution took place decades after the photograph first stole a fugitive march on literature's storage monopoly, only once the 1880s and 1890s had consolidated phonography, typography, and the cinema as the emblematic Edisonian media constellation of the new century. But by that time photography had already become an ambivalent medium straddling both regimes of sense, common to both and yet somehow native to neither. There is thus a kind of "obtuse" angle specific to photography, in regard to both of the dominant discourse networks that crystallized on either side of its invention and popularization. It belongs equally to the world of Tennyson, Dickinson, and their obscure contemporary Rosa Coldfield as it does to the world of Quentin and Shreve's Harvard and the Hollywood writers' pens of 1935.

In that latter regard, it pays to recall Joseph Urgo's argument that "Quentin and Shreve, as collaborators, must have originated [in Faulkner's] successful record as an employee in the Hollywood studio system."[110] Since our task is to

---

[108] Gérard Genette, *Narrative Discourse Revisited*, trans Jane E. Lewin (Ithaca, NY: Cornell University Press, 1988), 88.
[109] Roland Barthes, *Image Music Text*, trans. Stephen Heath (New York: Hill and Wang, 1978), 53.
[110] Joseph Urgo, "*Absalom, Absalom!*: The Movie," *American Literature* 62.1 (March 1990), 56.

specify the nature of Quentin's status as writer, this argument has a compelling logic to it. The fact that the various narrative points of view on offer in *Absalom* "are folded over one another to provide a single, recognizable text, or series of pictures, *by two of the narrators themselves*" (59), surely raises more than a subliminal relationship to that industrial scene of collaborative screenwriting in which Faulkner was recurrently situated throughout the writing of *Absalom* (and which would be reimagined symptomatically in Hollywood's self-reflections, from *Sunset Boulevard* (1950) and *In a Lonely Place* (1950) to *Singin' in the Rain* (1952) and down to *Barton Fink* (1991), in which Faulkner's own avatar is so crudely manhandled as to suggest that Meta Carpenter wrote all of his screenplays and novels during the Hollywood sojourn). Urgo is bold enough in his hypothesis to have forced the issue: Quentin oversteps the bounds of magazine writing altogether, since he is already committed to a "potential visual production" whose "only [conceivable] medium" is film itself (60). This willful anachronism, in which 1935 and 1909 form a strange loop, certainly helps to clarify why it is that Rosa's "long-elapsed periods of time are conveyed in an instant" in Quentin's visual imagination, his screenwriter's "filmic images communicating instantaneously what a 'printed tale' would take much longer to evoke" (60). Our own argument, meanwhile, has sought to slow down this rush to the cinematic and uncover a substratum of photographic tropes in which the "continuous, gliding, almost hallucinatory effect of true slow motion photography" that Alan Spiegel once detected in Faulkner's prose is mortified and disarticulated into its constitutive motor ataxia.[111] Further, we have contrived to demonstrate that the resultant "image-text" has as much to do with the goat-glanding of early sound cinema as it does with the scene of writing itself. The point remains valid that, as Peter Lurie has put it in another idiom, the "acceding of speech to the visual" in Rosa's monologue for Quentin gives rise to "visual images or [. . .] shadows endowed with motion" that can scarcely be disentangled from "certain properties or effects of film."[112] If, however, Quentin is indeed anachronistically engaged in the process of conjuring a film production from a narrative that cannot be listened to, it still remains to be decided what the photographic trace, and its negative plate, might have to say about this screen adaptation internal to the narrative itself, and what speech's accession to visuality here might have to teach us about the persistence of romance in modernity. For, following Garrett Stewart, it is simply not enough to suggest that literature has gone the way of cinema, when cinema itself persistently enacts its material infrastructure in the photogrammic trace and the stutterings of synchronization.[113] What matters is

---

[111] Alan Spiegel, *Fiction and the Camera Eye: Visual Consciousness in Film and the Modern Novel* (Charlottesburg, VA: University Press of Virginia, 1976), 119.

[112] Peter Lurie, *Vision's Immanence: Faulkner, Film, and the Popular Imagination* (Baltimore: Johns Hopkins University Press, 2004), 118, 115.

[113] See, again, Stewart, *Between Film and Screen*.

to show how literature might have learned from cinema to expose its own mediatic unconscious in a network of textual signs that do for the novel what the photogram does for filmic motion, what the negative plate does for the photograph, and what the object voice does for both.

It makes sense, then, to reconsider Quentin's challenge from the direction of that other form contemporary to *Absalom*'s construction, cinema's other, the extended photo-essay, of which we have already said that its "ethics of form" was "imposed on the reader/viewer in the structural division of the photos and text. Our labor as beholders is as divided as that of Agee and Evans, and we find ourselves drawn, as they were, into a vortex of collaboration and resistance."[114] This seems as useful a point of comparison as the scene of Hollywood screenwriting, since here the complex "collaboration" is between text and picture per se, as well as between that dialectical interanimation and our own hermeneutic labors as readers. Given that Quentin and Shreve are the "readers," or hearers-without-listening, who react to the innermost tension between *récit* and affect in Rosa's narration by improvising an "ethics of form" of their own that contrives to get it right, this critical analogue in Agee and Evans (which took its own inspiration from Faulkner himself) is, if anything, more useful than the studio writers' pen. And here we can attempt a methodological fusion of the two multimedia analogies that work to relocate our critical attentions to 1935, rather than 1909 or 1864, as the true horizon of sense explored in *Absalom*'s figural economy. For it seems productive to think in unison the distinct roles of the photographic still image in sound cinema and the photographic essay, to see what that double exposure might have to offer an account of this great novel's mediatic unconscious.

It is indicative in this respect to recall Barthes's "third meaning," derived from sustained acts of attention to still frame photographs enlarged from the filmstrips of two Eisenstein films (that same Eisenstein whose directorial eye was to have passed over Faulkner's immediately contemporary treatment of *Sutter's Gold*, and whom Faulkner was to have evoked in his vision of American industrial hell, in "Wild Palms": "a scene like something out of an Eisenstein Dante"[115]). Once plucked from the automatic flow of cinema's illusory movement images, these reified photograms do something that they cannot achieve from within their functional role as "vanishing mediators" in the 24-frames-per-second exposure rate of the filmstrip. For in them it is suddenly possible to discern, not a literal, nor even a connotational value or sense, but "something *touching* . . . or *sensitive*"; which is to say that the enlarged photogram carries in it, against the grain of denotation and symbolization, an excessive affective charge, "a certain emotion," says Barthes, and "such emotion is never sticky,

---

[114] W. J. T. Mitchell, *Picture Theory*, 300.
[115] Faulkner, *If I Forget Thee, Jerusalem*, in *Novels 1936–1940*, 621.

it is an emotion which simply *designates* what one loves, what one wants to defend: an emotion-value, an evaluation."[116] At which point it seems advised to jump-cut to that other contemporary photo-value, which we specified in relation to Denning's account of the documentary aesthetic of the 1930s: "less a triumph of realism than a sign of the failures of narrative imagination."[117] The photograph, as deployed by Bourke-White or Agee and Evans, was a visual supplement to that faltering of narrative imagination in the midst of a crippling social crisis; it supplied the missing architectonic, the ingredient without which there was no story to tell, since it communicated in a hot instant exactly what the narrative text could not supply, namely (and precisely) "an emotion which simply *designates* what one loves, what one wants to defend: an emotion-value, an evaluation." And this permits us to rejoin our earlier discussion of Jameson's theory of affect as what cancels the narrative temporality of the *récit* and substitutes for that "faltering narrative imagination" of romance a visual and well-nigh photographic punctum: "the realm of the visual begins to separate from that of the verbal and conceptual and to float away in a new kind of autonomy. Precisely this autonomy will create the space for affect."[118] Three theoretical events, directly attending to the moment at which something in the nature of a "timeless" photographic intensity emerges to forestall or displace a "faltering" or suspended narrativity, and all of which converge on affectivity, or "an emotion-value" that cannot be reduced to words, but which is precisely what the words desire most ardently to attain.

It all accords with Rancière's analysis of the "aesthetic regime" of modernity in terms of an epochal sundering of the "literary" authority classically bestowed upon the visual arts, from those arts themselves, now free to engage any-space-whatever on their own terms. "The power of words is no longer the model that pictorial representation must take as its norm. It is the power that hollows out the representative surface to make the manifestation of pictorial expressiveness appear on it."[119] In this transformational context, words (romance, poetry) have lost their legislative sway over the rights of the image, and henceforth rather "amend the surface by causing another subject to appear under the representative subject" (76). A new logic of conjoining words and images arises. Here we are putting into theoretical focus a distended moment in cultural and literary history, during which poetic narrative can no longer totalize, or legislate the distribution of the sensible. New media have sapped literature of both visual and vocal essences, leaving it the options of either mechanically marking time

---

[116] Barthes, *Image Music Text*, 59.

[117] Denning, *The Cultural Front*, 119.

[118] Jameson, *Antinomies of Realism*, 55.

[119] Jacques Rancière, *The Future of the Image*, trans. Gregory Elliott (London & New York: Verso, 2009), 76.

or intervening in the new regime of sense by "becoming text" or typescript, and "hollowing out the representative surface" it once filled in with hallucinations of plenitude. It is this textual excavation, this deliberative faltering of narrative discourse on its own ground, that allows for "pictorial expressiveness" to appear in a new modality—as affect, intensity, modernism.

Twin sistered

At the organizational center of the novel's nine chapters is a chapter almost entirely presented in italics, a massively sustained stretch of narrative prose that terminates in the refrain "But Quentin was not listening" (142), before the chapter abruptly ends and we are transported to Harvard. The transition out of the italicized immanence that defines this unique chapter involves a brief return to its central knot, "something which he [Quentin] could not pass," namely, "that door, the running feet on the stairs beyond it almost a continuation of the faint shot, the two women, the negress and the white girl in her underthings" (142). It is the greatest moment of romantic catharsis in the whole Sutpen story, but which the witness-narrator herself had signally failed to flesh out—Henry's boudoir confession of murder to his now "widowed" sister over Bon's bloodied corpse, before he flees to parts unknown. Quentin cannot "pass it" because he has, at last, contracted the virus of romance. His desire to "see" the scene that was not seen is so intense that he writes it himself: the two siblings, of "a terrific, an almost unbearable similarity, speaking to one another in short brief staccato sentences like slaps, as if they stood breast to breast striking one another in turn," in italics of his own:

> *Now you cant marry him.*
> *Why cant I marry him?*
> *Because he's dead.*
> *Dead?*
> *Yes. I killed him.* (143)

As a prefiguration of the remainder of the novel's narrative method—the speculative filling in of gaps in the romance plot—the moment is precise, and precisely located. For what it concludes is, in fact, the novel's most extraordinary departure from the very aesthetic ideology that Rosa is supposed to embody; what it shows is that Quentin's "not listening" has taken a new path, away from its passive ability to conjure photographs from the object voice, and towards an active and replenished narrative imagination. Quentin (and Shreve) can assume control from this point on, because there has been an effective transference, and perhaps even a chiasmic reversal of roles.

What first detains us at a formal level is the strange discursive texture of the lengthy italicized text that precedes this dramatic rupture and symbolic tearing away from the "Aunt's" verbal teat. John Matthews is precise in his characterization of this most exhausting of all the book's narrative materials: it is "as if we're overhearing Quentin's mental recapitulation of what Rosa has said to him."[120] Noel Polk and Joseph Urgo take that point a little further—"The italics may [...] suggest that the content of the monologue represents Quentin's reconstruction, conscious or unconscious, of all that he has heard from various sources," engaging in a tactic of narrative anachronism including "sexually specific language" and a "very twentieth-century attempt to understand Rosa in psychoanalytical terms."[121] Their impression that "Quentin throughout is visualizing what Rosa describes rather than hearing or processing each individual word" (57) would, if true, certainly make of this chapter the central exhibit in the novel's to-and-fro pulses of energy between verbal narration and visual hypostases, before the formal break of this "co-equality" at its conclusion and the resumption of a more purely narrative mode. For argument's sake, then, we will adopt the hypothesis that the italics of this central chapter designate a zone of narratological ambivalence that can best be characterized as a "double exposure" or "composite portrait" of two generationally distinct storytellers, now equally invested in the material's fortunes; quite unlike the dramatic separation of father and son in the preceding few chapters, and of Quentin and Shreve in the book's second half—who although they certainly do blur (and blur into Mr. Compson as well), nevertheless remain characterologically distinct in a manner that cannot be claimed for Chapter Five's startling compaction of "Quentin-Rosa."

What might this entail? We can insist at once that it has something to do with "that door" as a significant point of resistance within the romance topology itself. The entire chapter hinges on "that door's" closure and the consequent inaccessibility and apocryphal status of any scene that might have taken place behind it. Rosa's privileged narratological status as first-hand witness of the events is compromised just at the very point where it ought most decisively to have been vindicated: she arrives too late to prevent the death of Bon, and (curiously) "too soon" to exonerate herself from the ultimate crisis of the dynastic plot (112), without for all that directly witnessing any of its crucial moments. And it is clear that this temporally paradoxical "too soon" that will graft her, not just as aunt but as potential mother-in-law, onto the accursed Sutpen stock is related spatially to "that door" that shuts her out from the incident-heavy "stream of event." The door functions metaphorically as the emblem of what is

---

[120] John T. Matthews, *William Faulkner: Seeing Through the South* (Chichester: Wiley-Blackwell, 2009), 177.

[121] Noel Polk and Joseph Urgo, *Reading* Absalom, Absalom! (Jackson, MS: University Press of Mississippi, 2010), 56.

at stake for Rosa in the cancellation and sublation of narrative time itself, as we have read before: *"there had been no shot. That sound was merely the sharp and final clap-to of a door between us and all that was, all that might have been—a retroactive severance of the stream of event: a forever crystallized instant in imponderable time"* (131). This is a decisive moment in the text, since it elevates a symbolic narrative function (the closing of a door) into a self-allegorical figure for what (I have been arguing) the modernist novel most wants to win from the living corpse of romance: the retroactive transfiguration of narrative temporality into a "forever crystallized instant" of affect. The closing of a door is Rosa's choice metaphor for that *hysteron proteron* "shot heard only by its echo," which she continues, honestly, to believe is the central event of her story. That she is wrong, that she has in fact mistaken the true, cardinal event of this text for that ersatz moment of fratricidal melodrama, is what the curiously "double-exposed" narrative discourse of Chapter Five will ultimately prove, against the very grain of its compulsive narrative logic. How it does so is "Quentin-Rosa's" greatest achievement, and perhaps the greatest single achievement of all American literature.

Quentin and Rosa both converge on a palpable sense of something, a door, that "cannot be passed." We are situated at a barricaded threshold here, to which access has been denied; quite plausibly it is one of those places where "as you know, one must pronounce *shibboleth* properly in order to be granted the right to pass."[122] If there is something missing here, it is that unpronounceable word whose meaning would matter less "than, let us say, its signifying form once it becomes a password, a mark of belonging, the manifestation of an alliance" (20). Derrida traced the history of such a word into the context of the Spanish Civil War (which began in February 1936, just as Faulkner put the finishing touches on *Absalom*), where it became, "not a word in passing, but a silent word transmitted like a *symbolon* or handclasp, a rallying cipher, a sign of membership and a political watchword" (23). But here, on the fading echo of the "last shot" of the American Civil War, *"I saw a closed door but did not enter it"* (121) because of one of those *"occurrences which stop us dead as though by some impalpable intervention,"* and because there is no available word that would open it; no *shibboleth*. Only, of course, there is.

What impedes passage through the closed door and into a fully hallucinated romance plenitude takes the *hysteron proteron* form of a Sutpen off-print, *"Sutpen coffee-colored face enough there in the dim light, barring the stairs [. . .] not swimming up out of the gloom, but already there, rocklike and firm and antedating time and house and doom and all"* (113). Clytie has here absorbed into her own being something of the newly dead Charles Bon's figurative status as the text's

---

[122] Jacques Derrida, "Shibboleth: for Paul Celan," in Thomas Dutoit and Outi Pasanen, ed. and trans., *Sovereignties in Question: The Poetics of Paul Celan* (New York: Fordham University Press, 2005), 1.

negative plate; she who "antedates time" and was always "already there" inevitably recasts the "Sutpen face" she wears as somehow derivative of her own gloom-bound ur-face. She is next forced into classical form, cast as *"the cold Cerberus"* of the Sutpen netherworld his mansion has become (113). But there is something so compelling about the *hysteron proteron* figure of the coffee-colored Sutpen face that cannot be easily displaced. Its work is to derange the coordinates of narrative telling so radically that the temporal warp and weft of the *récit* form is turned inside out. For while the typical romance works by alternating the time of the scene with the time of accelerated action, here scene-time (hypothetically isomorphic with the time of narration) slows to such a degree that for six of the most packed pages in world literature, at most thirty seconds of story time transpires. The obstacle before the door is also a kind of wound in narrative time, which allows the breathless momentum of the story to dissipate and its tissues to unravel. Quentin-Rosa's "I" is separated from its own material support in a body: the latter "still advanced, ran on," while "I, myself" is stopped "dead" by the black face that antedates time (113). This *"furious yet absolutely rocklike and immobile antagonism which had stopped me"* (113) also disables the narrative's capacity to absorb it. Like one of those "failures of narrative imagination" that typified the 1930s for Michael Denning, here we find a clear instance of a crisis that so rattles the "knowable communities and settled social relations" of a world that something other than narrative is called for.[123] If some *shibboleth* is not spoken, this "immobile antagonism" will swallow the known universe.

She tries. *"I was crying not to someone, something, but (trying to cry) through something"* (113), to articulate some password to the *"profoundly attentive and distracted listening to or for something which I myself could not hear"* (114) that Clytie now embodies. Far from having performed *shibboleth*, however, the cry and the listening form a disjunction, and into that disjunction there suddenly interposes a romance hallucination of what lies behind the door (much like Quentin's at the end of the chapter), with all the expected props intact: *"nuptial couch,"* *"pale and bloody corpse,"* *"bowed and unwived widow"* (114). But "Quentin-Rosa" seems to be aware that this is a narrative *cul-de-sac*, using the self-characterization of *"self-mesmered fool"* (114) to condense and pass an entire new media ecology's judgment on the one it has extinguished: romance hallucinations are henceforth a folly. And what puts an unpassable bar across them is this *"cold implacable mindless"* negative plate, or dark *"replica"* of the Sutpen face, which now takes the ultimate step of crossing what Melville had called, in a comparable context, the *deadly space between*. As is well known, while the discretionary narrator of "Billy Budd" takes the prudent path of "indirection" in his lengthy traversal of

---

[123] Denning, *The Cultural Front*, 119.

the "deadly space between" Claggart's nature and that of our "normal natures," Billy himself crosses it in a fatal flash: "quick as the flame from a discharged cannon at night, his right arm shot out, and Claggart dropped to the deck."[124] And so it is now with Clytie, one nature to another: *"Then she touched me, and then I did stop dead"* (115).

Of touching, it has been written that it is "a question of life and death," since "some kind of reserve," a "certain tact" is "inscribed a priori, like a first commandment, the law of originary prohibition."[125] Derrida continues: "Ritual prohibitions would then come to be determined, afterward, and only on the background of an untouchability as initial as it is vital, on the background of 'Thou shalt not touch, not too much'" (47). Prior even to the taboo against incest, this originary proscription against tactless touching would seem to be the very foundation of law itself. Situated as it is on the threshold between one body and its other, touch violates the sanctity of observed boundaries in such a way that both Eros and Thanatos are invoked. Touch violates, but in so doing makes things such as dynasties possible. As Bon puts it to himself (in Shreve's speculation), the legal fiction of paternity itself might, in touch, be at once posited and proven; craving as he does "the living touch of that flesh warmed before he was born by the same blood which it had bequeathed him to warm his own flesh with, to be bequeathed by him in turn to run hot and loud in veins and limbs after that first flesh and then his own were dead" (263). Of course, what he gets is nothing, "no shock, no hot communicated flesh that speech would have been too slow even to impede—nothing" (264). His photogenesis, we have said, precludes him from such a haptic shudder. But here at last is *"something monstrous and immobile, with a shocking impact too soon and too quick"* (115), a momentous touch that, in one unstoppable access, blooms into the most radiant and consequential affect that it will have been possible for *Absalom, Absalom!* to wring from the faltering machinery of its romance plot:

> *Because there is something in the touch of flesh with flesh which abrogates, cuts sharp and straight across the devious intricate channels of decorous ordering, which enemies as well as lovers know because it makes them both:—touch and touch of that which is the citadel of the central I-Am's private own: not spirit, soul; the liquorish and ungirdled mind is anyone's to take in any darkened hallway of this earthly tenement. But let flesh touch with flesh, and watch the fall of all the eggshell shibboleth of caste and color too.* (115)

---

[124] Herman Melville, *Billy Budd, Sailor* (London & Chicago: Chicago University Press, 1962), 99.

[125] Jacques Derrida, *On Touching—Jean-Luc Nancy*, trans. Christine Irizarry (Stanford, CA: Stanford University Press, 2005), 47.

The word is spoken; "Quentin-Rosa" has pronounced *shibboleth*, and in the very context it most needed to be spoken. Only not to Clytie, not to that *"attentive and distracted listening,"* but to us and to literature itself, where these astonishing periods will strain to preserve Clytie's shattering gesture against time. To Clytie, of course, "Quentin-Rosa" can speak only that other "password, a mark of belonging, the manifestation of an alliance" whose historical conditions of possibility have just now, with the "last shot of the war," finally begun to unravel. It is a watchword whose function is to shore up the very edifice of "caste and color" that the South's military defeat has, just yesterday, rattled to the foundations: *"Take your hand off me, nigger!"*

The extraordinary wonder of the scene, however, is that the *hysteron proteron* construction has pre-empted this reactionary and restorative password of the plantocracy, with that *"fall of all the eggshell shibboleth of caste and color too"* that Clytie's touch has instigated in the present. In the paradoxical tense now occupied by the "Quentin-Rosa" narrator, it is too late to retreat behind the fortress of *"nigger,"* since it is implacably *"joined by that hand and arm which held us, like a fierce rigid umbilical cord, twin sistered to the fell darkness which had produced her"* (116). The unexpected appearance of the umbilicus as a figure precognizes its subsequent use in the parable of the pool ripples, which are linked, we will recall, by "a narrow umbilical water-cord" that allows them to propagate from one to the other: a maternal media hook-up. Here, the most improbable effects are engendered by the figure's application to a sustained touch—the photogenetics are radicalized, miraculously permitting Clytie and Rosa to have been "twin sistered" to the *"fell darkness which had produced her."* We are impelled in the first instance to conceive of this as a metaphor for Sutpen himself, reminded that Clytie's face was *"at once both more and less than Sutpen"* (116), and given that it matches any number of other metaphors for him as emanating from hell. And yet the umbilical figure that binds the two women in this protracted instant of touch must also conjure up a vision of that maternal slave womb in which both, black and white, are suspended, itself just as surely a *"fell darkness"* in the additional sense of being black both inside and out. Given that Rosa's own childhood is described shortly after as *"some projection of the lightless womb itself"* (119), we are being situated in a most ambivalent tropological space, where the photogenetic figure of the negative plate is conjoined to a gestative and umbilical figure, in order to allow Rosa finally to speak those most improbable words to the "Cerberus-nigger" whose function it is to withhold from her the romance plenitude of *"what I could not, would not, must not believe"* (116). Finally, a *shibboleth* equal to the touch itself, "a silent word transmitted like a *symbolon* or handclasp": *"perhaps not aloud, not with words . . . I cried 'And you too? And you too, sister, sister?'"* (116)

This is the singular moment of metalepsis in which "Quentin-Rosa" achieves the coordinate-shattering "emotion-value" that stitches 1864 to 1909 (and

1935, and 2017) in an affection-image along two medial seams simultaneously: photographically, the negative plate of Clytie has "developed" into its white double in a logic that is not filiative but affiliative, and which permits the positive print (now both Quentin and Rosa) to hail its dark "twin" across the "*shibboleth of caste and color too*," not to mention history itself; and narratively, in the dimension of voice, Rosa's "object voice" has finally obtruded far enough into Quentin's capacity to "imagine" the scene that the *shibboleth*—"*you too, sister, sister*"—is precisely his own, as every reader of *The Sound and the Fury* already knows. The point is that this metaleptic node of multiple transferences is occasioned by a touch that obtains, not between two of the protagonists of the Sutpen dynastic-romance plot, but between the childless primary narrator and the longest-lived, childless, most "minor" Sutpen herself, both alive in 1909, and due to touch one last time. Their 1864 touch takes place, formally, in order to forestall the rushing descent of the 1909 narrative into outright cliché behind the closed door; it is a device, coined in 1935, for the interruption of that narrative drive, in order to suspend what Jameson called the "system of the récit" (73), so that "the space for affect" (55) might be cleared. Blocking "that door" to the "stream of event," it opens instead "*a forever crystallized instant in imponderable time*" (131) that will take precisely eight months of story time, and twenty pages of close-typed text, to close. This, the most distended and elaborated affect in the novel, emerges from a touch that triggers the most protracted suspension of narrative energies in its plot—"*So we waited for him*" (128).

The extraordinary thing about the eight-month aftermath of what I am now going to call the singular event of *Absalom, Absalom!*—Clytie's touching of Rosa, and Rosa's answering *shibboleth* "sister, sister"—is how it develops the affiliative logic of that cry in directions that must be understood as both political and ethical. The suspension of the dynastic plot is at the same time the removal of the patriarch and heir apparent, along with the pretender himself. It is, indeed, the removal of all the cardinal points of the romance, barring the intended herself who, retroactively transfigured by this multiple subtraction, is absorbed instead into the "twin sistered" affection-image of Rosa and Clytie. But all this is amplified and raised from the level of the ethical to that of the political by the historical situation that this hiatus in narrative time precisely occupies; namely, the end of the war, the defeat of the South, and the necessity of surviving prior to Reconstruction. This is that unthinkable "non-event" in whose shadow Faulkner's tortured romances play out their tropological and elliptical games, but here it is superimposed upon an event of the first order: the tendentious collapse of an entire ideological superstructure given the outrage of "*that black arresting and untimorous hand on my white woman's flesh*" (115). Upon which, of course, "*I stopped dead*," but only because "I" has miraculously transformed into "we": "*We did not need him...*" (128).

"We" lived "*amicably, not as two white women and a negress, not as three negroes or three whites, not even as three women, but merely as three creatures [. . .] in whom sex was some forgotten atrophy like the rudimentary gills we call the tonsils*" (128). The touch has cut across not just the shibboleths of caste and color, but of gender and sex as well, not to mention age; and it has spread from two to three, the basis of a collective, not a couple. Indeed, nothing could so clearly demonstrate the quality of event specific to this miraculous touch, which here behaves like that stupefying world-historical interpellation of St. Paul: "There is neither Jew nor Greek, there is neither slave nor free, there is neither male nor female," of which Badiou has written that it founds a political collective on the basis of *universal singularity*, where "slaves, women, people of every profession and nationality will [. . .] be admitted without restriction or privilege."[126] "*It was as though we were one being, interchangeable and indiscriminate, which kept that garden growing, spun thread and wove the cloth we wore, hunted and found and rendered the meagre ditch-side herbs*" (129). Who was then a gentleman, when Adam delved and Eve span? A plantation has become a self-sustaining commune, thanks extrinsically to the temporary subtraction of patriarchal authority and the rule of law and the market, and the permanent disestablishment of the institution of slavery; but intrinsically to the contagious egalitarian logic of a single touch. It is here, from within the "one being," that Judith's nobility is transfigured into something worthy of commemoration: "*who (and abetted by Clytie) would cook twice what we could eat and three times what we could afford and give it to anyone, any stranger in a land already beginning to fill with straggling soldiers who stopped and asked for it*" (129). This redistributive Franciscan logic is the consequence of an event, a touch, whose immense affective radiance seems capable of remaking the very world itself—until after eight months, the patriarch returns, and the plot takes its satirical turn; or, after twenty pages, the interregnum falters, the romance hallucination is revived, and the scene of narration shifts to Harvard, where there is no question of any woman who, having survived the aftermath of war on a feminist commune, might wish further to communicate the "molecularity" of that event in any form whatever.

The difference between this "still" image of universal singularity in *Absalom, Absalom!* and the comparable scenes in *Gone With the Wind* where Scarlett takes up spade and hoe and turns to the land with her former slaves is everything this chapter has been committed to establishing: the extraordinary formal lengths in tropology, mediatic self-awareness, and structural organization that Faulkner's text has gone to in order to engineer and justify this moment as the romance narrative's photo-affective *punctum* or "third meaning," cutting athwart the dynastic plot at an oblique angle in order to conjure an astonishing

---

[126] Alain Badiou, *St. Paul: The Foundation of Universalism*, trans. Ray Brassier (Stanford, CA: Stanford University Press, 2003), 13–14.

affection-image. Whereas Mitchell's text places her scenes of female farm labor within a simple continuity of romance conventions and forms, in a manner that establishes her protagonist's enduring heroism, Faulkner's are functionally epiphenomenal, serving no end other than their own immanence, exhausting themselves in their own intensity, prior to the resumption of narrative business as usual (however unusual it may be). Indeed, it is only once the entire text is read, and re-read, that this touch and its consequences come into proper focus as the text's most resonant "post-meaning," situated at its navel, but arrived at only after "travers[ing], as though the length of an initiatic way, the whole meaning, in order to extenuate it, to exempt it."[127]

That is to say that, without the Sutpen romance plot in all its profuse complexity and elaboration, this protracted moment is unthinkable; the touch and its brief aftermath of subjective fidelity between three women are plausible and meaningful only as extenuations or exemptions of the melodramatic materials that hold them, precariously and delicately, in place at the very center of the novel. After all, what it interrupts is the otherwise irresistible momentum of "the truly obscene ideas of patrimony, inheritance, heredity, superiority on the basis of birth, blood or race" that constitute the genetic sequence of all romance ideologies; but it is only through interrupting it, forcing a vacuum into its broiling heart, that it can be perceived as such.[128] And in that sense, it is possible to say that this touch is the invaluable impress, made upon the American novel form in 1935, of a truth whose real fortunes are always to come, promissory rather than actual. A truth *for us*. Such a truth "demonstrates the normative operation of the existing symbolic order precisely by falling out of it," and asks of us (its potential subjects) how the world will appear if "we" represent it to one another as something to form a *sensus communis* around and follow through to its end.[129] Of course, we come across the evidence of this touch amid a truly vast circulation of generic tropes, mediatic figures, and formal tensions internal to the production of the art-novel in 1935, and at a point in the text where a metaleptic "falling out" of the compulsions of romance is precisely what has been prepared for by the material. The great success of those procedures ensures that what survives a reading of *Absalom, Absalom!* is a "single, inexistent—albeit real—point, which, once it's been identified and spotlighted, will change everything and bring about the truth" of what can only be called the *communist idea*.[130] This is very far from saying that William Faulkner was personally animated by such an idea—though his nostalgic ruminations on the divine trust placed in

---

[127] Barthes, *Roland Barthes*, 87.

[128] Alain Badiou, *Plato's Republic: A Dialogue in 16 Chapters*, trans. Susan Spitzer (New York: Columbia University Press, 2012), 158.

[129] Kenneth Reinhard, Introduction to Badiou, *Plato's Republic*, xix.

[130] Alain Badiou, *Plato's Republic*, 165.

human beings certainly tend in that direction: "He made the earth first and peopled it with dumb creatures, and then He created man to be his overseer on the earth and to hold suzerainty over the earth and the animals on it in his name, not to hold for himself and his descendants inviolable title forever, generation after generation, to the oblongs and squares of the earth, but to hold the earth mutual and intact in the communal anonymity of brotherhood."[131] Rather, it is to suppose that great literature may well be impelled, by its own immanent aesthetic logic, to brush up against that idea at points where its innermost tensions and contradictions are straining hardest, as here. To conceive of this touch in constellation with the "sperm-squeezing" cry of *Moby-Dick*'s Chapter 94, and with the "master plan of sexual love" in the fifty-third chapter of *Gravity's Rainbow* is to acknowledge the periodic brushing of the communist idea against American literature, not in terms of its political organization or rhetoric, but as the upsurge of an "unpredictable event" from within artistic deformations of the world of opinion. Such events, such crystals of aesthetic energy, survive the historical collapse of those "eggshell shibboleths" of race, class, and gender, and seize us with an unrealized futurity that implicates us, one and all: "No one has ever changed or will ever change, merely through moral lessons," Badiou's Socrates declares, "a character that's been set in stone by prevailing opinion. Philosophy can only be effective if the political divine has intervened first, if some event interrupts the consensual routine" (188). So it is with the novel, too, whose aesthetic events are sprung from the obscure void of that "ordinary confused babble of opinion" (190), thanks to the ambiguous tropology of the form's mediatic unconscious.

---

[131] Faulkner, "The Bear," in Malcolm Cowley, ed., *The Portable Faulkner*, revised and expanded (New York & London: Penguin, 2003), 229.

INDEX

Note: Page numbers in **Bold** indicate a sustained discussion of the subject.

Ackermann, Zeno 18–19, 21
Adams, Richard 88
Adorno, Theodor W. 108, 171, 173, 177–8, 203, 211, 214
Agee, James
 and Evans, Walker 229–31, 241, 271–2
Anderson, Benedict 202
Apollinaire, Guillaume 227
Aronowitz, Stanley 167
Auden, W. H. 57, 82
automobile **86–113, 124–41**
aviation 44
 as mediation 54–64, **66–82**

Badiou, Alain 230, 280–2
Bal, Mieke 228
Bankhead, John Hollis 89
Bakhtin, Mikhail M. 41, 86
Ballard, J. G. 76
Banjo on My Knee, A 216
Barthes, Roland 39–40, 194, 258, 268–9, 271–2
Barton Fink 270
Bassett, John 6
Baudelaire, Charles 60
Bazin, André 258
Beckett, Samuel 188, 213
Benjamin, Walter 40n110, 135, 238, 258
Berardi, Franco "Bifo" 178
Bergson, Henri 264
Blotner, Joseph 56
Brecht, Bertolt 57, 81
Brennan, Teresa 108
Brooks, Cleanth 4, 25, 190, 214
Browning, Robert 37
Burton, William Meriam 131

Cain, James M. 208
Caldwell, Erskine
 and Bourke-White, Margaret 229, 272

capitalism 119–215
 and finance 67–9
 uneven development of 14–15, 21
cavalier, as figure 49–52, 54, 63, 81–3, 87, 102–3
Cavell, Stanley 258–9
Cervantes, Miguel de
 Don Quixote 87
Chandler, Raymond 153–4, 157
Chaplin, Charlie 40–1
Charles I of England 49
Chase, Richard 16–17, 106
Citizen Kane 222
Connor, Steven 172
Conrad, Joseph 38–9, 41, 43, 236–7
Cowley, Malcolm 9
Crane, Hart 57, 82
Cromwell, Oliver 49
Cunningham, Seymour 88

Delaunay, Robert 57, 82
Deleuze, Gilles 194, 224–5
 with Guattari, Felix 111–12
Derrida, Jacques 221, 225, 259–60, 275–7
Denning, Michael 230, 246, 272, 276
DeVoto, Bernard 8
Dewey, John 122
Dickinson, Emily 231, 269
Doctorow, E. L. 104n31
Dos Passos, John 211, 236
Dolar, Mladen 188, 235
Dreyer, Carl Theodor 187
Duck, Leigh Anne 25

Eagleton, Terry 39
Edison, Thomas 174, 179, 228, 233, 240, 269
electricity 168–71, **175–85**, 194–5, 200–4
Eliot, T. S. 42, 213, 227
Evans, Jessica 256
everyday life 11–12, 24, 238

Fadiman, Clifton 7–8
Falkner, William Clark 30–2
Farrell, James T. 7
Faulkner, William
  and romance **4–15**, 17, 30–3
  and modernism 24, **32–43**, 112, 213–15
Faulkner, William: texts by
  Absalom, Absalom! 9, 34, 42, 46–7, 50, 145, 168, 183, **216–82**
  "Ad Astra" 63
  "All the Dead Pilots" 61–3, 242–3
  "L'Après-Midi d'un Faune" 30
  As I Lay Dying 7, 40, 45–6, 115, 143–6, 168–9, **180–99**, 202–8
  "Death Drag" 41, 73–6, 78
  "Evangeline" 245, 248–50
  Flags in the Dust/Sartoris 44, 51–4, 63, 74, 84–5, 87–8, **91–106**, 109, 112, 118–20, 130, 133–4, 142, 156
  "Flying the Mail" 69–71
  Go Down, Moses 29
  Hamlet, The 34–5
  Idyll in the Desert 65–7
  If I Forget Thee, Jerusalem 217
  Knight's Gambit 31, 106
  Light in August 8, 34, 50, **145–52**, 176, 262
  Marble Faun, The 30
  Marionettes, The 30
  Mayday 30
  "Mule in the Yard" 41
  Pylon 29, 42–3, 46, 72, **77–83**, 103, **216–24**, 241
  Review of *Test Pilot* 76, 221
  Sanctuary 29, 34, 42, 45, 144–6, **152–81**, 183, 187, 202–3
  Sound and the Fury, The 27–8, 34, 41–2, 44–5, 84–5, 87, **107–42**, 142, 145, 151, 279
  "The Leg" 248
  Unvanquished, The 41, 51, 53, 216–18
  "Vendée" 35
  "War Birds" 63–5
Fitzgerald, F. Scott 229
Flaubert, Gustave 12
Flesch, Hans 174, 176
Forbes, B. C. 179
Freud, Sigmund 13, 53, 108, 166, 188, 196, 251, 266
Frow, John 19

Gannett, Lewis 8
Genette, Gérard 209, 268
Genovese, Eugene 21
Gershwin, George 145
Gilbreath, William S. 90
Gitelman, Lisa 169, 178, 228
Godden, Richard 3, 5, 217
Goethe, Johann Wolfgang von 224, 242, 269
Gone With the Wind 280
gothic 7–10, 123, 145–6, 150, 219, 234
gramophone 45, 149–53, 171–7, 195, 229

Green, Martin 214
Greeson, Jennifer 24
Gunning, Tom 200

Hagood, Taylor 26
Hardinge, Emma 184
Hartley, Marsden 59
Hawks, Howard 64
Hawthorne, Nathaniel 16, 21
  The Scarlet Letter 208
Hegel, Georg Wilhelm Friedrich 257–8, 260
Heidegger, Martin 74
Hemingway, Ernest 165, 167, 218, 236
Hilmes, Michelle 202
Howards End 99
"Hugh Selwyn Mauberley" 30

In a Lonely Place 270

James, Henry 16, 36, 151–2
Jameson, Fredric 11, 13, 22, 26, 29, 34, 37, 39, 86, 94, 108, 152, 236, 238–9, 243, 272, 279
jazz 28, 144–5, 155–6, 164–5, 170
Jazz Singer, The 228
Joyce, James 13, 119, 160, 213, 231, 236–7

Keats, John 156
Kennedy, John P. 18, 50
Kenner, Hugh 85, 237, 239–40
Kittler, Friedrich 167, 173–5, 181, 225–7, 232, 235, 240, 257–8, 269

Lacan, Jacques 159, 188–9, 192
Last Slaver, The 216
Latham, Sean 87
Lefebvre, Henri 116–17
Levin, Thomas Y. 173, 176
Lippmann, Walter 226–7
Lord Jim 38
Löwy, Michael 20
Lukács, György 113–14

Malevich, Kazimir 59
Mallarmé, Stéphane 30, 37–8, 224–5
Marinetti, Filippo Tommaso 58, 72, 76, 82, 112
Marx, Karl 139
  Capital 75
McCoy, Horace 208
McGurl, Mark 218
McHaney, Thomas 216–17
McKeon, Michael 22
media 1–2, 6, 27–30, 33–4, 43–4
Melville, Herman 16–17, 217, 276, 282
Millgate, Michael 123
Mitchell, Margaret 9
Mitchell, W. J. T. 224, 230
modernism 10–15, 23, 30, 32–4, 48, 85, 112, 151, 157, 193, 203, 230–1, 239–41, 268, 272–3, 275
Moholy-Nagy, László 176–7

money as mediation 138–9
Moretti, Franco 11–12, 115
motorcar 97–100, 125–42
Murphy, Dudley 248

news and literature 218–41
Niedecker, Lorine 143–4
Nietzsche, Friedrich 62n35, 199
Norris, Frank 15–16
novel form 11–15, 24, 35

O'Brien, Flann 75
oedipus complex 196–9, 205
O'Neill, Eugene 213

Pearson, Josephine Anderson 89
petroleum 130–2
photography 54–63, **222–70**
   negative plate 223, 250–3, **256–63**
Polk, Noel 51, 274
Porter, Carolyn 217–18
posthumanism 77–83, 269
Pound, Ezra 30, 32–3, 213
Pynchon, Thomas 282

radio 45, **143–86**, **193–215**
Rampton, David 193
Rancière, Jacques 37, 92, 272–3
realism 11–15, 23, 114, 238–40
récit 207–9, 236–43, 268–73
Renard, Maurice 173, 235
Rickels, Laurence 179
Rilke, Rainer Maria 227
Road to Glory 216
Rodowick, D. N. 259
romance 1–2
   American **15–22**, 150
   encounter/event 87, 98, 124, 244, 280–2
   European 22–3
   in Faulkner **4–15**, 30–3, 48, 64–5
   narrative logic of 39, 86–7
   plot 273–82
   realism 114
   Southern 3, **17–22**, 29–33, 48, **89–106**, 121–2, 149, 252–3
Romine, Scott 25
Ross, Stephen 191, 212
Rosskam, Edwin 229
Ryle, Gilbert 74

Sartre, Jean-Paul 34, 39
Schwartz, Lawrence H. 25–6
Sconce, Jeffrey 149, 179, 198–9
Scott, Sir Walter 17–20
Sensibar, Judith 247–8
Shakespeare, William
   Hamlet 123
Shelley, Percy 156

shibboleth 275–82
Shipp, Cameron 8
Simms, William Gilmore 18, 50
Singin' in the Rain 270
Slave Ship 216
smell 107–10, 127–37, 157
Snelling, Paula 8
Socrates 282
Sollors, Werner 128
South, as region 24–30, 48–9, 86–90, 152, 199–200
Stein, Gertrude 14, 240, 242, 263
Stone, Geoffrey 7–8
Story of Temple Drake, The 162, 167
Stott, William 229–30
streetcar 119–30
Sundquist, Eric 180–1, 190
Sunset Boulevard 270
Sutter's Gold 216, 271
Swift, Jonathan 77

Talbot, Henry Fox 244, 257–8, 269
Taylor, William R. 49
Tennyson, Lord Alfred 32, 231, 269
transportation 44–5
Trotter, David 86, 87, 99
Trilling, Lionel 9
Tucker, George 18
Tucker, Nathaniel 19
Twain, Mark (Samuel Clemens) 17–18

U.S. postal system 67–9

Virilio, Paul 55, 60

Warner, Saul Bass 120, 229
Wasson, Ben 84
Watson, Jay 24–5
Watson, Richie 21
Welles, Orson 210
Westbrook, Wayne 137–8
White Rose of Memphis, The 17, 30–2
Whitman, Walt 57
Williams, Raymond 20, 95
Williamson, Joel 54, 253
Witkiewicz, Stanislav Ignacy 266–7
Wollen, Peter 59
Wooden Crosses 216
Wordsworth, William 36
Wright, Richard 21, 229
Wurtzler, Steve 170–1, 175, 201

yankee, as figure 49–52
Yeats, W. B. 57, 81

Zeitlin, Michael 81
Žižek, Slavoj 132, 188
Zola, Émile 239
Zukofsky, Louis 143–4

www.ingramcontent.com/pod-product-compliance
Ingram Content Group UK Ltd.
Pitfield, Milton Keynes, MK11 3LW, UK
UKHW042006230426
12048UKWH00009B/577